Foreign Policy Breakthroughs

Foreign Policy Breakthroughs

Cases in Successful Diplomacy

EDITED BY ROBERT HUTCHINGS

and

JEREMI SURI

To Lisa,

Physics, Dance, and Diplomacy are the secret of success! Good luck.

Yours,

12-3-15

OXFORD
UNIVERSITY PRESS

To Lisa, with best wishes,

Robert Hutchings

OXFORD
UNIVERSITY PRESS

Oxford University Press is a department of the University of Oxford.
It furthers the University's objective of excellence in research, scholarship,
and education by publishing worldwide. Oxford is a registered trade mark
of Oxford University Press in the UK and in certain other countries

Published in the United States of America by
Oxford University Press
198 Madison Avenue, New York, NY 10016,
United States of America

Library of Congress Cataloging-in-Publication Data
Foreign policy breakthroughs : cases in successful diplomacy / edited by Robert Hutchings and Jeremi Suri.
p.   cm.
Summary: "Diplomacy is essential to the conduct of foreign policy and international business in the twenty-
first century. Yet, few international actors are trained to understand or practice effective diplomacy. Poor
diplomacy has contributed to repeated setbacks for the United States and other major powers in the last
decade. Drawing on deep historical research, this book aims to 'reinvent' diplomacy for our current era. The
original and comparative research provides a foundation for thinking about what successful outreach, negotiation, and relationship-building with foreign actors should look like. Instead of focusing only on failures, as
most studies do, this one interrogates success. The book provides a framework for defining successful diplomacy and implementing it in diverse contexts. Chapters analyze the activities of diverse diplomats (including
state and non-state actors) in enduring cases, including: post-WWII relief, the rise of the non-aligned movement, the Nuclear Non-Proliferation Treaty, the U.S. opening to China, the Camp David Accords, the reunification of Germany, the creation of the European Union, the completion of the North American Free Trade
Agreement, and relief aid to pre-2001 Afghanistan. The cases are diverse and historical, but they are written
with an eye toward contemporary challenges and opportunities. The book closes with systematic reflections
on how current diplomats can improve their activities abroad. Foreign Policy Breakthroughs offers rigorous
historical insights for present policy"— Provided by publisher.
Summary: "This book provides a framework for defining successful diplomacy and implementing it in diverse contexts"— Provided by publisher.
ISBN 978-0-19-022611-4 (hardback) — ISBN 978-0-19-022612-1 (paperback) 1. Diplomacy—
History—20th century—Case studies. 2. Diplomacy—History—21st century—Case studies. 3. World
politics—1945-1989—Case studies. 4. World politics—1989—Case studies. I. Hutchings, Robert L.,
1946- editor of compilation. II. Suri, Jeremi, editor of compilation.
D843.F569 2015
327.2—dc23

2014047622

3   5   7   9   8   6   4   2

Printed in the United States of America on acid free paper

To Kim and Alison

CONTENTS

ABOUT THE CONTRIBUTORS

Rafael Fernández de Castro

Rafael de Castro Medina is the Founding Chair of the Department of International Studies at Mexico's Instituto Tecnológico Autónomo de México (ITAM). He holds the Jay and Debe Moskowitz Chair at Syracuse University's Maxwell School of Citizenship and Public Affairs. He served as foreign policy adviser to Mexican President Felipe Calderón. His work focuses on Mexican foreign policy, Mexico-U.S. relations, and issues of economic development and political economy. He is also founding editor of *Foreign Affairs Latinoamerica* and has published numerous articles and books, including *The United States and Mexico: Between Partnership and Conflict* (with Jorge I. Dominguez). He was the coordinator for the UNDP's 2013–14 Human Development Report, *Citizen Security with a Human Face: Evidence and Proposals for Latin America*. Fernández de Castro holds a Ph.D. in political science from Georgetown University as well as an MPAff from the Lyndon B. Johnson School of Public Affairs at the University of Texas at Austin.

Mark Dawson

Mark Dawson is the Professor for European Law and Governance at the Hertie School of Governance in Berlin. He holds degrees from the Universities of Edinburgh and Aberdeen as well as a Ph.D. from the European University Institute in Florence. He has been a visiting scholar at the Institute for Global Legal Studies of the University of Wisconsin and a Visiting Fellow at the Harvard Kennedy School. Before joining the Hertie School, he was an Assistant Professor at Maastricht University. His research has focused on the relationship in the EU between law and policymaking—he recently published a book on "New Governance and the Transformation of European Law" (Cambridge

University Press, 2011) and a further edited volume on judicial activism at the European Court of Justice (Edward Elgar, 2013).

Galia Golan

Dr. Galia Golan is Darwin Professor emerita of the Hebrew University of Jerusalem, where she was head of the Political Science Department. Presently she is Head of the MA and the Program in Diplomacy and Conflict Studies at the Interdisciplinary Center Herzliya. Her eleventh book is entitled *Israeli Peacemaking since 1967: Factors Behind the Breakthroughs and Failures*. Her coedited book with Walid Salem, *Non-state Actors in the Middle East—Factors for Peace and Democracy*, is also available through Routledge. One of her earlier books of note is *Israel and Palestine: Peace Plans and Proposals from Oslo to Disengagement*.

Jonathan Hunt

Jonathan Hunt is a historian of America and the world, having received his doctorate from the University of Texas at Austin in 2013. He has received fellowships from the Woodrow Wilson International Center for Scholars, the Eisenhower Institute, and the Center for International Security and Cooperation at Stanford University. A student of international nuclear and environmental history, he has written for the *Bulletin of the Atomic Scientists*, *Passport*, the *Huffington Post*, and the *National Interest*. He is currently writing a book-length study of the golden age of nuclear diplomacy during the Cold War and its enduring legacy for international security and politics, entitled *Faustian Bargain: The United States and the World's Pursuit of Nuclear Order from Atoms for Peace to the Iraq War*. He has recently been named a Stanton Nuclear Security Fellow at RAND Corporation.

Robert Hutchings

Robert Hutchings is Dean of the Lyndon B. Johnson School of Public Affairs at the University of Texas at Austin. Before joining the LBJ School in 2010, he was Diplomat in Residence at Princeton University, where he also served as Assistant Dean of the Woodrow Wilson School of Public and International Affairs. During a public service leave from Princeton in 2003–05, he was Chairman of the U.S. National Intelligence Council. His combined academic and diplomatic career has included service as Fellow and Director of International Studies at the Woodrow Wilson International Center for Scholars, Director for European Affairs with the National Security Council, and Special Adviser to the Secretary of State, with the rank of ambassador. He is author of

American Diplomacy and the End of the Cold War, among many other books and articles. A graduate of the U.S. Naval Academy, he received his Ph.D. from the University of Virginia.

Christopher J. Lee

Christopher J. Lee is based at the Wits Institute for Social and Economic Research (WISER) at the University of the Witwatersrand, Johannesburg. He is the editor of *Making a World After Empire: The Bandung Moment and Its Political Afterlives* (2010) and the author of *Unreasonable Histories: Nativism, Multiracial Lives, and the Genealogical Imagination in British Africa* (2014).

Stephen R. Porter

Stephen R. Porter is an Assistant Professor of U.S. and International history at the University of Cincinnati, having earned his Ph.D. from the University of Chicago in 2009. He is completing a book manuscript entitled *Benevolent Empire? Refugees, NGOs and the American State,* which examines the public and private dimensions of U.S.-led refugee aid initiatives and related humanitarian endeavors in the twentieth century. He elaborates on the broader international dimensions of these phenomena in an essay in the forthcoming *Cambridge History of the Second World War* (2015). He has directed a degree program on international human rights at the University of Cincinnati and has been a research fellow at the Institute for Historical Studies at the University of Texas-Austin, Social Science Research Council, Miller Center of Public Affairs, Hurst Institute in Legal History, and Taft Research Center.

Beatriz Leycegui

Beatriz Leycegui has over twenty-four years of experience in the private, public, and academic sectors. Beatriz is a partner at SAI Law & Economics, an economics, legal, and investment banking consulting firm, which she rejoined in 2013 as Head of the International Trade and Investment Practice Group. Beatriz's work focuses on advising domestic and international companies, as well as federal, state, and foreign governments on the World Trade Organization and free trade agreements obligations and dispute settlement, investment, customs, and public policy matters. She had previously worked at SAI from 1999 to 2006. Beatriz served as Mexico's Undersecretary for Foreign Trade between December 2006 and August 2011. She also was Director of Legal Analysis of the Office in Charge of Negotiating NAFTA between 1990 and 1992. Beatriz graduated as a lawyer from the Escuela Libre de Derecho in

Mexico City and holds a Master's Degree in International Affairs from Columbia University.

Paula R. Newberg

Paula R. Newberg is a Clinical Professor of Government and Fellow of the Wilson Chair, University of Texas at Austin. A scholar and practitioner with wide-ranging experience in multilateral and nongovernmental organizations, she served as Special Adviser to the United Nations in Asia (including Afghanistan), Europe and Africa. Formerly a Senior Associate at the Carnegie Endowment for International Peace, where she cofounded its Democracy Project, and a Guest Scholar at the Brookings Institution, Newberg was the Director of the Institute for the Study of Diplomacy at Georgetown University. Newberg's work focuses on human rights, democratic governance, and foreign policy in crisis and transition states. She has written extensively on constitutional development and jurisprudence, the politics of assistance in and to conflict and postconflict states, and rights in conditions of insurgency. A former contributing columnist for the *Los Angeles Times* and *The Globe and Mail*, she writes for Yale Global Online, and is an adviser to a number of nonprofit organizations working in the rights and democracy fields.

Jeremi Suri

Jeremi Suri holds the Mack Brown Distinguished Chair for Leadership in Global Affairs at the University of Texas at Austin, where he is a professor in the Lyndon B. Johnson School of Public Affairs and the Department of History. Suri has written five books on American politics, history, and foreign policy, including *Power and Protest: Global Revolution and the Rise of Detente, Henry Kissinger and the American Century,* and *Liberty's Surest Guardian: American Nation-Building from the Founders to Obama.* Suri writes for newspapers and magazines, including the *New York Times, Foreign Affairs,* and *Wired Magazine.* He also appears frequently on radio and television. Suri blogs at http://jeremisuri.net.

ACKNOWLEDGMENTS

This book began as an idea, became a project, and then inspired a conference. Our goal was to help scholars and practitioners "reinvent diplomacy" after more than a decade of disappointing diplomatic performance by Americans and other international actors. We recognize that the conditions of the international system, domestic politics, and the modern media make sustained diplomacy difficult. That is why it is more important than ever to develop a new body of scholarship, helping current leaders to understand the practice of diplomacy. The strongest and wealthiest actors—including the United States, the European Union, and China—will need to promote more skilled diplomacy in the coming years for the protection of their national interests. The same is true for smaller states and nongovernmental actors who seek to reform the international system. This volume is one piece of a larger scholarly and policy project to improve the foundations for global statesmanship in the twenty-first century. We hope to build on this foundational volume with more conferences, training opportunities, and publications. These continuing activities are central to the "Reinventing Diplomacy" initiative at the Lyndon B. Johnson School of Public Affairs.

Many people and institutions made this book possible. The editors are fortunate to work with stimulating and supportive colleagues at the LBJ School and the Department of History at the University of Texas at Austin. Both supported this project (intellectually and financially) from its beginnings, and the LBJ School has been especially generous in its support of the conference that produced this volume. The Institute for Historical Studies in the Department of History at the University of Texas was a vital early partner, helping us to bring many of the contributors to this project together on our campus. Additional financial support came from the Center for European Studies and the European Union Center of Excellence at the University of Texas. We also received generous funding from Livingston Kosberg. We are grateful for all of our generous supporters.

A number of colleagues served as insightful commentators on the chapters in this volume. They include David Adelman, Kamran Ali, Joshua Busby, Robert Chesney, Geoffrey Connor, Yoav Di-Capua, Jonathan Fine, William Inboden, Patrick McDonald, Simon Miles, Larry Napper, Larry O'Bryon, Rosalba Ojeda, Jason Parker, Lorinc Redei, Bartholomew Sparrow, Alan Tully, and Catherine Weaver. Beth Rutter and Liliana Merubia helped with organizing much of our work on this project. David McBride, our editor at Oxford University Press, offered encouragement and sage guidance.

We owe deep thanks to Dr. Jenny Knowles Morrison. At every step, she helped us to bring this project to fruition, as an intellectual contributor and a scholarly manager. Thank you, Jenny.

1

Introduction

ROBERT HUTCHINGS AND JEREMI SURI

The international system is experiencing the most profound power shift in more than sixty years. The collapse of the Cold War order, the rise of China and India as global powers, and the advent of new transnational challenges have all combined to overturn old verities and assumed points of reference. Who imagined that the Cold War, during which both sides had mobilized as if for war, would end with the peaceful capitulation of one side, or that the post–Cold War era, which was supposed to be characterized by "soft power" and economic interdependence, would prove to be so violent? Where will the next challenges appear, and how shall we prepare for them? Strategists, scholars, and government leaders have reason to be humble in their predictions. The only certainty is that the future will surprise us. Forward-looking leaders must equip themselves with the knowledge and skills to adapt to unexpected changes and work with unfamiliar groups.

This diplomatic capability appears most lacking in contemporary foreign policy leadership. With major flux in East Asia, Europe, South Asia, and, of course, the Middle East, virtually every country around the world is facing a new set of political, economic, and social pressures. Yet there seems to be a global deficit in strategic responses to these challenges—at the very time that such action is most urgently needed. Stalemate hinders even incremental progress in global negotiations over climate change, the Doha trade round, nuclear arms reductions, a global energy forum, and almost every other major issue. International institutions from the United Nations Security Council to the international financial institutions to regional organizations like NATO, the European Union, and the many Asia-Pacific security forums have shown themselves unable to make urgently needed reforms. The World Bank and the International Monetary Fund continue to maintain the cozy arrangement under which an American always leads the former and a European, the latter— despite repeated calls for opening these institutions up to the emerging economic powers. The UN Security Council continues to reflect the political arrangements of the immediate post–World War II period rather than twenty-first-century population and power realities. Security Council reform not only failed, it never began.

In the United States, the Cold War produced some lingering bad habits. The existence for more than forty years of a known external threat discouraged scholars and statesmen from undertaking a rigorous strategic reappraisal of their nation's evolving interests. Also, because that long conflict had such a substantial military component, and because countries on both sides of the East–West divide built large military arsenals, it became tempting to view every strategic challenge, then and now, through the same lens. Domestic political posturing about American strength and righteousness reinforced this tendency.

The response to the terrorist attacks of September 11, 2001—the so-called global war on terror—reflected and reinforced the inherited strategic distortion in American thinking. Policymakers reached for a misguided war metaphor because it was the only one they could imagine. Policymakers emphasized military responses because those were the tools they were most accustomed to wielding in the face of existential foreign threats. As a result, American foreign policy tactics and strategy were both underanalyzed and overmilitarized in the early twenty-first century. These shortcomings had profound effects in misdirecting American power, alienating allies, and discrediting worthy goals, including democratization and development.

The Importance of Diplomacy

America has the world's most sophisticated and ubiquitous military—present in every corner of the globe, and performing missions from border protection to rural development to counterterrorist operations. At the same time, the United States has a deficient diplomatic corps—underfunded, minimally trained, and frequently overmatched by the breadth and scope of problems the country faces throughout the world. Annual defense spending dwarfs that of the State Department and USAID combined. The Defense Department's 2008 budget was more than twenty-four times as large as that of the State Department and USAID combined ($750 billion compared with $31 billion). Only $7.5 billion went to the State Department's diplomatic and consular programs. The Defense Department has more lawyers than the entire U.S. diplomatic corps.[1] As then Defense Secretary Robert Gates argued in 2008, the U.S. government risks the "creeping militarization" of its foreign policy by giving such overwhelming priority to the Pentagon.[2]

Now that U.S. ground forces have returned home from two of the country's longest wars, in Iraq and Afghanistan, there is an urgent need to reassess strategic priorities and capabilities. What international role should the United States play in the twenty-first century? How, and with what tools, should the United States engage the rest of the world? What role does America's still-unrivaled military power play, and how can U.S. leaders better use the formidable nonmilitary elements of American power and influence? How, in particular, can scholars and practitioners, working together, resurrect diplomacy from the musty archives of the past and make it more relevant to the present and future?

Scholars and practitioners have produced a substantial body of literature on international economics and military strategy, but they have not done the same for diplomacy and statecraft, for which the literature is less systematic and richly developed. There is good material on certain aspects of diplomacy—such as negotiation, decision-making, and national negotiating "styles"[3]—but there are few good synthetic treatments that bring these and other dimensions together.[4] The rich memoir literature—from statesmen as well as working-level professionals—rarely provides the deep analysis needed for serious understanding, and it is usually confined to a particular era that does not lend itself to application in other times and places. Seminal works by Dean Acheson, George Kennan, Henry Kissinger, and others— memoirs as well as diplomatic history—sometimes offer general observations about diplomatic practice, but these are usually brief asides rather than systematic analyses.[5]

At the other end of the spectrum, studies of diplomatic theory and practice tend to be too general and abstract, illustrating theory by brief examples rather than deep research. Several single-authored or coauthored studies, some by scholars, others by former diplomats, fall into this category.[6] These works generally have the virtue of coherence, theoretical grounding, and logical exposition, but they tend to be too distant and detached from the drama, disorder, and confusion of diplomacy as it actually happens. Historical cases are presented briefly to illustrate particular points, but without detail or depth. Few studies have attempted to combine theoretical rigor and deep research in the manner of Graham Allison's early study of the Cuban missile crisis or Margaret MacMillan's recent examination of the origins of the First World War.[7]

Several recent compendia—large multiauthor volumes—are notable for the breadth of their coverage, but individual chapters tend to be too brief to allow for deep and persuasive research.[8] Reading fifteen pages on public diplomacy and another fifteen on economic diplomacy may be useful for introducing students to the field, but it cannot yield a broad understanding of the making and implementation of foreign policy. Such volumes, even the better ones, suffer from having dozens of different authors producing brief chapters of uneven quality. Many of the more narrowly focused multiauthor works suffer from the same liability.[9]

An underlying conceptual impediment is that diplomacy, foreign policy, and national security strategy have tended to be compartmentalized. Diplomacy, in this schema, is what diplomats do, foreign policy is what politicians do, and the management of national security is what nameless administrators do. This book takes a profoundly different approach, arguing that the segmentation of these various activities cannot produce a full understanding of the conduct of international diplomacy. The foreign policy challenges covered here required politically astute statesmanship, careful implementation of policy decisions, and close management of diverse actors. The activities of a U.S. arms control negotiator, for example, cannot be understood without an appreciation for the political support that existed at the highest levels of government, the foreign policy strategy within which arms negotiations fit, the management of the multiple foreign policy agencies (and their divergent interests) involved in arms control, and so on. Key diplomatic actors, from the president or prime minister down to senior staff, are at one time or another national security strategists, managers of the foreign policy process, policymakers, diplomats, and negotiators.

The very term "diplomacy" presents problems because it tends to connote a more limited set of activities than the editors and authors intend. Other terms—statecraft, foreign policy, and national security policy—present similar difficulties. Absent a better alternative, this work also employs the term "diplomacy," but as the authors of the various case studies make clear, we mean by that term a very broad set of activities by which political leaders, senior foreign policy officials, staff members of the foreign policy agencies, diplomats, and negotiators conceive of, develop, and implement foreign policy.

Among most students and scholars of international relations, diplomacy hardly exists as a serious field of inquiry or as an academic course of study. At the undergraduate level, few universities offer a single course on diplomacy. Diplomatic education at the graduate level is not much better. Even in public policy schools, including those with "diplomacy" and "foreign service" in their titles, there is nothing that could be called a curriculum in this field. Most of them offer no courses at all in diplomacy; those few such courses that do exist are not comparable in rigor or breadth to the rest of the curricula in those schools.

At the professional level, diplomacy is similarly undervalued, underanalyzed, and underresourced. Although diplomatic training occurs in foreign service institutes and academies of diplomacy around the world, this is mostly confined to foreign language and area studies training, with a thin veneer of "how to" training for junior diplomats. Indeed, few diplomats, American or other, have ever enrolled in a course in diplomacy—before or after entering diplomatic service. Even as they rise to the highest levels of diplomatic service, they are expected to learn "on the job" rather than as part of a rigorous program of professional preparation. Contrast this to the professional training their military counterparts receive all the way through their careers.

This volume aims at making a contribution, albeit modest, to "reinventing diplomacy" as a subject of serious study by students, scholars, and practicing diplomats alike. It proceeds from the premise that the study of diplomacy, strategy, and statecraft needs to be more comprehensive in scope, better informed by history, and more global in outlook. One of its aims is to "internationalize" the study and practice of statecraft so that American and Chinese diplomats, for example, can be trained in similar, or at least mutually comprehensible, ways. Such a synthesis occurs in the academic study of international relations but not in strategy and statecraft. It is a strange irony that international relations scholars from around the world speak a common professional language—read the same books, debate the same theories—but their statesmen and diplomats do not. Of course, there are common manners of diplomatic discourse that facilitate communication among governments, but these are matters of form rather than substance. The cultural and philosophical foundations of diplomatic practice are divergent in the extreme, even in the case of neighboring countries like France and Germany or Mexico and the United States.

In particular, the present volume aims to make a contribution to the study of diplomatic case studies, and their application to contemporary statecraft. Once a staple of international relations, this literature has thinned out considerably in the past decade. In particular, the widely used Pew Case Studies in International Affairs have not been adequately replenished since Pew Charitable Trusts ended its sponsorship several years ago.[10] This volume will fill a scholarly void, and it will push the study of diplomatic practice in promising new directions.

We have assembled a diverse group of scholars and practitioners, representing a variety of perspectives, time periods, and geographic areas. Some depict diplomacy at the highest level; others focus on the second- and third-tier working-level diplomats whose activities had a decisive influence on policy. Some cases have a strong U.S. dimension; others do not.

The cases presented here are ones that we considered examples of successful diplomacy. There are, of course, many assessments of diplomatic failure— every failure attracts critics, who, like vultures, peck away at the vulnerable remains of human frailty. Studies of diplomatic success, however, are far less common because success is difficult to pin down. Success for whom? Who was responsible? The guiding insight of this volume is that we should continue to examine diplomatic failures, but we must also try to learn from successful diplomatic efforts. Otherwise, we diminish the possibilities of diplomacy (as is common), and we fall into the cynical "creeping militarism" that Robert Gates astutely identified in our own time.

Creating a rigorous comparative framework for the study of successful (as well as unsuccessful) diplomacy is integral to the prevention and resolution of violent conflicts. Diplomacy is not an alternative to war, nor is it simply the work that precedes the onset of war or follows war's conclusion. Diplomacy is an ever-present and always essential element of effective statecraft, under conditions of war, peace, and everything in between. Until states and their leaders define their national interests reasonably rather than extravagantly, and pursue their goals through rational strategies and effective tactics, the struggle to avert or contain violent conflict is lost before it begins. The study of diplomacy will not produce perpetual peace, but it might help reduce the dysfunction and misperception that sometimes give rise to conflict.

What Is Diplomacy?

Diplomacy is a concept rooted in history. In its contemporary manifestations, it reflects the efforts by states to exercise power in ways that engage more potential partners, expanding possible points of consensus. Diplomacy emphasizes mutual gains, relationships, and compromises for larger purposes. It implies a repeated set of interactions and a process of mutual learning between actors. Diplomacy includes coercion and threats, but it also requires discussion and room for bargaining between participants. Diplomacy, therefore, rejects quick and final solutions to complex international problems.

Diplomacy is an ongoing process and a recurring mode of interaction, more than a specific tactic or maneuver. Louis XIV's distinguished diplomat François de Callières used this insight as the foundation for his remarkable and still widely read treatise on negotiation and statecraft:

> A powerful prince who maintains a constant system of diplomacy served by wise and instructed negotiators in the different states of Europe, and who thus cultivates well-chosen friendships and maintains useful sources of information, is in a position to influence the destiny of neighbouring foreign states, or to pursue war where it is favourable to his design. In all these concerns, the prosperity of his plans and the greatness of his name depend first and last on the conduct and qualities of the negotiators to whom he entrusts his services.[11]

Callières treated diplomacy as a crucial determinant of state power and as a contributor to all forms of policy: alliance, entente, rivalry, and even warfare.

He described diplomacy by the personal interactions of state envoys in foreign territories and the qualities of thought behind those interactions. The skilled diplomat, for Callières, studied the history of his peers closely, learning to make his state's interests compatible with the fears, hopes, and personalities of others. Diplomacy was a social game for Callières, with fine food and wine at lavish banquets that broke down barriers, and it was an arena for intellectual artistry, where the diplomat brought together different political techniques and cultural styles for carefully chosen purposes. Above all, Callières explained that successful diplomacy helped a ruler to achieve his aims, and often reduce his costs, in both peace and war.

Sir Harold Nicolson, the great early twentieth-century British scholar of diplomacy, concurred. He emphasized the personal elements of diplomacy, and he described how they contributed to the interests of the state and its people. Writing with his typical directness, Nicolson explained: "Diplomacy is neither the invention nor the pastime of some particular political system, but is an essential element in any reasonable relation between man and man and between nation and nation."[12] The history of modern diplomacy for Nicolson, as for the contributors to this book, is the history of relations between individuals serving larger political groups—both state and nonstate.

Nicolson applied his concept of diplomacy to the study of two moments in the modern era when the negotiations and relationships between diplomats transformed the international system: the Congress of Vienna in 1815 and the Paris Peace Conference in 1919. A century apart, these two postwar gatherings of state representatives sought to replace years of destructive warfare with enduring cooperation and peace. The two conferences captured the great potential and the frustrating challenges for modern diplomacy. They also illustrated why the quality and context of diplomacy are crucial to the evolution of the international system.[13]

The successful diplomacy at the Congress of Vienna, dominated by Austrian Foreign Minister Clements von Metternich, established a system of consultation and compromise (the "Congress System") between the four big European powers: Austria-Hungary, Prussia, Russia, and Great Britain. They managed disputes on the European continent through negotiation for more than fifty years. With the revival of France under new monarchs, they also integrated Paris into a European-wide diplomatic process. The cooperative relationships established at the Congress of Vienna ended a century filled with warfare on the European continent, opening a half-century of unprecedented peace between powerful neighboring states.

The Congress System was not perfect, as the Crimean War of 1853–1856 revealed, but it preserved peace in Europe and allowed the states on the continent to grow and prosper as they had not in the decades before 1815.

The leaders of Europe did not abandon their traditional ambitions—on the continent, and especially in their expanding overseas empires. Under the Congress System, however, they calibrated their actions to respect the legitimate interests of other states and preserve cooperative relations. The Congress System used diplomacy to support and coordinate diverse European state interests.[14]

The Congress System broke down as social and economic changes within societies replaced the diplomats of the early nineteenth century with leaders intent on pursuing more aggressive policies. The newly unified countries of Germany and Italy benefited from a shift in industrial and military power, and they no longer wished to play by the conservative rules set out in 1815. In the scramble for empire, all the major European powers emphasized military expansion over careful diplomacy. The rejection of Congress diplomacy by Otto von Bismarck in Germany, Louis Napoleon in France, William Gladstone in Great Britain, and Nicholas I in Russia opened a new era that A.J.P. Taylor aptly described as a "struggle for mastery." Rivalry and conflict among the European powers contributed to escalating violence and the "Great War" that destroyed much of the continent in the early twentieth century.[15]

The Paris Peace Conference in 1919 did not replicate its predecessor in Vienna, but it drew on the same determination to replace decades of conflict with renewed cooperation. The Paris Peace Conference also articulated an idealistic vision of international relations based on law and freedom, not privilege and military repression. The victors from the First World War sought to announce a "new diplomacy" that emphasized arms reductions, compromise on territorial disputes, and the managed breakup of empires. Under pressure from American president Woodrow Wilson, the Treaty of Versailles created the League of Nations to institutionalize diplomacy, emphasizing collective security over unilateralism and war. The settlement at the end of the Great War promised a hopeful new beginning for Europe, the United States, and other parts of the world.[16]

These idealistic aspirations were widely popular, especially among intellectuals, but the Paris Peace Conference failed to give diplomacy a real chance. Too many key actors from Germany, but also from Russia, China, and other emerging states, were excluded. Despite later accusations, the terms of the treaty were *not* unduly harsh on those who lost the war. What was missing from the final settlement was a process for reconciling the costs of rebuilding the victors' societies with the needs and the pride of those who had lost the war. Countries like France required an infusion of reparations money to overcome the damage to their society from the war, but Germans were unwilling to accept that they should pay and accept complete responsibility for the damage. The treaty felt imposed, it fell short of Wilsonian promises for broader international participation, and it failed to create a process for continued negotiation and trust building. Unlike the Congress of Vienna, the Paris Peace Conference sought to implement political and legal solutions rather than seed relations and ongoing negotiations for mutual gain. Nicolson was one of many to diagnose more miscommunication and diversion at the Paris Peace Conference than direct diplomatic dialogue.[17]

President Woodrow Wilson and his successors were shattered by the experience of the Paris Peace Conference. They initially sought to avoid further entanglements in international diplomacy of this kind. With the rise of fascism and the Second World War, however, President Franklin Roosevelt was one of many Americans to realize that the future of the United States required a new commitment to diplomacy, on an unprecedented scale. In fact, the United States as a nation exhibited its most serious commitment to diplomacy in the middle of the twentieth century. This was, perhaps, the "golden age" of American internationalism. Although many of the key elements of midcentury American internationalism remained controversial, especially within the United States, Washington's diplomacy helped set a new pattern for postwar international relations.[18]

Postwar American diplomacy is not necessarily a model for today, but it is an inspiration and a useful point of departure for reinventing the concept. A brief overview of this history highlights the key elements of diplomacy as we employ the concept in this volume. A focus on this period, in its historical context following the Congress of Vienna and the Paris Peace Conference, captures many of the inspirations for how we define, narrate, and advocate diplomacy in the chapters of this book.

The Postwar Moment

In the aftermath of the Second World War, the United States possessed unmatched military and economic leverage over the largely destroyed and starving countries of Western Europe. Many observers in Washington believed that the United States should use its extraordinary power to force a new future on the societies that had embroiled the United States in two terrible world wars. This was the thinking behind Secretary of the Treasury Henry Morgenthau's plan to "pastoralize" Germany. Morgenthau argued that the United States should deploy its power to solve "the German problem" in Europe by keeping the Germans down. Morgenthau had many supporters in Washington, especially among those who wished to avoid another world war and focus American capabilities at home.[19]

The Soviet Union modeled a different use of power within the parts of Eastern Europe occupied by the Red Army. Soviet forces used their power to extract resources from Eastern Germany and other former Nazi-occupied areas. The Soviets installed leaders trained in Moscow and loyal to Josef Stalin wherever they could. They ruled with an iron fist that emphasized control and mobilization over recovery and growth.[20]

Morgenthau's proposal had an intuitive appeal to President Harry Truman, a politician who had initially made a name for himself through his participation in congressional efforts to identify and prosecute "war profiteers" in American society. Stalin's approach, although officially condemned by Washington, also had appeal for those who wanted to ensure control over Europe after a terrible world war. Those who advocated a deal with Stalin to divide the continent into Soviet and American spheres, for purposes of geopolitical stability, implicitly accepted the repressive exercise of power in postwar Europe.

In the end, however, the United States chose to use its power in Europe, and other parts the world, differently. Emerging from a decade of economic depression followed by four years of war, many leading American figures believed that the nation had to build international consensus around common approaches to political and economic affairs. This was the "New Deal" approach to the world. It emphasized open markets, industrial growth, political freedoms, and state-centered regulations to manage "boom and bust" cycles. New Dealers recognized that building consensus around these practices, particularly in Europe and East Asia, required much more than brute force. It required, as it had at home, skillful and consistent diplomacy.

The New Deal was a political style that encouraged diplomatic uses of power. Franklin Roosevelt embodied this approach in his efforts to build a "grand alliance" with Great Britain and the Soviet Union during the war. He also modeled diplomacy in his creation of numerous "alphabet" agencies (they became known by their initials), both at home and abroad, to give diverse actors a stake in an American-led postwar order. This was the shared goal of the National Recovery Administration, aimed at unemployed workers in the United States, and the World Bank, devoted to improving circumstances in poor countries after the war. The multiplying agencies of the New Deal, and their spaghetti web of constituents, were the frustrating genius of American diplomacy in this era. Engagement and connection substituted for coherence and clarity. This approach seemed to work, at least in comparison to the politics of scarcity and conflict that brought such suffering in the decade before.[21]

America's postwar diplomacy was multidimensional and long-lasting. It did not grow out of a single document or plan. Most of the key diplomats then, as now, had limited formal training in diplomacy as a subject of study. What they possessed was a *sensibility* and a *set of experiences* that encouraged a "magnetic" approach to power. Postwar American leaders believed that the nation's unprecedented power would work most effectively and efficiently when it attracted support and nurtured new relationships. They used coercion and intimidation when necessary, especially in excluding communist sympathizers from power, but they instinctively emphasized inclusion, consultation, and compromise. They looked to engage former enemies, rather than alienate or even contain. They hoped to build more policy stakeholders in a postwar society of growth, freedom, and stability.[22]

The postwar American diplomats found effective and courageous partners in Western Europe. Without these partners on the ground, American efforts never could have succeeded. In many cases, postwar European leaders pushed Americans to broaden their commitments and invest more in societies that were, in fact, very far removed the American vision of democratic capitalism. Diplomats such as Jean Monnet and Robert Schuman in France, Ernest Bevin and Anthony Eden in Great Britain, Alcide De Gasperi in Italy, and Konrad Adenauer and Ludwig Erhard in West Germany built enduring personal relationships with American leaders that nurtured trust, cooperation, and friendship. Although a desire to contain Soviet advances short of war motivated much of the American commitment to Western Europe in the Cold War, the close diplomatic connections on the ground channeled assistance in creative, effective, and sustainable directions.

Americans did more to help rebuild and secure Western Europe than they could have imagined in 1945 because of the deep diplomatic commitments on both sides of the Atlantic. This was indeed a "golden age" for U.S.–Western European diplomacy. Leaders acted out of self-interest. They worked together to create cooperative mechanisms that helped all the major actors in the long run. Forward-thinking and cooperative self-interest of this kind was a more effective foundation for peace and prosperity than the idealistic alternatives proposed in prior decades. Diplomacy was indeed realistic.[23]

W. Averell Harriman—a wealthy businessman who served as America's ambassador to the Soviet Union during the Second World War, then a key leader for American postwar aid in Europe through the Economic Cooperation Administration (ECA), and then a frequent diplomatic troubleshooter for Cold War presidents—articulated the self-conscious mix of influence, restraint, and consensus building within U.S. policy circles:

> The bigger the stick, the more it must be kept in the closet. It is a fundamental principle of American foreign policy that the more power we have, the more considerate we should be of the sovereignty of other nations. I think you will agree that no one has greater determination than I have to encourage and press the OEEC [Organization for European Economic Cooperation] and the different countries to

do what we think is needed to attain European recovery and greater integration of European organization. This can only be done with the greatest of skill, patience, and real diplomacy.[24]

"Real diplomacy" began during the war, when American leaders accommodated the concerns of figures such as British prime minister Winston Churchill, Field Marshal Bernard Montgomery, and General Charles de Gaulle, despite their nearly complete dependence on U.S. assistance. President Franklin Roosevelt and General Dwight Eisenhower consulted closely with these men to strengthen a common war effort. They did not dictate strategy.[25]

"Real diplomacy" also occurred when Americans encouraged a primary role for national and local West European leaders in disbursing precious development funds allocated by Washington after the war. The European Recovery Program ("the Marshall Plan") seeded joint councils staffed by mixed nationalities to set common priorities, procedures, and forms of accountability. The Marshall Plan rebuilt productive economies on the foundation of new mutually beneficial relationships. The cooperation mattered, in the end, more than the money.[26]

"Real diplomacy" was also the origin for what became the most successful alliance in history: the North Atlantic Treaty Organization (NATO). The initiative for the alliance came from the Europeans, not the Americans. The alliance pooled resources for collective security despite vast disparities in capabilities. Most of all, the alliance gave all participants a strong voice in decision-making, despite the obvious deference to American military primacy. NATO has held together for more than sixty years and expanded successfully because it is an alliance of unequal military powers that share a commitment to serious consultation and common security interests. Americans negotiate with their NATO partners, they adjust to the needs of their NATO partners, and they pool skills and experiences for common goals, as in the recent NATO deployments in Afghanistan. History is filled with powerful military alliances, but NATO has succeeded as others have not because of its diplomatic foundation—embraced by the United States and its less powerful allies.[27]

A similar and perhaps more impressive example of postwar diplomacy is the formation of the European Union (EU)—a set of institutions designed to build common practices for all residents of the European continent. Begun as a mechanism for managing access to scarce industrial resources after the Second World War, the EU emerged slowly over the next six decades to increase trade, labor mobility, business and university collaboration, and health and environmental cooperation for an expanding number of states—twenty-eight as of 2015. The EU includes a directly elected parliament, a court of justice, a central bank, and a shared currency. Despite frequent economic difficulties and obvious political frictions, the EU has brought together most of the large and small states in Europe, many of whom were long-standing adversaries, for cooperative purposes. The EU functions through a continuing process of consultation and compromise, mediated through multiple institutions. Even when disagreements over social welfare programs or regional defense are most intense, the leaders on the continent have nurtured an overriding commitment to resolving their differences through mutual respect and accommodation. The states of Europe, which spent more than three hundred years fighting one another for continental supremacy, have, through the EU, redefined their relations around peaceful diplomacy.[28]

Diplomacy is about toughness and disagreement, as much as aid and alliance building. What distinguishes diplomatic uses of power is the emphasis on relationships, repeated interactions, and efforts to find mutual benefits, even among former adversaries. The United States adopted this approach with remarkable success and consistency in postwar Europe.[29] So did the leading European states, with transformative effects on a continent that had been dominated by war.

The history of other regions is, of course, very different for the postwar period. The nature of diplomacy differs across both space and time. Our point is not to offer an exhaustive survey, but to draw insights from the recent history of diplomacy in a variety of areas, not exclusively Europe, for contemporary global challenges. We have a lot to learn from these cases. They are valuable and influential, although they are not complete.

Successful Diplomacy (Not Diplomatic Success)

We frequently read about diplomatic failures—in the Middle East, around North Korea, and between the United States and emerging powers. Rarely do we read about diplomatic successes. The most commonly agreed instances of American diplomatic success are probably postwar Western European reconstruction and the resolution of the Cuban missile crisis, joined perhaps by the Camp David accords and the American opening to Communist China. The relative neglect of diplomatic successes in the scholarly literature is attributable to actual deficiencies in diplomatic practice—a concern that is indeed part of the rationale for this book. More deeply, scholarly neglect is a consequence of inadequate reflection about what constitutes success or failure. We have already argued that we should learn from our successes as well as our failures. To do so, we need to recalibrate and develop a more realistic way of assessing success and failure. If almost everything is considered to be a failure (or simply irrelevant), we risk learning nothing at all.

In this book we distinguish *diplomatic success* from *successful diplomacy*. The former is outcome driven: if things turned out well, the case in question must have been a success; if things turned out badly, we label it a failure. The Bay of Pigs was a failure because the invasion was repulsed; the Cuban missile crisis was a success because nuclear confrontation was averted. Had the invasion of Cuba somehow succeeded, President Kennedy might well have received praise for his boldness and courage in the face of uncertain odds. By the same token, had the Cuban missile crisis led to a U.S.–Soviet nuclear exchange, Kennedy might well have been condemned for reckless brinkmanship with a less-than-stable Soviet leader. Conflating outcomes with policy process—failing to distinguish diplomatic success from successful diplomacy—produces an intellectual muddle.

The same is true of "intelligence failures," real or alleged. When a national security disaster or "strategic surprise" occurs, it is quickly and indelibly labeled an "intelligence failure." Rarely are the right questions asked before rendering such a severe judgment. What, precisely, was the alleged failure? Could the outcome have been prevented with reasonably good intelligence performance based on the information available at the time, guarding against the false clarity of hindsight bias after the event?

"Diplomatic success," defined by outcome, is often ambiguous and subject to differing assessments owing to broad historical factors that diplomats do not control. Such judgments also tend to shift over time. In answering President Nixon's question about the impact of the French Revolution, Zhou Enlai is said to have replied that it was "too early to say." Zhou may have misunderstood the question in giving his memorable answer,[30] but the story illustrates the point nonetheless. It is certainly appropriate for scholars and practitioners to weigh the historical record of diplomatic or foreign policy successes and failures, which is why most of the literature is focused in this direction, but this kind of approach often does not shed much light on how successful the diplomatic practice actually was. Outcomes alone do not elucidate the quality of the diplomacy during the course of events.

"Successful diplomacy" is a more useful concept. That is our focus in this book. Political leaders set objectives for their diplomats (or other foreign policy officials); if those objectives are achieved, the diplomacy can be judged successful, quite apart from the ultimate consequences of the actions undertaken. Of the cases in this volume, one could debate whether the Camp David accords solved fundamental regional problems, but one can assert with much more confidence that this was an instance of successful diplomacy in that the negotiations—from the American perspective at least—achieved what they were intended to achieve.

"Successful diplomacy" deals with the actions of human agents, acting individually or in concert, to affect outcomes. The question of agency is critical here. Diplomats and others inherit objective realities—the "structure" of the situation—that constrain or enable action. At one extreme are cases in which the objective realities diplomats face defy successful resolution, no matter how skillful the diplomacy. At the other end are cases wherein forces were converging toward a happy outcome that even a diplomatic bungler could have seen through to a successful end. In between are the most interesting cases, in which a proverbial "window of opportunity" opens to allow a diplomatic breakthrough when no such possibility may have existed before. At such times, diplomats have an opportunity to alter the course of history, or at least nudge it in a favorable direction. American diplomacy at the end of the Cold War in Europe, another case covered in this volume, was one such case of a fleeting opportunity, seized by American (and German) diplomats.

Distinguishing agency from structure is a key challenge. A focus on diplomats leads to an inflation of their agency and a downplaying of structural factors; a focus on systemic forces tends to encourage retrospective determinism, whereupon individual agency accounts for little more than "residual variance." Our cases strive to steer between these two extremes, to give a rigorous accounting of both structure and agency.

Specifying the "unit of analysis" is critical. "Mexico" was not an actor in our case on the North American Free Trade Agreement (NAFTA); individuals acting in the name of the government of Mexico were. Which actors? In which agencies? What did they do? How and to whom did they do it? (This is Lenin's *"Kto kogo?"* question: "Who [did what to] whom?") Diplomatic case studies understandably focus on presidents, prime ministers, and foreign ministers. Sometimes this is fully warranted, but it can also be a consequence of the ease of retrieval because more is discoverable about the actions of senior leaders than of their able lieutenants. Yet the majority of policy ideas (good and bad) originate well below the level of the seniormost political leaders, as do most of the actions required to implement policies. Even in cases like the Camp David negotiations and the American opening to Communist China, characterized by diplomacy at the highest level, the initiatives involved much more than the personal roles of Anwar Sadat, Menachem Begin, and Jimmy Carter or Richard Nixon, Henry Kissinger, Mao Zedong, and Zhou Enlai. Each of these leaders relied on countless advisers, aides, and forgotten diplomats.

One of the key issues affecting successful diplomacy has to do with the "principal–agent" problem: decision-makers (principals) and their diplomats (agents) have different or "asymmetrical" interests and information, and they often act at cross-purposes. As Fred Iklé explained in his classic book *How Nations Negotiate*, negotiators "have personal ambitions which are rarely, if ever, identical with the interests of their country"[31]—or, he might have added, with those of the presidents or prime ministers who sent them to do their bidding.

Diplomatic practice is replete with examples of negotiators who are sent abroad without the full backing or attention of their senior leaders, or without a consensus among cabinet-level officials, making it hard to represent a government position that has not fully formed. At the other extreme, there are many examples of negotiators acting as free agents, going well beyond their mandates in their zeal to reach an agreement, whether or not it serves the objectives they were sent to advance.

Successful diplomacy demands disciplined and coherent government, in which the various foreign policy departments and their "agents" operate within a common strategic framework. One cannot understand the role played by diplomats without reference to their larger organizational context. Diplomats represent the characteristics of their government, as well as its official positions.

The role of political leadership is both critical and inadequately understood. Most of the leaders covered in this volume were not larger-than-life Hegelian "world-historical" figures. Effective political leadership is not necessarily or usually a consequence of charismatic personality. The case studies presented here probe the question of political leadership to determine what attributes, from the heroic to the mundane, were decisive; they identify the most critical actors—and the interactions among them—that contributed to effective negotiations, compromises, and relationships. That is the essence of successful diplomacy.

Historical Case Studies

We have chosen cases that illustrate the conduct of diplomacy in very different settings. They begin with the development of the post–World War II order and conclude with the contemporary challenge of providing development assistance to Afghanistan. The settings span five continents; the actors range from presidents and prime ministers of powerful states to representatives of struggling postcolonial countries and relatively unknown lower-level officials in international organizations. Some cases deal with epochal issues like the end of the Cold War in Europe; others, with the convening of a single conference. Our hope in presenting such a diverse set of cases is to identify some general principles of effective diplomacy that transcend particular settings.

Stephen Porter's case examines the creation of UNRRA, the United Nations Relief and Rehabilitation Administration, a fascinating, complex joint effort among forty-four countries and numerous nongovernmental organizations. This little-known case of multilateral negotiation and coordination set the stage for the many other humanitarian relief agencies and indeed for the

UN system itself. Christopher Lee's examination of the 1955 Bandung conference, half a world away from UNRRA's main operations, marked the first effort toward solidarity among the newly independent postcolonial states, joined by other leaders of what would become the Non-Aligned Movement.

The efforts at multinational solidarity in Bandung were a precursor to an even larger diplomatic effort at global nuclear arms control. Jonathan Hunt's chapter recounts the motivations, challenges, negotiations, and innovations that led to the signing of the Nuclear Non-Proliferation Treaty (NPT) in 1968. Hunt recounts how perseverance, compromise, and coercion contributed to what he aptly calls a "nuclear community." Diplomacy was crucial in turning what looked like a race for the bomb into a more managed international order.

The next two cases involve well-known examples of diplomacy at the highest levels. Jeremi Suri's study of the Nixon-Kissinger opening to China in the early 1970s covers the elements of what might be called classical diplomacy—strategy, secrecy, patience, and face-to-face negotiations among dominant political figures. The opening also involved numerous probes by U.S. diplomats with their Pakistani, Romanian, and Polish counterparts, as well as the behind-the-scenes work of a skilled and disciplined National Security Council staff. Similarly, Galia Golan's chapter highlights how the diplomacy of the Camp David accords centered on the interactions among Sadat, Begin, and Carter, while also involving complex "two-level games" in which management (and manipulation?) of Israeli and Egyptian public opinion played a critical role. The Camp David case raises interesting questions about what constitutes "success" in international diplomacy. Was this a success for all parties equally, or did assessment of success depend on one's vantage point?

Robert Hutchings's case study of American diplomacy and the end of the Cold War in Europe looks inside the foreign policy apparatus of the U.S. government to explore the interactions among the White House and the Departments of State and Defense. Hutchings focuses on the strategic planning and complex negotiations that contributed to successful diplomacy. The roles of President George H.W. Bush and Secretary of State James Baker were indispensable, but this is a case involving many dozens of actors and agencies. In similar fashion, Mark Dawson's account of the formation and evolution of the European Community and its expansion eastward is a story not so much of visionary political leaders, but of European magistrates and Brussels-based bureaucrats creating a community of law. It is also an account of the creation of the European Union as an altogether new type of international body, and of such institutions as the International Court of Justice and the European Commission as independent actors in their own right.

Beatriz Leycegui and Rafael Fernandez de Castro examine the negotiation of the North American Free Trade Agreement (NAFTA) from the Mexican perspective, a neglected dimension in the scholarly literature. "Two-level games" were particularly important here, and the case shows how attentive Mexican negotiators were not only to domestic stakeholders in Mexico but also to those in the United States. The authors also bring the story up to the present, examining the lessons of NAFTA as applied to ongoing negotiations toward a Pacific Alliance among Chile, Colombia, Peru, and Mexico.

Finally, Paula Newberg's case explores multilateral diplomatic efforts in Afghanistan during the 1990s. This is an emblematic post–Cold War case, involving interactions with a weak and often hostile government pursuing a fundamentalist religious agenda. The case acquires particular salience in light of the so-called Arab Awakening, in which religious influences overlap with ethnic divisions in a region likely to be characterized by weak or failed states. This also brings our diplomatic survey almost full circle, back to the legacy of the European colonial empires depicted in Christopher Lee's study of the Bandung Conference.

The conflict and uncertainty in the contemporary Middle East, as in other regions, offer compelling rationales for our historical focus in this volume. Military force and development aid alone will not bring peace and stability to the modern international system. Contemporary foreign policy requires more successful diplomacy. This volume examines the nature of successful diplomacy, drawing lessons grounded in past practice for current challenges. We conclude this volume with some explicit lessons for twenty-first-century diplomats and their princes.

Notes

1. J. Anthony Holmes, "Where Are the Civilians? How to Rebuild the U.S. Foreign Service," *Foreign Affairs* 88, no. 1 (January–February 2009): 150. By 2012, the State Department and USAID budget had risen to $47 billion (Office of Management and Budget, *The Federal Budget 2012*), but the disparity remained nearly as wide.
2. "Gates Again Urges Funding for Diplomacy," *Los Angeles Times*, July 16, 2008.
3. The publications of the U.S. Institute of Peace, particularly its series on national negotiating behavior, deserve special mention.
4. Paul Gordon Lauren, Gordon A. Craig, and Alexander L. George, *Force and Statecraft: Diplomatic Challenges of Our Time*, 4th ed. (New York: Oxford University Press, 2006) is a partial exception, but it takes on so much (diplomatic history as well as statecraft) that it is can serve as little more than an introduction to the subject matter. Alexander George's *Bridging the Gap: Theory and Practice in Foreign Policy* (Washington, DC: U.S. Institute of Peace Press, 1993) is another exception, but it is now rather dated, and it, too, is rather cursory in its treatment of key concepts related to "coercive diplomacy."
5. Dean Acheson, *Present at the Creation: My Years at the State Department* (New York: W.W. Norton & Co., 1987): George F. Kennan, *Memoirs, 1925–1950* (New York: Little,

Brown & Co., 1967); Henry A. Kissinger, *Diplomacy* (New York: Simon & Schuster, 1994), as well as his memoir trilogy: *White House Years, Years of Upheaval,* and *Years of Renewal.* There are also shorter works that distill general lessons for diplomacy: e.g., Abba Eban, *Diplomacy for the Next Century* (New Haven: Yale University Press, 1998); Chas. W. Freeman, Jr., *Arts of Power: Statecraft and Diplomacy* (Washington, DC: U.S. Institute of Peace Press, 1997). The memoir literature and the literature on diplomatic history are too vast to allow for a thorough accounting in these notes, which are limited to works explicitly focusing on diplomatic theory and practice.

6. R.K. Barston, *Modern Diplomacy,* 4th ed. (New York and London: Longman, 2013); G.R. Berridge, *Diplomacy: Theory and Practice* (London: Palgrave, 2nd edition, 2002); Keith Hamilton and Richard Langhorne, *The Practice of Diplomacy: Its Evolution, Theory and Administration* (London: Routledge, 1995); Kishan S. Rana, *21st Century Diplomacy: A Practitioner's Guide* (New York: Continuum, 2011); Shaun Riordan, *The New Diplomacy* (Cambridge: Polity Press, 2003); Joseph M. Siracusa, *Diplomacy: A Very Short Introduction* (Oxford: Oxford University Press, 2010); Monteagle Stearns, *Talking to Strangers: Improving American Diplomacy at Home and Abroad* (Princeton, NJ: Princeton University Press, 1996).

7. Graham T. Allison, "Conceptual Models and the Cuban Missile Crisis," *American Political Science Review* 63, no. 3 (September 1969): 689–718; Graham T. Allison, *Essence of Decision: Explaining the Cuban Missile Crisis* (New York: Little, Brown and Company, 1971); Margaret MacMillan, *The War That Ended Peace: The Road to 1914* (New York: Random House, 2013).

8. See, e.g., Andrew F. Cooper, Jorge Heine, and Ramesh Thakur, eds. *The Oxford Handbook of Modern Diplomacy* (Oxford: Oxford University Press, 2013); Andrew G. Cooper, Brian Hocking, and William Maley, eds., *Global Governance and Diplomacy: Worlds Apart?* (London: Palgrave Macmillan, 2008); Pauline Kerr and Geoffrey Wiseman, eds., *Diplomacy in a Globalizing World: Theories and Practices* (Oxford: Oxford University Press, 2012).

9. G.R. Berridge, Maurice Keens-Soper, and T.G. Otte, *Diplomatic Theory from Machiavelli to Kissinger* (London: Palgrave, 2001); Brian Hocking, ed., *Foreign Ministries: Change and Adaptation* (London: Palgrave Macmillan, 1999); Brian Hocking and David Spence, eds., *Foreign Ministries in the European Union: Integrating Diplomats* (London: Palgrave Macmillan, 1999); Kishan Rana, *Asian Diplomacy: The Foreign Ministries of China, India, Japan, Singapore and Thailand* (DiploFoundation, 2007, Baltimore, Maryland); Paul Sharp and Geoffrey Wiseman, eds., *The Diplomatic Corps as an Institution of International Society* (London: Palgrave, 2008).

10. The case studies are now managed by the Institute for the Study of Diplomacy at Georgetown University (http://faculty.guisd.org/), but the supply has been dwindling, partly because of the pressure, on younger scholars in particular, to publish in refereed journals rather than in a case study series.

11. François de Callières, *De la manière de négocier avec les souverains* (originally published in France in 1716), reprinted in English as *The Practice of Diplomacy,* ed. A. F. Whyte (London: Constable and Company, 1919), 18.

12. Harold Nicolson, *Diplomacy* (Oxford: Oxford University Press, 1977 ed., originally published in 1939), 4.

13. See Harold Nicolson, *The Congress of Vienna* (New York: Harcourt, Brace, 1946) and *Peacemaking* (Boston: Houghton Mifflin, 1933). Nicolson attended the Paris Peace Conference as a young British foreign service officer. He wrote his account of that conference first, before turning to the history of the Congress of Vienna.

14. See Paul Schroeder, *The Transformation of European Politics, 1763–1848* (New York: Oxford University Press, 1994). Henry Kissinger's Ph.D. dissertation and first book remains an important account of this period. See *A World Restored: Metternich, Castlereagh, and the Problems of Peace, 1812–1822* (Boston: Houghton Mifflin, 1957).

15. See A.J.P. Taylor, *The Struggle for Mastery in Europe, 1848–1919* (Oxford: Oxford University Press, 1954). See also Paul Kennedy, *The Rise and Fall of the Great Powers* (New York: Random House, 1987), chaps. 4 and 5.

16. See Margaret MacMillan, *Paris 1919: Six Months That Changed the World* (New York: Random House, 2003); David A. Andelman, *A Shattered Peace: Versailles 1919 and the Price We Pay Today* (New York: Wiley, 2007); Erez Manela, *The Wilsonian Moment: Self-Determination and the International Origins of Anticolonial Nationalism* (New York: Oxford University Press, 2007).

17. See Nicolson, *Peacemaking*; Manfred F. Boemeke, Gerald D. Feldman, and Elisabeth Glaser, eds., *The Treaty of Versailles: A Reassessment after 75 Years* (New York: Cambridge University Press, 1998).

18. See Robert Divine, *Second Chance: The Triumph of Internationalism in America during World War II* (New York: Antheneum, 1967); Robert Dallek, *Franklin D. Roosevelt and American Foreign Policy, 1932–1945* (New York: Oxford University Press, 1979).

19. See Warren F. Kimball, *Swords into Ploughshares? The Morgenthau Plan for Defeated Germany, 1943–1946* (New York: Lippincott, 1976); William Hitchcock, *The Bitter Road to Freedom: The Human Cost of Allied Victory in World War II Europe* (New York: Free Press, 2008), chap. 5.

20. See Norman Naimark, *The Russians in Germany: A History of the Soviet Zone of Occupation, 1945–1949* (Cambridge, MA: Harvard University Press, 1995).

21. See Robert Dallek, *Franklin Roosevelt and American Foreign Policy, 1932–1945*, rev. ed. (New York: Oxford University Press, 1995); Elizabeth Borgwardt, *A New Deal for the World: America's Vision for Human Rights* (Cambridge, MA.: Belknap Press of Harvard University Press, 2005).

22. The best account of American diplomacy in the early Cold War is Melvyn P. Leffler, *A Preponderance of Power: National Security, the Truman Administration, and the Cold War* (Stanford, CA: Stanford University Press, 1992). The best theoretical exploration of this period is G. John Ikenberry, *After Victory: Institutions, Strategic Restraint, and the Rebuilding of Order After Major Wars* (Princeton, NJ: Princeton University Press, 2001).

23. See Geir Lundestad, *The United States and Western Europe since 1945: From "Empire" by Invitation to Transatlantic Drift* (Oxford: Oxford University Press, 2003); Jeremi Suri, *Henry Kissinger and the American Century* (Cambridge, MA: Belknap Press of Harvard University Press, 2007), chap. 2.

24. W. Averell Harriman, Paris, Office of Special Representative in Europe, Economic Cooperation Administration to Paul G. Hoffman, Administrator, Economic Cooperation Administration, February 6, 1948, folder 3, box 267, W. Averell Harriman Papers, Library of Congress Manuscript Reading Room, Washington, DC.

25. See Mark A. Stoler, *Allies and Adversaries: The Joint Chiefs of Staff, the Grand Alliance, and U.S. Strategy in World War II* (Chapel Hill: University of North Carolina Press, 2000).

26. See Greg Behrman, *The Most Noble Adventure: The Marshall Plan and the Time When America Helped Save Europe* (New York: Free Press, 2007); Michael J. Hogan, *The Marshall Plan: America, Britain, and the Reconstruction of Western Europe, 1947–1952* (New York: Cambridge University Press, 1987).

27. See John Lewis Gaddis, *We Now Know: Rethinking Cold War History* (New York: Oxford University Press, 1997), chap. 2; Andreas Wenger, Christian Nuenlist, and Anna Locher, eds., *Transforming NATO in the Cold War: Challenges beyond Deterrence in the 1960s* (London: Routledge, 2007).

28. See William Hitchcock, *The Struggle for Europe: The Turbulent History of a Divided Continent, 1945 to the Present* (New York: Random House, 2003); James J. Sheehan, *Where Have All the Soldiers Gone? The Transformation of Modern Europe* (New York: Houghton Mifflin, 2008).

29. See Jeremi Suri, *Liberty's Surest Guardian: American Nation-Building from the Founders to Obama* (New York: Free Press, 2011), chap. 4.

30. See Richard McGregor, "Zhou's Cryptic Caution Lost in Translation," FT.com, June 10, 2011.

31. Fred Charles Iklé, *How Nations Negotiate* (New York: Harper & Row, 1964), 143.

2

Humanitarian Diplomacy after World War II

The United Nations Relief and Rehabilitation Administration

STEPHEN R. PORTER

The close of the Second World War sparked a burst of international institution building on a scale arguably not seen before or since. From the last stages of hostilities through the first few years of a tense and qualified peace, the Allied victors in particular created a galaxy of civilian-based organizations and attendant collaborative systems that, along with anticolonialism and an emerging Cold War, helped to usher forth a new international order. Shaping the field of global capitalism for decades to come, for instance, were the International Monetary Fund and the International Bank for Reconstruction and Development (later, part of the World Bank). The International Court of Justice and the war crimes trials in Nuremberg and Tokyo, furthermore, joined the Universal Declaration of Human Rights and conventions on genocide and refugees in institutionalizing international law concerning postconflict justice and rights protection. Addressing a panoply of other matters were such entities as the United Nations Educational, Scientific and Cultural Organization and the Food and Agriculture Organization of the United Nations, both operating with significantly more robust mandates than their institutional predecessors from the pre–World War I and interwar eras had been able to boast. Shadowing and often enveloping them all, of course, was the United Nations, chartered during the spring of 1945 in San Francisco.[1]

Viewed skeptically, these developments represented little new, but instead masked a traditional realpolitik approach to international relations. The participating states that built these institutions were, after all, undeniably motivated by their respective self-interests and worked in an environment shaped by the disproportionate influence of the great powers. The differences in the states' respective goals were legion, cleaving especially over colonialism and intensifying East–West tensions. Valid as this critical perspective is, however, it invites an incomplete rendering of the story. For it is also important to recognize that, to varying degrees, the states that built these institutions and related systems pursued national interests and power through processes requiring a remarkable willingness to engage in diplomatic exchange and multilateral innovation. Confronting a world that seemed to have nearly destroyed itself, state officials found a common desire amidst their myriad differences to secure a more stable, peaceful, and prosperous future. The international institution emerged in unprecedented fashion as a key vessel for pursuing these ends.[2]

Although a vibrant array of scholarship has analyzed the import of these phenomena for the history of diplomatic relations, one area of international institution building, civilian war relief, has often been either neglected as a diplomatic achievement or else treated largely as a cautionary tale for how *not* to approach interstate collaboration.[3] This study aims to help rebalance the discussion. It argues that the Allied and Associated states of the Second World War—and especially the "Big Four" powers of the United States, Great Britain, the Soviet Union, and China—engaged in a sustained and challenging but ultimately successful exercise of multilateral diplomacy to address the worst humanitarian crisis that the world has ever known. It concentrates on a three-year window of opportunity between late 1940 and late 1943 when representatives of the Big Four found points for consensus and compromise among significant differences to turn vague conceptions for postwar humanitarian relief into, by far, the largest intergovernmental aid organization in history, the United Nations Relief and Rehabilitation Administration (UNRRA). Managing wartime alliances with one another and with less powerful states, the diplomat-architects of UNRRA, as it was commonly known, built the first of many large civilian-based "United Nations" endeavors to follow. The oft-overlooked UNRRA, that is, was remarkable not only for its utterly unprecedented size and scope but also for its role in inaugurating a moment in geopolitics when solutions to a broken world's problems were often sought through broadly inclusive multilateral institutions.

Even though the World War II–era project of relief has earned an array of valid criticisms, UNRRA's positive impact was nevertheless profound in terms of its amelioration of human suffering, stabilizing influence on wrecked economies and political systems, and development of new models of diplomatic and administrative interaction between states when more violent approaches had recently proven all too appealing. Many millions of people owed their security, health, and often life to this intergovernmental agency of unprecedented size and reach. In reducing the scope of the war's immediate humanitarian impact—from Europe across North Africa and the Middle East through swaths of East Asia—UNRRA created a critical degree of relative stability for national and multilateral structures of government, production, and exchange to rebuild. In hindsight, for example, UNRRA might arguably be considered as having served as a short-term crisis management prerequisite for the implementation of such longer-term rebuilding, integrative, and reconciliation projects as the Marshall Plan and the European Coal and Steel Community. Created in 1943, UNRRA also served as the first major diplomatic and governing template for the flurry of postwar international entities operating under the banner of the United Nations, wherein Great Power influence would be joined by that of smaller states in managing international affairs through typically peaceful, if often contentious, multilateral engagement. Finally, UNRRA bequeathed important legacies to international projects of refugee management and related forms of humanitarian aid and development assistance for decades to come.[4] What UNRRA accomplished and helped to spawn should be better understood alongside the organization's deficiencies, especially when acknowledging the complex enormity of the challenge.

Contextualizing "Success"

Though the process that led to UNRRA's emergence should be deemed an exercise in *successful diplomacy,* as the next section argues, what about the work of the institution produced through that process? In other words, was UNRRA a *diplomatic* and *administrative success*? The verdict here is decidedly more mixed, but a contextualized assessment that considers the challenges alongside the ideals and the accomplishments with the limitations yields a qualified "yes." A critical assessment requires an appreciation of both what the organization managed to do and the nearly unfathomable scope of the crisis that it faced.

Despite deep geopolitical tensions among the Allied countries, forty-four states participated in UNRRA's founding meeting, representing 80 percent of the world's population. These included two critically important countries that had remained largely absent from international humanitarian management— or many other forms of multilateral innovation—during the interwar years: the Soviet Union and the United States. The forty-eight states eventually serving on UNRRA's policymaking council oversaw an organization that spent $3.7 billion (unadjusted) and employed over twenty thousand people hailing from nearly fifty countries during its core operational tenure from late 1943 through 1947. UNRRA coordinated thousands more personnel from the dozens of civil society "voluntary agencies" affiliated with it. Operating in the sixteen countries of former Axis occupation across Europe, Asia, North Africa, and the Middle East, UNRRA assisted at least twenty million refugees and other civilians left vulnerable from hostilities. The organization supplied food, shelter, medical care, transportation, educational programs, and agricultural and technical assistance, along with other forms of aid, often making the difference between destitution and relative comfort, and for many, between life and death. The UNRRA-run "Displaced Persons" camps in the Western zones of occupied Germany alone housed 715,000 people at a single time, with scores of thousands more residing in similar camps in China, the Middle East, Austria, Italy, and beyond. The organization, furthermore, accomplished all of this while promoting a hiring policy that forbade discrimination based on sex, race, religion, nationality, or political creed, a position that sparked some of the criticism it received from those distraught over the number of women, Jews, and pacifists working for UNRRA. Reflecting on UNRRA's work several years after the organization's dissolution, one observer noted that although "the long-range results of this first large-scale international operation cannot yet be estimated," it should be considered "the first blueprint of the post-war order." It was responsible for "preventing epidemics and famine, rehabilitating transportation, industry and agriculture, restoring confidence and morale, and enabling the victims of aggression to begin to help themselves."[5]

Although often relatively overlooked in the subsequent historical record, UNRRA should also be considered a progenitor of the better-known international organizations and other systems of international collaboration that emerged in such force at the war's end. Formally established at a conference of forty-four nations in Atlantic City, New Jersey, in November 1943, UNRRA predated the United Nations organization by a year and a half.[6] (The "United Nations" in the former's name had been coined by Franklin Roosevelt in late 1941 as a synonym for the Allied and Associated countries.) In early 1942, a British state document predicted that "post-war relief will afford the first opportunity for renewed international collaboration and will be a first step toward post-war reconstruction." The document suggested that such relief operations would represent a concrete manifestation of the multilateral spirit advanced through the Atlantic Charter proclamation by the United States and Britain in August 1941.[7]

As much as UNRRA accomplished and as important as it became as a model for postwar collaboration, the needs and challenges of the postwar world proved vastly greater than UNRRA could ever have been expected to meet. As hostilities ceased in 1945, a staggering sixty million people remained displaced from their homes and homelands, constituting a major source of the humanitarian, economic, and political instability produced by the war.[8] UNRRA, related relief organizations, and Allied militaries were tasked with helping to care for these people in makeshift camps and other sites of displacement, repatriate them to their homelands when possible, and, especially after 1946, seek out options for resettlement to new nation-states when the authorities responsible for the refugees deemed repatriation impossible or a poor option. This was in addition to massive feeding, child care, and medical and educational programs that these organizations operated on behalf of vulnerable civilian and prisoner of war populations that were not displaced.[9]

These were massive charges for a massive crisis, not only because of the material and logistical demands but also for the daunting diplomatic challenges involved. In the highly charged geopolitical milieu of the period, organized humanitarian aid could be used both as a "weapon" against a state's adversaries, in the words of one U.S. diplomat, and a salve to heal the "festering wounds" afflicting "the whole of international society," as British politician and academic Harold Laski opined.[10] The displaced, in particular, were imbued with remarkable political, economic, and cultural value—both positive and negative—by the nation-states engaged with the refugee organizations. States cared very much what happened to the displaced, whether the goal was repatriation, resettlement, or exclusion. Categorized by states variously as national citizens, common laborers, skilled experts, intelligence assets, family members of co-nationals, excludable undesirables, and state enemies in need of punishment or extermination, refugees garnered a symbolic power that could significantly inflame or ameliorate tensions in the international system. When accounting for the nature and scale of these challenges, some key areas of the post–World War II civilian relief project should be considered a qualified success in terms of diplomacy and governance, even when some very real shortcomings are acknowledged.

Like UNRRA's positive accomplishments, its shortcomings can be viewed through three, often overlapping, categories: the politics of domestic and international relations, administration (or governance), and humanitarian ethics. Like most of the era's other new international institutions and related endeavors, for instance, neither UNRRA nor the broader field of humanitarian management that it joined prevented the tensions between a Soviet-backed East and U.S.-backed West from morphing into the Cold War. In fact, relief affairs did indeed often serve as a "weapon" wielded by the emerging superpowers and their respective allies against one another. This occurred especially over the issue of repatriating unwilling refugees to former homelands in the Soviet East, where many feared a legitimate threat of persecution. UNRRA and the Allied militaries repatriated millions of people before the Western powers began to insist on resettlement elsewhere by later 1946 and early 1947. Furthermore, although UNRRA was regularly heralded by its advocates as an enterprise that placed international cooperation above the internal politics of states, the former was frequently placed in the service of the latter. This occurred, for instance, when UNRRA relief supplies were used by officials affiliated with Mussolini's former regime to reestablish and legitimize a discredited Italian state,[11] or when recently elected right-wing officials in Greece diverted relief away from needy civilian areas supportive of leftist political factions.[12] UNRRA also earned a reputation, even among some of its advocates, for being inefficiently administered and often at odds with the military authorities with which it had to work, illegitimately prioritizing the economic gain of its commercial contributors and staffing itself with an army of inexperienced and sometimes unruly personnel.[13] Although UNRRA officials often boasted that their organization prioritized need over politics, UNRRA was not in fact a neutral actor, but rather an organization run by and largely for the Allied victors. The millions of displaced and suffering German civilians, for instance, were not originally eligible for UNRRA aid, leading one scholar to suggest that at times the organization threatened to become a "conquerors' relief wing."[14] (In late 1944, however, Jews of German origin became eligible for UNRRA support.)[15] Moreover, the Soviets never allowed UNRRA to operate refugee camps in its zone of German occupation, instead quickly and often brutally repatriating millions to former homelands shadowed by a rising Iron Curtain, many against their will, and to grave futures in Siberian gulags when they were not executed outright.[16]

These are sound, significant criticisms that must be taken seriously by anyone interested in learning from the experience of UNRRA, but a more positive overall verdict emerges when framing our criteria for success with a realistic assessment of what was possible given the profound challenges faced by the historical actors at the time. Even had the major powers involved in UNRRA's European operations agreed with one another over such ultimately divisive issues as forced repatriation, the politics of resource allocation, and respective civil liberties in the camps, Europe's humanitarian, economic, and infrastructural devastation would still have presented a logistical challenge never previously witnessed on such a scale. Former New York governor and UNRRA director-general Herbert Lehman offered a useful reminder to skeptics of the organization while addressing a U.S. House committee in late 1945 that threatened to cut off U.S. funding to the enterprise. Urging the representatives to adopt a more realistic set of expectations, Lehman observed that managing a humanitarian crisis of the scope and sort confronting the world at that moment was "a hard game." It was, Lehman counseled, "the toughest game."[17] Moreover, UNRRA's official historian, George Woodbridge, not long after the organization's 1947 dissolution, observed, "UNRRA operated in a world which it did not and could not control. . . . If it was expected that a wartorn world should, in about two years, be transformed into a paradise of prosperity, the work certainly failed." But Woodbridge went on to caution that to deem UNRRA a failure would be "ridiculous."[18]

Whatever one's assessment, the challenges confronting the organization's very emergence and subsequent administration were undeniably great. The diplomats who brought the agency into existence represented governments with sometimes profoundly divergent goals. UNRRA's participating states faced an enormous and profoundly chaotic crisis, one whose natural state leaned toward entropy rather than governability. Furthermore, whereas the deliberations between the two new superpowers offered little more than obstinate acrimony after the war, whether regarding bilateral matters between them or broader international endeavors such as the United Nations, the two states more often than not managed to convert their tensions into productive ones during the diplomatic process that conceived UNRRA. Some of the factors explaining this difference are structural, of course. The U.S. needed Soviet sacrifices on the battlefield to defeat Germany. The Soviets in turn grew to understand that they would desperately need American contributions of relief supplies upon the cessation of hostilities. As Dean Acheson, perhaps the most important American diplomat in relief planning, later observed, he and his colleagues "did rather better with the USSR in our negotiations than many of our successors have done since, not due, I hasten to add, to our skill but to the Soviet desire for relief assistance."[19] Each state had more to lose than gain by embracing stalemate. But if there is an overriding lesson to Soviet-American deliberations over postwar relief planning within the context of a looming Cold War, it is that the relevant officials recognized their structural interconnectedness. Relative to East–West relations after the war, a group of Soviet and American diplomats often fueled their labors with a sense of empathy for their tenuous ally, an empathy that they believed could enhance their respective national interests. However strong a case can be made for UNRRA's limitations and missteps, its accomplishments appear at least as remarkable when considering the nature of the challenges faced by the organization.

Making UNRRA an Intergovernmental Reality

UNRRA owed its creation to the deliberation of representatives from dozens of Allied states, but those most responsible during its three-year gestation period from late 1940 to late 1943 were a cluster of officials from the foreign ministries of the Big Four: Britain, the Soviet Union, China, and the country with the most leverage over the diplomatic process by virtue of its ability to contribute more resources to postwar relief than all of the others combined, the United States. Secretary of State Cordell Hull and Assistant Secretary of State for Economic Affairs Dean Acheson of the United States collaborated in garnering domestic and international political support for the relief organization as well as in formulating broad U.S. policy approaches to postwar relief. Hull left most of the day-to-day interactions between the United States and its Allies to Acheson, a respected lawyer and administrator of the Lend-Lease program. American ambassador to Britain John Winant liaised with his State Department superiors and British officials in London, and former New York governor and future UNRRA director-general Herbert Lehman worked with Acheson in fine-tuning American positions in the late stages of the negotiations that would produce UNRRA in November 1943. Directing British interests were Foreign Secretary Anthony Eden, economist Frederick Leith-Ross, and British ambassador to Washington Lord Halifax (Edward Wood), with John Maynard Keynes periodically providing a philosophical counterbalance to the conservative Leith-Ross over the appropriate roles that states and private philanthropy should play in relief initiatives. Two Chinese ambassadors to the United States, Hu Shih and Wei Tao-ming, doggedly, and ultimately successfully, lobbied to expand what had been conceived initially as a purely European endeavor to include significant relief operations in China.[20] Ambassador Ivan Maisky communicated Soviet positions to officials of the British and exiled European governments in London, and Maxim Litvinov and Andrei Gromyko served as the Soviet ambassadors in Washington.

Learning from past relief operations for the earlier conflict marks the first of several key factors helping to explain UNRRA's creation as an exercise in successful diplomacy. The experience of the First World War, in fact, loomed large in the minds of most of those centrally responsible for the emergence of UNRRA. By the outbreak of the Second World War, the massive humanitarian operations directed by Herbert Hoover during the First World War and its aftermath had become mythologized in large reservoirs of popular memory. Already a renowned international mining engineer by the time that hostilities began in 1914, Hoover's first relief endeavor, the Commission for Relief in (German-occupied) Belgium (CRB), demonstrated his stunning ability to manage vast and complex systems of food procurement and distribution amidst the fighting. Following the example of the CRB were several other Hoover-led civilian relief organizations, the last of which, the American Relief Administration for a Russian famine, operated until 1923. Each entity relied on various degrees of support from the American state, governments allied with the United States, civil society organizations, and other charitable contributions. Hoover's organizations and various other operations affiliated with them collectively affected the lives, often profoundly, of over two hundred million people in a seven-thousand mile expanse across Europe, parts of the Near East, and North Asia. These activities represented major breakthroughs in international humanitarianism, whether in times of war or otherwise.[21]

Impressive as these feats were, however, the architects of humanitarian aid for the Second World War saw the Great War experience as something to avoid as much as emulate. Even while admiring Hoover's efforts, there was a near consensus by key relief planners in the Second World War that in the Great War's immediate aftermath, relief efforts often came too late, with insufficient resource support from participating states (especially the U.S. Congress) and an insistence by the largest contributor, the United States, on keeping firm control over what were often supposed to be internationally collaborative ventures.[22] Also tarnishing the legacy of the Great War relief efforts was Hoover's insistence that recipient nations either pay for the supplies—mostly drawn from enormous U.S. food surpluses amassed during the war—or take on debts that would ultimately contribute to caustic environments of economic and political instability. In the assessment of some, then, the relief efforts of the Great War era sewed the seeds for future conflict even while ameliorating the suffering of millions.[23]

Soviet officials during the Second World War were especially sensitive to this history of relief activities from the Great War era. The missions in Russia and the Ukraine directed by Hoover, the American Red Cross, and other American philanthropies sometimes blatantly used food and other relief provisions as a weapon against the Bolsheviks in the Russian Civil War. Litvinov possessed a deep personal knowledge of the frustrations born from the American relief efforts of the earlier war, having been tasked with negotiating the controversial entry of American relief missions into Russia. Along with Gromyko and the ambassadors' boss in Moscow, Foreign Minister Vyacheslav Molotov, the Soviets adopted a hard line early in the Second World War that recipient countries (the Soviet Union would clearly be a major one) maintain wide authority over the distribution of relief provisions within their sovereign territories.[24] It ultimately proved a demand that the United States was more open to, if not always pleased with, than in the era of the Great War.

Early planning marked a second factor differentiating the relief efforts of the Second World War from those of the First. It gave the statesmen architects of the organization time not only to predict the complex array of postwar relief needs but also, crucially, to digest and often find ways to accommodate each other's differing positions on how aid operations should run.[25] The process began in earnest in August 1940, when British prime minister Winston Churchill declared that his nation would begin the deliberate stockpiling of food reserves and other potential relief supplies from all over the British Empire in anticipation of postwar relief needs, encouraging other food-producing nations to do the same. It was a rather audacious time to speak of plans for managing liberated territories, considering that the Allied war effort was on the defensive in the summer of 1940. But Churchill and his advisers believed that publicizing the planning of postwar relief could both curry favor among populations living under Axis rule, thereby potentially aiding the Allied war cause, and offer economic outlets after liberation for the vast quantities of "surplus" wheat and other raw materials held by Britain, the United States, Canada, Argentina, and other Allies as a result of the British naval blockade and oceanic warfare. "The shattering of Nazi power," he promised, would bring "immediate food, freedom, and peace" to the liberated populations. (Although Churchill "deliberately" stated that Allied relief would extend to the German and Austrian peoples, they were ultimately left out of UNRRA's purview.)[26]

A third factor contributing to UNRRA's emergence was a belief among key Allied statesmen in forging a more *multistate response to relief efforts* than witnessed after the First World War. Soon after Churchill's speech, a full year before the United States would enter the war, Frederick Leith-Ross initiated conversations with U.S. assistant secretary of state Henry Grady and then Grady's successor, Dean Acheson, to urge the Americans to plan for the acquisition and distribution of wheat and other raw materials for postliberation relief needs. At about the same time, in late 1940, Britain's chief economic adviser, Frederick Leith-Ross, inaugurated a series of meetings at St. James Palace in London with the Allied European governments exiled there. These sessions took some modest, preliminary steps toward making the provisioning of food and other aid supplies a collaborative endeavor rather than one in which each liberated country competed on the international marketplace for itself, a path that some had already begun exploring.[27]

British economist John Maynard Keynes generally welcomed these initiatives but found the approach taken by his economic counterpart Leith-Ross and others in Winston Churchill's Conservative Administration insufficient. By early 1941, as evidence mounted that the scope of the humanitarian needs of the war might even surpass that of the First World War, Leith-Ross remained convinced that private charities and well-regulated private markets would be able to manage the bulk of aid operations. State governments would offer critical direction and resource support, but their role would be more supplemental than central. Keynes, at that point an informal, though influential adviser to the British Treasury, shuttled between London and Washington to convince both British and American officials that, on the contrary, the situation demanded a heavier hand by participating states. Acheson later recalled that the "seeds" planted for a larger state presence in postwar relief "sprouted simultaneously" on both sides of the Atlantic in the summer of 1941. Keynes proved influential in convincing Leith-Ross, British secretary of state for foreign affairs Anthony Eden, and Acheson that planning for postliberation aid required greater prioritization within the various interested governments, especially those of Britain and the United States.[28]

In short order Acheson disentangled relief planning from the thick bureaucratic web that comprised—and in Keynes's estimation, constrained—most other postwar planning within the State Department concerning international trade, finance, law, military alliances, and, above all, a nascent United Nations organization to replace the League of Nations. Acheson's Special Research Division began operating a full three months before the Japanese invasion of Pearl Harbor prompted the United States to enter the war as an official member of the Allies.[29] At about the same time, the United States began hosting regular meetings in Washington of the International Wheat Council, composed mostly of representatives from the food-producing countries of Britain, the United States, Canada, Australia, and Argentina.[30] And in September 1941, Leith-Ross's committee in London formalized itself as the Inter-Allied Committee on Post-war Requirements, asking the exiled governments there to prepare estimates of their humanitarian requirements during the first half-year after Axis liberation so that foodstuffs and other critical materials could be procured, stored, and earmarked for eventual distribution. A contemporary observer opined of these initiatives that "here was the first official international effort to implement freedom from want and a forecast of an intergovernmental relief organization."[31] These were confident endeavors, perhaps surprisingly so considering that Allied victory still seemed neither imminent nor, perhaps, even likely. Such developments would lead Leith-Ross to predict that "coordination after this war will have had no parallel since the Thirty Years' War."[32]

Keynes's influence in convincing Acheson and other American officials of the importance of a capacious role for states in postliberation relief initiatives serves as a reminder that these affairs should be considered not just as matters of U.S. foreign policy but also as within the domestic milieu of American politics. The American interest in early multilateral planning for postwar relief needs was informed by a broader commitment by the Roosevelt administration, heavily influenced by the ascendant economic theories of Keynes and tested through domestic New Deal programs, to organizing large-scale, multiagency state solutions for massive social and economic problems. Along with such U.S.-propelled endeavors as the Atlantic Charter and the various projects affiliated with the formation of the United Nations, the Roosevelt administration's interest in the postwar planning process that would culminate in UNRRA represented a desire to offer, as one historian phrased it, "a New Deal for the world." This philosophy coalesced with economic Keynesianism in Britain and Soviet Socialism in the East to make the internationalization of "social security"—an international "welfare state," as UNRRA was called by another historian—a highly valued goal among the Allies for a more prosperous, stable, and peaceful postwar world.[33] To some of their advocates, well-planned war relief operations came to represent a concrete manifestation of the multilateral spirit advanced through the Atlantic Charter proclamation by the United States and Britain in August 1941.[34]

Perhaps no element was more important to forging UNRRA's robust multilateral response to postwar relief than the *involvement of both the Soviet Union and the United States*. Along with Britain, they were the most important states in UNRRA's emergence and brief maturation. (Although China was considered one of the Big Four, and as such its representatives consulted and kept apprised of developments, in the earlier stages of UNRRA's development, especially, the Chinese representatives played a more modest overall role than their counterparts from the other three powers.) The degree and types of participation played by the Soviets and Americans proved a far cry from World War I relief initiatives. The Russian Revolution and ensuing Civil War meant that Soviet Russia had participated in Great War initiatives only as an occasional, though significant, recipient. Even at that, the American-dominated relief efforts were often steered away from Soviet factions and toward their enemies.[35] U.S. congressional skepticism of international commitments during the Great War era meant that the American state's support of relief efforts, although significant, often arrived late and with a great many unilateral strings attached. During the Second World War, even though both emerging superpowers demonstrated considerable ambivalence toward UNRRA as well, each critically chose to pursue national interests through a robust association with the international organization.

As the Western Allies were taking various initial steps toward postliberation relief, the Soviets leapfrogged them. On January 13, 1942, Soviet ambassador to Britain Ivan Maisky gave British secretary of state for foreign affairs Anthony Eden the first comprehensive proposal of the war for a powerful centralized international organization. The massive and vicious German advance into Eastern Europe left little doubt that the Soviet Union and the states in its sphere of influence would require tremendous amounts of aid upon the war's cessation. Beyond humanitarian concerns, Foreign Minister Molotov and his diplomatic corps well understood that controlling key features of such an institution—especially the distribution of aid—could yield considerable economic and political influence over not just the territories of the Soviet Union but neighboring regions as well. The Soviets were keen to support friendly regimes with relief supplies and to keep such provisions away from adversarial factions. It was a position buttressed by the experience of American relief efforts in Eastern Europe in the 1910s and 1920s. The Soviet proposal represented an early attempt to set some of the terms of the discussion over relief so that the Soviet Union might both maximize the amount of aid it received after the war and gain influence over how such aid was distributed to the smaller states in its geographical orbit, while at the same time avoiding giving the Americans outsized power.[36]

Although some aspects of the Soviet proposal proved unacceptable to the Americans and the British, others offered *room to build consensus and compromise*, another important element to the diplomatic process that transformed nascent relief planning into a massive, multilateral institution. Most problematic was the proposed membership, consisting of the Soviets, Britain, other European Allies, Canada, India, Australia, New Zealand, and South Africa. Conspicuously missing—though not for long—were all of the presumed donor states of North America except Canada (the omission of the United States was particularly glaring) and the various Asian and Middle Eastern countries expected to be in dire need of receiving aid upon liberation.[37]

Unacceptable as the proposed organization's exclusive membership proved to be for Britain, the United States, and others, three additional aspects of the Soviet vision for postwar relief ultimately found their way into UNRRA's final form. First, Foreign Minister Molotov and his associates worked to balance the disproportionate political authority that the British had been exercising over Leith-Ross's Inter-Allied Committee by proposing a highly centralized bureaucracy with a strong central committee. It would be composed of a small number of member states, with the Soviets and British clearly expected to deploy considerable influence, that would exercise administrative control over the distribution of aid. This was a different model from the Inter-Allied Committee, in which more traditional political negotiations between state diplomats (dominated by the British thus far) were expected to determine the shape of relief efforts. Second, to avoid what Soviet officials saw as the Americans' disregard for national sovereignty in the relief missions of the Great War era, the Soviets insisted that the government of a recipient state give its consent to any proposed operation and play a major role, where possible, in the distribution of international aid.[38] A third Soviet demand that ultimately materialized, by and large, was broached in the early planning stages for postwar relief, but given full articulation in the Potsdam Agreement of 1945. Namely, the Soviets insisted that the proposed relief organization be required to repatriate all Soviet citizens as quickly as possible after the enemy territory where they temporarily resided had been liberated. This policy over repatriation ultimately meant that UNRRA would repatriate not only millions of willing and eager refugees back home but also hundreds of thousands more who feared that returning would—and often did—endanger their livelihoods and their lives.[39] If the initially proposed membership of the organization unsurprisingly proved noxious to the Americans, British, and others, these three other matters offered an acceptable starting point for negotiations, a common terrain on which the various parties could work, a lingua franca through which they could speak.

After the American ambassador to Britain, John Winant, received the Soviet proposal from the British, the Americans initiated a yearlong approach that might fairly be called "benign delay," which proved to be a further factor in fostering a diplomatic environment that eventually produced UNRRA. Assistant Secretary of State Acheson and his staff, backed by Secretary of State Hull, took nearly a year to respond to the Soviet proposal with anything approaching a formal one of their own. The first half of 1942 was spent with Acheson's staff conducting tedious studies of the Soviet plan.[40] The Americans' deliberately slow pace in responding to the Soviet proposal with an official one of their own was not conducive to the diplomatic process because it hindered progress. In May, for instance, Winant alerted Hull with some alarm that Leith-Ross and his British colleagues had grown "anxious" and found it "embarrassing" to promise the Allied governments exiled in London that the American response to the Soviet proposal was imminently forthcoming. The exiled statesmen were eager to earmark food and other supplies for their countries upon liberation.[41] The Dutch and Norwegians, in particular, had begun to chafe at the requests of the British, occasionally echoed by the Americans, to wait for the emergence of the relief organization to handle such things in a more organized and collaborative fashion rather than turning the procurement of supplies into a competitive free-for-all on the international markets. Without American action, it was generally understood that relief operations simply could not exist on a scale approaching that of the looming humanitarian crisis.[42]

Even though the slow American response frustrated representatives of Allied and Associated states, it ultimately fostered a productive diplomatic environment for the emergence of UNRRA in two related ways. First, it provided time for the United States to get on the same page with its close British ally before entering into sometimes difficult negotiations over the final shape of the relief organization with the Soviets and other Allied and Associated states. In Frederick Leith-Ross's estimation, the Soviets sought to "obtain a vested interest" in the proposed organization by virtue of taking the lead on its development. The result would be that the Soviets would lay claim to the "final form [of] inter-allied control" over relief operations. Ambassador Winant agreed, opining that the proposal "would give undue influence to Russia through military-geographical factors which might result in pressure on refugee governments" exiled in the West from Eastern Europe.[43] The Americans' tactic of benign delay represented a deliberate attempt to make time work for their interests without jeopardizing the goal of a genuinely multilateral relief endeavor. And from the American perspective, in particular, before the Allied victories in North Africa late in the year, there were few civilian populations yet to manage anyway, so planning could proceed at a modest pace.

The second rationale for the deliberate approach by the Americans was a more domestically focused version of the first. Cordell Hull was especially keen to avoid turning the issue of a largely U.S.-supported postliberation relief institution into a highly publicized—and thus, politicized—matter before absolutely necessary. The secretary of state, along with Acheson and others within the department, gauged little appetite in the country—not just in the public, but also among certain congressmen and military leaders—for the U.S. government to bankroll humanitarian missions when it was already bankrolling so much of the Allied military cause. As Hull explained to Leith-Ross in August of 1942, "at this critical stage of the war" any formal announcements by the State Department would risk "unfair criticism in the press, which would be followed by political opposition," threatening to "obstruct the post-war program in its entirety."[44]

The Americans, however, remained acutely aware of the need to both maintain close working relations with the British and avoid alienating a tenuous but enormously important Soviet ally, not to mention the Chinese, whose value as a military ally was also critical and whose humanitarian needs would be tremendous. Finally, on May 7, Acheson's subcommittee tasked with studying the Soviet proposal cabled its informal response to London. Copies were also forwarded for reaction up the chain of command in Washington, to Secretary of State Cordell Hull and Vice President Henry Wallace. Although it is unclear whether FDR saw it, the president asked to be kept informed of its development. Some revisions were implemented the next month after consultation with the British, but notably, no official sanction from the U.S. government was given for it, a practice that Hull and Acheson followed diligently over the next half-year. Acheson's draft was, for the moment, to remain just that: a draft for further, informal consideration but not determinative action.[45]

Although changes were eventually made to the informal American proposal to accommodate the interests of the foreign ministries of both large and small states, Allied militaries, and legislatures (especially the U.S. Congress), "Acheson's draft" of June 1942 would serve, to a striking degree, as the blueprint for the UNRRA draft agreement the following November. The American proposal echoed the Soviet desire for a strong, centralized bureaucracy with a small but powerful central committee largely governing most relief operations. It left the door open to the Soviet insistence regarding recipient-government consent and in-country distribution of supplies, something that would be given more definite form over the coming year through negotiation and compromise. Differing from the Soviet proposal, however, and generally echoing British desires, the American draft insisted that the relief organization be a far more inclusive and international endeavor, composed of the several dozen Allied and Associated states now referred to as the "United Nations," not limited to European states. Rather than having the Soviets and British dominating the central committee, as was proposed in the Soviet plan, the Americans added themselves and China, making it a secretariat controlled by the Big Four. A powerful director-general would oversee relief operations, and, with the strong support of the British, it was assumed that the director-general would be an American. Finally, and critically for the actual operations of UNRRA in the coming years, the American draft called for the relief organization to utilize the human and material resources of voluntary agencies, as the contributions from member states would likely fall short of vast relief requirements.[46]

As work on the American draft crawled deliberately ahead in the second half of 1942, the Americans honed techniques in another factor contributing to the successful diplomacy that produced UNRRA the following November: *alliance management in relief planning.* Acheson and his corps regularly worked with Leith-Ross, Lord Halifax (Britain's ambassador to Washington), and other British officials to refine the draft in line with the many points of consensus between the groups while finding ways to make it more responsive to the concerns, both voiced and anticipated, of other governments and of pertinent administrative, military, and legislative sectors within their own governments. Managing the alliance proved a delicate game and demanded the careful handling of foreign officials sensitive to the large and growing influence of their wartime American ally and its close relationship with the British. Western officials regularly apprised their Eastern counterparts of developments, occasionally asked for their input, and assured them that the draft being refined by the Americans and British was merely "tentative" and "unofficial," subject later to broader scrutiny and revision.[47]

In one example of this phenomenon, shortly after Frederick Leith-Ross paid a quiet visit to Washington in mid-1942 to try to prod the United States to a quicker pace, Secretary of State Hull invited Ambassador Litvinov of the Soviet Union and Ambassador Hu Shih of China in for a meeting. Secretary Hull and Assistant Secretary Acheson sensed a growing anxiety from their Allies to the East that the British and Americans were colluding on the shape of postwar relief while neglecting Soviet and Chinese interests. Although the Soviets had offered the first formal proposal for the relief organization a half-year prior, the balance of power now seemed to tilt toward the Anglo-American partnership, albeit not completely. As the Soviets and Chinese remained critical Allies in the war, Hull and Acheson well understood that they would also hold considerable leverage in the negotiations over postwar relief in the coming months. Hull assured the Eastern diplomats that during the recent U.S.-British discussions, "we had kept them in mind from the beginning" and "that no definite plans had yet been reached for a program." Secretary Hull promised that the United States and Britain "would let them see every tentative suggestion we reduced to writing and keep them advised of any phase of the conversations." Hull finished the meeting with an explanation that before a formal proposal could be offered to other states for formal consideration, it would be necessary "to assemble the pertinent facts [on postwar relief needs], to discuss them and appraise them, and then to consider what concrete program might be gradually developed." In other words, the Eastern Allies would be asked for some input, but would generally need to continue to wait while the Americans and British fine-tuned their designs for the organization. Hull then had Acheson meet with the two ambassadors to similarly mollify their concerns.[48]

Present at the Creation

The dramatic Allied military advances of late 1942 in North Africa finally kicked the American planning machine into a higher gear. First, Roosevelt created a special office in charge of relief, the Office of Foreign Relief and Rehabilitation, placing New York governor Herbert Lehman in charge of it. It was already understood by the Big Four that an American would assume the directorship of the proposed international organization, and Lehman's appointment signaled that it would be him.[49] Next, for the first half of 1943, Acheson chaired regular meetings in Washington to finalize a draft agreement for the entity that had now taken the name: the United Nations Relief and Rehabilitation Administration. No longer were the Americans hashing out plans only with Halifax, Leith-Ross, and other British officials, however. Now Litvinov and the new Chinese ambassador and legal scholar, Wei Tao-ming, became part of the official discussions. The politically savvy Wei would prove instrumental in the coming months and years in ensuring that China would become a major recipient of UNRRA aid, not the forgotten Ally of the Far East that the original Soviet plan envisioned.[50]

The meetings benefited from two dynamics: one, broad and structural, the other, more particular to the group of diplomats involved. As to the former, both the Soviet Union and the Chinese desperately coveted the vast supplies that UNRRA would have at its disposal and well understood that the United States would furnish more of the organization's material and capital resources. So, for instance, much as Litvinov tried to toe the Kremlin line that no UNRRA project could move forward without the unanimous consent from the organization's members, or at least from its central committee, he appreciated the

need for pliancy with the wishes of Washington on this and many other matters. On a more human scale, although the small group of diplomats possessed
contrasting personalities, the men nonetheless built a productive working rapport. Acheson would even recall it as "congenial." The American diplomat especially appreciated the "roly-poly" and "voluble" Litvinov as "an old-school
Russian" who "understood the forms and uses of courtesy" and "presented an
amusing antithesis" to the more reserved Lord Halifax. The working relations
between the men crossed into social affairs that included dinner with the diplomats' families and regular painting sessions between the wives of Litvinov
and Acheson, the former being English-born. When negotiations got stymied
by disagreements over details, the four developed a habit of stepping back to
ruminate on broader issues of consensus: in Acheson's words, "the world
which was to be."[51]

When in June 1943 an official draft proposal was released to the representatives of the other forty members of the United Nations for their consideration
and comment, it was offered as an agreement forged by the Big Four, not just
by the Anglo-American alliance that had been primarily responsible for the
rather tedious pace of planning developments during most of 1942. Although
the draft agreement for the organization was born of genuine compromise, it
nevertheless betrayed significant imprints of the British and, especially, American planners. Between its release for comment in June and UNRRA's inaugural meeting in Atlantic City, New Jersey, that November, the draft agreement
would be modified relatively modestly through additional negotiations with
the broader group of member states along with the American military, Congress, and other sectors of the U.S. federal government that would be responsible for the United States' disproportionately large role in the organization.
With Herbert Lehman assuming a powerful director-generalship, UNRRA
would be headquartered in New York with regional European operations managed through a London office. And though UNRRA's relief supplies would,
when possible, be distributed by the recipient governments—a Soviet sticking
point since the beginning—Director-General Lehman and his subordinates
would maintain considerable oversight authority.[52] It fell largely to the assistant U.S. secretary of state for Latin American Affairs, Adolf Berle, to assuage
Soviet foreign minister Molotov's concerns over the significant imprint the
Americans had on the organization. Berle asked Ambassador Litvinov to explain to his boss in Moscow that such moves were necessary in order to secure
political support from an American public and Congress leery over the contributions that the United States was being asked to make to the institution.[53]

Berle's explanation was not merely a sales pitch to the Soviets, but an honest
recognition of the need for thoughtful diplomacy on the American home front
as well. Advocates for UNRRA within the Roosevelt administration looked

both warily backward to Wilson's failures with the U.S. Congress over American membership in the League of Nations and to current factions in Congress that were leery of extending America's support for its Allies beyond direct military requirements. As such, they mounted a vigorous campaign to ensure that the mistakes of the past would not be repeated on the American home front. This forged the domestic side of a *two-level game* of diplomacy, in which the international and intranational tactics of a political endeavor are deployed in deliberate concert with one another by representatives of a liberal democracy to achieve a broader strategic goal. Theorized by political scientist Robert Putnam, the two-level game played by the Americans proved to be a final factor that helped to make the deliberations over UNRRA an exercise in successful diplomacy.

Administration officials, especially Dean Acheson, kept Congress regularly informed of the progress over UNRRA, both while the organization was being proposed and once it was operational after late 1943. The administration made one significant departure from this tact, and had administration officials not quickly realized their gaffe and reversed course, it might have cost them congressional support for UNRRA. Shortly after the June draft agreement was released for consideration, Roosevelt made a rather uncharacteristic political miscalculation in announcing that the United States would become a party to UNRRA not through congressional approval but through a simple executive order. Roosevelt perceived the approach as an executive end-around the legislative process that had stymied Wilson's plans for the League of Nations. Key congressmen were furious, most notably, Michigan Republican senator Arthur Vandenberg. As an influential member of the Foreign Relations Committee, Vandenberg had recently abandoned his long-held isolationism and was deemed a critically important ally in shoring up political support for UNRRA. Even if FDR had managed to make the United States a signatory to the new organization through executive order, it would still have fallen to Congress to approve funding for the organization. With all signs suggesting that the United States would be expected to contribute the lion's share of UNRRA's operating budget, the results of FDR's tactic could have proven fatal to the organization's actual administration.[54]

With Vandenberg and others voicing outrage, the administration withdrew the plan and the State Department redoubled its efforts at mollifying its colleagues on the Hill. Acheson regularly invited key Republicans on the Senate's and House's respective foreign relations committees to advise on the drafting and administration of UNRRA. Requests from Congress were passed onto UNRRA's preparatory council, and as the United States was expected to foot two-thirds of UNRRA's bill, Congress's wishes were usually incorporated.[55] In early 1944, just months after UNRRA's official creation, Vandenberg promised congressional support for the new organization and praised the State Department for its outreach efforts, calling them "amazingly cooperative, almost without precedent." Soon thereafter, Congress quickly agreed to deliver its first installment of UNRRA funding, $1.3 billion.[56]

The campaign directed itself not just toward Congress but to the American public more generally. Former Republican president and World War I relief czar Herbert Hoover was conspicuously brought in as a consultant on UNRRA planning and operations. This was part of a broader message that the organization would not play the part of an American "Santa Claus" to the world, but instead encourage receiving countries to use UNRRA relief as a first step to securing their own "rehabilitation." Relief operations were discursively linked to the patriotic fervor behind the war effort. Hull, Acheson, and Lehman publicly insisted time and again that America's contributions to the new organization could be used for both humanitarian good and for the strategic interests of the country.[57] As Lehman put it, since "shattered economies, pestilence, starvation and death breed riot and anarchy," the United States "must use food, clothing, shelter and the necessities of life as a real weapon to win complete and overwhelming victory and to secure the peace which must follow."[58] Even though UNRRA had its persistent detractors, a poll of 1,260 Americans conducted in the autumn of 1945 found a full 82 percent of respondents approved of Congress committing additional funds to the organization.[59] Capturing the net import of such phenomena, if not the overall complexity of American opinions about UNRRA, Dean Acheson opined the year before that "the Congress of the United States and the people of the United States are unreservedly behind this Administration."[60] In extraordinarily challenging domestic and international environments, the diplomatic processes that made UNRRA a reality were indeed remarkable.

Legacies

Although the circumstances surrounding UNRRA's creation and operation were unique enough to prevent their direct, wholesale application to other diplomatic challenges, the organization did leave several pronounced footprints on the world to come that collectively demonstrate the potential benefits of pursuing such a bold and innovative exercise in multilateral diplomacy. Some of UNRRA's effects can be measured in the short-term stability that they offered to dangerously unstable environments, which in turn provided space for other projects of economic reconstruction, political rejuvenation, and diplomatic engagement over the *longue durée*. UNRRA food, medical care, specialized aid to the displaced, and agricultural and industrial expertise all allowed governments, often new and fragile, to concentrate on rebuilding their economies, infrastructures, and political systems rather than only trying to keep their populations alive. This was true not only for Western Europe, where the resources of the Marshall Plan, the European Coal and Steel Community, and other transnational projects would find solid enough terrain for rebuilding, and not just sustaining, that region of the continent. It also applied, if more equivocally, to the Soviet-occupied East and to China. The latter would receive considerable UNRRA assistance for its suffering populations, even while mired in a revived and devastating civil war. UNRRA had a stabilizing impact even where its reach proved limited. Although German citizens were controversially disqualified from receiving direct UNRRA aid, for instance, the 921 Displaced Persons camps operated by the organization for non-German refugees in the Western zones of occupation allowed both temporary and more permanent ruling authorities in an emerging West Germany to direct limited resources to other critical needs.[61] And though such postwar and early Cold War entities as the Marshall Plan and NATO are commonly credited with fostering a U.S.-led coalition of liberal democracies in the West for decades to follow, UNRRA—its budget and personnel ranks swelled by American contributions—arrived first and belongs more squarely in that conversation. When considered alongside the various UN endeavors described at the beginning of this essay that UNRRA also foreshadowed, it becomes evident that the organization offered models and channels of interstate engagement that helped to make the postwar years and decades, for all their troubles, a less volatile time than might have emerged.

UNRRA also made a lasting impact on subsequent approaches to governing humanitarian crises. When the strains of an emerging Cold War helped to splinter the coalition supporting UNRRA in 1947, in its place emerged a number of other international endeavors designed to assist vulnerable populations. Much of their staffs, administrative architectures, and resource bases were, to varying degrees, effectively transferred from UNRRA. Paramount among these were the World Health Organization[62] and, for assisting displaced populations, the International Refugee Organization (1947–1952) and the United Nations High Commissioner for Refugees (1951–present). Although subject to many valid criticisms, these latter two entities, along with attendant international agreements and related organizations, built upon UNRRA's massive Displaced Persons operations to ensure that the protections afforded to refugees in the postwar world would remain, by and large, much stronger than during the interwar period. Furthermore, the civilian agencies that emerged in UNRRA's member states often developed into permanent bureaucracies dedicated to international humanitarianism, development, and similar endeavors. And even though leaders in the Allied militaries often resented what they perceived as UNRRA's intrusion into territories that their forces had recently taken, in the assessment of one study, "UNRRA established relief work as an essential part of all future military planning."[63]

A final word on UNRRA's legacy belongs to the organization's impact on a wide host of civil society organizations engaged in refugee aid and related humanitarian endeavors. In an acknowledgment that the contributions of member states would fall far short of predicted needs, UNRRA planners early on arranged for the significant involvement of nonstate voluntary agencies in the organization's operations. One hundred twenty-five voluntary agencies from some twenty countries formally helped to implement UNRRA programs, exercising near complete administrative control of many Displaced Persons camps. Often at the request of UNRRA officials and those of its member states, these philanthropies organized themselves in national and international federations.[64] Over the ensuing years and decades, these developments made later incarnations of these nongovernmental organizations more capable of running increasingly robust humanitarian missions across the globe, contributing to what has been called an "NGO revolution." Some of these organizations have additionally built a degree of political heft and independence that has allowed them, frequently through discourses of human rights, to challenge the very nation-states that had helped to nurture their maturation in the era of the Second World War. In this sense, one of UNRRA's more intriguing legacies may be that an interstate venture played a seminal role in the unprecedented growth of today's thriving global civil society.[65]

Notes

1. Important examples from this extensive literature are Elizabeth Borgwardt, *A New Deal for the World: America's Vision for Human Rights* (Cambridge, MA: Belknap Press, 2005); Mark Mazower, *No Enchanted Palace: The End of Empire and the Ideological Origins of the United Nations* (Princeton, NJ: Princeton University Press, 2009); Mazower, *Governing the World: The History of an Idea* (New York: Penguin, 2012), 191–213; Akira Iriye, *Global Community: The Role of International Organizations in the Making of the Contemporary World* (Berkeley: University of California Press, 2004); Evan Luard, *The History of the United Nations* (New York: St. Martin's, 1982); Paul F. Diehl, ed., *The Politics of Global Governance: International Organizations in an Interdependent World* (Boulder, CO: Lynne Reinner, 1997); Benn Steil, *The Battle of Bretton Woods: John Maynard Keynes, Harry Dexter White, and the Making of a New World Order* (Princeton, NJ: Princeton University Press, 2013); Elizabeth Borgwardt, "A New Deal for the Nuremberg Trial: The Limits of Law in Generating Human Rights Norms," *Law and History Review* 26, no. 3 (Fall 2008): 679–705; Timothy P. Maga, *Judgment at Tokyo: The Japanese War Crimes Trials* (Lexington: University Press of Kentucky, 2001); Mary Ann Glendon, *Making the World New: Eleanor Roosevelt and the Universal Declaration of Human Rights* (New York: Random

House, 2001); Akira Iriye, Petra Goedde, and William I. Hitchcock, *The Human Rights Revolution: An International History* (New York: Oxford Univerisity Press, 2012); Samantha Power, *A Problem from Hell: America in the Age of Genocide* (New York: Basic Books, 2002); Michael R. Marrus, *The Unwanted: European Refugees in the Twentieth Century* (New York: Oxford University Press, 1985).

2. See references in note 1.
3. Some important literature on the history of organized refugee aid during the era includes Marrus, *The Unwanted*; "Relief Work in the Aftermath of War," special issue, *Journal of Contemporary History* 43, no. 3 (July 2008) (hereafter, July 2008 *JCH*); Sharif Gemie, Fiona Reid, and Laure Humbert, *Outcast Europe: Refugees and Relief Workers in an Era of Total War, 1936–1948* (London: Continuum International, 2011); William I. Hitchcock, *The Bitter Road to Freedom: The Human Cost of Allied Victory in World War II Europe* (2009) 215–248, New York: Free Press; Susan E. Armstrong-Reid and David Murray, *Armies of Peace: Canada and the UNRRA Years* (Toronto: University of Toronto Press, 2008); George Woodbridge, *UNRRA: The History of the United Nations Relief and Rehabilitation Administration*, vol. 1–3 (New York: Columbia University Press, 1950); Jacques Vernant, *The Refugee in the Post-War World* (New Haven, CT: Yale University Press, 1953); Malcom J. Proudfoot, *European Refugees: A Study in Forced Population Movement* (Evanston, Il: Northwestern University Press, 1956); Louise W. Holborn, *The International Refugee Organization: A Specialized Agency of the United Nations, Its History and Work, 1946–1952* (London: Oxford University Press, 1956); Grace Fox, "The Origins of UNRRA," *Political Science Quarterly* 65, no. 4 (1950): 561–584.
4. Although tracing these legacies is largely beyond the scope of this chapter, some of the organizations that can count UNRRA as a fairly direct institutional progenitor include the International Refugee Organization, the UN High Commission for Refugees, and the World Health Organization.
5. Woodbridge, *UNRAA*, vol.2, 67–78, 492, 535–552; Gemie, Reid, and Humbert, *Outcast Europe*, 298, 316, 357; Jessica Reinisch, "Introduction: Relief in the Aftermath of War," July 2008 *JCH*: 371–404 (especially 390). On the criticisms of the diversity of UNRRA's staff, see Gemie, Reid, and Humbert, 322–323, 327, 332. Quote from Fox, *Origins of UNRRA*, 561.
6. Executive Order 9453, Providing for the Participation of the U.S. in the Work of UNRRA; President Roosevelt, *First Report to Congress on U.S. Participation in Operations of UNRRA, as of September 30, 1944* (Washington, DC: GPO, 1945), 14–15.
7. U.S. Department of State. *Foreign Relations of the United States: Diplomatic Papers, 1942,* vol. 3 (Washington: GPO, 1960), 93 (hereafter *FRUS*).
8. *U.S. Senate Hearings on H.J. Res. 192, UNRRA Participation*, February 1944 (Washington, DC: GPO, 1944), 22.
9. Woodbridge, *UNRRA*; Fox, *Origins of UNRRA*; Robert H. Johnson, "International Politics and the Structure of International Organization: The Case of UNRRA," *World Politics*, 3, no. 4 (July 1951): 520–538.
10. "Lehman Discusses Food as a Weapon," *New York Times*, February 1, 1943; Quote from Reinisch, *Aftermath of War*, 379.
11. G. Daniel Cohen, "Between Relief and Politics: Refugee Humanitarianism in Occupied Germany," July 2008 *JCH*, 437–449; Frank Snowden, "Latina Province: 1944–1950," July 2008 *JCH*, 509–526.
12. Katerina Gardikas, "Relief Work and Malaria in Greece," July 2008 *JCH*, 493–508.
13. Gemie et al., *Outcast Europe*, 362–363, 488; Reinisch, "Introduction", 386.
14. Gemie et al., *Outcast Europe*, 311; Reinisch, "Introduction", 387.
15. Other state and civil society organizations emerged to care for the other parts of the ethnically German population not covered by UNRRA's umbrella. This population included the twelve million *Volksdeutsche* forcibly deported from the Soviet Union and Central Europe to Germany (where many had never previously lived) as part of Potsdam Agreement of 1945 between the Soviet Union, Britain, and the United States. The organizations taking responsibility for them included the Council of Relief Agencies Licensed to Operate in Germany (CRALOG), a federation of American voluntary agencies, and the U.S.

Government and Relief in Occupied Areas (GARIOA), a U.S. government agency that also delivered aid in Austria and Japan. Gerard Daniel Cohen, *In War's Wake: Europe's Displaced Persons in the Postwar Order* (New York: Oxford University Press, 2012); R. M. Douglas, *Orderly and Humane: The Expulsion of Germans after the First World War* (New Haven, CT: Yale University Press, 2012).

16. Woodbridge, *UNRRA*, vol. 2, 485; Gemie, 355.

17. Gemie, 325–326.

18. Woodbridge, *UNRRA*, vol.1, 535, 537.

19. Dean Acheson, *Present at the Creation: My Years in the State Department* (New York: W.W. Norton, 1969), 69.

20. UNRRA also operated in the Philippines, Korea, the Middle East (including North Africa), and Ethiopia. Woodbridge, vol. 2, 81–93, 334–341, Gemie et al., *Outcast Europe*, 371–465.

21. See, for example, George H. Nash, *The Life of Herbert Hoover: The Humanitarian, 1914–1917* (New York: W.W. Norton, 1988), 362–365; Nash, *The Life of Herbert Hoover: Master of Emergencies, 1918–1919* (New York: W.W. Norton, 1996); Frank M. Surface and Raymond L. Bland, *American Food in the World War and Reconstruction Period: Operations under the Direction of Herbert Hoover, 1914 to 1924* (Stanford, CA: Stanford University Press, 1931); Suda Lorena Bane and Ralph Haswell Lutz, eds., *Organization of American Relief in Europe: 1918–1919* (Stanford, CA: Stanford University Press, 1943); Merle Curti, *American Philanthropy Abroad: A History* (New Brunswick, NJ: Rutgers University Press, 1963), 244–300.

22. Royal Institute of International Affairs, *Relief and Reconstruction in Europe, the First Steps: An Interim Report by a Chatham House Study Group* (London: Royal Institute of International Affairs, 1942). Medical and technical experts were convinced that getting a jump on feeding, sanitizing, and, with the introduction of DDT, pesticide operations would—and, in fact, did—dramatically reduce the horrific instances of famine and disease that plagued the era of the Great War. Ben Shephard, "'Becoming Planning Minded': The Theory and Practice of Relief, 1940–1945," July 2008 *JCH*, 407–408.

23. British and American economists additionally sought greater economic integration after the war through freer trade rather than a return to the high tariffs of the interwar period. Susan Armstrong-Reid and David Murray, *Armies of Peace: Canada and the UNRRA Years* (Toronto: University of Toronto Press, 2008), 17–18, 39; Shephard, "'Becoming Planning Minded,'" 409–410.

24. *FRUS, 1942*, v. 1, 159–162; Ben Shephard, *The Long Road Home: The Aftermath of the Second World War* (London: The Bodley Head, 2010), 33–35, 48; Bertrand M. Patenaude, *The Big Show in Bololand: The American Relief Expedition to Soviet Russia in the Famine of 1921* (Stanford, CA: Stanford University Press, 2002).

25. Others have made a contrary point. Ben Shephard, for instance, has argued that the early planning for postwar relief ultimately made UNRRA a clumsy, bureaucratic behemoth. Although it is beyond the scope of this essay to engage thoroughly with this contention, one can at least as easily imagine that waiting to begin the planning for postwar relief until the war's end would have also presented obstacles to postwar relief efforts, possibly with the effect of thwarting the emergence of a large, multilateral entity like UNRRA. For whatever adverse effects early planning may have had on the eventual administrative efficiency of UNRRA, this essay suggests that time was an important factor in fostering familiarity and understanding between state diplomats. This, in turn, nurtured opportunities for compromise and consensus that ultimately allowed UNRRA to emerge as the massive international relief institution that it became, even if, perhaps unsurprisingly, it could also be a remarkably inefficient one. Shephard, *Long Road Home* and "'Becoming Planning Minded.'"

26. Acheson, *Present at the Creation*, 64–65; Shephard, *Long Road Home*, 31–33; Shephard, "Becoming Planning Minded," 408–409, 412. For Churchill's speech, Royal Institute of International Affairs, *Bulletin of International News* 17, no. 18 (September 7, 1940): 1153–1156.

27. *FRUS, 1940*, vol. 3, 138–42; *FRUS, 1941*, vol. 3, 98–112; Acheson, *Present at the Creation*, 64–5.

28. *FRUS*, 1941, vol. 3, 98–112; Acheson, 65. On the divergent positions by Leith-Ross and Keynes on the proper role of the state in controlling raw materials during this phase of the war see, John Cunningham Wood, ed., *John Maynard Keynes, A Critical Assessment: Second Series* (New York: Routledge, 1994), 85–88.

29. Acheson, 64–65; Elizabeth Clark Reiss, *The American Council of Voluntary Agencies for Foreign Service, ACVAFS: Four Monographs* (New York: The Council, 1985), 6; Division of Public Information, OFRRO, "The Office of Foreign Relief and Rehabilitation Operations, Department of State," Washington, DC: GPO, 1943), hereafter, OFFRO official report, 1943; *U.S. Senate Hearings on H.J. Res. 192, UNRRA Participation*, February 1944 (Washington, DC: GPO, 1944), 30; *U.S. House Hearings on UNRRA Participation*, December 1943 to January 1944 (Washington, DC: GPO, 1944); "Planning for Peace Seen Gaining in U.S.," *New York Times*, February 28, 1943.

30. *Frus, 1941, vol. 1*, 530–556; Woodbridge, *UNRRA*, vol.1, 7–9; Fox, 562–564; Acheson, *Present at the Creation*, 64–65.

31. Fox, "The origins of UNRRA", 564.

32. Francesca Wilson, *Advice to Relief Workers: Based on Personal Experiences in the Field* (London: John Murray & Friends Relief Service, 1945), 5.

33. Borgwardt, *A new Deal for the World*; Reinisch, "Introduction", 365–366, 388; Cohen, "Between Relief and Politics."

34. See, for instance, *FRUS*, 1942, vol. 1, 93.

35. Patenaude, *Big Show in Bololand*; Surface and Bland, *American Food in World War*.

36. *FRUS*, 1942, vol. 1, 89–162.

37. Fox, "The origins of UNRRA", 563–564; Armstrong–Reid and Murray, *Armies of Peace*, 18–19; Shephard, "'Becoming Planning Minded,'" 409; Acheson, *Present at the Creation*, 66.

38. Agreement for the United Nations Relief and Rehabilitation Administration, November 9, 1943, in Woodbridge, v.3, Appendix; *FRUS*, 1942, vol. 1, 155; Fox, 562–563.

39. UNRRA was not permitted to find resettlement possibilities for those who refused repatriation or else had no existing nation-states to return to. The forced repatriation after the war of many hundreds of thousands of people to the Soviet sphere became a major source of criticism of UNRRA. Along with claims that the Soviets were using UNRRA supplies to help support communist states in Eastern Europe, the issue of repatriation convinced a majority in Congress to stop funding the relief organization in 1946. In its place arose another largely U.S.-funded humanitarian entity, the International Refugee Organization, which, without the membership of an emerging Eastern Bloc, was able to be more overtly controlled by its American benefactor. Chief among the differences between UNRRA and the successor IRO, the latter was tasked with resettling the one million refugees in the Western Allied zones of occupation in Germany and elsewhere, a major early battle of the Cold War. See: UNRRA Agreement; Holborn; Marrus; Woodbridge; Vernant; Proudfoot.

40. *FRUS*, 1942, vol. 1, 89–162; Armstrong-Reid and Murray, *Armies of Peace*, 18–19.

41. Fox, "The origins of UNRRA", 574.

42. *FRUS*, 1942, vol. 1, 101

43. Though the responsibility for enemy victims of the war was ultimately and largely disregarded by UNRRA, Winant nonetheless reminded his superiors that the fourth article of the recently issued Atlantic Charter demanded that there be "no difference with respect to relief between victor and vanquished." See *FRUS*, 1942, vol. 1, 89–92 (quotes from 91–92).

44. *FRUS*, 1942, vol. 1, 133.

45. *FRUS*, 1942, vol. 1, 89–130; Fox, 573–575.

46. Woodbridge, *UNRRA*, vol.1, 67–78; Fox, "The origins of UNRRA", 574.

47. *FRUS*, 1942, vol. 1, 89–130.

48. *FRUS*, 1942, vol. 1, 115–118. Quotes from 115–116.

49. Armstrong-Reid and Murray, *Armies of Peace*, 18–19; Fox, "The origins of UNRRA", 566.

50. Acheson, *Present at the Creation*, 68; UNRRA, *UNRRA in China: 1945–1947* (New York: UNRRA, 1948).

51. Acheson, *Present at the Creation*, 68.

52. In reality, however, the Soviet Union and other governments sometimes were able to control the distribution of UNRRA supplies without much actual regulation from UNRRA.

The Committee of Records of War Administration, "The United States at War: Development and Administration of the War Program by the Federal Government, Bureau of the Budget" (Washington, D.C.: GPO, 1946); OFRRO official report, 1943; *FRUS*, 1942, vol. 1, 148–149; Woodbridge, vol. 3.

53. "War Victim Relief Setup is Drafted," *Washington Post*, January 11, 1943; *FRUS*, 1942, vol. 1, 128–130.

54. Acheson, *Present at the Creation*, 71–72; UNRRA, *Report of the Director General: Second Session of the Council, Montreal, September 1944, Part 1* (London: His Majesty's Stationary Office, 1944), 133–139.

55. See, for example, UNRRA, *Report of the Director General: Second Session, September 1944, Part 1*, 133–139.

56. *Senate Hearings on UNRRA Participation*, February 1944, 11–13 (13 for quote); Acheson, 80.

57. For example, "The Lehman OFRRO Blueprints Its Task," New York Times, January 7, 1943.

58. "Lehman Discusses Food as a Weapon." On the connection between Americans' support for the war effort and their willingness to accept unprecedented expansions of federal authority, see James T. Sparrow, *Warfare State: World War II Americans and the Age of Big Government* (New York: Oxford University Press, 2011).

59. National Opinion Research Center, University of Chicago, October 1945, USNORC.450135.R18A.

60. UNRRA, *Report of the Director General*, September 1944.

61. Woodbridge, *UNRRA*, vol.1, 81–256, 361–453, 469–532 (on "DP" camp numbers, 502); Michael J. Hogan, *The Marshall Plan: America, Britain, and the Reconstruction of Western Europe, 1947–1952* (New York: Cambridge University Press, 1987).

62. Gemie, 334.

63. Gemie et al., *Outcast Europe*, 425.

64. Woodbridge, *UNRRA*, vol.1, 67–78.

65. There is a long history to the collaboration between state and voluntary associations in the name of humanitarianism, dating especially from the early nineteenth century. For a good overview of this phenomenon, see Michael N. Barnett, *Empire of Humanity: A History of Humanitarianism* (Ithaca, NY: Cornell University Press, 2011). These issues are elaborated in Stephen R. Porter, *Benevolent Empire? Refugees, NGOs, and the American State* (forthcoming).

3

The Rise of Third World Diplomacy

Success and Its Meanings at the 1955 Asian-African Conference in Bandung, Indonesia

CHRISTOPHER J. LEE

From April 18 to 24, 1955, twenty-nine countries from Asia and Africa convened in the city of Bandung, Indonesia, to address pressing issues their respective continents faced during the early Cold War period. Formally named the Asian-African Conference, this diplomatic meeting of independent and nearly independent countries was the largest of its kind up to that point, ostensibly representing 1.4 billion people, or almost two-thirds of the world's population at the time by some estimates. Only the United Nations, which had seventy-six members in 1955, was larger in numeric representation and in terms of geographic and political magnitude. The Bandung conference furthermore offered a global stage for the rise of such statesmen as Ahmed Sukarno of Indonesia, Jawaharlal Nehru of India, Gamal Abdel Nasser of Egypt, and Zhou Enlai of the People's Republic of China, all of whom promoted personal, national, and international interests with varying degrees of success. Sponsored by Indonesia, Burma (present-day Myanmar), Ceylon (present-day Sri Lanka), India, and Pakistan, official delegations in attendance were sent from the People's Republic of China (PRC), Egypt, Turkey, Japan, Libya, Lebanon, Jordan, Syria, Iran, Iraq, Saudi Arabia, Yemen, Afghanistan, Nepal, Laos, Cambodia, Thailand, North and South Vietnam, the Philippines, Ethiopia, the Gold Coast (present-day Ghana), Sudan, and Liberia.[1]

Though regional conflict in Southeast Asia, specifically between North and South Vietnam, provided the initial catalyst for holding the conference, the program for the meeting ultimately included broader issues concerning American and Soviet influence in Asia and Africa, the consequent importance of sovereignty for those states that had recently achieved postcolonial independence, and remaining questions over the upsurge of decolonization then occurring,

Illustration 3.1 Outside the conference hall for the 1955 Asian-African Conference in Bandung, Indonesia. Permission to use from the Asian-African Conference Museum, Bandung, Indonesia.

particularly in Africa. The origins and purposes of the meeting were therefore multifaceted geographically and politically, reflective of the expansive continental representation at hand.

Indeed, the scale and sweep of these urgent topics underscored the opportunities and challenges present, further indicated and defined by the diversity of delegations (Illustration 3.1). Of the twenty-nine countries in attendance, most had achieved self-government, though there were others, such as Sudan (independent in 1956) and the Gold Coast (independent in 1957), that still remained under the last vestiges of colonial rule. Further constituting this varied spectrum were increasingly influential states of the postcolonial world—such as India and the host country Indonesia—as well as countries that had only recently dropped their own imperial ambitions—like Japan, which lost its empire after its defeat at the end of World War II, and Turkey, which similarly experienced the dissolution of the Ottoman Empire and its territories across the Middle East and North Africa at the end of World War I. Some countries had experienced intensive European colonization over many decades and, at times, centuries—the Gold Coast, Egypt, and India, for example—and other states in attendance had experienced Western imperial influence in far more limited ways—such as Ethiopia, China, Thailand, and Liberia. Still, what provided a sense of solidarity among participants was recognition that, first, the global political order was experiencing profound change during the 1950s and that, second, countries in Asia and Africa had the most to gain, and potentially lose, within this shifting context. Decolonization and the decline of European empires had converged with the rise of a new great power rivalry between the United States and the Soviet Union. Political leaders in Africa and Asia—in particular Sukarno, Nehru, Nasser, and Zhou, as cited before—quickly recognized that new diplomatic strategies were essential to confront and manage these emergent trends, lest their countries fall once more under the influence of external powers.[2]

This chapter positions the 1955 Asian-African Conference as a diplomatic meeting that achieved limited practical success in the short term, yet one that attained great symbolic success in the long term. These contrasting assessments point to two key dimensions of the meeting—the importance of promoting and accomplishing diplomatic agendas of immediate regional urgency, while also acknowledging and celebrating the unparalleled novelty of an international conference involving twenty-nine countries from Africa and Asia, a moment signaling and legitimating the decisive rise of a new era of Third World diplomacy. The conference attendees themselves recognized this historic significance, as cited in a number of opening addresses.[3] This chapter consequently broadens the definition of successful diplomacy by not only examining a case study located outside the West—thus extending a political geography of international diplomacy that has often gravitated toward the United States and Europe—but also highlighting different variables that make successful diplomacy—among them, the role of social capital, the impact of political timing, and the distinction between and function of symbolism and *realpolitik*.

To draw out these points, this chapter in particular appraises the international conference as a modular form within diplomatic practice and statecraft. International diplomacy requires a setting and audience. Political leaders as agents of history need a stage, often literally. As a result, international conferences provide an indispensable format for enabling successful diplomacy—by facilitating conditions for addressing circumstances of immediate crisis, as well as structuring diplomatic routine over time. Recognizing the role of format for constructing diplomatic engagement not only presents another dimension for evaluating successful diplomacy but also underscores an essential aspect of international relations that tends to be overlooked in favor of more charismatic, yet often analytically enigmatic, factors, such as personal leadership style. As this chapter demonstrates, international conferences can *produce* leadership and *generate* historical precedent, as much as confirm them.

The International Conference as a Modular Form

The international conference is a prosaic, yet requisite, feature of modern diplomacy. Indeed, this political format is so intrinsic to interstate practices that it has typically escaped explicit consideration as a specific custom that has evolved historically, served a number of purposes, and, as a result, been universally embraced. To regard international conferences in this conscientious way therefore raises questions of comparison and definition. Broadly construed, the practice of diplomacy can occur between individuals representing states, nongovernmental organizations, and political communities that reside within and among nation-states, to list three possibilities. Diplomacy can consist of bilateral engagement or multilateral discussions, depending on the issue and goal at hand. Furthermore, such engagements can be focused and crisis oriented—seeking the end of violent conflict, for example—or they can form part of a diplomatic routine—the scheduled meetings of the UN, to offer another example. In sum, these distinct qualities regarding actors involved, the nature of engagement, and the role of timing explain the provisional uses of diplomatic conferences—from addressing pressing emergencies at one end of the spectrum to generating positive and consistent interstate relations on the other. These three areas thus present an initial set of criteria for making empirical distinctions and creating a working taxonomy for analyzing conferences and their role in successful diplomacy.

But historical context and precedent also play vital roles in defining the uses and meaning of international conferences. The international conference as a practice and form must be understood as emerging concurrently with the rise of the nation-state since the early modern era and maturing particularly after 1945. This assertion is not to claim that diplomatic meetings did not occur in earlier historical periods. Rather, the argument put forward here is that the institutionalization of international conferences started only once the nation-state form itself gained acceptance and widespread currency. The international conference as a diplomatic format has consequently taken shape over at least two hundred years. It is distinctly modern. Indeed, the international conference is not merely an *effect* of the rise of the nation-state. This diplomatic practice helped *produce* the nation-state through facilitating recognition of the rights of sovereignty and equal membership within a community of nations, among other tasks. But how did this production happen? And how does it relate to (and what is meant by) the term "modular"?

In his classic study *Imagined Communities: Reflections on the Origin and Spread of Nationalism* (1983), Benedict Anderson argues that twentieth-century nationalisms have possessed "a profoundly modular character." They "draw on more than a century and a half of human experience. . . . The very idea of 'nation' is now nestled firmly in virtually all print-languages; and nation-ness is virtually inseparable from political consciousness."[4] As Anderson outlines in detail, nationalism materialized historically as the result of both intellectual endeavor and political activism alike—political imagination, enabled through shared language and modern media, provided the crucial means for generating identities that transcended local commitments, thus politically binding geographically disparate peoples into a common territorial community. But what made nationalism modular—that is, universally embraced politically and ubiquitous geographically—was gradual recognition and acceptance of the nation-state as the preeminent modern political form. The principle of national self-determination—as established by revolutions in the United States and Haiti, for example, during the late eighteenth century and later consecrated by the League of Nations (established in 1919) and the United Nations (established in 1945)—challenged the legitimacy of prevalent empire-states to affirm nationalism and a new political order based on the nation-state.[5] Over time, this modularity reinforced this status quo to the exclusion of political alternatives. Questions remain, however, regarding the techniques for establishing and maintaining this pattern of governance. If explanations are still being pursued as to how the nation-state transitioned from being a rare political form during the early modern era to being omnipresent by the end of the twentieth century, Anderson's idea of modularity must be interrogated further to understand what other political structures, instruments, and practices became routine concurrent with the evolution of the nation-state.

The international conference constitutes one of these techniques. Meetings of this kind were not a result of an international system of nation-states—a secondary consequence of its formation—but instead played a vital role in its creation. A brief history can be outlined. The diplomatic meetings that resulted in the Peace of Westphalia (1648) are commonly viewed as crucial to the rise of state sovereignty through a general acceptance of the right of territorial control as a basic political principle. Though the treaties that were reached achieved little in diminishing empire as a political form, which was not their intention, the format of the interstate conference remained.[6] Indeed, the seventeenth century witnessed decisive European expansion overseas to North America, Africa, and Asia, reflecting unabated imperial ambitions— political aspirations that contributed to intracontinental tensions and global competition that, in turn, compelled further diplomacy. Similar to Westphalia, which ended the Thirty Years' War (1618–1648) and the Eighty Years' War (1568–1648), diplomatic meetings during this later period produced the Treaty of Utrecht (1713), which sought to end the War of the Spanish Succession, which embroiled the major powers of Western Europe, and the Treaty of Amiens (1802), which sought to stabilize an uneasy relationship between France and the United Kingdom involving not only continental affairs but also imperial concerns over the disparate territories of the Dutch West Indies, Trinidad, Egypt, Ceylon, and the Cape Colony in South Africa. The most significant diplomatic meeting of this early modern period was the Congress of Vienna (1814–1815), which lay the groundwork for a new European community in the wake of the Napoleonic Wars (1803–1815) and the end of the Holy Roman Empire in 1806. In contrast to the diplomatic occasions of the preceding centuries, this international conference not only sought to end conflict and summon a balance of power in Europe—it intended to create an institutional means for ensuring future peace through a structured routine of regular diplomatic conventions. The Concert of Europe (1815–1914), also known as the Congress System, thus materialized through a sequence of diplomatic conferences across a range of continental locales, such as Verona (1822), London (1832), and Berlin (1878). It served as a fundamental precursor to the League of Nations (1919–1945).[7]

The nineteenth century, therefore, proved to be a crucial period in the rise of the international conference as a technique for reconciling interstate tensions and balancing power. The twentieth century witnessed a wider proliferation in theme, purpose, and actors involved. Indeed, this political format became ubiquitous globally due, once more, to the ascendance of the nation-state as the preeminent political form. Imperial ambition among European states, paradoxically, proved to be the catalyst for this emergence. The Berlin Conference (1884–1885), which divided the African continent for the acquisition and use of Western powers, guaranteed that European aspirations for political and economic dominance would continue to play out across a global imperial landscape. But overseas expansion equally influenced the rise of new states through the introduction of liberal ideals of individual rights and political equality that resulted in struggles for self-determination. The American (1775–1783) and Haitian Revolutions (1791–1804), as cited previously, are exemplary cases of early efforts toward this end, which resulted in the birth of new nation-states. But such attempts at self-determination were not always successful. Conflict could ensue, effecting diplomatic meetings yet again and a compromised status quo. One of the first diplomatic meetings of the twentieth century occurred after the South African War (1899–1902, also known as the Anglo-Boer War) between Great Britain and the Afrikaner republics of the Orange Free State and the South African Republic (also referred to as the Transvaal Republic), a war that ended with the Treaty of Vereeniging, which established British control and led to the 1910 formation of the Union of South Africa as a self-governing dominion in the British Empire.

Peace, therefore, remained a central theme for twentieth-century international conferences. The importance of routine equally carried over. The Treaty of Versailles (1919), which formally ended World War I at the Paris Peace Conference, created the League of Nations with the intention of maintaining a balance of power similar to the Concert of Europe, albeit at a much broader scale encompassing sovereign countries around the world. The ultimate failure of the League in preventing the global conflict of the Second World War produced another round of conferences even more ambitious in scope. The United Nations Conference on International Organization (1945) in San Francisco founded the UN as an institution, with subsequent conferences establishing and maintaining the International Court of Justice, the World Health Organization, the World Food Programme, and the UN Educational, Scientific and Cultural Organization (UNESCO), among many other institutional bodies and associations. The Bretton Woods Conference (1944) similarly founded two global financial institutions—the World Bank and the International Monetary Fund—that in turn would influence global economic coordination through the format of routine international meetings. The Second World War and the groundswell of decolonization across Asia and Africa that followed thus initiated a proliferation of international conferences—a reflection of the global reach of conflict and devastation that had occurred at midcentury, the rapid emergence of new nation-states across the world, and the persistent nineteenth-century belief that international meetings between states could restore and maintain a sense of balance and order.[8]

But a different order of conferences also transpired during the first half of the twentieth century, indicating that international meetings were not the exclusive province of sovereign governments alone. The Pan-African Congresses that took place beginning in 1900, the 1911 Universal Races Congress in London, the League against Imperialism meeting held in Brussels in 1927, and the two Pan-Asian People's Conferences held in Nagasaki (1926) and Shanghai (1927) embraced this political format to represent communities that had experienced political exclusion or disenfranchisement by states in some form.[9] These assorted meetings involving the participation of racial minorities, colonial subjects, and people of color more generally demonstrate not only the rise of international politics that worked through a different social and political strata but equally how such marginalized groups seized upon this political form, practice as an instrument to circumvent local political limitations, such as colonial rule and racial oppression, which they confronted. Ideological political movements of pan-Africanism, pan-Asianism, and communist internationalism, while ineluctably involving states as a political backdrop and at times as sources of support, sought to place their political aspirations in identity-based communities that extended beyond the formal boundaries of nation-states. Frequently guided by an ambitious intellectual leadership, these transnational endeavors sought to collect and stand for the hopes of broadly defined social groups that faced political restrictions locally and globally. Although these movements ultimately dissolved, the historical significance of their international conferences should not be overlooked. These meetings facilitated a context for geographically dispersed people to meet, converse, and produce positions of political solidarity. These international conferences, attended by persons often without official political capacity, still engaged with matters of self-determination.

And they acquired symbolic value as a result, doing so through broadly conceived political imaginations anchored in shared experiences of racial discrimination, cultural prejudice, and political suppression. These meetings solidified the role and importance of transnational identity groups as influential sociopolitical formations during the twentieth century.

The question of their failure lingers, however. These international conferences at the grassroots level raise questions as to how successful diplomacy is to be properly defined, if the decline of these transnational movements ultimately indicates unconditional diplomatic failure as a result. This chapter resists the latter view. Although this set of populist politics did wane after the Second World War, these early conferences must be understood as generative, producing a political consciousness against Western norms and power that would persist and gain further ground once countries in Asia and Africa achieved independence. The 1955 Asian-African Conference belongs to this alternative tradition. Yet, the Bandung meeting also shares affinities with the diplomatic history emanating from Europe since the nineteenth century, as described earlier. The Bandung conference consequently marks an important intersection between early twentieth-century social movements and the emergence of global diplomacy after the Second World War. Indeed, it symbolizes a key transitional moment from populist forms of transnationalism to the mainstream international diplomacy of sovereign nation-states. Political communities in Asia and Africa that were once without representation quickly gained recognition during the era of decolonization, with Bandung highlighting this transformation.

But international conferences provide more than ceremonial occasions for mutual recognition and political legitimacy. They also build social capital—a primary limitation of earlier grassroots conferences and a recurrent opportunity for postcolonial states during the Cold War. This concept presents an additional method for understanding the stakes of diplomatic engagement and the reasons for diplomatic success, or failure. Furthermore, it reinforces the modern character of international conferences—their capacity to facilitate and build interstate networks of trust through political, economic, and intellectual resources.[10] The remainder of this chapter provisionally employs this concept to assess the 1955 Asian-African Conference and its legacies.

Success and Limitation: The 1955 Asian-African Conference in Perspective

The popularity of social capital as an analytic concept has largely been a recent phenomenon. It has also found use beyond academia, to measure economic growth and formulate policy by organizations like the World Bank. But it is a fluid concept that has been subject to debate. The history of its use is deep, extending back to thinkers such as Max Weber, Emile Durkheim, Jeremy Bentham, and John Dewey, among others—all of whom sought to elaborate Karl Marx's introductory use in 1867 that intended to understand financial capital from a social perspective.[11] More recent attention has been placed on the relationships between social capital, social networks, and prosperity.[12] As Pierre Bourdieu has argued, social capital interacts with other forms of capital—financial capital being the classic example, but also human capital (the physical capacity to produce) and cultural capital (determined by credentials of education, knowledge, and heritage). These different types of capital, which might also include personal and political capital, work together with one another to increase wealth and well-being.[13] As with financial capital, a key characteristic of social capital is its capacity to generate growth and productivity. Community is vital in this regard. Social capital is created and accumulated through membership in social networks. To offer one definition, James Farr has described social capital as "the network of associations, activities, or relations that bind people together as a community via certain norms and psychological capacities, notably trust, which are essential for civil society and productive of future collective action or goods, in the manner of other forms of capital."[14]

This section considers how international conferences supply one institutional venue for such capital accumulation. International meetings present occasions for building interstate networks of trust and community, drawing from and aggregating forms of capital—social, political, and economic alike—that are possessed by individual countries. Indeed, the rapid emergence of the conference format among newly independent countries after the Second World War can be understood through this lens. Whereas metropole–colony diplomacy typically played a key role in negotiating independence, international conferences provided an alternative means of recognizing sovereignty and network building.[15] Meetings like the 1947 Asian Relations Conference in Delhi, the 1953 and 1956 Asian Socialist Conferences in Rangoon and Mumbai, and the 1958 and 1960 All-African People's Conferences in Accra and Tunis, to offer just a few examples, enabled new patterns of political networking among states and liberation movements during the early postcolonial period.[16] The location of these international conferences in Asia and Africa strikingly indicated a new political geography that had emerged from the shadows of Western colonial rule (Illustration 3.2). These diplomatic moments must be recognized as taking place during a critical period of transition between colonial and postcolonial periods, amid a passing era of modern European imperialism and a new era of Cold War rivalry and intervention. They transpired during a time of both existential uncertainty and opportunity,

Illustration 3.2 Indonesian Prime Minister Ali Sastroamidjojo (right) with Egyptian leader Gamal Abdel Nasser (center) at the Bandung airport. Permission to use from the Asian-African Conference Museum, Bandung, Indonesia.

signaling attempts by countries in Asia and Africa to intervene in the global politics then taking shape. Furthermore, although these postwar occasions belong to a chronology of conferences, including such precursors as the Pan-African Congresses and the League against Imperialism meeting, they also highlight a fundamental shift from these earlier events, given that their attendees primarily represented sovereign nation-states. Struggles for self-determination remained in parts of Africa and Asia. But the increasing involvement of autonomous states facilitated a different set of political possibilities to come into view—a result of political independence and the resources that went with it—in contrast to previous conferences where those who gathered had little actual political power or social capital to draw upon.

The Asian-African Conference formed a part of this budding diplomatic landscape. It built upon the 1927 League against Imperialism meeting and the 1953 Asian Socialist Conference, both of which involved Asian and African participation. But, in addition to these preceding events, the Bandung meeting must be placed against the backdrop of two parallel developments. First, two conferences in 1954 proposed and planned the idea of convening countries from Asia and Africa for a major diplomatic event—the Colombo Conference

(April 28 to May 2, 1954), held in Colombo, Ceylon, and the Bogor Conference (December 28–29, 1954), held in Bogor, Indonesia. With the support of President Ahmed Sukarno (1901–1970), Prime Minister Ali Sastroamidjojo (1903–1976) of Indonesia spearheaded the effort, which reflected the regional ambitions of Indonesia, concern over the situation in Vietnam with the French departure and the Geneva Conference (April 26 to July 20, 1954) occurring the same year, as well as the belief that Asian and African countries were experiencing "a great awakening" with a concomitant "search for unity."[17] The choice of Bandung can be understood in this regard. It was one of the most important cities in Indonesia, where Sukarno had received his university education and had started his political career, helping found the Partai Nasional Indonesia.[18] Bandung also offered a degree of security, being outside Jakarta, but located close enough to the capital to facilitate coordination. Additionally, unlike the other Colombo Powers (so named after the 1954 meeting) that sponsored the conference, Indonesia had not been part of the British Empire and remained something of an outsider within the group. As a result, it provided a pragmatic alternative to India, a more likely venue given Prime Minister Jawaharlal Nehru's authority and India's previous role as host to the Asian Relations Conference. India, however, maintained tense relations with its regional neighbors of Pakistan and the PRC, which could have jeopardized participation and the overall success of the meeting.

The preceding observation relates to a second backdrop of importance. On April 29, 1954, India and the PRC signed an agreement, after months of negotiation starting in December 1953, known as the Five Principles of Peaceful Co-existence (referred to in India as the Panchsheel Treaty). Intended to resolve a border dispute between the two countries following the PRC's acquisition of Tibet in 1950, its principles included mutual respect for territorial integrity and sovereignty, mutual nonaggression, mutual noninterference, beneficial cooperation, and peaceful coexistence.[19] This platform would go on to inform the final communiqué of the Bandung meeting.

In sum, the Asian-African Conference must be situated within this immediate regional context, in addition to the broader historical framework as outlined before. Indeed, as insinuated earlier, the embrace and use of the international conference format must not be interpreted as derivative, but as a vital revision of form and purpose for a new global order (Illustration 3.3).

The Bandung conference was the largest of its kind, ostensibly representing 1.4 billion people or almost two-thirds of the world's population. In contrast to the Asian Relations Conference and the later All-African People's Conferences, the Bandung meeting decisively involved both continents. Only the Non-Aligned Movement (established in 1961) and the UN were larger numerically. Its significance must therefore be recognized not only in terms of

Illustration 3.3 Indian Prime Minister Jawaharlal Nehru addressing the conference delegates. Permission to use from the Asian-African Conference Museum, Bandung, Indonesia.

historic timing but also through its geographic and political magnitude. These immediate qualities produced both hopes and constraints for individual attendees, as well as for the conference agenda as a whole. Those African countries in attendance, for example, were outnumbered by Asian participants. Of the twenty-nine delegations, only six were African—the Gold Coast, Egypt, Libya, Ethiopia, Liberia, and Sudan. Geographic representation was thus decidedly tilted toward Asia. Furthermore, among the Asian countries in attendance, a clear majority—thirteen total—were from South and Southeast Asia, leaving the Middle East and East Asia more marginal within that continental grouping. This regional participation can be attributed to the sponsorship of the five Colombo Powers, as well as concern over escalating tensions between North and South Vietnam, recently divided by the Geneva Accords reached in July 1954. The signing of the Manila Pact in September 1954, which would lead to the formation of the U.S.-sponsored Southeast Asia Treaty Organization (SEATO), also spurred the involvement of regional countries, even those such as the Philippines and Thailand, whose governments were sympathetic to American interests. In fact, this agreement had further motivated the organization of an Asian-African conference to counter growing American influence.[20]

These political and territorial factors ultimately informed the successes and limitations of the meeting. Although the participation of so many countries generated an atmosphere of excitement and political possibility, the broad inclusiveness and ambition overwhelmed the prospect of more modest achievements. Taking place between April 18 and 24, 1955, this weeklong period allowed time for public speeches, informal meetings, and working groups to occur. Intentions to encourage intercontinental goodwill, to discuss shared socioeconomic problems, to consider the issue of postcolonial sovereignty vis-à-vis the West, and to determine the role Africa and Asia might have in promoting peace in a world polarized by the Cold War provided several unifying themes for the diverse set of assembled delegations. It is clear the conference offered a unique venue to build networks among countries in Asia and Africa along political, economic, and sociocultural lines. Unlike the UN with its Western and Soviet supervision, the meeting actively excluded, at least formally, these superpower influences. As in preceding conferences that represented different social movements, the opportunity to meet, converse, and exchange ideas in person had political value. But the broad themes of the conference were also stage-managed by specific leaders who attended. The Bandung meeting introduced, legitimated, and entrenched recognized heads of state (Illustration 3.4). Though a range of unofficial delegations and nonstate participants attended, the conference was similarly exclusive, and elitist, in this regard.[21]

Of the leaders present, four proved to be crucial in defining the meeting's short-term and long-term success—Ahmed Sukarno of Indonesia, Jawaharlal

Illustration 3.4 Indonesia President Ahmed Sukarno outside the conference hall. Permission to use from the Asian-African Conference Museum, Bandung, Indonesia.

Nehru (1889–1964) of India, Zhou Enlai (1898–1976) of the People's Republic of China, and Gamal Abdel Nasser (1918–1970) of Egypt.[22] Each played different roles and achieved different outcomes. Each had different sources of capital—personal, political, and economic—to draw upon. As the host, Sukarno played an indispensable part to ensure the conference's success along with Prime Minister Sastroamidjojo, who attended more prosaic organizational matters of scheduling, diplomatic arrivals, and so forth. Sukarno's opening address captured the immediate symbolism of the conference:

> What can we do? We can do much! We can inject the voice of reason into world affairs. We can mobilise all the spiritual, all the moral, all the political strength of Asia and Africa on the side of peace. Yes, we! We, the peoples of Asia and Africa, 1,400,000,000 strong, far more than half the human population of the world, we can mobilise what I have called the Moral Violence of Nations in favour of peace. We can demonstrate to the minority of the world which lives on the other continents that we, the majority, are for peace, not for war, and that whatever strength we have will always be thrown on to the side of peace.[23]

Sukarno's unusual, yet vivid, phrase the "Moral Violence of Nations" to achieve world peace set the tone for how Asian and African countries could participate in the evolving global order. Indeed, peace emerged as a clear theme in the final communiqué of the conference—not just a regional peace for Southeast Asia or Asia generally, but world peace broadly construed, thus genuflecting toward past conferences in Europe during the nineteenth century. This excerpted passage also illustrates what became known as the Bandung Spirit: a feeling of political and global possibility when Asian and African countries collected their interests together. This spirit of Third World solidarity would form one of the long-term successes of the meeting. The Asian-African Conference—or simply "Bandung" for shorthand—would continue to be cited as a symbolic moment of Third World unity in the decades ahead.[24]

Though other leaders would embrace this sentiment, a sense of realpolitik also held sway. Nehru and Zhou, in particular, pursued complementary agendas that reflected the recent Panchsheel agreement, as well as broader goals within the overlapping contexts of global decolonization and the Cold War (Illustration 3.5). They arguably shared the most political capital of any of the leaders in attendance, based on their personal reputations and the countries they represented. India and China were two of the largest countries in territorial size, with resources and economic wealth that not only affirmed their hegemonic influence in the regions of South and East Asia but also added to their

Illustration 3.5 PRC Foreign Minister Zhou Enlai (left) with President Sukarno (center). Permission to use from the Asian-African Conference Museum, Bandung, Indonesia.

political and economic clout in the decades ahead. Combined with this dimension were the remarkable political histories that both countries possessed. India held the distinction of being the first major colony of Great Britain to achieve independence, along with Pakistan following partition in August 1947. Under the leadership of Nehru and Mohandas Gandhi, the Indian National Congress, and India more generally, attained an anti-imperial symbolism and moral authority widely admired by other colonial countries. In fact, Nehru had participated in the 1927 League against Imperialism meeting, so he understood the importance of intercolonial connections and the new possibilities that could emerge at Bandung. The PRC similarly attracted attention for the Chinese Communist Revolution in 1949, after a twenty-year period of conflict with Chinese nationalists under the leadership of Chiang Kai-shek (1887–1975). This armed struggle—informed by Marxism and supported by peasants and workers who pursued tactics of guerrilla warfare—provided a contrast to the popular nonviolent resistance of Gandhi but proved no less influential to anticolonial movements in Asia and Africa. Maoism—the revolutionary thought and strategy of China's communist leader Mao Zedong (1893–1976)—inspired and sustained political activism across both continents.

As a consequence of these factors, both Nehru and Zhou perceived Bandung as an occasion to consolidate their standing among regional neighbors and globally. In addition to the PRC's invasion of Tibet in 1950, which added a tense quality to their relations, the PRC had intervened in the Korean War (1950–1953) the same year and supported Ho Chi Minh and the Việt Minh during the anticolonial struggle in Vietnam. In short, the territorially expansive ambitions of the PRC were readily apparent in the years prior to Bandung. Still, Nehru had insisted that China be invited to the meeting, given the recent Panchsheel Treaty. The high-profile participation of Nehru and Zhou served to reinforce this pact. But they also had individual agendas. Although the Non-Aligned Movement would not formally take shape until the Belgrade Conference of Non-Aligned States (hereafter, the Belgrade Conference) convened in 1961, Nehru promoted the idea of "non-alignment"—a term first coined by India's UN ambassador V. K. Krishna Menon, but also emerging from Nehru's earlier experience with the anticolonial strategy of noncooperation during the 1920s. Nonalignment with the United States and the Soviet Union marked the transformation of a tactic of anticolonial resistance to one of diplomatic principle. Zhou's intentions were no less ambitious in scope. He sought wider diplomatic recognition for the legitimacy of the PRC, given that Taiwan (formally known as the Republic of China) retained UN status as China, a situation that would last until 1971. Tensions between the PRC and Taiwan were such that Zhou barely survived an assassination attempt in Hong Kong on his way to Jakarta when the original Air India flight he was on exploded. Zhou's commitment to attending the meeting underscored its political importance to the PRC. Whereas Nehru and India's legitimacy appeared unquestioned, Zhou and the PRC viewed the Asian-African Conference as another vital step toward wider recognition in the international community, given its exclusion from the UN.[25]

Other leaders faced questions of legitimacy of a different type. For Gamal Abdel Nasser, Bandung offered an opportunity for gaining international recognition, enabling him to ascend to a status equivalent to statesmen like Nehru, despite the ambiguities of the coup that placed him in power in 1952. The period between the 1952 Revolution led by the Free Officers and April 1955 was a complex one for Nasser. Though he played a key role in the revolt and served as vice-chairman of the Revolutionary Command Council under President Muhammad Naguib, it was not until late 1954—after ongoing disputes with Naguib and surviving a failed assassination attempt in October of that year—that Nasser effectively ascended to the presidency. A new constitution approved in 1956 would formalize this status.[26]

Nasser had grown concerned with the continued influence of Great Britain in the Middle East, especially after the signing of the Baghdad Pact in February 1955, which arranged a series of military agreements between Britain, Iraq, Iran, Turkey, and Pakistan—the last four, it should be noted, were attendees at the Bandung Conference. Egypt had been an observer at the 1947 Asian

Relations Conference, and Nasser had reached out to Nehru in the weeks prior to the Asian-African Conference, with mutual diplomatic visits to Cairo and Delhi. The Bandung meeting solidified this effort on the part of Nasser, with the elder Nehru assuming a mentorship role.

Indeed, the relationship between Nehru and Nasser points to another type of imbalance among delegates: generational differences. Nehru was sixty-six years old at the conference; Nasser was only thirty-seven. This generational element provided opportunities and constraints. Although Nasser had little political capital to offer Nehru, opportunity reigned for Nasser, with distinct gains through his friendship with Nehru indicated in the years ahead, particularly through the formation of the Non-Aligned Movement in 1961.[27]

The Asian-African Conference, therefore, captured an intersection of individual and group aims. It solidified the leadership roles of some, as in the cases of Nehru and Zhou. It marked the public ascent of others, such as Sukarno and Nasser. Each achieved varied degrees and definitions of success. But the immediate outcome of the conference was a final communiqué that stated the broad desire for economic cooperation and cultural exchange, recognition for human rights and self-determination, the condemnation of new and future forms of imperialism, and the pursuit of policies that would promote world peace. It consisted of seven parts. The first part, Section A, prioritized economic cooperation and technical assistance, acknowledging "the urgency of promoting economic development in the Asian-African region." Specific recommendations included establishing cooperative efforts and funds for development assistance (Item 3); stabilizing trade and commodity prices (Items 4–7); nationalizing banks and creating regional financial institutions (Item 8); and making energy policies concerning oil and nuclear power (Items 9 and 10). Second to economic growth was cultural cooperation (Section B), which recognized the cultural diversity of Asia and Africa (Item 1) and the impact Western colonialism and racism had had in suppressing the cultural progress of these continents (Item 2). The founding of "educational, scientific and technical institutions" (Item 4), in addition to sponsoring forms of cultural exchange, was viewed as aiding "the promotion of world peace and understanding" (Item 3). Section C, "Human Rights and Self Determination," stated explicit support for the 1948 Universal Declaration of Human Rights (Item 1) and specifically criticized ongoing practices of racial discrimination and segregation in the world, especially apartheid in South Africa (Item 2). Section D, "Problems of Dependent Peoples," went further to acknowledge the continued existence of colonialism in the world, and Section E, "Other Problems," listed specifically the Palestinian question, as well as political situations in Aden and West Irian (Western New Guinea).[28]

The final two parts of the communiqué—Section F, "Promotion of World Peace and Cooperation," and Section G, "Declaration on the Promotion of World Peace and Cooperation"—in hindsight capture the strongest qualities of the conference, even if these aspirations proved largely rhetorical in nature. These sections urged not only inclusion of future Afro-Asian states as members of the UN but also that Asian and African countries play a role on its Security Council. Furthermore, Section F stated that "disarmament and the prohibition of the production, experimentation and use of nuclear and thermonuclear weapons of war are imperative to save mankind and civilization from the fear and prospect of wholesale destruction," thus acknowledging the profound new military threat that the Cold War presented, one potentially more dangerous than past colonialism. Japan's involvement at Bandung and its firsthand experience of nuclear devastation at Hiroshima and Nagasaki ensured the presence of this section. Section G's final ten-point summary, also referred to as the Ten Principles or the *Dasa Sila Bandung*, concluded with an argument that the aforementioned issues were all interrelated, that respect for human rights, state sovereignty and territorial integrity, racial equality, and the promotion of economic and cultural cooperation would help surpass the recent imperial past, as well as enhance security in the future. "The Asian and African Conference declares its conviction that friendly cooperation in accordance with these principles would effectively contribute to the maintenance and promotion of international peace and security," the communiqué stated, "while cooperation in the economic, social and cultural fields would help bring about the common prosperity and well-being of all."

In sum, the Asian-African Conference concluded with wide-ranging aims that reflected the equally expansive geography and politics of those who attended. Though it originated with a set of regional crises, it emerged with a broader political vision that perceived the situation in Southeast Asia as emblematic of a new and dangerous Cold War nuclear age. The final communiqué underscored these concerns and indicated that Asian and African countries would be involved in future diplomatic efforts to seek the security of their respective continents.

Historical judgments since the meeting have sharply contrasted, at times tending toward a kind of utopianism—Bandung being a shining instance of Third World solidarity—and on other occasions leaning toward dismissiveness—a conference that ultimately accomplished little. Its significance naturally rests somewhere between these two positions. The weaknesses of Third World solidarity positioned against Cold War rivalries were immediately apparent. Bandung proved to be a moment of limited social and political capital. It is important to stress once more that nonalignment as a stated principle shared by all in attendance was not an outcome of Bandung, a reflection of the formal and informal security agreements, such as SEATO and the Baghdad Pact, that a number of participants had already engaged. Only India, Burma, and Indonesia supported the idea explicitly. Turkey had additionally been a member of the North Atlantic Treaty Organization (NATO) since 1952, thus aligning itself with the U.S. and Western Europe. SEATO would continue to make regional inroads, resulting in the escalation of American involvement and eventually the Vietnam War. A number of other countries also had unilateral relations with the United States, including Saudi Arabia and Japan, and others had strong ties with the Soviet Union, such as China and North Vietnam. On a different track, China and India remained tense neighbors, a rivalry that soon exploded with the 1962 Sino-Indian War. In this view, the Bandung meeting did not succeed, either in terms of the final communiqué or through the continuation of friendly relations that personal diplomacy could offer.

But other developments also occurred. Pre-existing alignments with the First and Second Worlds did not preclude other options. Regional conflicts did not prevent other relationships from taking shape. If the geographic balance of the meeting tilted toward Asia, the future of Asia-Africa relations quickly moved to the continent of Africa. Nasser gradually positioned himself as a leader of the Third World, a status enhanced by the support Egypt garnered during the 1956 Suez Crisis, when Great Britain and France failed to regain control over the Suez Canal after Nasser nationalized it. In December 1957, the Afro-Asian Peoples' Solidarity Organization (AAPSO) was established in Cairo, marking a new intercontinental endeavor in the wake of Bandung. AAPSO proved to have even wider involvement, including a range of organizations rather than only official state delegations from African and Asian countries. The conferences it organized between 1958 and 1965 sought to continue the spirit of Bandung by emphasizing professional exchange, cultural promotion, women's coalitions, and youth participation. Furthermore, its meetings were held within an expanding range of locales, including Guinea, Ghana, and Tanzania.

Most significant, however, was the trajectory of nonalignment. Although it had a limited impact at Bandung, it soon gained momentum through its embrace by Yugoslavia's Josip Broz Tito and Ghana's Kwame Nkrumah. The Belgrade Conference of Non-Aligned States, convened in 1961, formalized this solidarity. Besides Tito and Nkrumah, key figures included Nehru, Nasser, and Sukarno, with Zhou and the PRC notably absent. A second Non-Aligned Movement (NAM) conference was held in Cairo in October 1964 with delegations from forty-seven states in attendance, a numeric growth resulting from the wave of decolonization in sub-Saharan Africa.

The efforts at sustaining a Third World bloc thus achieved a high point by 1964, a culmination compromised a year later with the failure to coalesce a proposed second Asian-African conference. The NAM ultimately super-seded the Asian-African Conference—drawing upon it symbolically, but marking a different configuration of nation-states that would meet routinely in the decades ahead. Nevertheless, the Bandung conference succeeded in initiating this set of political possibilities—the building of social and politi-cal capital through intercontinental networking—even if it proved to be a one-time diplomatic moment, rather than establishing an enduring diplo-matic routine.[29]

Lessons in Successful Diplomacy from Bandung to the Present

With the colonial period receding and postcolonial autonomy better under-stood, the initial fervor of Afro-Asian solidarity in 1955 shifted and declined during the 1960s, though it did not entirely disappear. The Vietnam War, the anti-apartheid movement in South Africa, and the Arab-Israeli conflict con-tinued to offer reasons for protesting against Western intervention. New connections were also fostered, particularly in Latin America with the 1966 founding of the Afro-Asian Latin American People's Solidarity Organiza-tion in Havana, Cuba. But these later developments do not fully account for the successes, or failures, of Bandung. The Asian-African Conference did not establish a diplomatic routine like the NAM or AAPSO. In this regard, the Bandung meeting approximates European diplomatic occasions that sought regional peace, rather than the institutionalization of good relations through scheduled diplomacy. To interpret the event as a failure due to its singularity therefore risks overestimating the ambitions and purpose of the conference—and it overlooks how similar European conferences also failed to establish an enduring peace. Furthermore, while those in attendance did agree to a final communiqué of wide-ranging ideals, measuring success or failure by the achievement of those high ideals neglects a more prosaic aspect of the meeting and international conferences more generally: the opportu-nity to meet, converse, and develop relations with other leaders and diplo-mats. As discussed, leaders brought strengths and weaknesses—different forms of political, economic, and social capital—to the diplomatic table. These imbalances created both opportunities and constraints for leaders, countries, and the conference as a whole. But one of the more momentous results of the meeting was the opening of a new political horizon through this first occasion of political networking and Third World solidarity.

In contrast to many present-day understandings, the "Third World" was a positive term and virtue at the time, designating a new coalition of independent nations and an alternative to past and contemporary forms of imperialism. Although the origins of the expression "Third World" preceded the conference, Bandung captured its meaning in palpable form.

In keeping with the purpose of this edited volume, several concluding lessons can be drawn. First, international conferences must be viewed as comprising a particular institutionalized form in the world of diplomacy and statecraft. They are an indispensable aspect of successful diplomacy, and they have a history, evolving concurrently with the rise of the modern nation-state. Indeed, they have provided a vital means for generating and maintaining state sovereignty during times of war and peace alike. The Asian-African Conference is a case in point. During an uncertain period of multiple transitions in the international community, the Bandung meeting affirmed the independence of sovereign nation-states in Asia and Africa in the face of a receding period of Western imperialism and emerging rivalries of the Cold War. The Bandung conference succeeded in asserting this principle.

Second, in similar fashion, conferences create a stage for public leadership and diplomatic agency—two essential features of successful diplomacy. Bandung illustrates this point as well. A range of leaders arrived at the conference with different histories and different agendas. Bandung provided an occasion for delegates to promote the interests of their own countries, but it also allowed for broader ideas of community to take shape, even if in nascent form. Nehru's pursuit of nonalignment and Sukarno's notion of unity in diversity, which drew from his perspective on Indonesia's national identity, looked beyond their own nation-states to more expansive notions of political community. Leaders such as Nasser, in turn, were keen to participate in such projects, as a means of bolstering their national and international reputations. Leaders viewed the Asian-African Conference as a diplomatic stage for these different ideas, and the conference format presented a moment of agency to pursue them. It enabled the success of these leaders.

Third, conferences must be understood as important occasions for networking and building social capital, thus helping to ensure successful diplomacy in the future. The nascent independence of many of these nation-states meant that the economic and political capital these countries could bring to the diplomatic table in 1955 was limited. Still, some leaders, such as Nehru, Sukarno, and Zhou, represented countries that had extensive resources and economic capital, whereas others, such as Nasser and Nehru, once more possessed forms of personal capital, based on their individual histories, which added to their stature. These variables, if at times elusive and difficult to measure, nevertheless point to reasons that explain the authority of certain leaders and delegations over others.

These factors also clarify why diplomatic success in the short term was unclear, and diplomatic gains in the long term were more significant, as argued in the introduction. Despite anti-Western rhetoric and emerging claims of nonalignment, the countries in attendance did not have the political and economic resources in 1955 to establish the durable networks necessary to create a sustainable, alternative community of nations beyond external influence. Pre-existing connections with former European colonial powers, as well as new relations with the United States and the Soviet Union, proved more appealing and productive in the short term. Domestic politics also proved important. The initial limits of political and economic capital not only blunted interstate network formation during the early postcolonial period but also contributed to a domestic focus on economic development and consolidating wealth internally. Efforts to build diplomatic networks did continue, as the NAM demonstrates. But uncertainty remained ever present, as it was at Bandung. As Nehru said in passing, in an address given on April 22, 1955, "We rely on nobody except on the friendship of others; we rely on ourselves and none others."[30] This balance of cooperation and individualism would become more pronounced in the years ahead.

Yet, these ideas of the past have become more viable over time. The end of the Cold War has witnessed the opening of possibilities for reviving past projects, if in revised form. Since 2000, the Forum on China-Africa Cooperation (FOCAC) has hosted a series of conferences to encourage investment and trade between China and African countries. The Asian-African Conference has been a key historical reference point for this present-day endeavor, although with a crucial difference—greater wealth and power.[31] The BRICS economic bloc—unifying the economic and political interests of Brazil, Russia, India, China, and South Africa—has similarly posed a challenge to the hegemony of Euro-American economies and financial institutions, through escalating economic growth in Asia, Africa, and Latin America.[32] The period since 1955 has therefore been one of gestation and maturation for generating the economic and political capital necessary for the strength of current relations. The sequence of international conferences put in motion by FOCAC and BRICS has built a new set of networks with more resources than existed at Bandung. This history of the present, within this intercontinental context, ultimately signals the continued vitality of international conferences and their role in reinforcing the nation-state, as well as enabling broader communities of political possibility, as once exemplified in April 1955.

Notes

1. An invitation was also sent to the Central African Federation (contemporary Malawi, Zambia, and Zimbabwe), then under British colonial rule. It should be noted that this figure (twenty-nine) has also been debated, given that unofficial delegations also attended, such as those from Algeria and South Africa. Mark Philip Bradley, for example, incorrectly cites a figure of thirty in a recent essay: Mark Philip Bradley, "Decolonization, the Global South, and the Cold War, 1919–1962," in *The Cambridge History of the Cold War, Volume 1*, ed. Melvyn P. Leffler and Odd Arne Westad (Cambridge: Cambridge University Press, 2010), 479. On the unofficial attendance of South African and Algerian delegations, see, respectively, Brian Bunting, *Moses Kotane, South African Revolutionary: A Political Biography* (London: Inkululeko Publications, 1975), chap. 12; Alistair Horne, *A Savage War of Peace: Algeria 1954–1962* (New York: NYRB Classics, 2006), chap. 6.

2. For recent depictions of Bandung, its origins, and legacies, see Kweku Ampiah, *The Political and Moral Imperatives of the Bandung Conference of 1955* (Leiden: Brill, 2007); Roland Burke, *Decolonization and the Evolution of Human Rights* (Philadelphia: University of Pennsylvania Press, 2013), chap. 1; Christopher J. Lee, ed., *Making a World After Empire: The Bandung Moment and Its Political Afterlives* (Athens: Ohio University Press, 2010); Derek McDougall and Antonia Finnane, eds., *Bandung 1955: Little Histories* (Melbourne: Monash Asia Institute, 2010); Seng Tan and Amitav Acharya, eds., *Bandung Revisited: The Legacy of the 1955 Asian-African Conference for International Order* (Singapore: NUS Press, 2008).

3. The speeches from the meeting have been published in a number of volumes. See, for example, George McTurnan Kahin, *The African-Asian Conference: Bandung, Indonesia, April 1955* (Ithaca, NY: Cornell University Press, 1956).

4. Benedict Anderson, *Imagined Communities: Reflections on the Origin and Spread of Nationalism*, rev. ed. (London: Verso, 2006 [1983]), 137.

5. For discussion of this issue, see, for example, Frederick Cooper, *Colonialism in Question: Theory, Knowledge, History* (Berkeley: University of California Press, 2005), chap. 6.

6. Jane Burbank and Frederick Cooper, *Empires in World History: Power and the Politics of Difference* (Princeton, NJ: Princeton University Press, 2010), 182, 183.

7. On the Concert of Europe, see Mark Mazower, *Governing the World: The History of an Idea, 1815 to the Present* (New York: Penguin, 2012), epilogue plus chaps. 1 through 4; Jennifer Mitzen, *Power in Concert: The Nineteenth-Century Origins of Global Governance* (Chicago: University of Chicago Press, 2013).

8. On the UN's history, see Paul Kennedy, *The Parliament of Man: The Past, Present, and Future of the United Nations* (New York: Random House, 2006); Mazower, *Governing the World*, chap. 7; Mark Mazower, *No Enchanted Palace: The End of Empire and the Ideological Origins of the United Nations* (Princeton, NJ: Princeton University Press, 2009); Stanley Meisler, *United Nations: The First Fifty Years* (New York: Atlantic Monthly Press, 1995).

9. On the Pan-African Congresses, see P. Olisanwuche Esedebe, *Pan-Africanism: The Idea and Movement, 1776–1991* (Washington, DC: Howard University Press, 1994). On the Universal Races Congress, see, for example, Mansour Bonakdarian, "Negotiating Universal Values and Cultural and National Parameters at the First Universal Races Congress," *Radical History Review* 92 (2005): 118–132; Susan D. Pennybacker, "The Universal Races Congress, London Political Culture, and Imperial Dissent, 1900–1939," *Radical History Review* 92 (Spring 2005): 103–117; Paul Rich, "'The Baptism of a New Era': The 1911 Universal Races Congress and the Liberal Ideology of Race," *Ethnic and Racial Studies* 7, no. 4 (1984): 534–550; Universal Races Congress, *Record of the Proceedings of the First Universal Races Congress, held at the University of London, July 26–29, 1911* (London: P.S. King & Son, 1911). On the League against Imperialism, see Vijay Prashad, *The Darker Nations* (New York: New Press, 2007), chap. 2; Robert J. C. Young, *Postcolonialism: An Historical Introduction* (Oxford: Blackwell, 2001), 176–177. On Pan-Asianism—which, it must be noted, also contributed to Japan's imperial ambitions—see

Cemil Aydin, *The Politics of Anti-Westernism in Asia: Visions of World Order in Pan-Islamic and Pan-Asian Thought* (New York: Columbia University Press, 2007); Prasenjit Duara, "The Discourse of Civilization and Pan-Asianism," *Journal of World History* 12, no. 1 (2001): 99–130; Sven Saaler and J. Victor Koschmann, eds., *Pan-Asianism in Modern Japanese History: Colonialism, Regionalism and Borders* (London: Routledge, 2007).

10. On networks and global politics, see Miles Kahler, ed., *Networked Politics: Agency, Power, and Governance* (Ithaca, NY: Cornell University Press, 2009).

11. James Farr, "Social Capital: A Conceptual History," *Political Theory* 31, no. 1 (2004), 7, 8.

12. Alejandro Portes, "The Two Meanings of Social Capital," *Sociological Forum* 15, no. 1 (2000), 2.

13. Pierre Bourdieu, "The Forms of Capital," in *Handbook of Theory and Research for the Sociology of Education*, ed. J. G. Richardson (New York: Greenwood, 1985): 241–258. See also James S. Coleman, "Social Capital in the Creation of Human Capital," *American Journal of Sociology* 94, Supplement (1988): S95–121; Simon Szreter, "The State of Social Capital: Bringing Back in Power, Politics, and History," *Theory and Society* 31, no. 5 (2002): 573–621.

14. Farr, "Social Capital," 9.

15. For a study of such negotiations, see Matthew Connelly, *A Diplomatic Revolution: Algeria's Fight for Independence and the Origins of the Post–Cold War Era* (New York: Oxford University Press, 2002).

16. On the these conferences, see "All-African People's Conferences," *International Organization* 16, no. 2 (1962): 429–434; George M. Houser, "At Cairo: The Third All-African People's Conference," *Africa Today* 8, no. 4 (1961): 11–13; Homer A. Jack, "Ideological Conflicts," *Africa Today* 6, no. 1 (1959): 11–17; G. H. Jansen, *Nonalignment and the Afro-Asian States* (New York: Praeger, 1966), 265, 266; J. A. McCallum, "The Asian Relations Conference," *The Australian Quarterly* 19, no. 2 (1947): 13–17; J. A. McCallum, "Personalities at the Asian Relations Conference," *The Australian Quarterly* 19, no. 3 (1947): 39–44.

17. "The Afro-Asian Conference," *Pakistan Horizon* 8, no. 1 (1955): 306.

18. Prashad, *Darker Nations*, 34, 35.

19. "No. 4307. India and [the] People's Republic of China," *Treaty Series* 299, Nos. 4303–4325 (1958): 57–81.

20. On SEATO, see Damien Fenton, *To Cage the Red Dragon: SEATO and the Defense of Southeast Asia, 1955–1965* (Singapore: NUS Press, 2012). On U.S. policy toward the Bandung meeting, see Jason Parker, "Cold War II: The Eisenhower Administration, the Bandung Conference, and the Reperiodization of the Postwar Era," *Diplomatic History* 30, no. 5 (2006): 867–892.

21. Among the better-known unofficial delegates were African-American participants Richard Wright and U.S. Congressman Adam Clayton Powell, Jr. See Nico Slate, *Colored Cosmopolitanism: The Shared Struggle for Freedom in the United States and India* (Cambridge, MA: Harvard University Press, 2012), 210–212; Richard Wright, *The Color Curtain: A Report on the Bandung Conference* (Oxford, MS: University Press of Mississippi, 1995 [1956]). Unofficial delegates representing liberation struggles in Algeria and South Africa also attended, as mentioned earlier. See Bunting, *Moses Kotane*, chap. 12; Connelly, *A Diplomatic Revolution*, 81, 85, 93–96.

22. On the leaders present, see Amitav Acharya and See Seng Tan, "Introduction: The Normative Relevance of the Bandung Conference for Contemporary Asian and International Order," in Tan and Acharya, *Bandung Revisited*, 1–18.

23. "Speech by President Sukarno of Indonesia at the Opening of the Conference," *Collected Documents of the Asian-African Conference, April 18–24, 1955* (Jakarta: Department of Foreign Affairs, 1983), 8.

24. This symbolism has been particularly demonstrated through different memoirs and commemorations of the meeting. See, *inter alia*, Roeslan Abdulgani, *The Bandung Connection: The Asia-Africa Conference in Bandung in 1955* (Singapore: Gunung Agung, 1981); Donald K. Emmerson, "A New Spirit of Bandung?" *Pacific Forum/CSIS*, April 29, 2005; Jamie Mackie, *Bandung 1955: Non-Alignment and Afro-Asian Solidarity* (Singapore: Editions

Didier Millet, 2005); Volker Matthies, "The 'Spirit of Bandung' 1955–1985: Thirty Years Since the Bandung Conference," *Intereconomics* 20, no. 5 (1985): 207–210.

25. For a recent appraisal of Zhou and his career, see Gao Wenqian, *Zhou Enlai: The Last Perfect Revolutionary* (New York: Public Affairs, 2007).

26. For a recent biography of Nasser, see Saïd K. Aburish, *Nasser: The Last Arab* (New York: Thomas Dunne Books, 2004).

27. Rami Ginat, *Syria and the Doctrine of Arab Neutralism: From Independence to Dependence* (Sussex: Sussex Academic Press, 2010), 105, 113–115.

28. For a complete copy of the communiqué, see "Final Communique of the Asian-African Conference," *Collected Documents of the Asian-African Conference, April 18–24, 1955* (Jakarta: Department of Foreign Affairs, 1983), 137–144.

29. On the history of nonalignment, see, for example, J. W. Burton, ed., *Nonalignment* (London: Andre Deutsch, 1966); Cecil V. Crabb, Jr., *The Elephants and the Grass: A Study of Nonalignment* (New York: Praeger, 1965); G. H. Jansen, *Nonalignment and the Afro-Asian States* (New York: Praeger, 1966); Lawrence W. Martin, ed., *Neutralism and Nonalignment: The New States in World Affairs* (New York: Praeger, 1962); Natasa Miskovic, Harald Fischer-Tiné, and Nada Boskovska, eds., *The Non-Aligned Movement and the Cold War: Delhi-Bandung-Belgrade* (New York: Routledge, 2014); Robert B. Rakove, *Kennedy, Johnson, and the Nonaligned World* (New York: Cambridge University Press, 2012).

30. Kahin, *The African-Asian Conference*, 65.

31. For two overviews of contemporary China-Africa relations, see Deborah Brautigam, *The Dragon's Gift: The Real Story of China in Africa* (New York: Oxford University Press, 2010); Howard W. French, *China's Second Continent: How a Million Migrants Are Building a New Empire in Africa* (New York: Knopf, 2014).

32. On BRICS, see Vijay Prashad, *The Poorer Nations: A Possible History of the Global South* (London: Verso, 2012), 221–225.

4

The Birth of an International Community

*Negotiating the Treaty on the Non-Proliferation
of Nuclear Weapons*

JONATHAN HUNT

By 1963, the accelerating spread of nuclear knowledge and technology across
the globe was setting off fears that a cascade of states would build "the ultimate
weapon." On March 21 of that year, U.S. president John F. Kennedy answered
a question from members of the press, who had gathered in the State Department's public auditorium to learn whether a comprehensive nuclear test-ban
treaty (CTBT) that U.S. negotiators were trying to hammer out with Soviet
officials in Geneva was within reach. Kennedy took the occasion to peer into
his crystal ball and make a more global forecast: "I see the possibility in the
1970s of the President of the United States having to face a world in which 15
or 20 or 25 nations may [have] these weapons." He warned that this would be
"the greatest possible danger and hazard."[1] More than fifty years later, those
states fielding nuclear weapons still number less than ten thanks in part to a
landmark phase of multilateral efforts to broker a nuclear nonproliferation
treaty and thereby inaugurate a global regime under whose auspices nuclear
power has been managed ever since.

The Treaty on the Non-Proliferation of Nuclear Weapons (NPT) opened
for signature on July 1, 1968, five years after Kennedy first rang the alarm bells
and almost a decade since Irish foreign minister Frank Aiken proposed a "non-
dissemination" pact to the United Nations General Assembly (UNGA).[2] The
NPT's record in stopping more states from acquiring these weapons of mass
destruction is mixed; since 1968, Israel, South Africa, India, Pakistan, and
North Korea have all produced them. Yet, these five proliferators are a far cry
from Kennedy's forecast of "15 or 20 or 25," and the ranks of the nuclear-armed
have also periodically dwindled, such as when South Africa decommissioned
its nuclear weapons in 1989 or Kazakhstan, Belarus, and Ukraine gave up

those inherited from the Soviet Union by 1996. The NPT's importance in how the international community tries to confront suspicious nuclear activities is, by contrast, incontrovertible. It inaugurated a system of safeguards on fissile materials that power nuclear reactors and could also fuel a bomb, most worrisomely uranium-238 and plutonium-239, which is run by the International Atomic Energy Agency (IAEA). It also authorizes the UN Security Council to apply sanctions, or force, against countries found in violation of those safeguards, or pursuing clandestine work on nuclear weapons. The treaty has sometimes legitimated extralegal acts, including Israel's preemptive strikes against Iraqi and Syrian nuclear facilities, and, most infamously, the American invasion of Iraq in 2003 based on allegations of secret nuclear activities, which eventually proved spurious. The NPT nonetheless remains central to debates about whether nonsignatories, such as India, deserve full access to nuclear technology, or whether Iran and North Korea have breached their obligations as signatories and, if so, what ought to be done.

The negotiation of a nuclear nonproliferation treaty in the 1960s demanded careful coordination among scores of nation-states at a watershed moment in world politics; like vastly complex clockwork, untold moving parts would need to align.[3] The Second World War gave rise to an international community of nation-states steeped in liberal values.[4] The ascent to superpower status of two countries—the United States and the Soviet Union—whose constitutional principles denounced colonialism, together with the costs of waging six years of total war, had bankrupted Europe's empires, ethically and financially.[5] Decolonization witnessed the replacement of their colonial holdings with dozens of new Afro-Asian nation-states. These postcolonial nation-states were welcomed into an expanding complex of international organizations, transnational linkages, nongovernmental organizations, and multinational forums with the UN at its heart.[6] This process enriched the diversity of representative bodies such as the UNGA, tilting the balance of voting rights within them away from the capitalist and communist blocs and toward the Global South as nearly forty new nation-states joined the organization between 1957 and 1967.[7]

The rise of an international community was the decisive context in which the NPT was written.[8] As a consequence, success had three interlocking prerequisites. The first was to open a window of opportunity between the superpowers. Given their preeminence, collaboration between the United States and the USSR was vital. The second was to find a broadly "acceptable balance of mutual responsibilities and obligations" among the various groups of states with interests at stake in nuclear security, energy, and politics. Allies' opposition could be just as damaging as that of adversaries. Washington and Moscow therefore consulted their partners routinely before taking offers to the other side. Nonaligned views grew increasingly salient once the East and West found common ground on language relating to European security. Because nuclear power then symbolized the glittering future for global energy markets and military power, commercial and security interests were often compelling. The final prerequisite was for diplomats to overcome "barriers to resolution" even as they demarcated a "zone of potential agreement" among the various stake-holders. Barriers to resolution are usually psychological in nature and can be-devil all efforts at conflict resolution or overcoming the "collective-action problem," whereby discrete actors find it difficult to trust one another enough to make joint commitments to pursue common and mutually beneficial goals.[9] Such barriers are surmountable, however, by "improving the relationship be-tween the parties so that it ceases to exacerbate, and ideally begins to attenu-ate, the barriers in question."[10] The roots of U.S.-Soviet cooperation in promoting a nonproliferation treaty sprang in part from cultivating better rela-tions between their Geneva delegations.

Superpower collaboration was necessary, yet nevertheless insufficient, for constructing a global nonproliferation regime. A final settlement re-quired general and lasting support from an international community newly born of decolonization and the United Nations' founding. UNGA Resolu-tion 2028 outlined the guiding negotiating principles in 1965: "the treaty should embody an acceptable balance of mutual responsibilities and obliga-tions of the nuclear and non-nuclear Powers."[11] In reality, the zone of pos-sible agreement needed to encompass five sets of states—the superpowers, allied regional powers, nonaligned regional powers, nuclear exporters, and nuclear importers—with most states belonging to multiple groups.[12] Non-proliferation diplomacy was consequently a slow and cumbersome process mired in legal technicalities and punctuated by endless plenary sessions. In six years of negotiations, the three multinational bodies in which the treaty was drafted met more than four hundred times.[13] Students of diplomacy should accordingly learn two lessons whose effects are hard to measure yet whose adoption is critical for diplomacy to succeed. The first is the impera-tive of perseverance and continuous diplomacy. Consensus takes time to coalesce and turns of fortune are often key to one side shifting policy and unlocking progress. When the United States sought the Federal Republic of Germany's (FRG) backing after Washington nixed a NATO nuclear force cherished by Bonn, for example, the West German disarmament minister, Swidbert Schnippenkoetter "made a point of stressing" how grateful he and his colleagues were for the "patience with which [the United States had] answered our many questions."[14] Practicalities tend to dictate a govern-ment's choice, but a failure to communicate can derail negotiation before it gets going.

As Steven Miller has observed, "international legal regimes depend on consent."[15] The second point is even the best agreements are doomed without partisans of diplomacy. The NPT would ultimately live or die according to the fate of a UNGA resolution endorsing the final text and whether the parties believed that the treaty continued to reflect their interests and their understandings of its original purpose. The establishment of the U.S. Arms Control and Disarmament Agency (ACDA) and the Eighteen Nation Disarmament Conference (ENDC) added new institutional and social platforms on which negotiators could build more promising nuclear relations between the United States and the world. A partisan of diplomacy was not necessarily an enemy of the military, however, and ties to the military-industrial complex proved surprisingly useful. The connections that ACDA director William "Bill" Foster had in the Pentagon from his days as deputy secretary of defense helped him recruit Secretary of Defense Robert McNamara as an ally.[16] Time and again, diplomatic progress occurred thanks to individuals whose worldview and career were rooted in international solutions. The Mexican deputy foreign minister, Alfonso García Robles, had spent fifteen years working in Turtle Bay (the UN's Manhattan neighborhood) before becoming active in nuclear diplomacy. This experience helped him rally nonaligned votes in the UNGA behind the treaty's endorsement in 1968.[17] The fact that only four states have chosen not to sign (or chosen to leave) the NPT since it entered into force in 1970, testifies to the durable consensus these partisans of diplomacy built.

A Global Chain Reaction

After the Second World War ended with two atomic bombs falling on Japan, the world struggled to manage the nuclear revolution amid two tectonic shifts in world affairs—the Cold War and the twilight of Europe's empires. The first attempt to govern the nuclear age began while Hiroshima and Nagasaki were still no-man's-lands. The Acheson-Lilienthal report drawn up by U.S. scientists and officials proposed a United Nations Atomic Energy Commission to regulate nuclear technology. The commission would own all sources of uranium ore needed to build the revolutionary weapons or produce electricity from a nuclear pile that could yield a second, unnatural, transuranic element—plutonium—that could also yield an atomic bomb. The international control of atomic energy would take hold once the United States dismantled its nuclear stockpile. Nuclear disarmament would thus preempt an arms race. Advanced in June 1946, the plan combined the stick of preemptive action with carrots such as full exchange of scientific information with peaceful uses. Drafted mainly by the Manhattan Project's scientific director, J. Robert

Oppenheimer, its chief negotiator, Bernard Baruch, raised the bargaining price when he arrived in Geneva, demanding inspections backed by a UN-sanctioned force unrestrained by a Soviet veto in the UN Security Council.[18] Soviet authorities rejected the Baruch Plan, however. Stalin had already launched a fast-track military program, which meant that adopting the plan would place the Soviet Union in violation and thus subject to sanction and military action by the UN.[19] The postwar failure to internationalize atomic energy lessened the role that global governance would play in international security. "A cause and a consequence of the Cold War," the Baruch Plan became a "symbol of the mutual mistrust in Soviet-American relations."[20]

A nuclear arms race ensued. The Soviets tested a fission weapon in 1949, a feat the U.S. trumped in 1952 by testing the world's first thermonuclear weapon, which harnessed exponentially more powerful energies released when atoms were fused rather than split. The hopes vested in atomic energy for economic progress nevertheless inspired many to champion international cooperation in peaceful nuclear enterprises. In December 1953, U.S. president Dwight D. Eisenhower informed the UNGA of his desire to apply his country's "entire heart and mind to finding the way by which the miraculous inventiveness of man shall not be dedicated to his death, but consecrated to his life."[21] Eisenhower's "Atoms for Peace" signaled an enduring U.S. commitment to promoting nuclear science and technology by means of technical assistance, experimental reactors, and training programs for foreign scientists and engineers.[22] The initiative led to the IAEA's founding in 1957 and expedited the global distribution of nuclear know-how and reactors.

Nuclear globalization also increased the odds of proliferation. Research reactors' reliance on enriched uranium and generation of weapons-grade plutonium together with the education of thousands of nuclear scientists and engineers multiplied those states capable of launching a military program expeditiously.[23] In 1966, the State Department's Policy Planning Council identified five "principal nuclear capable countries"—West Germany, India, Israel, Japan, and Sweden—and five more threshold states—Australia, Egypt, Pakistan, South Africa, and Switzerland.[24] India and West Germany caused the most concern owing to their advanced nuclear programs, territorial disagreements with Pakistan and East Germany, respectively, and proximity to nuclear-armed neighbors, the Soviet Union and China, also respectively. In Latin America, Argentina and Brazil possessed sizable nuclear sectors. All told, the worrisome countries consisted of four regional powers allied to the West (Australia, the FRG, Israel, and Japan), six nonaligned regional powers (Argentina, Brazil, Egypt, India, Pakistan, and South Africa), and two advanced albeit small European states (Sweden and Switzerland). Among them, West Germany, Sweden, and Japan had plans for nuclear exports, and the rest would probably be importers. American companies were nonetheless predominant in the global nuclear market, and France, the United Kingdom, and the Soviet Union were close behind.[25]

Recurrent nuclear crises illustrated the perils of inaction. Frank Aiken, the Irish foreign minister, proposed the first "non-dissemination" resolution to the UNGA on the heels of the Second Taiwan Straits Crisis in August 1958, when Communist Chinese troops lobbed shells against Nationalist Chinese positions on the tiny islands of Quemoy and Matsu.[26] These barrages precipitated a standoff between Taiwan and China as U.S. planes loaded with atomic bombs circled the nearby skies. International observers were already worried about Mao Tse-tung's claim that a thermonuclear war would lead to communism's triumph notwithstanding the hundreds of millions killed. Aiken warned that "if general war is brought upon the world for any motive . . . it will neither democratize nor communize it; it will annihilate it." The August crisis confirmed that a "rogue state" represented a threat to world peace.[27] Aiken's proposal nonetheless stalled in the UNGA because of French nuclear ambitions and U.S.-Soviet discord relating to NATO's nuclear defense. Nuclear crises on the periphery of the Cold War nevertheless underscored two dangers. First, the spark that could set off a thermonuclear war could come from anywhere. Second, nuclear globalization would slowly yet inexorably put more and more fingers on the button.

Attention focused more on limited steps and less on radical solutions as the nuclear club steadily grew. The United Kingdom became the third country to test a nuclear weapon, in 1952. Prevailing opinion was that France and China would soon follow, and scholars started pondering the "Nth-country" problem, hypothesizing that each new nuclear weapon state would prompt more to follow.[28] The first French nuclear test in North Africa in 1960 and French and Chinese criticism of the Limited Test Ban Treaty, which Kennedy and Khrushchev signed in August 1963, proved that even superpowers could not freeze the status quo by themselves. Forecasts that nuclear globalization would breed proliferation and the arrival of thermonuclear warheads one thousand times more powerful than those which razed Hiroshima and Nagasaki convinced even skeptics that the time for international control had come.[29]

Hard-Nosed Internationalism

International institutions and ideas about global order would guide the negotiations involving nuclear nondissemination. Aiken persuaded the nuclear powers to back his resolution in 1961. By then, the nuclear question had outstripped any one state's ability to contain it.[30] U.S. commitment to an international regime was necessary given the country's postwar ascendancy. American faith in internationalism had peaked in the war's immediate wake as the country helped found the United Nations, World Bank, International Monetary Fund, and International Court of Justice. Once the Cold War set in, however, the American tradition of pursuing progressive values abroad waned, and its inclination to expand its influence through a world-spanning network of military alliances, bases, and forces waxed.[31] Voices espousing more reliance on the UN still sounded in domestic politics, most famously in the eloquent tones of two-time Democratic presidential candidate Adlai Stevenson. International luminaries such as Indian prime minister Jawaharlal Nehru also called for greater cooperation among states and less confrontation between the rival blocs. The Eisenhower administration worried about the nuclear arms race as well.[32] Secretary of State Christian Herter bemoaned the lack of a dedicated office in charge of moderating conflict rather than steeling for it. He formed the ACDA to foster "continuity and depth in the review, development, and negotiation of [arms control] policy," which institutionalized the practice in Foggy Bottom.[33]

Three developments vaulted the agency into the cockpit of U.S. foreign policy. First, the 1960 elections transformed the office into an autonomous entity when arms control became a major issue in the Democratic primary. After Kennedy's victory, presidential advisers debated where to slot the bureau into the bureaucratic machinery. An executive agency would display seriousness of purpose, but another stakeholder might bog the process down and render the agency a dwarf among titans—the State Department and the Defense Department. The acting deputy director of the ACDA, Edmund Gullion, wanted the office in Foggy Bottom to keep the Pentagon at bay and harmonize arms control and disarmament policy with other issues areas.[34] However, John McCloy, a longtime power broker, overruled him. Now Kennedy's special adviser on arms control and disarmament, he concluded that the State Department's compartmentalized focus on specific regions and countries would impede the pursuit of bigger schemes. Kennedy split the difference, making the ACDA a semiautonomous agency reporting to the secretary of state, but also enjoying separate statutory authority, its own budget, and direct access to him upon the secretary's notification. This "two-hat arrangement" empowered the agency to play a central, coordinating role until its reabsorption into the State Department in 1999.

The second development driving the ACDA's foreign policy prominence were the individuals chosen to wear those hats. Kennedy named William Foster the agency's director in September 1961. Foster had two decades of experience in the belly of the military-industrial complex and combined business acumen with a cosmopolitan outlook and ethos of public service. His first government post was helping transition the country from isolationism to internationalism by shifting American industry from consumer products to tanks, guns, and warplanes amid the Second World War.[35] His membership in the Republican Party helped, too, by shielding the agency from partisan attacks. An engineer by training, Foster broke off his studies at MIT to serve in the U.S. Army Air Corps during the First World War, founding a steel company afterward.[36] His knowledge of U.S. airpower brought him to the attention of Robert Lovett, who served with McCloy as Secretary of War Henry Stimson's right hand during the war. Lovett needed help rallying manufacturers behind the effort to build enough warplanes to wage the war. Foster moved from a consultant on the War Production Board to director of the army's purchases division, ending the war as Stimson's special representative for aircraft procurement. His wartime performance and business sense landed Foster his next job as Under Secretary of Commerce from 1946 to 1948, when Secretary of State George C. Marshall recruited him to administer the Marshall Plan as deputy special representative in Europe. He then went to work in the Pentagon as deputy secretary of defense when the Korean War began to escalate. Under Eisenhower, Foster and his "old friend" McCloy worked as special advisers on disarmament and the threat of surprise nuclear attack.[37] This background gave him the social capital and credentials needed to court the Pentagon and oppose the Joint Chiefs of Staff when needed, allowing the ACDA to function as a "bureaucratically independent conscience."[38] Because arms control meetings often took place overseas, a highly capable deputy was also needed. Adrian "Butch" Fisher was a Washington lawyer who began government service as McCloy's wartime lieutenant. He then helped stand up the U.S. Atomic Energy Commission as its chief counselor before becoming Secretary of State Dean Acheson's legal adviser during the second Truman administration.[39] Foster and Fisher were an effective team, often swapping places and roles so that "one mind[ed] the store when the other [was] doing the negotiating."[40] They flew across the Atlantic to attend plenaries in Geneva and New York City, advised friendly governments around the world, and testified before congressional committees on Capitol Hill.

The final element of the ACDA's rise to foreign policy prominence was the apogee of a security-first branch of liberal internationalism in U.S. foreign policy based on promoting international cooperation while zealously guarding the nation's security. American views of the world had always been exceptional owing to the country's geographical isolation and liberal ideology. Acheson would warn against "two contrary and equally unrealistic ideas" between which U.S. foreign policy seemed to oscillate—George Washington's farewell address cautioning against "entangling alliances" and Woodrow Wilson's quest

for world peace through collective security.[41] A postwar generation of statesmen had sought to balance power and principle in an outgoing foreign policy
that reflected a cosmopolitan and commercial worldview as well as faith that
international agreements were desirable under strict conditions. Stimson and
Acheson had played leading roles in building the U.S. national security state
and nuclear arsenal. Now, two apprentices strove to preserve an active role in
the world despite the resulting dangers. "A country with the world-wide commitments of the United States," Foster wrote in a 1964 article in *Foreign Affairs*,
could not afford to remain aloof if a conflict was dire enough to provoke the use
of nuclear weapons. The "price" of inaction "would be a renunciation of our
commitments and involvement all over the world: an attempt to return to isolationism at a time when the world is shrinking so rapidly as to make any such
policy at best wishful thinking and quite possibly a blueprint for disaster."[42]

Foster's desire to preserve his country's ability to affect the world was
matched by a growing anxiety among experts that more states acquiring nuclear weapons would lead to catastrophe. Nuclear strategists believed that the
world would become exponentially more dangerous with every new finger
placed on the button. They deduced as well that less-developed states such as
the PRC would have less to lose than industrialized countries such as the
United States or the USSR in the event of a nuclear crisis. Beneath these judgments lurked chauvinistic presumptions about race and modernity. Nevertheless, the scheme of mutual assured destruction looked far riskier when analysts
factored in the superpowers' alliance commitments and entanglements in
such global hot spots as the Middle East, Southeast Asia, and the Caribbean.
Nuclear crises on the Cold War's "periphery" underscored two dangers. First,
the spark needed to set off a thermonuclear war might come from anywhere.
Second, nuclear proliferation would introduce more variables into the already
demanding calculus of nuclear crisis management. The 1961 Berlin Crisis and
the 1962 Cuban Missile Crisis dramatized how quickly "catalytic nuclear
wars" could erupt if regional crises or proxy wars escalated into superpower
confrontations.[43] In Foster's words, "The use of a few nuclear weapons by any
power—even of one such weapon and even with an intent to localize the
effect—might lead to their use in large numbers by other powers, with cata-
clysmic consequences."[44]

Scholars and practitioners often assume a firm opposition between internationalism and a realism based on national interest.[45] Foster and his compatri-
ots, however, regarded international means as robust, practical means to help
attain national ends. A nonproliferation treaty could achieve what the country
could not do alone. Furthermore, the trust needed to negotiate the treaty
would become institutionalized as the regime it authorized enforced common
rules and administered effective safeguards. Modern critics often cite slow

progress toward the general and complete disarmament promised by Article VI of the NPT as proof of the treaty's duplicity, and those dubious of an equivalence among nuclear nonproliferation, rights, and disarmament in the "grand bargain" downplay its importance altogether. At the time, a nonproliferation treaty was considered a collateral step toward disarmament.[46] The disarmament ideal remained meaningful, which signified, according to Foster, "our ultimate goal": "a difficult—yet—possible possibility" for which "more readily achievable approximations" might "pave the way."[47] The treaty would help keep a window on a nuclear-free world cracked. First, though, Soviet and U.S. officials needed to overcome years of acrimony in order to pry it open.

Opening a Window

Talks between the United States and the Soviet Union accelerated and then stalled in 1964. The main impediment was a U.S. proposal to share control over nuclear weapons with West European allies in a NATO force consisting of "mixed-manned" (carrying men from different NATO nations) submarines or cruisers. This multilateral nuclear force (MLF) would buttress Atlantic security after the scares in Berlin and Cuba and help dissuade European allies from seeking their own nuclear deterrents.[48] Initially, Khrushchev affirmed his willingness to sign if Washington pledged that Bonn would not obtain "the possibility of being in charge of nuclear weapons."[49] Moscow's allies in Eastern Europe were aghast, however, and Polish leader Wladyslaw Gomulka conveyed his "deeply troubling thoughts" to Khrushchev: acquiescence was tantamount to "silent consent," undercut disarmament, further split a Communist camp already weakened by discord between the Soviets and Chinese, aided the FRG's quest to reunify Germany, and brought the Germans one step closer to nuclear weapons.[50] Khrushchev had demanded a weak exit clause in compensation; Gomulka complained that he should "prohibit the creation of multilateral nuclear forces now, and you will not [need to] reserve yourself the right to tear up the treaty!"[51] The Soviets reversed course, forbidding any scenario in which the FRG had more access to nuclear arms. The two sides were soon at loggerheads over the exact meaning of nonproliferation. The lack of fidelity in Soviet-American interactions, which were still mainly ad hoc, worsened matters. The superpowers would remain at odds for two years as they worked to rebuild relations even as the Vietnam War erupted.

Kennedy's assassination in November 1963 shocked the world. His successor, Lyndon Baines Johnson, felt beholden to his record in nuclear arms control, including the MLF.[52] The gridlock began to clear when the U.S. negotiating team brought a package of collateral arms control proposals to Geneva in January 1964, including a nonproliferation treaty.[53] Though sincere, the package was crafted mainly "for atmosphere" and to signal the new president's intention to find a small expanse of common ground to start.[54] National Security Adviser McGeorge Bundy described the initiative's motive as showing that "the way to begin is to begin."[55] It was clear when the Soviets unveiled their own package that nonproliferation was the place to begin, but the MLF remained an obstacle. "Washington was preoccupied with China and Moscow with the MLF," Foster observed; consequently, the matter was discussed only "in a narrow fashion."[56]

A window of opportunity began to open because of the social space that Geneva afforded. The Swiss city was a place where Soviet and American delegates could get acquainted, and, in time, the two contingents came to enjoy warm, productive relationships. Years later, the ACDA general counsel, George Bunn, recalled how mistrust gave way eventually to friendship:

> When I first came to Geneva in 1962, the Cold War seemed to be still on. . . . The negotiators were very . . . challenging, hostile, belligerent. . . . Even in a cocktail party, . . . they seemed to be trying to make points against you. By the end of my period there . . . in '68, I had learned how to drive a Volga automobile, and drunk a good deal of vodka with . . . fellow Soviet negotiators. There was just a complete change in the attitudes and relationships between the two delegations.[57]

Soviet diplomat Roland Timerbaev remembered similarly, remarking that "fortunately, we did not turn into 'opposite numbers' representing two rival 'superpowers' of the Cold War era, which was typical for that time." Instead, they found themselves "likeminded people" who "deeply believed in the vital need to stop the proliferation of nuclear weapons, and [who] did our utmost to achieve that goal."[58] These low-level relationships would bear fruit when treaty articles baffled higher-ups in Washington and Moscow. Committee procedures in Geneva also helped the two sides coordinate. Foster and Soviet negotiator Semyon Tsarapkin served as the ENDC's cochairs, which afforded them opportunities to speak outside the Council Chamber, where the plenary met in the Palace of Nations. The city's social milieu and the cochairmen meetings created an international middle ground where Soviet and U.S. arms controllers explored solutions at a distance from their capitals. According to Foster, it was "the only place where we have a continuing contact with the Soviet Union outside of normal diplomatic channels" as well as "the only place, too, where we can take broad soundings on opinions and ideas of the non-aligned nations." Geneva served "as a university in a sense . . . a citadel of learning for representatives in the

ENDC—indeed for all."[59] Mohamed Shaker, one of Egypt's junior delegates, witnessed diplomats from disparate societies develop a sense of common cause and camaraderie. Nonaligned delegates saw themselves as drafted into a historic struggle against a universal threat.[60] They also prized their inclusion in multilateral talks on issues of war and peace because their countries had historically been excluded from such councils. Their continued support was critical since a nonproliferation treaty would demand the "lion's share" of them.[61]

The arrival of a third aspirant to global hegemony was another impetus for cooperation. Soviet and U.S. positions began to sync up once Moscow began worrying about Beijing. By 1963, U.S. intelligence had concluded that China would test its first nuclear device soon. The Soviets were themselves intimately familiar with the program, having supplied it with technical assistance until 1959.[62] The two sides felt each other out about how to forestall the event, including at cochairman meetings, where the Soviets often apologized for broadsides in the full sessions, in which the Vietnam War and the Sino-Soviet split often prompted them to attack U.S. foreign policy. In February 1964, Foster proclaimed in the plenary that "the interests of both nuclear sides" and "of the non-nuclear powers overlap with each other and with the existing nuclear powers" for reasons of "moral sense and national self-interest." Tsarapkin shot back by denouncing the MLF and West German revanchism so sharply that Foster lamented a "return of the Cold War."[63] Yet, their private conversations belied the theatrics. Days later, Tsarapkin assured Foster that his remarks "did not amount to [a] return to [the] Cold War" and intimated that a superpower condominium was possible and desirable:

> He reiterated time and again that our two countries are self-sufficient and therefore have ... no need to encroach upon each other, that they both bore great responsibility for what went on in [the] world and ... they had to pay [the] price for this responsibility. They took [the] line that all other countries including France, China, India, UAR, ... even [the] G.D.R., were playing [the] U.S. and U.S.S.R. against each other and were trying to obtain advantage from differences and contradictions between them; they could do it in present circumstances but if [the] U.S. and U.S.S.R. were to agree with each other everybody else would have no choice but to fall in line.[64]

If the United States as the "world's gigantic power and also [the] large Soviet Union were to reach agreement," he concluded, "all troubles in [the] world could be readily controlled by us."[65]

These frank exchanges gave Foster a uniquely clear reckoning of Soviet attitudes. When Johnson and his chief advisers met to decide between the NPT

and the MLF in April, however, Europe watchers in the State Department res-
cued the multilateral force from the guillotine. Foster emphasized that the Soviets held a "strongly negative view" of the scheme, which could end up "tying
U.S. hands in such [a] way that it could be immobilized in future disarmament
and non-disseminations discussions." When the U.S. ambassador to the Soviet
Union, Foy Kohler, related "no evidence" of such a view, Foster insisted that
Kohler's view "did not coincide with his impressions from his talks" in
Geneva.[66] Foster failed to persuade the president to bury a long-standing project of major importance to a key ally; nevertheless, his argument was heard.
By November, Bundy was reminding Johnson that the MLF represented "a
means, and not an end in itself," and the president warned his diplomats against
twisting the Europeans' arms to get them on board.[67]

The long-anticipated Chinese nuclear test on October 16, 1964, underscored the merits of superpower collaboration, but also its limits. The Joint
Chiefs of Staff had begun to formulate plans for the Chinese threat, up to and
including a preemptive strike, in the summer of 1963. The plan required Soviet
acquiescence, however, which Bundy twice solicited from the Soviet ambassador in Washington, Anatoly Dobrynin. At first, Dobrynin asserted that the
MLF "did not make it easier for the Soviet Government to deal with the question of Chinese nuclear ambitions."[68] Even so, according to Robert Kennedy's
sources, "the Soviets were determined not to permit the development of a Chinese nuclear weapon."[69] The Johnson administration thus had reason to believe in "many possibilities for joint action with the Soviet Government,"
including a joint warning, finalizing a CTBT, or "even a possible agreement to
cooperate in preventive military action."[70] When Bundy approached Dobrynin the second time, however, the Soviet ambassador "gently remarked"
that the Sino-Soviet mutual defense treaty remained in effect.

The window that began to open peered out upon a world governed by rules
and institutions rather than preemptive strikes and superpower condominium.
The renewal of regular contacts between the capitalist and communist giants had
allowed an official channel for frank communication to open and a social site
where diplomats could break down negotiating barriers to develop. These investments yielded dividends as global elites began to contemplate seriously how to
strike the right balance among a range of national interests in the nuclear realm.

Striking a Balance

The Johnson administration reacted to China's feat by establishing a blue-
ribbon committee led by former deputy secretary of defense Roswell Gilpatric. Although those who remained wedded to the MLF eventually buried the

report, its conclusions would nevertheless frame the ensuing debate.[71] Its authors thus wrote the playbook for crafting a nonproliferation treaty by evaluating how to win over various types of states: the Soviet Union; allied regional powers such as West Germany; nonallied regional powers such India; nuclear exporters such as members of the European Atomic Energy Community (Euratom); and nonaligned states such as Mexico. Most significant, it enshrined an unspoken policy of opposing nuclear proliferation regardless of strategic circumstances, when some senior officials were pondering the merits of treating it on a case-by-case basis.

Washington knew that the new Soviet leadership duo, Leonid Brezhnev and Alexei Kosygin, wanted real concessions on Europe's nuclear future. The crux, Gilpatric recognized, was "what, if any, modifications . . . would be acceptable as a price to get the USSR to go along with a nonproliferation agreement," including "abandoning the MLF?"[72] The full committee regarded nonproliferation as conditional on "two basic 'ifs': Soviet cooperation and future Chinese behavior."[73] U.S. actions, they judged, could encourage the former, if not the latter. The final report recommended a higher priority on nonproliferation and better U.S.-Soviet relations. Concluding that "the Soviet Union . . . shares with us a strong interest in preventing the further spread of nuclear weapons," the report counseled the government to "undertake new initiatives to obtain such support," such as a battery of arms control measures. Significantly, a nonproliferation treaty "should not wait, or be dependent upon, the resolution of any issues relating to an Atlantic nuclear force."[74]

West Germany's response to the MLF's possible euthanization was key. Walt Rostow, chairman of the State Department's Policy Planning Council, envisaged the force in one stroke granting "prestige along with participation" to the FRG and "increasing credibility to the deterrent." McCloy highlighted "the urgent need for increasing communications with the Germans and implicating them in a collective approach to planning for the future of the Alliance," if the MLF were indeed scrapped.[75] The demise of a NATO nuclear force would demand a great deal of sugarcoating and scapegoating. They substituted the "hardware" option with two "software" options: the Nuclear Planning Group, in which NATO defense ministers would discuss nuclear policy, and the "McNamara Committee," tasked with determining "overall NATO guidelines for the deployment and use of NATO's nuclear weapons."[76] Washington thus cushioned the blow by finding other ways to enhance West German "prestige and participation." Furthermore, they strove not to "rub the Germans' noses in it" and let Britain and France, who were nearly as hostile as the Soviet Union to the scheme, do most of the dirty work.[77]

India's support depended on what impact a settlement would have on its security and status. New Delhi found its long-standing policy of nuclear forbearance under siege by nationalist forces at home and Communist China next door.[78] Its eventual decision not to sign the treaty would attest to how dissimilar national interests and conceptions of global order were not always reconcilable. India asked for two concessions for which neither superpower proved willing to incur the military or diplomatic costs. First, three successive Indian prime ministers demanded a CTBT and a fissile material cutoff treaty in combination with a nonproliferation treaty so that the notional regime would address vertical (i.e., the nuclear arms race) and horizontal (i.e., new nuclear powers) proliferation together. Second, Indian authorities wanted security guarantees in exchange for their nuclear renunciation. Yet, U.S. officials warned that "a nuclear umbrella . . . might be too much temptation for Indian adventures."[79] Nuclear assurances were difficult for another reason. India's foreign policy since independence rested on two pillars—nuclear forbearance and nonaligned leadership. Together, these traditions deprived India of a nuclear defense because assurances without an alliance were not "so clear or easy."[80] Last, therefore, the superpowers could not agree on what form assurances should take. India wanted a universal guarantee to retain its nonaligned status, but Moscow refused to cover NATO countries where U.S. nuclear weapons were stationed and Washington resisted categorical pledges while its military was bogged down in Vietnam.[81] A more equitable regime and more robust assurances might have won India over. Instead, India never signed the treaty, testing a "peaceful nuclear explosive" in 1974 and unveiling a military weapon in 1998.

The peaceful uses of nuclear technology meant that a treaty would impinge on the fabled global market as well. By early 1967, the United States and the Soviet Union had in conference with allies agreed to language that would bar collective nuclear forces but permit nuclear sharing and equivocate on a hypothetical European Union nuclear force. But the legal relationship between the global safeguards that the IAEA would handle and the regional safeguards that Euratom already operated was still unclear. Euratom's membership mirrored that of the European Community: Belgium, France, Italy, Luxembourg, the Netherlands, and West Germany. In light of France's military program, export aspirations, and skepticism toward global governance, the Euratom issue implicated a thicket of political problems related to European integration. Equally important were fears about competitiveness versus the global leader, such as the possibility that foreign inspectors might commit industrial espionage on behalf of their home countries. German officials explained that the spying they feared "might well be from an inspector named Ivanovich. It might also be a fellow named Johnson."[82]

To level the playing field, Foster and Fisher prevailed upon the president to invite inspectors from the IAEA into the country's own nonmilitary nuclear facilities. When Moscow resisted full autonomy for Euratom, the new warmth among Soviet and U.S. negotiators in Geneva manifested itself in low-level, ad referendum talks about Article III (i.e., the treaty's safeguards article). There was a freedom to improvise on friendly excursions that high-level consultations lacked. While hiking in the Alps, Bunn and Timerbaev discussed the IAEA's overseeing and verifying Euratom much as "certified public accountants" audited "corporation bookkeepers." Each delegation then presented the initiative to its bosses as the other's "informal suggestion." This caused some miscues, such as when U.S. official Llewellyn Thompson mentioned the new "Soviet proposal" to Andrei Gromyko and the Soviet foreign minister was taken aback: "What do you mean, Soviet delegation proposal? I thought that was an American delegation proposal!" Nevertheless, the eight months during which U.S. diplomats "fought and bled" for language that would permit groups of states to negotiate collectively with the IAEA managed to appease West Germany without displeasing countries such as Japan, which wanted uniform rules. The episode illustrated how political necessity often trumped sound policy as U.S. officials "fought mainly for the interests of only one of our allies, as against our own national interests and those of most of the rest of our allies and most of the rest of the world."[83] West Germany was simply that crucial.

Soviet and U.S. officials tabled a joint draft treaty to the ENDC on January 18, 1968. Personal goodwill in Geneva had smoothed the way. After a frenetic last few days of give-and-take yielded a consensus draft, Fisher and his fellow delegates raced to alert the White House on the eve of the president's State of the Union address. On the way to the U.S. consulate, his car got stuck in a snow bank. The Russian deputy ambassador leapt to his aid with words of encouragement: "Now, look you fellows got to get a telegram out. You can't afford to waste your time pushing a car. Here, let me give you a ride."[84]

Endowing Legitimacy

The NPT was a product of the UN system. Because the treaty would restrict nuclear "have-nots" more than "haves," heeding their views was crucial. In 1961, UNGA Resolution 1722 (XVI) had constituted the ENDC, which included eight neutrals and integrated the Afro-Asian bloc, already the largest international grouping, into the workings of global nuclear diplomacy.[85] The committee's exclusivity and autonomy was a boon, reducing the scale of consensus needed while preserving certain superpower prerogatives. The inclusion of nonaligned states was as well; they quickly proved "a stabilizing factor."[86]

Their relative impartiality helped detoxify an environment contaminated by U.S.-Soviet vitriol. And by representing a broader segment of an emerging international community, they helped draft a more equitable and therefore more resilient treaty. In 1965, they seized upon discord between the East and West to push through UNGA Resolution 2028, which called for a treaty to provide "a step towards the achievement of general and complete disarmament and, more particularly, nuclear disarmament" and to reflect a "balance of mutual responsibilities and obligations of the nuclear and non-nuclear Powers."[87]

Following the ad referendum success in August 1967, Rusk informed Johnson that "the game" would "move to the non-nuclear powers" in the ENDC: Brazil, Burma, Ethiopia, India, Mexico, Nigeria, Sweden, and the United Arab Republic.[88] Fruitful talks depended on nonaligned members' acquiescence, with the neutral delegations serving as "first responders" concerning the treaty's global acceptability.[89] Their views largely coincided, though the regional powers, Brazil and India, wanted more. India's plenipotentiary, V.C. Trivedi, insisted on firmer security guarantees, and the Brazilian ambassador, Alfonso da Costa Guimaraes, demanded a loose definition for peaceful nuclear explosives (PNEs), whose basic equivalence to nuclear weapons meant that permitting them would open a major loophole in the treaty.

This made the backing of neutral states with a record of promoting internationalism, such as Mexico and Sweden, particularly vital. Swedish disarmament minister Alva Myrdal continually pushed for an accompanying CTBT to equalize nuclear rights and responsibilities between the nuclear "haves" and "have-nots," but the superpowers were loath to curtail their own nuclear weapons programs. Other suggested amendments met with greater approval. The most significant were those forwarded by Mexican diplomat Jorge Castañeda in September. In addition to bolstering the article laying out an "inalienable right" to "nuclear energy for peaceful purposes," he championed references supportive of nuclear-free zones, such as that then being finalized in Latin America, and an international service to supply PNEs to countries desirous of them. His most far-reaching proposal was the inscription of an explicit link in the treaty between nuclear proliferation and disarmament meant to formalize a "solemn recognition ... of the special responsibility of the nuclear Powers:"[90]

> In short, the nuclear Powers cannot actually undertake to conclude future disarmament agreements among themselves; but they certainly can undertake to endeavor to do so; that is, they can certainly undertake to initiate and pursue negotiations in good faith in order to conclude such agreements. ... It would be an imperfect obligation, since it would not be accompanied by sanctions, but it would be more than a statement of intention.[91]

Myrdal likened the language to a "promissory note."[92] The other nonaligned delegations rallied behind the Mexican amendments, whose contents would eventually find expression in Article IV, which invoked an "inalienable right" to peaceful nuclear technology; Article V, which promised an international PNE service; Article VI, which registered the "promissory note"; and Article VII, which upheld nuclear-free zones. Latin American countries had held talks to bar nuclear weapons from their region after the Cuban missile crisis. When the Treaty for the Prohibition of Nuclear Weapons in Latin America and the Caribbean (aka the Treaty of Tlatelolco) opened for signature on February 14, 1967, the Global South showed that it could manage nuclear weapons without the superpowers. Washington and Moscow had supported the Latin American initiative partly in hopes of imparting some momentum on nonproliferation proceedings when they were floundering.[93] In hindsight, though, the concurrent negotiations boxed them in on what constitutional rights a nonproliferation treaty would recognize.

The final year of talks featured meaningful revisions and substantial trade-offs as various coalitions—formal and informal—hustled to ensure they could live with the outcome. Non-nuclear weapon states wanted a regime that would maximize their benefits and minimize their costs. The growing sense of a treaty's imminence led stakeholders to seek a regime that would be responsive to their future needs as well. Concerns about legal procedures thus joined demands for a CTBT, or a fissile material cutoff treaty, clear rights to peaceful nuclear explosives, or more robust security assurances. Japanese foreign minister Takeo Miki's proposal that conferences review the treaty's efficacy and fairness every five years gained widespread approval.[94] These NPT review conferences, or "RevCons," which are preceded by two preparatory conferences, or "PrepCons" the two years before, have become a fixture of international nuclear diplomacy. These meetings exemplified how even formal treaties are not absolute, but are instead subject to continual debate. Nuclear have-nots continue to insist that the NPT do more than "disarm the unarmed." Meanwhile, those worried about current proliferation trends call for more intrusive inspections of state's nuclear facilities.[95] In fact, the continual diplomacy that brought the treaty into being never stopped.

The diplomatic endgame represented how power and principle cohere when international rules are made. Collaboration between the superpowers was increasingly glaring in Geneva and New York, where delegations expressed mounting "irritation at Soviet-American collusion."[96] It was nonetheless essential for whipping the necessary votes in the ENDC and the UN. Brazil and India were particularly displeased. The Indian demand to "impose equal obligations on all" was impossible to reconcile with an intrinsically discriminatory treaty.[97] And Washington and Moscow were unwilling to offer binding security assurances or endorse an inalienable right to PNEs. The superpowers pledged to push through a UN Security Council resolution that would bind them to respond expeditiously to nuclear aggression or threats, but most observers saw it as an empty gesture. Collectively, these decisions narrowed the zone of possible agreement to the point that it excluded Brazil and India. Other neutral states were also unconvinced of the treaty's merits. When ACDA director William Foster and Soviet envoy Alexei Roshchin put forward a plenary motion to endorse the draft treaty, it failed to win a majority. It was instead "referred" to the UNGA with Brazil, India, and Romania pointedly abstaining.

A favorable resolution in the United Nations would still legitimate the treaty. The UN met exclusively to debate the treaty in April 1968. Nuclear have-nots had set an implicit deadline by pushing through a resolution sponsoring a Conference of Non-Nuclear-Weapon States. The superpowers had managed to push the meeting back to August 1968, which meant it was a race to finish the treaty lest "the non-nuclear powers [get] together and hav[e] an advance caucus for making a rather high price with going along."[98] The support of certain regional blocs would be key to winning a positive outcome in the Political Committee and the General Assembly of the United Nations. Moscow pressed its allies and neutral friends, and Washington leaned on its NATO allies, along with Japan, Israel, and South Africa (among many others) to hold the line against any further amendments. Foreign delegates joked that "the only thing" the Soviets and Americans "didn't do was hold hands."[99] Even so, Latin American, African, and the Middle Eastern delegations put up more of a fight than anticipated, which produced a change of heart toward revisions. First, the Soviet ambassador promised to restrain Israel's nuclear ambitions in exchange for opening the floor to amendments.[100] The Latin American and African blocs, which possessed 24 and 32 members, respectively (almost half of the then 124-member body), were the main prizes, however. With Argentina and Brazil irreconcilable, Mexico was now the bellwether for the rest of Latin America. Fresh off his triumph in successfully mediating the nuclear-free-zone talks in Mexico City, Deputy Foreign Minister Alfonso García Robles set forth his conditions: signing of Protocol II of the Treaty of Tlatelolco by the nuclear powers, obligating them to honor the agreement; a conspicuous invocation of the principle of "pacific settlement of disputes" in the nonproliferation treaty's preamble; an added inalienable right to "equipment and material" in Article IV; PNE assistance "as soon as possible;" and a more forceful Article VI compelling nuclear haves to cease the nuclear arms race. All but the last demand was eventually met, which brought to an end the treaty's journey from a superpower diktat to what is now called "the grand bargain." By contrast, the African bloc asked for two ill-fated concessions: Western support for a resolution that would censure South Africa's occupation of South West Africa and assurances that Pretoria would stay nonnuclear; they received only the latter, which would ultimately prove hollow.

Opinion in Turtle Bay thus held that the new treaty had been formulated mainly to win over the hearts and minds of Latin American delegations, twelve of which would serve as eventual cosponsors. As for African intransigence, U.S. intermediaries reassured South Africa that the IAEA would not regulate its uranium-mining industry, and Pretoria's professed support placated its neighbors, for now.[101] García Robles's interventions were crucial in securing the Latin American vote, but the U.S. ambassador, Arthur Goldberg, lionized the new international community, portraying the treaty as "the creation of all nations, large and small." He also underscored the "good faith and willingness to compromise" displayed by the nuclear powers and ended by affirming his hope that the NPT would promote equitable access "to the peaceful blessing of nuclear energy" and the promissory note written by the nuclear powers:

> My country believes that the permanent viability of this treaty will depend in large measure on our success in the further negotiations contemplated by Article VI. . . . Following the conclusion of this treaty, my government will, in the spirit of Article VI . . . pursue further disarmament negotiations with redoubled zeal and hope and with promptness.[102]

The constant business of outreach, conciliation, reassurance, horse-trading, and outright badgering by Soviet and U.S. officials had reached its end. But it had also incurred costs. To pursue a goal together with others without coercion entails compromise, and multilateral action always has a price. The French ambassador in New York judged that concessions had "served as a pretext for a number of delegations, under intense Soviet and U.S. pressure, to join the draft resolution, as revised."[103] There were grounds for cynicism; after all, between 1958 and 1968, the United States and the Soviet Union added nearly 20,000 warheads and 8,500 warheads to their nuclear stockpiles, respectively.[104] But the bargain struck between nuclear haves and have-nots also spurred the Johnson and Nixon administrations and their counterparts in Moscow to negotiate the Strategic Arms Limitation Treaty (SALT I) in 1972, which for the first time placed a ceiling on the number of delivery vehicles possessed by each side. (Driven in part by Article VI's promissory note, the United States and post–Soviet Russia would finally agree in 2010 to reduce their deployed warheads to 1,550 apiece).[105]

On June 10, 1968, the Political Committee approved a resolution commending (as opposed to recommending) the NPT as now drafted: ninety-two votes in favor and four against. Pro-treaty forces were elated and relieved. A full plenary confirmed the near consensus two days later. President Johnson surprised the gathering by making a personal appearance in the dome-vaulted General Assembly Hall, where he hailed the next step: "the limitation of strategic offensive and defensive nuclear weapons." He praised the accomplishment of a multilateral compact that might halt the further spread of nuclear weapons. When he signed the treaty in the East Room of the White House three weeks later, his remarks sounded providential: the treaty "keeps alive and keeps active the impulse toward a safer world."[106] In truth, that impulse had animated proceedings from the beginning, as U.S. and Soviet negotiators overcame years of animosity to start building a worldwide system of nuclear governance among a broadly representative community of nation-states.

Conclusion: Fostering a Nuclear Community

The Treaty on the Non-Proliferation of Nuclear Weapons today serves as a "cornerstone" of global efforts to regulate nuclear technology in hopes of restricting the nuclear franchise. Its legacy is evident in efforts to roll back North Korea's nuclear arsenal, ongoing negotiations between the United States and five kindred world powers and the Islamic Republic of Iran to pacify its nuclear program, and the troubling legacy of the 2003 Iraq War waged in the treaty's name. The treaty is a living testament to how multilateral diplomacy can yield common rules that buttress collective security by authorizing international institutions to enforce them through regulation, consultation, economic sanction, and legitimate compulsion. Thanks in large part to its entry into force in 1970, Kennedy's fear of a world abounding with nuclear powers never came to pass.

The negotiations were a model in successful multilateral diplomacy. Success had three determinants. First, institutions at home and abroad facilitated trust building, communication, and cooperation among the principal stakeholders. One key to success was the continuous nature of the enterprise. The establishment of the ACDA ensured that nuclear arms control and nonproliferation were always on Washington's agenda, and that of the ENDC institutionalized the practice of global nuclear diplomacy. Second, Soviet and U.S. officials heeded the views of an assorted and overlapping set of states—allies, neutrals, exporters, and importers. Through patient and conscientious diplomacy, arms controllers from around the globe outlined a zone of potential agreement in which every group save a handful of regional powers were accommodated. Last, superpower negotiators cooperated with leaders from the postcolonial world who served as gatekeepers to the new international community. Bearing in mind colonialism's legacy, they graced the treaty with a firm basis in international consensus by striking a tolerable balance between nuclear rights and responsibilities. Such carrots and sticks were proof that multilateral dialogue and international institutions were not ends in themselves, but rather tools with which to make world affairs more consensual, predictable, and manageable.

It was no accident that the accord was struck in the 1960s. The arrival of dozens of new Afro-Asian states galvanized the search for nuclear order by raising the specter of proliferation. This development also transformed the negotiating process by compelling the superpowers to work through multilateral channels and respect the interests and outlooks of developing nations in the Global South. If the NPT was the fruit of a postcolonial world, it also confirmed that multilateral diplomacy could flourish at a time of decolonization and superpower hostility. The United States, then as now the world hegemon, embraced a hard-nosed brand of liberal internationalism at a transformative moment, when global society grew sufficiently integrated and representative to police itself through the rule of law rather than the rule of force. American leadership sprang from a long tradition of promoting free markets, common security, and self-determination. It was spurred on by Latin American nuclear diplomacy and President Johnson's hunger for peace laurels as the Vietnam War tore the country apart.[107]

Multilateral diplomacy draws strength from the belief that states can be trusted, if the circumstances are right. Henry Stimson once remarked that "the only way you can make a man trustworthy is to trust him; and the surest way to make him untrustworthy is to distrust him and show your distrust."[108] The ten-year journey to draft a nuclear nonproliferation treaty illustrated how this outlook entails not idealism but rather a higher form of realism once called "enlightened self-interest." As Stephen C. Neff, a leading scholar of international law, has observed, although "the efficacy of international law is not something to be taken for granted, . . . one of the more remarkable facts of world history . . . is how well this precarious mechanism of largely voluntary compliance actually works in practice."[109] Those tasked with brokering multilateral deals have to identify the incremental means that will bring them slowly yet steadily closer to their loftier ends. The NPT's drafters succeeded by embracing multinational forums as diplomatic middle grounds, where representatives could constantly build trust among themselves and their governments through socialization, as well as incubators, through which they could devise ingenious solutions to tough policy puzzles. Foster once described his work as, at heart, "the task of creating community and avoiding anarchy." The project of building communities, he concluded, was "constantly pitched on broader and broader levels."[110] Multilateral diplomacy is driven by a search for commonality and connection in a fraught and anarchic world. It begins with individuals, and through continuous efforts ideally expands to envelop foreign ministries, governments, heads of state, nations, international bodies, and perhaps even global society. Global nonproliferation diplomacy prospered because the international community arose in those years after empire and before the "unipolar moment" when the United States stood alone in its superpower. But it also helped bring that community into being by impelling the world's nation-states to recognize and act upon their common interest in combatting "this tremendous and most threatening of all forces."[111]

Notes

1. John F. Kennedy, "News Conference 52," March 21, 1963, State Department Auditorium, Washington, D.C., http://www.jfklibrary.org/Research/Research-Aids/Ready-Reference/Press-Conferences/News-Conference-52.aspx.
2. Frank Aiken was a staunch Irish anticolonialist and internationalist, who first conceived of and proposed a "non-dissemination treaty." His imprint on the NPT has been largely overlooked. The best treatments of Irish diplomacy at the United Nations more generally in this period are Joseph Morrison Skelly, *Irish Diplomacy at the United Nations, 1945–1965: National Interests and the International Order* (Dublin: Irish Academic Press, 1997) and T. D. Williams, "Irish Foreign Policy, 1949–1969," in Joseph Lee, ed., *Ireland 1945–70* (Dublin: Gill and Macmillan, 1979). For Frank Aiken himself, the definitive work is Bryce Evans and Stephen Kelly, *Frank Aiken: Nationalist and Internationalist.* (Dublin: Original Writing, 2014).
3. The best previous effort to analyze and account for the dynamics of multilateral consultations went with a ranching metaphor instead: Chester A. Crocker, Fen Osler Hampson, and Pamela R. Aall, eds., *Herding Cats: Multiparty Mediation in a Complex World* (Washington, DC: United States Institute of Peace Press, 1999).
4. G. John Ikenberry, *After Victory: Institutions, Strategic Restraint, and the Rebuilding of Order after Major Wars* (Princeton, NJ: Princeton University Press, 2001), chap. 6.
5. Much ink has been spilt on this historical subject. Three good books with which to start for readers desirous of better understanding the ideological and geopolitical contexts in which decolonization unfolded are William Roger Louis, *Imperialism at Bay 1941–1945: The United States and the Decolonization of the British Empire* (Oxford: Clarendon Press, 1977) and Elizabeth Borgwardt, *A New Deal for the World: America's Vision for Human Rights* (Cambridge, MA: Belknap Press of Harvard University Press, 2005); Odd Arne Westad, *The Global Cold War: Third World Interventions and the Making of Our Times* (Cambridge: Cambridge University Press, 2005).
6. Akira Iriye, *Global Community: The Role of International Organizations in the Making of the Contemporary World* (Berkeley: University of California Press, 2002).
7. Ryan M. Irwin, *Gordian Knot: Apartheid and the Unmaking of the Liberal World Order* (Oxford: Oxford University Press, 2012), 10.
8. The historical literature on the Nuclear Non-Proliferation Treaty is voluminous and has undergone four waves. Those who negotiated the treaty for the United States and the Soviet Union were focused mainly on bilateral affairs, nuclear weapons' intrinsic risks, and in the case of chairman of the U.S. Atomic Energy Agency, Glenn Seaborg, technical and economic considerations: McGeorge Bundy, *Danger and Survival: Choices about the*

Bomb in the First Fifty Years (New York: Random House, 1988); George Bunn, *Arms Control by Committee: Managing Negotiations with the Russians*, Studies in International Security and Arms Control (Stanford, CA: Stanford University Press, 1992); Roland Timerbaev, *Rossiiai iaadernoe nerasprostranenie (Russia and Nuclear Nonproliferation): 1945–1968* (Moskva: Nauka, 1999); Glenn T. Seaborg, *Stemming the Tide: Arms Control in the Johnson Years* (Lexington, MA: Lexington Books, 1987). Postrevisionist accounts focusing on geopolitical trend lines actually predated revisionist explanations assigning more significance to superpower shenanigans or U.S. hegemony. Postrevisionist accounts treated the NPT primarily as a facet of U.S.-Soviet détente: John Lewis Gaddis, *The Long Peace: Inquiries into the History of the Cold War* (New York: Oxford University Press, 1987); Marc Trachtenberg, *A Constructed Peace: The Making of the European Settlement, 1945–1963* (Princeton, NJ: Princeton University Press, 1999); Francis J. Gavin, "Blasts from the Past: Proliferation Lessons from the 1960s," *International Security* 29, no. 3 (Winter 2004): 100–135; Glenn T. Seaborg, *Stemming the Tide: Arms Control in the Johnson Years* (Lexington, MA: Lexington Books, 1987). A strain of critical, revisionist takes on the NPT originated with a book by the Swedish disarmament minister involved in the events: Alva Myrdal, *The Game of Disarmament: How the United States & Russia Run the Arms Race*, rev. ed. (New York: Pantheon, 1982). The most recent historical synthesis has called attention to the continuity of monopolistic behavior by the United States: Shane J. Maddock, *Nuclear Apartheid: The Quest for American Atomic Supremacy from World War II to the Present* (Chapel Hill: University of North Carolina Press, 2010). Scholars are beginning to pay increasing attention to the other states that were involved or were affected by the bargaining. See author's "Into the Bargain: The Triumph and Tragedy of Nuclear Internationalism during the mid-Cold War, 1958–1970" (Ph.D. diss., University of Texas at Austin, 2013).

9. Bryon Bland, Brenna Powell, and Lee Ross, "Barriers to Dispute Resolution: Reflections on Peacemaking and Relationships between Adversaries," in Ryan Goodman, Derek Jinks, and Andrew K. Woods, eds., *Understanding Social Action, Promoting Human Rights* (New York: Oxford University Press, 2012), 265–291.

10. Ibid., 266.

11. Reproduced in Mohamed Shaker, *The Nuclear Non-Proliferation Treaty: Origin and Implementation, 1959–1979*, vol. 3 (New York: Oceana Publications, 1980), 934–936. Shaker's book is the definitive codex of public statements and proposals made during the NPT proceedings.

12. Roger Fisher and William Ury, *Getting to Yes* (New York: Penguin, 1983); Roy J. Jewicki, John Minton, and David Saunders, "Zone of Potential Agreement" in *Negotiation*, 3rd ed. (Burr Ridge, IL: Irwin-McGraw Hill, 1999).

13. The ENDC met approximately 380 times between March 14, 1962, and March 14, 1968; the UN First Committee, General Assembly, and Security Council met more than thirty times in the final stage of negotiations. Final verbatim records of the Conference of the Eighteen-Nation Committee on Disarmament are available here: http://quod.lib.umich.edu/e/endc/. UN records of NPT preparatory documents and relevant sessions are accessible here: http://legal.un.org/avl/ha/tnpt/tnpt.html.

14. Roger Tubby, REFTEL Geneva to Washington, DC, "FRG Views of NPT," February 25, 1967, Lyndon Baines Johnson Presidential Library, National Security Files, Files of Francis M. Bator, box 10 (hereinafter LBJ, NSF).

15. Steven E. Miller, *Nuclear Collisions: Discord, Reform & the Nuclear Nonproliferation Regime* (Cambridge, MA: American Academy of Arts and Sciences, 2012), 1.

16. William Foster to Robert S. McNamara, "Resignation as Secretary of Defense," January 30, 1968, folder 1, box 13, William Foster Papers, George C. Marshall Library (hereinafter Foster Papers, GCML).

17. Paul M. Kennedy, *The Parliament of Man: The Past, Present, and Future of the United Nations* (New York: Random House, 2006); Jonathan R. Hunt, "'Among Nations, Respect for the Rights of Others Is Peace:' Mexican Nuclear Diplomacy and the NPT Grand Bargain, 1962–1975," in Andreas Wenger, Roland Popp, and Liviu Horowitz, eds., *The Making of a Nuclear Order: Negotiating the Nuclear Non-Proliferation Treaty* (forthcoming).

18. The quasi-official account of the Acheson-Lilienthal and the Baruch Plan is Richard G. Hewlett and Oscar E. Anderson, Jr., *The New World, 1939–1946*, vol. 1., *A History of the United States Atomic Energy Commission* (University Park: Pennsylvania State University Press, 1962). For a more skeptical reading of the proposal, read Barton J. Bernstein, "The Quest for Security: American Foreign Policy and International Control of Atomic Energy, 1942–1946," *Journal of American History* 60 (March 1974).

19. David Holloway, *Stalin and the Bomb: The Soviet Union and Atomic Energy, 1939–1956* (New Haven, CT: Yale University Press, 1994).

20. Bernstein, "Quest for Security," 1044.

21. Press Release, "Text of the Address Delivered by the President of the United States before the General Assembly of the United Nations in New York City Tuesday Afternoon, December 8, 1953," Dwight D. Eisenhower Presidential Library, http://www.eisenhower. archives.gov/research/online_documents/atoms_for_peace/Binder13.pdf

22. Richard G. Hewlett and Jack M. Holl, *Atoms for Peace and War, 1953–1961: Eisenhower and the Atomic Energy Commission* (Berkeley: University of California Press, 1989); Ira Chernus, *Eisenhower's Atoms for Peace* (College Station: Texas A&M University Press, 2002).

23. Matthew Kroenig, *Exporting the Bomb: Technology Transfer and the Spread of Nuclear Weapons*, Cornell Studies in Security Affairs (Ithaca, NY: Cornell University Press, 2010); William C. Potter, *Nuclear Power and Nonproliferation: An Interdisciplinary Perspective* (Cambridge, MA: Oelgeschlager, Gunn & Hain, 1982); Matthew Fuhrmann, *Atomic Assistance: How "Atoms for Peace" Programs Cause Nuclear Insecurity*, Cornell Studies in Security Affairs (Ithaca, NY: Cornell University Press, 2012).

24. U.S. Department of State Policy Planning Council, "The Further Spread of Nuclear Weapons: Problems for the West," February 14, 1966, National Security Archive, The Nuclear Vault, http://www2.gwu.edu/~nsarchiv/nukevault/ebb253/doc01.pdf

25. Bertrand Goldschmidt, *The Atomic Complex: A Worldwide Political History of Nuclear Energy* (La Grange Park, IL.: American Nuclear Society, 1982).

26. Frank Aiken, *Ireland at the United Nations, 1958* (Dublin: Brún agus Ó Nualláin Teo, 1958), 31–46.

27. Francis J. Gavin, "Blasts from the Past: Proliferation Lessons from the 1960s," *International Security* 29, no. 3 (Winter 2004): 100–135.

28. Albert Wohlstetter, "Nuclear Sharing: NATO and the N+1 Country," *Foreign Affairs* 39, no. 3 (April 1961), 355–387. As Benoît Pelopidas infers, the metaphor of proliferation, which soon replaced dissemination to connote an increase in the number of nuclear weapon states to embody a force of nature rather than the sum of state choices, took hold around this time. Nuclear "optimists" and "pessimists" alike have erred in assuming an inexorable trend toward ever-more nuclear weapon states, conflating the history of nuclear things with a history of proliferation. The globality and automaticity ascribed to proliferation at the time, however, also commended the regional and international approaches that were inscribed in the Treaty of Tlatelolco and the NPT. As Matthew Kroenig has observed, whether a great power can project its power over a potential proliferator is the primary determinant of whether it tried to rein in that country's nuclear ambitions. My research suggests that a history of conflict or cultural predispositions can also be determinant at times. Benoît Pelopidas, "The Oracles of Proliferation: How Experts Maintain a Biased Historical Reading That Limits Policy Innovation," *The Nonproliferation Review* 18, no. 1 (March 2011): 297–314; Matthew Kroenig, "Force or Friendship? Explaining Great Power Nonproliferation Policy," *Security Studies* 23, no. 1 (January 2014): 1–32.

29. Campbell Craig, *Glimmer of a New Leviathan: Total War in the Realism of Niebuhr, Morgenthau, and Waltz* (New York: Columbia University Press, 2003).

30. Scholars debate whether international organizations and treaties help resolve the "security dilemma," whereby gains in one state's military power threaten others' security. John H. Herz, "Idealist Internationalism and the Security Dilemma," *World Politics* 2, no. 02 (January 1950): 157–180 and Robert Jervis, "Cooperation under the Security Dilemma," *World Politics* 30, no. 02 (January 1978): 167–214.

31. Melvyn P. Leffler, *A Preponderance of Power: National Security, the Truman Administration, and the Cold War,* Stanford Nuclear Age Series (Stanford, CA: Stanford University Press, 1992).

32. Foggy Bottom is the Washington, D.C., neighborhood where the State Department is located and whose name is synonymous with the bureau. Evan Thomas, *Ike's Bluff: President Eisenhower's Secret Battle to Save the World* (New York: Little, Brown, 2012); Campbell Craig, *Destroying the Village: Eisenhower and Thermonuclear War* (New York: Columbia University Press, 1998).

33. Edmund A. Gullion, Memorandum for the Kennedy Administration, "A United States Arms Control Administration," undated, ACDA, President's Office Files, John F. Kennedy Presidential Library, 3 (hereinafter ACDA, POF, JFKL). Gullion cautioned that it was "probably true that Defense views would prevail more strongly under this arrangement [of autonomy] than under another."

34. Edmund A. Gullion to John F. Kennedy, December 15, 1960, ACDA, POF, JFKL.

35. Walter Isaacson and Evan Thomas, *The Wise Men: Six Friends and the World They Made* (New York: Simon & Schuster, 1986).

36. "William C. Foster, Former Arms Control Aide," October 16, 1984, *New York Times*: http://www.nytimes.com/1984/10/16/obituaries/william-c-foster-former-arms-control-aide.html; www.arlingtoncemetery.net/wcfoster.htm; krepon.armscontrolwonk.com/archive/3091/william-c-foster.

37. William Foster, Oral History, August 5, 1964, JFKL, 4.

38. Fred Iklé, conference address, in "Arms Limitation and Disarmament: Seventeenth Strategy for Peace Conference Report," Stanley Foundation, October 7–10, 1976: http://files.eric.ed.gov/fulltext/ED148666.pdf.

39. "Obituary; Adrian S. Fisher, 69, Arms Treaty Negotiator," March 19, 1983, *New York Times*: http://www.nytimes.com/1983/03/19/obituaries/obituary-adrian-s-fisher-69-arms-treaty-negotiator.html.

40. Adrian Fisher, Oral History Interview, part 2, November 7, 1968, LBJL, 8–9.

41. Isaacson and Evans, *The Wise Men,* 179–181.

42. William Foster, "New Directions in Arms Control and Disarmament," *Foreign Affairs* 43, no. 4 (July 1965): 590.

43. Herman Kahn, *Thinking about the Unthinkable* (New York: Horizon, 1962), 60–61, 228.

44. Foster, "Arms Control and Disarmament," 591.

45. Glenda Sluga, *Internationalism in the Age of Nationalism* (Philadelphia: University of Pennsylvania Press, 2013).

46. David Tal, *The American Nuclear Disarmament Dilemma, 1945–1963* (Syracuse, NY: Syracuse University Press, 2008).

47. William Foster, "Possible Remarks for World Council," draft, June 15, 1964, Foster Papers, GCML, 1–3.

48. Hal Brands, "Non-Proliferation and the Dynamics of the Middle Cold War: The Superpowers, the MLF, and the NPT," *Cold War History* 7, no. 3 (August 2007): 389–423; Marc Trachtenberg, *A Constructed Peace: The Making of the European Settlement, 1945–1963* (Princeton, NJ: Princeton University Press, 1999), 146–400.

49. Douglas Selvage, "The Warsaw Pact and Nuclear Proliferation, 1963–1965" (working paper, Cold War International History Project, Woodrow Wilson International Center for Scholars, Washington, D.C., April 2001, pp. 20–21.

50. Ibid., 20–24.

51. Ibid., 21.

52. According to then chairman of the U.S. Atomic Energy Agency, Glenn T. Seaborg, "The circumstance under which Lyndon Johnson assumed the presidency implied a strong obligation to carry forward the policies and programs of his predecessor." *Stemming the Tide: Arms Control in the Johnson Years* (Lexington, MA: Lexington Books, 1987), 6.

53. Ibid., 9–11.

54. Fisher, Oral History Interview, part 2, p.1.

55. McGeorge Bundy to Robert McNamara, January 14, 1964, *Foreign Relations of the United States, 1964–1968,* vol. 11, pp. 3–5 (hereinafter *FRUS* 11).

56. P. O. Alphand to Paris, "Foster's Views," January 15, 1964, box 768, cote 517INVA, Archives du Ministere des Affaires Étrangères de France (hereinafter AMAEF).

57. George Bunn, "Have and Have-Nots," in War and Peace in the Nuclear Age series, WGBH Media Library & Archives (interview, November 30, 1986): http://openvault. wgbh.org/catalog/wpna-ffebb0-interview-with-george-bunn-1986.

58. Roland Timerbaev, "In Memoriam: George Bunn (1925–2013)," Arms Control Today, June 2012.

59. Memorandum, "Your Interview with Dan McAuliff, ABC," folder 8, box 17, Foster Papers, GCML, 2. Emphasis in the original.

60. Mohamed Shaker, interview by the author, April 9, 2013, Washington, D.C.

61. Ibid.; transcript, "Remarks by Mr. Foster at Lunch by UN Society of Schlosshotel Gehrhus," July 3, 1966, folder 18, box 17, Foster Papers, GCML, 5.

62. John Wilson Lewis, China Builds the Bomb (Stanford, CA: Stanford University Press, 1988).

63. William Foster, "Statement to the 164th Plenary Meeting of the ENDC," box 16, Foster Papers, GCML, 4; Herve Alphand to Paris, "ENDC," February 7, 1964, Box 768, cote 517INVA, AMAEF.

64. William Foster to Dean Rusk, "Memorandum of Conversation with Tsarapkin [2 of 2]," February 11, 1964, box 11, subject files—Disarmament, NSF, LBJL (hereinafter SF—D).

65. William Foster to Dean Rusk, "Memorandum of Conversation with Tsarapkin [1 of 2]."

66. Memorandum of White House discussion, "MLF," April 10, 1964, FRUS, 1964–1968, vol. 13, pp. 35–37.

67. "NATO Nuclear Policy," November 8, 1964, box 2, Memos to the President, NSF, LBJL.

68. William Burr and Jeff Richelson, "Whether to 'Strangle the Baby in the Cradle': The United States and the Chinese Nuclear Program, 1960–64," International Security 25, no. 3 (Winter 2000), 71.

69. "Attorney General Robert Kennedy's Luncheon with Soviet Ambassador Dobrynin" (memorandum), July 7, 1964, box 3, Files of McGeorge Bundy, NSF, LBJL, pp. 1–2.

70. "Chinese Nuclear Weapons" (memorandum), September 15 1964, FRUS, 1964–1968, vol. 30, pp. 94–95.

71. Francis J. Gavin, "Blasts from the Past: Proliferation Lessons from the 1960s," International Security 29, no. 3 (Winter 2004): 100–135; Hal Brands, "Rethinking Nonproliferation: LBJ, the Gilpatric Committee, and U.S. National Security Policy," Journal of Cold War Studies 8, no. 2 (January 2006): 83–113.

72. Memorandum, "Major Issues," November 6, 1964, box 10, Gilpatric Papers, JFKL. Quoted in Brands, "Rethinking Nonproliferation," p. 93.

73. Committee on Nuclear Proliferation, Minutes, January 7–8, 1965, FRUS 11, 166–168.

74. Committee Report, "Nuclear Proliferation," January 21, 1965, FRUS 11, 173–182.

75. Draft Minutes, "Discussion of the Second Meeting of Committee on Nuclear Proliferation," December 13–14, 1964, FRUS 11, 145–150.

76. Defense Affairs Committee, North Atlantic Treaty Organization: http://archives.nato. int/nuclear-defence-affairs-committee-2;isaarNuclear

77. Seaborg, Arms Control in the Johnson Years, 195.

78. Itty Abraham, The Making of the Indian Atomic Bomb: Science, Secrecy and the Postcolonial State (New York: St. Martin's, 1998) and George Perkovich, India's Nuclear Bomb: The Impact on Global Proliferation (Berkeley: University of California Press, 1999).

79. Committee on Nuclear Proliferation, Minutes, pp. 166–168.

80. Memorandum of Conversation, "Secretary McNamara's Meeting with Committee on Non-Proliferation," January 7, 1964, FRUS 11, 154.

81. Dean Rusk to Adrian Fisher, "Kosygin Proposal and Security Assurances," March 5, 1966, box 13, SF—D, NSF, LBJL, p. 1. Some went so far as to oppose security assurances on the grounds that it would impede the United States from contemplating nuclear options in Vietnam and North Korea; see Walt Rostow to Johnson, "Proposed Soviet Security Declaration regarding NPT," April 19, 1967, box 128 [1 of 2], country file—India, NSF, LBJL.

82. Fisher, Oral History Interview, part 2, p. 13.
83. Dean Rusk to Lyndon Johnson, "Status of NPT Negotiations," [n.d.], *FRUS* 11, p. 533, fn. 2.
84. Fisher, Oral History Interview, part 2, p. 16.
85. Dimitris Bourantonis, *The United Nations and the Quest for Nuclear Disarmament* (Brookfield, VT: Dartmouth, 1993), 60–69.
86. Albert Legault and Michel Fortmann, *A Diplomacy of Hope: Canada and Disarmament, 1945–1988* (Montreal: McGill-Queen's University Press, 1992), 198.
87. Resolution 2028 (XX), Resolutions Adopted on the Report of the First Committee, November 19, 1965, UNGA, twentieth session: http://www.un.org/documents/ga/res/20/ares20.htm.
88. Walt Rostow to President Johnson, "NPT," August 10, 1967, *FRUS* 11, 494–495.
89. "The non-aligned states in Geneva" (note), October 20, 1967, box 769, cote 517INVA, AMAEF, 6–7.
90. Final Verbatim Record of the 331st Meeting of the Eighteen Nation Committee on Disarmament (ENDC), September 19, 1967, Geneva, ENDC/PV.331, pp. 4–11.
91. Ibid., pp. 9–10; *Documents on Disarmament, 1967*, pp. 394–395; George Bunn, R. M. Timerbaev, and James F. Leonard, *Nuclear Disarmament: How Much Have the Five Nuclear Powers Promised in the Non-Proliferation Treaty?* (Washington, DC: Lawyers Alliance for World Security, 1994), 18.
92. Spurgeon Keeny to Dean Rusk, "Report on the ENDC," April 1, 1968, box 5, Spurgeon Keeny Files, NSF, LBJL.
93. ACDA to Mexico City, "Meeting Proposed by Mexico to Discuss Denuclearization of Latin America," November 17, 1964, box 58, CF: LA-Honduras, NSF, LBJL.
94. *Documents on Disarmament, 1967*, 413–415.
95. ENDC/PV.430, p. 22.
96. Bernard de Chalvron to Paris, "Disarmament," February 29, 1968, box 768, cote 517INVA, AMAEF.
97. Embassy of Hungary in India to the Hungarian Foreign Ministry (report), March 30, 1968, Hungarian National Archives (Magyar Országos Levéltár, MOL). XIX-J-1-j Multilateral International Treaties, 1968, 107. doboz, 00617/18/1968. Obtained and translated for the Nuclear Proliferation International History Project by Balazs Szalontai, http://digitalarchive.wilsoncenter.org/document/112872
98. Fisher, Oral History Interview, part 2, p. 15.
99. "Appeals by U.S. and Soviet Open UN Atom Debate: Approval of a Treaty to Ban Spread of Nuclear Weapons Linked to Survival of World," April 27, 1968, *New York Times*.
100. Armand Berard to Paris, "Nonproliferation—Attitude of the U.A.R.," May 6, 1968, box 769, cote 517INVA, AMAEF.
101. Armand Berard to Paris, "Nonproliferation," June 3, 1968, box 769, cote 517INVA, AMAEF, p. 2.
102. "Appeals by U.S. and Soviet Open U.N. Atom Debate: Approval of a Treaty to Ban Spread of Nuclear Weapons Linked to Survival of World," April 27, 1968, *New York Times*.
103. Office of Political Affairs, "The Treaty on the Non-Proliferation of Nuclear Weapons" (note for the French minister of foreign affairs), July 10, 1968, box 769, cote 517INVA, AMAEF.
104. Robert S. Norris and Hans M. Kristensen, "Global Nuclear Stockpiles, 1945–2006," *Bulletin of the Atomic Scientists* 62, no. 4 (July 1, 2006): 64–66.
105. U.S. Department of State, "Treaty between the United States of America and the Russian Federation on Measures for the Further Reduction and Limitation of Strategic Offensive Arms," April 8, 2010, http://www.state.gov/documents/organization/140035.pdf.
106. Lyndon B. Johnson, "Remarks on Signing the Nuclear Nonproliferation Treaty, July 1, 1968, The Miller Center, http://millercenter.org/president/lbjohnson/speeches/speech-4037.
107. For the ideological and political determinants of American nonproliferation policy during the Eisenhower, Kennedy, and Johnson years, see the author's *The Bargain: America and the World's Pursuit of Perpetual Peace in the Nuclear Age* (forthcoming).

108. Sean L. Malloy, *Atomic Tragedy: Henry L. Stimson and the Decision to Use the Bomb against Japan* (Ithaca, NY: Cornell University Press, 2008), 34.

109. Stephen C. Neff, *Justice among Nations: A History of International Law* (Cambridge, MA: Harvard University Press, 2014), 478–479.

110. William Foster, "Possible Remarks for World Council" (draft), June 15, 1964, folder 1, box 17, Foster Papers, GCML, p. 3.

111. Kennedy, "News Conference 52."

5

From Isolation to Engagement

American Diplomacy and the Opening to China, 1969–1972

JEREMI SURI

In 1971 and 1972 the world seemed to turn upside down. In addition to the protests that convulsed every major society, prominent figures in the United States and the People's Republic of China who had made their careers by condemning the ideological degeneracy and threatening belligerence of their opposites, traveled great distances to announce a new era of cooperation, even friendship. The changes in perspective across the Pacific preceded substantive alterations in military and economic affairs. This was a political transformation made possible by diplomats working to bridge the personal and institutional divides between two highly antagonistic societies. Few diplomatic breakthroughs have generated as much attention—and controversy—as the dramatic opening of relations between Washington and Beijing in the early 1970s.[1]

Did Diplomacy Matter?

Henry Kissinger wrote the first authoritative account of the farsighted and flexible moves—largely orchestrated by Kissinger and his staff, in his account—to establish direct discussions between President Richard Nixon and Chairman Mao Zedong. Kissinger emphasized a series of secret and carefully orchestrated overtures, closely controlled by the president, his national security adviser, and a few trusted diplomats: Winston Lord, John Holdridge, and Vernon Walters. These National Security Council officials brought extensive regional knowledge and international experience to their work for Kissinger, and they operated effectively outside the traditional U.S. Department of State bureaucracy. They had focus and flexibility, and they were freed by the

Nixon administration to disregard many of the inherited ideological and institutional limitations on relations with Communist China.[2] The early historical assessments of the U.S. opening to China drew largely on Kissinger's memoirs and his heroic account of White House diplomacy.[3]

More critical scholars, who are less inclined to give Kissinger or Nixon personal credit for the breakthrough, have questioned the centrality of American decision-makers. These scholars have given more attention to the Chinese as the key actors, and they have also pointed to the geopolitical circumstances that encouraged Sino-American cooperation, regardless of who was in the White House. The rising military tensions on the long border between China and the Soviet Union, including a shooting war in 1969, and the chaos within China at the time encouraged the Communist leadership in Beijing to look to Washington for balance against external and internal challengers. New signs of friendship with American leaders would restrain Soviet aggression and, potentially, discredit some of the militants in China. According to this account, Mao Zedong orchestrated a rapid shift in China's strategic posture to increase his room for maneuver in a period of multiplying difficulties for his regime.[4] In retrospect, Mao's moves toward Washington anticipate the deeper Chinese Communist accommodation with capitalism later that decade.[5]

With the benefit of hindsight, some observers have contended that the U.S.-China opening was obvious, necessary, and almost inevitable (although no one said that at the time). The particular ideas and intentions of leaders mattered less than they seemed. From this perspective, personal overtures were not crucial, because the two countries had strong geostrategic reasons to come together: mutual efforts to contain Soviet power, shared interests in ending the Vietnam War, and a belated recognition that they were both better off with increased trade and communications. Sino-American conflict had become too costly. The strategic and economic benefits of cooperating to contain Soviet influence, manage Asian stability, and improve economic prospects outweighed inherited habits of threat and competition. Most of all, the citizens of both the United States and the People's Republic of China came to recognize, after more than twenty years of "nonrecognition," that the adversary was firmly entrenched in power. Echoing Robert Axelrod's research on the "evolution of cooperation," familiarity bred comfort and shared expectations.[6] This "realist" account privileges long-term circumstantial forces over charismatic personalities and short-term decisions. It contends that structure matters more than diplomacy.[7]

What is often lost in the Sturm und Drang of these debates is how difficult it was to bring the leaders of these societies together after more than twenty years of isolation, mutual threats, and direct military conflict around the Korean peninsula, the Taiwan Strait, and Indochina. Familiarity did not breed cooperation. Interests in strategic balancing did not easily override accumulated distrust. For all the obvious strategic logic behind a Sino-American opening, most of the bureaucratic, historical, and political pressures pushed in the opposite direction. The status quo standoff was much easier to maintain than it was to change. Institutional and ideological inertia favored conflict and isolation. Political leaders in Washington and Beijing had nurtured comfortable routines of recrimination, and they had developed confident repertoires of analysis that reinforced worst-case assumptions about the adversary. The ideological differences between the United States and China, the cultural distance between the societies, and the images of radicalism and militarism during the Cultural Revolution and the Vietnam War made it hard for many astute observers to imagine anything other than conflict between these countries. That was all most "expert" advisers had ever known.[8]

Moves to open relations between the United States and China were filled with uncertainty, risk, and fear. No president wanted to allow his domestic opponents to label him a "Communist appeaser," especially when Chinese society was engulfed in the evident radicalism of the Cultural Revolution during the late 1960s. This was particularly problematic for Democratic presidents, like Lyndon Johnson, who already confronted powerful domestic criticisms of their alleged foreign policy "weakness."[9] The Republic of China, America's traditional ally in Taiwan, lobbied forcefully against any "soft" overtures to the Communists on the mainland. Countering the logic of anti-Communism in Asia required quite a lot of courage. Few policy-makers could tolerate such strong political risks. Few diplomats had the authority to move in this dangerous direction.[10]

Understanding the Nixon Administration's Diplomacy to China

We still know very little about the diplomacy and planning within the People's Republic of China during the late 1960s and early 1970s. Without access to detailed and open archival materials, it remains difficult to assess how Mao Zedong, Zhou Enlai, and others around them organized their government to pursue friendlier diplomatic relations with the United States. It also remains difficult to assess their goals. Chinese Communist leaders had many reasons to see better relations with the United States as potentially beneficial, especially when they confronted worsening tensions with the Soviet Union and internal turmoil that threatened to undermine their regime. Nonetheless, suspicions about Washington's motives continued to run deep, and the escalation of American military activities in Southeast Asia expanded the potential danger on China's southern border.[11]

For the United States, we now have a full and easily accessible historical record for the period. Formerly classified documents from the White House, the State Department, and even many intelligence agencies are open in the National Archives, the Nixon Presidential Library, and various other repositories. In 2006 the Office of the Historian in the State Department published, as part of its highly regarded *Foreign Relations of the United States* (FRUS) series, an authoritative collection of many of the most important American documents for the opening to the People's Republic of China, 1969–1972. These materials allow historians to trace the inner development of U.S.-China diplomacy in the first Nixon administration.[12]

The available documents provide insightful details about what Nixon, Kissinger, and others hoped to achieve, and how they went about organizing the diverse (and often antagonistic) parts of the U.S. government to pursue—or at least not scuttle—their aims. The documents also offer a clear narrative of the evolving diplomatic moves that led from isolation when the Nixon administration began, to direct communications between Washington and Beijing two-and-a-half years later.

For later observers, that two-and-a-half-year time interval for policy change seems reasonable, perhaps even slow. In terms of the monumental strategic, institutional, and political transformation that the opening to China required, the shift was incredibly fast. Diplomatic revisions on such a large scale occur infrequently, and rarely with comparable speed and enduring effect.

The inherited obstacles to policy change were, in fact, enormous. Experts in the U.S. State Department who favored improved relations with Beijing, especially Assistant Secretary of State Marshall Green, feared Nixon and Kissinger's potentially "rash" actions. Seasoned diplomats favored a cautious gradualism ("small steps") over the quick shift that the president sought to create.[13] Similar worries came from members of Congress, especially Republican hard-liners, and citizen groups with a long history of condemning Chinese Communism. Advocates for the anti-Communist government in Taiwan, supported by Washington since before 1949, continued to dominate the domestic discussion of America's China policy when the new administration took office. President Nixon had relied heavily on their support throughout his career.

Despite all of these obstacles, the United States shifted its relations with a longtime adversary in less time than it takes most universities to launch a new academic program! Nixon and Kissinger forced change on a resistant policy bureaucracy and a reluctant public. They relied on their personal determination, their bureaucratic acumen, and, above all, their willingness to use various forms of secrecy, manipulation, and prevarication. They believed that they had no choice, if they wished to accomplish their strategic aims in a few short years.

Of course, the opening to China did not immediately produce productive relations between Washington and Beijing. Old suspicions and conflicting interests—especially around the Korean peninsula, the Taiwan Strait, and Indochina—continued to undermine cooperation. It took eight long years after Kissinger's icebreaking trip to Beijing in July 1971 before the two countries could establish official and full diplomatic relations in 1979. Progress stalled at many moments after the startling events of the first Nixon administration. Many inherited irritants and suspicions continue to undermine the stability of this relationship in the twenty-first century.

Nixon and Kissinger might have oversold the importance of their opening to China. They deserve enduring credit, however, for conceiving and implementing a major diplomatic breakthrough that contributed to the security and prosperity of the United States. They consistently and forcefully required the institutions of the U.S. government to align behind this shift in policy. When members of the government hindered their efforts, or challenged their leadership, they either hammered them into alignment or removed them from the process itself. This was often done with little tact, and it ruffled many egos, but it does appear necessary in retrospect for the fast-moving changes that Nixon and Kissinger wanted. Strong leadership matters for diplomatic effectiveness.[14]

Nixon and Kissinger pursued many parallel diplomatic tracks at the same time. They knew that they wanted to open relations with Beijing, but they also recognized that they lacked an easy and direct path. Most historians miss the surprising humility of Nixon and Kissinger in acknowledging their own ignorance of how best to engage Mao's government, especially during the continuing chaos of the Cultural Revolution.[15] In this context, the White House threw open numerous overtures for contact and discussion, relying on a wide variety of potential interlocutors—including the Romanians, the Dutch, the Norwegians, left-leaning French intellectuals, and, most famously, the leader of Pakistan, Yahya Khan. Nixon and Kissinger pursued multiple diplomatic tracks with energy and attention to details. They made sure those tracks did not contradict or undermine one another, but instead contributed to a larger coherent effort at reaching out to Beijing. Nixon and Kissinger managed to stay on message and send their message through many channels. Redundancy helped to get the message through, and it reinforced its sincerity.

Nixon and Kissinger recognized that a diplomatic opening to China had to begin with the big issues, not the smaller irritants that traditionally kept these countries apart. That was their most important insight. In many negotiations, the conventional wisdom is that you build confidence and trust by starting with the simpler things, leaving the deeply held principles and commitments for later discussion as the two sides build momentum. This is the pragmatic advice of starting small and creating new habits.[16]

To the frequent consternation of the more conventional diplomats in the U.S. State Department, Nixon and Kissinger ignored the issues that separated the United States and China on the future of Taiwan, control of Tibet, and the war in Vietnam. They also pushed ideological debates and concerns about internal issues to the side. Instead, Nixon and Kissinger demanded a razor focus on the importance of cooperation to ensure mutual respect, stability, and security in Asia. These were the biggest strategic issues. These were also the general positions that Nixon and Kissinger emphasized repeatedly in all communications. They articulated these general positions to show that the two countries, for all of their serious differences, faced an imperative need to work together. Nixon and Kissinger planned to work toward substantive agreements on other issues within this general framework. For Nixon and Kissinger, successful diplomacy was deductive: elucidating specific measures for cooperation and conflict avoidance after the leaders reached consensus on the main principles. The larger relationship drove the policy details, not vice versa.[17]

Getting Started

During his first day as president, Nixon conveyed to Kissinger and other close advisers that he wished to open relations with the People's Republic of China. This was a clear priority for the new president. His handwritten notes from his initial meetings contain the following words: "Chinese Communists: Short range—no change. Long range—we do not want 800,000,000 living in angry isolation. We want contact—will be interested in Warsaw meetings. Republic of China—cooperative member of international community and member of Pacific community."[18]

Nixon's phrase "Warsaw meetings" referred to the U.S.-China ambassadorial talks that began in the Polish capital in 1958 and continued intermittently through 1970. The president made it clear that he intended to elevate the importance of these never-ending meetings as a mechanism for encouraging improved relations between the two societies. The U.S.-China talks in Warsaw were the only direct contacts between representatives from Washington and Beijing. Although they did not accomplish anything concrete, the diplomats who met for more than a decade kept a mostly civil dialogue alive between the two governments, providing a foundation for talks of more substance when their leaders were ready.[19]

Nixon knew about the Warsaw meetings from his time as vice president. He did not want to be trapped by these discussions, but he recognized that he could build on the work of the obscure and midlevel diplomats toiling in the Polish capital. At the very least, the Warsaw meetings provided a direct channel for conveying his intentions to Beijing. Nixon instructed Kissinger, "We should give every encouragement to the attitude that this Administration is exploring possibilities of raprochement [sic] with the Chinese."[20]

The Central Intelligence Agency responded to these calls for Sino-American outreach with a negative prediction: "There is little prospect for change in China's attitudes and policies regarding the US while the present leadership obtains, and the US has a limited ability to influence these attitudes and policies." The CIA did not discourage diplomatic efforts from Washington, but it expected payoff only after a change of leadership in Beijing: "Any US 'overtures' to Communist China would be primarily intended to have an impact on China's post-Mao leadership."[21]

Nixon and Kissinger had contempt for this kind of conservative forecasting from the intelligence agencies. The president and his national security adviser had extensive experience as consumers of intelligence, and they generally believed that government agencies were more concerned with hedging their analyses, rather than anticipating major international shifts. According to Nixon and Kissinger, waiting for a change in the Chinese regime would mean stalling for many years. They were too impatient for that. They recognized that the negative CIA analysis was self-fulfilling, prolonging current unsatisfactory arrangements. Both Nixon and Kissinger were policy-makers who believed in the possibilities for targeted diplomatic risk taking. They proceeded to act in that way, often ignoring experienced analysts at the CIA, the Department of State, and other agencies.

In June 1969, only six months into his administration, Nixon signed National Security Decision Memorandum 17, initiating a series of unilateral measures to reduce restrictions on contact between the United States and the People's Republic of China. These initial measures were largely technical, involving the Foreign Assets Control and Export Control regulations. The measures had a real and obvious effect, facilitating trade in industrial goods and agricultural products between the countries, and among subsidiary corporations and allies. For a Chinese society in desperate need of grain and pharmaceuticals, Nixon's order was a very positive signal. It also opened the possibility for more travel among citizens of the two countries.[22]

As White House officials intensified their outreach to Pakistani and other foreign emissaries for help with contacting Mao's regime, these unilateral efforts to open trade and travel increased American credibility.

Reflecting on his strategy in a discussion with Kissinger in September 1969, Nixon displayed very clear thinking about the value of diplomatic overtures to Beijing:

> The President noted that we had made a small gesture toward the Chinese lately and it was interesting that the Chinese had not rejected this out of hand. We could go further and put the Chinese on the same basis as the Soviet Union concerning trade. This was something which should be considered.

Nixon went on to acknowledge serious differences between the United States and the People's Republic of China on many key issues, but he reiterated his focus on the importance of contact and the general principle of great-power cooperation. By the autumn of its first year in the White House, the Nixon administration had imposed this diplomatic approach on a foreign policy bureaucracy that had previously resisted similar thinking:

> The President said that, of course, there are issues such as U.N. membership for Communist China which are of concern, but these are short-run political problems which will be resolved eventually. In our own interests we must be prepared to deal with China on trade matters and other things which are of concrete importance.[23]

Mao's "Four Marshals"

As the Nixon administration reached out to Chinese diplomats and reduced limitations on trade and contact, Mao Zedong also began to turn Beijing's foreign policy in a new direction. He commissioned a secret internal study about the possibility of improving Beijing's relations with the Soviet Union and the United States. It is not clear precisely what motivated Mao's desire for a study at this time. China confronted rising tensions along its long border with the Soviet Union, and the war in Vietnam expanded to include more intensive fighting after early 1968. Even mentioning the possibility of improved relations with the United States would have sparked a storm of domestic criticism in China just months earlier. Although the strategic pressures on Beijing had not changed drastically, Mao seemed to recognize that perhaps the new Nixon administration in Washington was, despite the militant anti-Communist history of the president, open to cooperation. In retrospect, Mao's unprecedented decision in late January 1969 to allow uncensored domestic publication of Nixon's inaugural address was evidence of the Chinese leader's effort to reassess the new president. The American overtures during the first half of 1969 appear to have encouraged Mao's hopes.[24]

Affirming what their leader wanted to hear, four prominent Communist officials—the so-called four marshals chosen by Mao to report on international affairs—advised that Beijing could expect some positive diplomatic changes. Submitting their report to Mao in July 1969, the four marshals wrote, "In the foreseeable future it is unlikely that US imperialists and Soviet revisionists will launch a large-scale war against China, either jointly or separately." Both of these states, the authors explained, faced "crises at home and abroad" that limited their fighting capabilities.[25]

China did not require excessive preparation for war, but it needed to remain vigilant against foreign competitors, particularly those supported by Moscow. "The Soviet revisionists," the four marshals wrote, "have made China their main enemy, posing a more serious threat to our security than the US imperialists." The report alleged that the Kremlin's forces were "creating tensions along the long Sino-Soviet border, concentrating troops in the border area and making military intrusions. They are creating anti-Chinese public opinion, creating chaos on the international scene, while at the same time forcing some Asian countries to join an anti-China ring of encirclement."[26]

In response to Soviet challenges, the marshals advised that Beijing must maintain China's armed strength, while promoting "industrial and agricultural production." The future security of the People's Republic required that the nation become "a stronger economic power." For this purpose, the marshals suggested, "We should enhance our embassies and consulates in other countries, and actively carry out diplomatic activities." Breaking out of its isolation, China would expand the "international united front of anti-imperialism and anti-revisionism," while also acquiring more access to foreign imports, technology, and ideas.[27]

This analysis counseled for improved relations with the United States. Nixon appeared favorably disposed to new contacts, and Mao's advisers saw many advantages for their regime. The four marshals wrote, "Both China and the United States take the Soviet Union as their enemy." Working with Washington, leaders in Beijing could balance against Soviet power on "two-fronts," prohibiting the feared possibility of anti-Chinese superpower collaboration.[28]

Chen Yi, one of the four marshals, added a personal note to the final report: "It is necessary for us to utilize the contradiction between the United States and the Soviet Union in a strategic sense." He called for "a breakthrough in Sino-American relations." Chen admitted his ideas were somewhat "wild" in the context of standard anti-American rhetoric in Communist China (especially during the Cultural Revolution), but he recommended that state policy reflect how the "situation has changed today."[29]

The report of the four marshals shows that tensions with the Soviet Union played an important role in motivating Chinese leaders to consider new acts of friendship toward the United States. At the same time, the report also points to, without explicit evidence, the likelihood that the United States would receive Chinese overtures positively. This was not Beijing's experience since 1949.[30] What had changed to make Chinese leaders believe that the Nixon administration would be a willing partner, although its predecessors in the White House were not?

The four marshals and Mao might have acted out of instinct and desperation, but the Nixon administration's overtures from its first days in office must have encouraged Chinese inclinations to reach out to Washington, or at least watch for promising changes. We do not know for sure. We do know that the four marshals and Mao followed the shifts in American policy closely, and they listened to the president and his diplomats' words.[31]

Although Nixon and Kissinger anticipated that the Chinese would follow American moves closely, they did not have access to the report of the four marshals or other internal Chinese documents. The leaders of the two adversarial governments looked for the favorable signals that they desired, and they found evidence for what they wanted. Just as aggressive assumptions about an enemy often become self-fulfilling, guarded optimism can encourage congenial results. Much of diplomacy is driven by perceptions, expectations, and basic attitudes.

Ping-Pong Diplomacy

The diplomatic overtures from the United States in 1969 and the four marshals' report set the stage for the first public Chinese indication of interest. During 1970, Kissinger closely followed statements and signals from foreign interlocutors in Pakistan, Warsaw, Paris, Norway, and even Afghanistan. He saw many signs of Chinese reasonableness and restraint, despite continued acrimony. At times Kissinger was grasping at straws. At times he was astute to subtleties that could encourage a continuation of American efforts.

The first concrete evidence of Beijing's receptivity was the Chinese invitation for a U.S. table tennis team to visit the mainland. The American players were already in Japan for the World Table Tennis Championship when they received the offer, on April 6, 1971, to travel through China. The invitation appeared "out of the blue" to most observers, but Nixon, Kissinger, and high-ranking members of the administration immediately understood it in the context of their diplomatic overtures during previous months.[32] Kissinger's assistant for Chinese affairs, John Holdridge, commented, "The primary significance of the [Chinese] invitation is its reflection of Peking's openness and self-confidence in handling its foreign relations."[33]

The American media followed the table tennis players closely during their trip to China. The young American men and women were the first official American delegation to visit the mainland since the Communist Revolution in 1949. The youthful images of friendly competition and exotic locales in China captured the public imagination throughout the United States. This was a front-page story in newspapers and magazines. *Life* magazine provided glossy photo coverage of Americans and Chinese enjoying each other's company as they played and traveled near various historical sights.[34]

The American and Chinese players interacted favorably, they were well received in China, and they had an encouraging following in the United States and other parts of the world. The Ping-Pong diplomacy was significant because it created an alternative narrative to the acrimony and conflict that characterized most previous discussions of U.S.-China relations. Observers, including high-ranking policy-makers, could now begin to imagine an alternative set of relations between Washington and Beijing. Informal diplomacy mattered enormously, especially in breaking down inherited stereotypes and fears.

Nixon and Kissinger followed the Ping-Pong diplomacy with a new set of unilateral diplomatic overtures. On April 13, 1971, while the American table tennis players were still in China, the president signed National Security Decision Memorandum 105, implementing new "steps to increase personal and commercial contacts between the People's Republic of China and the United States." These steps were as follows:

1. Issuance of a public statement offering to expedite visas for groups of visitors from the People's Republic of China to the United States.
2. Relaxation of currency controls to permit Chinese use of American dollars.
3. Ending restrictions on American oil companies providing bunkers except on Chinese-owned or Chinese-chartered carriers bound to or from North Vietnam, North Korea, or Cuba.
4. Granting permission to U.S. vessels to carry Chinese cargoes between non-Chinese ports, and for U.S.-owned foreign flag vessels to call at Chinese ports.
5. Commencement of a relaxation of controls on direct trade between the United States and China by placing individual items under general license for direct export to the PRC, after an item-by-item interagency review to determine if they are of strategic significance.[35]

On April 19, 1971, Kissinger sent an additional memorandum (National Security Study Memorandum 124) to the secretaries of state and defense, as well as the director of the CIA, explaining that the president wanted them to suggest additional "possible diplomatic initiatives which the United States might take toward the People's Republic of China (PRC) with the objective of furthering the improvement of relations. These initiatives should explore the degree to which it is possible to build on recent progress. They should be put into the context of our relations towards other countries, especially the USSR and Japan."[36]

By the spring of 1971, two years into the Nixon presidency, the administration had encouraged the first serious reciprocal overtures between Beijing and Washington in more than twenty years. The Chinese seemed receptive. The images of Ping Pong Diplomacy contributed to a lessening of public tensions. The journey of the smiling table tennis players was connected to behind-the-scenes measures on trade, travel, and indirect communication pursued with consistent energy and determination by the president and his national security adviser. Despite internal resistance and limited immediate signs of progress, Nixon and Kissinger had persevered.

By April 1971, they had managed to direct all the main organs of government, and much of the American public, toward improving U.S.-China relations. The progress in the first two years was procedural and perceptual, and it also looks somewhat simple in retrospect, but it was complex, risky, and it required consistent diplomatic energy. Few previous White House occupants displayed such qualities.

The Kissinger Visit

Diplomacy is often like teaching. Success requires intensive preparation, continual adaptation, and extensive patience. Long periods pass without evident progress. Then, often when least expected, a breakthrough occurs. Old patterns of behavior finally fade away, and new modes of thinking take center stage. After many frustrations, the hard work and often unseen efforts appear to pay off.

For Nixon and Kissinger the moment of breakthrough came on the afternoon of April 27, 1971. Pakistani ambassador to the United States Agha Hilaly called Kissinger's assistant, Harold Saunders, with an "urgent message." Hilaly met with Kissinger at the White House from 6:12 to 6:30 p.m. Kissinger then walked over to the Oval Office to meet with the president from 7:00 to 7:37 p.m. These were all unplanned meetings that interrupted the crowded schedules of very busy policy-makers. These were meetings that carried U.S.-China discussions from the shadows into a bright new light.

Ambassador Hilaly conveyed a message from the Chinese prime minister, Zhou Enlai, to President Nixon, the first such direct message in at least a decade:[37]

> At present contacts between the peoples of China and the United States are being renewed. However, as the relations between China and the U.S.A. are to be restored fundamentally, a solution to this crucial question can be found only through direct discussions between high-level responsible persons of the two countries. Therefore, the Chinese Government reaffirms its willingness to receive publicly in Peking a special envoy of the President of the U.S. (for instance, Mr. Kissinger) or the U.S. Secretary of State or even the President of the U.S. himself for direct meeting and discussions. Of course, if the U.S. President considers that the time is not yet right the matter may be deferred to a later date. As for the modalities, procedure and other details of the high-level meeting and discussions in Peking, as they are of no substantive significance, it is believed that it is entirely possible for public arrangements to be made through the good offices of [Pakistani] President Yahya Khan.[38]

As if to underline the seriousness of this overture, officials in Beijing sent a subsequent message to Washington through Norway's ambassador to China, who dutifully passed it to his American counterparts. The Norwegian ambassador affirmed, "China is now prepared to start a wide range of contact activity with the U.S." He recounted that the Chinese leaders looked to the United States as a balance against continued tensions between Beijing and Moscow. The Norwegian ambassador also explained that Chinese leaders were impressed by the recent American "capacity to behave independently," rather than follow established Cold War routines. White House signals of change had reached their intended target.[39]

Nixon and Kissinger resolved quickly to accept the Chinese invitation for a high-level trip to Beijing. This trip would solidify a new cooperative working relationship between the two countries. It would also affirm the strategic leadership of Nixon and Kissinger in the eyes of the American people. With new friends in China and stronger support at home, the White House would gain additional leverage over the Soviet Union and North Vietnam, Nixon and Kissinger hoped. They sought to place the United States at the vertex of a new triangular relationship between Moscow, Beijing, and Washington. Such positioning would give the United States more flexibility than either Communist power.

Through skilled diplomacy, Nixon and Kissinger had indeed opened new options for American policy that served the nation's interests but did not necessarily require new deployments of force. They had carved out creative space for change in a formerly stagnant Cold War relationship. They had also neutralized the opposition of domestic figures (especially on the political right), skeptical U.S. government officials, and defenders of the Republic of China in Taiwan. The excitement of a diplomatic breakthrough unleashed a momentum that was difficult for reluctant observers to resist. The opening of direct talks turned presumptions upside down from what they had been just two years earlier.

Nixon's reply to Zhou Enlai, on May 10, 1971, captured the decisive turn in U.S.-China relations and the central role Nixon and Kissinger expected to continue to play in leading this process:

> President Nixon has carefully studied the message of April 21, 1971, from Premier Chou En-lai conveyed through the courtesy of President Yahya Khan. President Nixon agrees that direct high-level negotiations are necessary to resolve the issues dividing the United States of America and the People's Republic of China. Because of the importance he attaches to normalizing relations between our two countries, President Nixon is prepared to accept the suggestion of Premier Chou En-lai that he visit Peking for direct conversations with the leaders of the People's Republic of China. At such a meeting each side would be free to raise the issue of principal concern to it.
>
> In order to prepare the visit by President Nixon and to establish reliable contact with the leaders of the Chinese People's Republic, President Nixon proposes a preliminary *secret* meeting between his Assistant for National Security Affairs, Dr. Kissinger, and Premier Chou En-lai or another appropriate high-level Chinese official. Dr. Kissinger would be prepared to attend such a meeting on Chinese soil preferably at some location within convenient flying distance from Pakistan to be suggested by the People's Republic of China. Dr. Kissinger would be authorized to discuss the circumstances which would make a visit by President Nixon most useful, the agenda of such a meeting, the time of such a visit and to begin a preliminary exchange of views on all subjects of mutual interest. If it should be thought desirable that a special emissary come to Peking publicly between the secret visit to the People's Republic of China of Dr. Kissinger and the arrival of President Nixon, Dr. Kissinger will be authorized to arrange it. It is anticipated that the visit of President Nixon to Peking could be announced within a short time of the secret meeting

between Dr. Kissinger and Premier Chou En-lai. Dr. Kissinger will be prepared to come from June 15 onward.

It is proposed that the precise details of Dr. Kissinger's trip including location, duration of stay, communication and similar matters be discussed through the good offices of President Yahya Khan. *For secrecy, it is essential that no other channel be used. It is also understood that this first meeting between Dr. Kissinger and high officials of the People's Republic of China be strictly secret.*[40]

The emphasis on secrecy in discussions came from the United States, not China. Secrecy reflected Nixon and Kissinger's commitment to protect their diplomatic activities from domestic interference. They knew their early overtures to Beijing required centralization of power in the White House, and they continued to employ that tactic, often with obsessive qualities that became counterproductive over time.[41]

Nixon and Kissinger wanted to use their diplomatic achievements in China for policy purposes at home and abroad. They aimed to undermine their critics, pressure the Soviets, isolate the North Vietnamese, and spread American global influence at reduced costs. They had mixed success, but the high-level discussions with Chinese leaders gave them a very good start. Their diplomacy with China was open, but their politics were tightly closed and highly controlled.[42]

Kissinger and Nixon Go to China

Kissinger made his secret trip to China, through Pakistan, from July 9 to 11, 1971. The substance of the trip was less significant than the symbolism. When he and Nixon announced that he had been in China, they affirmed that leaders in both Washington and Beijing had begun a new cooperative relationship. Gone was the Cold War rhetoric about Communist treachery and capitalist "running dogs." Gone was the concern about appeasing the enemy. Most important, the leaders of the two former adversaries agreed that they had a greater interest in working together than denying each other's right to exist.

Kissinger's trip was an affirmation of diplomacy over ideology, and cooperation over containment. The accounts of his conversations with Zhou Enlai, which remained secret until the last decade, capture precisely this public shift in the relationship. The joint public announcement from Beijing and Washington on July 15, 1971 redefined the Cold War in Asia. Both sides agreed that they sought a "normalization of relations between the two countries." They explained that they met "to exchange views on questions of concern to the two sides."[43] The discussions were secret, but the real change was public, as it usually is with successful diplomacy.[44]

Following Kissinger's trip, in February 1972 President Nixon made the first official American state visit to the People's Republic of China. He intentionally visited China before traveling to the Soviet Union. He and Kissinger arrived in Beijing without advance agreement on an agenda, or even a basic schedule, with their Chinese hosts. This was a risky breach of protocol because it left the president's itinerary subject to the immediate control of leaders in Beijing. As in all of their dealings with the People's Republic, Nixon and Kissinger were willing to overlook key details for the purpose of building a working relationship.[45]

Chinese leaders reciprocated in their own terms. Soon after Nixon and Kissinger arrived in Beijing, Zhou Enlai whisked them to a meeting with Mao Zedong, in his study. The famous conversation of the four men (Mao Zedong, Zhou Enlai, Richard Nixon, and Henry Kissinger) seated in armchairs beside one another was entirely "philosophical," as Mao put it. They did not discuss particular policies, threats, or programs. They did not propose new initiatives. Instead, they focused on the need for cooperation in a complex domestic and international setting where, both Mao and Nixon admitted, they could not achieve very much acting alone.

Now an old and frail figure, the man who led the Chinese Communist Revolution criticized his own "big cannons" about "defeating imperialism" and "establishing socialism." Instead, Mao reflected, "I've only been able to change a few places in the vicinity of Beijing."[46] China needed the United States to anchor the regime in a sustainable global system of trade and security. The United States needed China to help ensure stability and security in East Asia as America's Vietnam War drew to a difficult conclusion. The Sino-American opening was a recognition of these "facts" by the leaders of the two societies, and a personal commitment to make cooperation replace years of destructive conflict.

Diplomatic Lessons

What do we learn about successful diplomacy from the Sino-American opening? First, *signals mattered*. Nixon and Kissinger's repeated measures to reduce restrictions on trade and travel with China, coupled with continued efforts at contacting Chinese leaders, convinced Mao Zedong and Zhou Enlai that they had to reconsider their view of American intentions. Perhaps the leaders of the United States were not trying to destroy China. Perhaps Nixon and Kissinger really wanted to cooperate. The Chinese leaders had strategic reasons to look for these signals at the time, but they still needed the confirmation that Nixon and Kissinger offered. Despite distance and distraction, American signals appeared to reach Beijing and encourage reciprocation, most especially in the Chinese invitation for Kissinger's visit in 1971.

Second, *flexibility mattered.* Nixon and Kissinger had a clear sense of American strategic interests in East Asia, and they retained a disdain for Chinese Communist ideology. Nonetheless, they recognized that effective policy was not driven by strategic interests and ideology alone. Leaders had to take risks, they had to experiment, and they had to shake things up. In China, and elsewhere, Nixon and Kissinger worked to break down existing patterns of behavior and create new ones. They nurtured diplomatic relationships over time, rather than pursuing "quick fixes" for major problems.[47]

The same appears to be true for the Chinese side. Mao and the four marshals showed flexibility in adjusting to new international pressures and openings. They observed American rhetoric and behavior closely. They reacted prudently to their reassessment of Washington's intentions. The Chinese were willing to take calculated risks for the purpose of enhancing their security.[48]

Third, and perhaps most important, *leaders mattered.* The most powerful people in both societies directed the diplomatic efforts. They formulated the ideas behind the opening. They managed a very delicate process. They pushed their subordinates to abandon their routines and follow through on new initiatives. The United States and the People's Republic of China would have remained hostile and isolated in the early 1970s if the leaders of these societies had not decided to take risks for change. Even if an opening in relations between these two countries was necessary, it would not have happened when it did without the determined diplomacy of their leaders.

Diplomacy only works on this scale when the most powerful figures in government understand it, encourage it, and support it. Presidents and prime ministers must seize their role as their country's diplomat-in-chief. Effective diplomacy starts at the top.

Notes

1. For an effort to place the opening to China in the context of broader international and domestic developments in the late 1960s and early 1970s, see Jeremi Suri, *Power and Protest: Global Revolution and the Rise of Détente* (Cambridge, MA: Harvard University Press, 2003). For an excellent account that places the U.S.-China opening in the context of social, cultural, and political developments in the United States during the 1970s, see Thomas Borstelmann, *The 1970s: A New Global History From Civil Rights to Economic Inequality* (Princeton, NJ: Princeton University Press, 2012). The best detailed diplomatic account of the U.S. opening to China is Chris Tudda, *A Cold War Turning Point: Nixon and China, 1969–1972* (Baton Rouge: Louisiana State University Press, 2012).

2. See Henry Kissinger, *White House Years* (Boston: Little, Brown, 1979), especially chap. 19. See also John Holdridge, *Crossing the Divide: An Insider's Account of the Normalization of U.S.-China Relations* (New York: Rowman and Littlefield, 1997).

3. See John Lewis Gaddis, *Strategies of Containment: A Critical Appraisal of American National Security Policy during the Cold War* (New York: Oxford University Press, 2005 ed., originally published in 1982), chaps. 9 and 10; Walter Isaacson, *Kissinger: A Biography* (New York: Simon and Schuster, 1992), especially chaps. 16 and 19.

4. I offered this interpretation in Suri, *Power and Protest*, 226–245. For more on the Chinese initiatives behind the opening, see Odd Arne Westad, *Restless Empire: China and the World since 1750* (New York: Basic Books, 2012), especially 365–438; Margaret MacMillan, *Nixon and Mao: The Week that Changed the World* (New York: Random House, 2007); Chen Jian, *Mao's China and the Cold War* (Chapel Hill: University of North Carolina Press, 2001), 238–276. For the best account of rising Sino-Soviet tensions, see Lorenz Lüthi, *The Sino-Soviet Split: Cold War in the Communist World* (Princeton, NJ: Princeton University Press, 2008).

5. On this point, see Chen, *Mao's China and the Cold War*, 277–283; Ezra Vogel, *Deng Xiaoping and the Transformation of China* (Cambridge, MA: Belknap Press of Harvard University Press, 2011).

6. Robert Axelrod, *The Evolution of Cooperation*, rev. ed. (New York: Basic Books, 2006).

7. See Aaron Friedberg, *A Contest for Supremacy: China, America, and the Struggle for Mastery in Asia* (New York: W.W. Norton, 2011). For systematic arguments about the importance of geopolitical structure over diplomacy in international affairs, see John J. Mearsheimer, *The Tragedy of Great Power Politics* (New York: W.W. Norton, 2001); Kenneth N. Waltz, *Theory of International Politics* (New York: McGraw-Hill, 1979).

8. See the overwhelming historical evidence for these points about the powerful ideological, institutional, and political barriers to Sino-American rapprochement, especially in the late 1960s: Michael H. Hunt, *The Genesis of Chinese Communist Foreign Policy* (New York: Columbia University Press, 1998); Warren I. Cohen, *America's Response to China: A History of Sino-American Relations*, 5th ed. (New York: Columbia University Press, 2010); Michael Schaller, *The United States and China: Into the Twenty-First Century*, 3rd ed. (New York: Oxford University Press, 2002).

9. On this general point about the domestic pressures for Democratic presidents, as well as Republicans, to embrace hawkish foreign policy positions during the Cold War, see Campbell Craig and Fredrik Logevall, *America's Cold War: The Politics of Insecurity* (Cambridge, MA: Belknap Press of Harvard University Press, 2009).

10. See Cohen, *America's Response to China*; Schaller, *The United States and China*.

11. On these points, see Qiang Zhai, *China and the Vietnam Wars, 1950–1975* (Chapel Hill: University of North Carolina Press, 2000); Zhihua Shen and Danhui Li, *After Leaning to One Side: China and its Allies in the Cold War* (Stanford, CA: Stanford University Press, 2011).

12. See *Foreign Relations of the United States (FRUS), 1969–1976*, vol. 17, China, 1969–1972 (Washington DC: U.S. Government Printing Office, 2006). The volume is available online: http://history.state.gov/historicaldocuments/frus1969-76v17.

13. See, for example, Secretary of State William Rogers's support for overtures to Communist China, but his articulation of the U.S. State Department's preference for careful and deliberate moves, involving consent from all major U.S. agencies, and potentially some American partners overseas. Memorandum from Secretary of State William Rogers to President Richard Nixon, December 2, 1969, *FRUS, 1969–1976*, vol. 17, doc. 49. Raymond Garthoff echoes Rogers's perspective: *Détente and Confrontation: American-Soviet Relations from Nixon to Reagan*, rev. ed. (Washington, DC: Brookings Institution Press, 1994), especially chaps. 6 and 7.

14. This is a point echoed in accounts by Patrick Tyler, *A Great Wall: Six Presidents and China* (New York: Public Affairs, 1999); James Mann, *About Face: A History of America's Curious Relationship with China, From Nixon to Clinton* (New York: Random House, 1998).

15. Jussi Hanhimäki makes this point very well in his book *The Flawed Architect: Henry Kissinger and American Foreign Policy* (New York: Oxford University Press, 2004), especially chap. 3.

16. For a recent statement of this perspective, see Cass R. Sunstein, *Simpler: The Future of Government* (New York: Simon and Schuster, 2013).

17. For Kissinger's deeper thinking about these issues as they related to diplomacy and foreign policy among the great powers, see Jeremi Suri, *Henry Kissinger and the American Century* (Cambridge, MA: Belknap Press of Harvard University Press, 2007), 138–248.

18. *FRUS*, 1969–1976, Vol. 17, doc. 3, fn 3.

19. Ambassadorial talks in Warsaw between representatives from the United States and the People's Republic of China began on September 15, 1958. See Kenneth T. Young, *Negotiating with the Chinese Communists: The United States Experience, 1953–67* (New York: McGraw-Hill, 1968).

20. *FRUS*, 1969–1976, vol. 17, doc. 3.

21. Ibid., doc. 12.

22. Ibid., docs. 14 and 19.

23. Ibid., doc. 31.

24. See Mao Zedong's comments on an article by a commentator of *Renmin ribao* (*People's Daily*) and *Hongqi* (*Red Flag*), January 1969, *Cold War International History Project Bulletin* (*CWIHP*), no. 11 (Winter 1998), 161. The text of Nixon's inaugural address appeared in the *People's Daily* and *Red Flag*.

25. Report by Four Chinese Marshals to the Central Committee, "A Preliminary Evaluation of the War Situation," July 11, 1969, in *CWIHPB*, no. 11 (Winter 1998), 166–168. The authors of the report were Chen Yi, Ye Jianying, Nie Rongzhen, and Xu Xiangqian. They each received the title "marshal" for military service on behalf of the Chinese Communist Party. For background on the report of the four marshals, see Chen, *Mao's China and the Cold War*, 245–249.

26. Report by Four Chinese Marshals to the Central Committee, July 11, 1969, in *CWIHPB*, no. 11 (Winter 1998), 166–167.

27. Ibid., 168.

28. Ibid., 167. See also the follow-up report, "Report by Four Chinese Marshals to the CCP Central Committee," September 17, 1969, *CWIHPB*, no. 11 (Winter 1998), 170.

29. Further Thoughts by Marshal Chen Yi on Sino-American Relations, in *CWIHPB*, no. 11 (Winter 1998), 170–171.

30. On this point, see Yawei Liu, "The United States According to Mao Zedong—Chinese-American Relations, 1893–1976," Ph.D. diss., Emory University, Atlanta, Ga., 1996.

31. See Mao Zedong's comments on an article by a commentator of *Renmin ribao* and *Hongqi*, January 1969, in *CWIHPB*, no. 11 (Winter 1998), 161.

32. Zhou Enlai later told Nixon that "the decision to invite the American table tennis team to China was made by Chairman Mao personally." See Memorandum of Conversation between Nixon, Kissinger, Zhou, et al., Beijing, February 21, 1972, available through the National Security Archive, George Washington University, Washington D.C.: http://www2.gwu.edu/~nsarchiv/NSAEBB/NSAEBB106/.

33. *FRUS*, 1969–1976, vol. 17, doc. 112.

34. *Life* 70 (April 30, 1971).

35. *FRUS*, 1969–1976, vol. 17, doc. 116.

36. Ibid., doc. 117.

37. Through intermediaries, the United States and the People's Republic of China had exchanged messages concerning conflict in the Taiwan Strait during the late 1950s. See John Lewis Gaddis, *We Now Know: Rethinking Cold War History* (New York: Oxford University Press, 1997), chap. 8.

38. *FRUS*, 1969–1976, vol. 17, doc. 118.

39. Ibid., doc. 123.

40. Ibid., doc. 125.

41. On the last point, see Garthoff *Détente and Confrontation*, especially chaps. 6 and 7; Hanhimäki, *The Flawed Architect*, especially chap. 15.

42. For more on this point, see Suri, *Power and Protest*, chap. 6; William Bundy, *A Tangled Web: The Making of Foreign Policy in the Nixon Presidency* (New York: Hill and Wang, 1998).

43. Richard Nixon, Remarks to the Nation Announcing Acceptance of an Invitation to Visit the People's Republic of China, July 15, 1971, *Public Papers of the President: Richard Nixon, 1971*, 819–820.

44. *FRUS, 1969–1976*, vol. 17, docs. 139–143.

45. On this point, see MacMillan, *Nixon and Mao.*

46. Memorandum of Conversation between Mao Zedong, Zhou Enlai, Wang Hairong, Tang Wensheng, Richard Nixon, Henry Kissinger, and Winston Lord, February 21, 1972, Mao's Residence, Beijing.

47. For Kissinger's deeper thinking about the importance of diplomatic and strategic flexibility, see Suri, *Henry Kissinger and the American Century*, chap. 4.

48. For a discussion of Chinese strategic flexibility in this period, see Chen, *Mao's China and the Cold War*, 238–276.

6

Sadat and Begin

Successful Diplomacy to Peace

GALIA GOLAN

Israel and Egypt fought five wars against each other before opting, finally, for a diplomatic solution to their conflict. Actually, there had also been diplomatic efforts even prior to some of these wars, conducted directly or indirectly by the two parties or by outside powers, for example, the two-power and four-power talks during the War of Attrition (1967–1970). There were even some diplomatic breakthroughs, most notably the acceptance by both Israel and Egypt of UN Security Council resolution 242 in November 1967. Yet, until the Camp David meeting of 1978, none of these efforts, including the successful but limited disengagement talks of 1974 and 1975, managed to produce a peace agreement. Assuredly these past endeavors contributed, perhaps each in its own way, to the eventual success of Camp David, but there were a number of factors that distinguished between what may be called the Camp David process and the earlier diplomatic efforts.

The key to the success was most likely—some might say undoubtedly—Sadat's dramatic gesture: his visit to Jerusalem and speech to the Knesset, which clearly broke down deeply ingrained psychological barriers—as they were intended to do. But there were other critical factors, both before, and especially after, this event; therefore, although it is impossible to know if the visit constituted an essential ("necessary") factor, one may more easily argue that it was not a "sufficient" factor to bring peace between the two countries. Leadership and personal diplomacy, most notably of U.S. president Jimmy Carter, became critical factors as talks faltered and personalities clashed in the bilateral discussions following Sadat's visit. At the same time, "spoilers," domestic critics in both Egypt and Israel, had to be dealt with. The negotiations were thus structured and conducted by the Americans to accommodate as many interests as possible. Indeed, the full range of diplomacy was employed, from language ambiguity, to separate assurances, to veiled threats, to appeals to out-side individuals and states or diaspora for intervention or assistance. Thus, both structure and agency became critical elements as well. At the base, how-ever, was the "political will" of the two leaders to achieve a diplomatic break-through: for Sadat, to gain the return of Egyptian territory without the obstacles inherent in more comprehensive talks including all parties and as-pects of the Arab-Israeli conflict; for Begin, to achieve relief from renewed warfare and from American pressure to deal with the Palestinian issue and relinquish the West Bank, which for him was part of the sacred Land of Israel (the biblical Eretz Israel). Furthermore, there were the personal and diplo-matic skills of President Carter.

The background factor that contributed significantly to the eventual diplo-matic success was not an act of diplomacy but rather the war of 1973, which changed the domestic and regional environment. The war, known as the Ram-adan War in the Arab world and as the Yom Kippur War in Israel, was viewed—and presented—in Egypt as a victory given the successful crossing of the Suez Canal and the blow to the aura of invincibility of the Israeli army. Indeed, on the seventh day of the war, Israel's prime minister Golda Meir was actually willing to call a cease-fire with Egyptian troops well dug in east of the Suez; Sadat refused (and went on to lose the war). Thus, it could now be said that the Egyptians had won back their honor and could now negotiate with Israel as equals. Indeed, Sadat himself suggested this upon occasion, referring to "new facts" created by the war, as the Egyptian people were no longer seen as a "life-less body."[1]

Yet, there is ample evidence that Sadat was in fact willing to negotiate with Israel for peace as early as 1971 and also in 1973 prior to the war. When he as-sumed power in 1970 following the death of Gamal Abdel Nasser, Sadat set about substituting the pan-Arab ambitions of his predecessor with a more Egypt-centered vision. Intent upon not only securing his own political power but also restructuring (one might say salvaging) the Egyptian economy and public morale, he clearly viewed the ongoing conflict with Israel as a serious obstacle to Egyptian well-being. In this sense, peace and economic progress were two parts of the same objective, because of the need to not only reduce the burden of defense and military spending but also to obtain sorely needed resources that would be available by replacing Soviet support with that of the United States. Student riots in the early 1970s, along with public pressure for moves to undo Egypt's 1967 humiliating loss of the Sinai, were an integral part of this picture. Thus, Sadat began almost immediately to remove his political challengers and to restructure the Egyptian economy and open secret chan-nels to Washington. He also initiated steps to regain Egyptian territory, whether by war or by diplomacy.

Following unsuccessful proposals for an interim, limited agreement to open the Suez Canal plus agreement to proposals by UN special envoy Gunnar Jarring regarding a future settlement with Israel, the more significant of the Egyptian peace offers was presented to the Americans by Sadat's national security adviser, Hafez Ismail, in Washington in February 1973. Secretary of State Kissinger conveyed it to the Israelis.[2] Although it is not clear from the U.S. documents of the meetings with Ismail that Egypt was willing to sign a separate peace agreement—in exchange for full Israeli withdrawal from Egyptian territory—the Israelis did view this as what Golda Meir's principal adviser, Israel Galili, termed "an offer of peace, with international guarantees."[3] However, even as they concluded that there was a serious threat of war, the Israelis turned down the offer in April 1973 because of their perceived need to hold on to the territory.[4] When a diplomatic breakthrough appeared unobtainable, as evidenced by the failure of the 1971 and 1973 offers and of Jarring's mission, along with the U.S.-Soviet détente call for what amounted to no more than continued status quo in the region, Sadat went ahead with a limited military action. His purpose was to break the status quo in order to revive a diplomatic path.

The war played a different role for Israel, changing the domestic environment in a manner that held some promise of greater flexibility. For Israelis, the Yom Kippur War was traumatic, primarily because of the surprise, the unpreparedness of the army, early defeats, the large number of casualties, and also the unreliability of the country's leadership. Public protests and an official commission of inquiry led to the resignation of Golda Meir's government in the spring of 1974, accompanied by a greatly reduced confidence in the country's military strength vis-à-vis the Arab states. The concept of "strategic depth" and "defensible borders" that the territories occupied in 1967 were purported to provide suffered something of a blow, in part because of the extended length of time and effort it took reservists and supplies to reach the embattled Israel Defense Forces at the Suez Canal.[5] The view of the territories as a security asset suffered a blow, apparently creating some readiness for territorial compromise, at least on the Egyptian front, along with the added incentive of avoiding another outbreak of war given the losses suffered. This was reflected in public opinion, which, just one month after the war, measured a significant drop (which was to become a trend) in opposition to returning the territories, particularly the Sinai.[6]

Early postwar diplomacy did not, however, produce a peace accord, perhaps because it was not intended to. In view of Kissinger's step-by-step approach, dictated by his wish to exclude the Soviets and avoid what he viewed as a futile effort for a comprehensive settlement, that is, peace agreements between Israel and all the parties involved, the Geneva Conference convened at the end of

1973, and even Kissinger's subsequent shuttle diplomacy was designed to obtain only limited disengagement of forces and reduction of tension. Israel did try to achieve a political concession, namely, a "non-belligerency" clause in the 1975 Egyptian-Israeli Interim Agreement, but Sadat was not willing to make such a concession while Israel continued to occupy a good part of the Sinai (including the strategically important port and naval base Sharm el-Sheikh). Indeed, it took an American suspension of the talks and what the United States called a "reassessment" of its relations with Israel just to achieve a partial withdrawal of Israeli forces to the middle of the Sinai.[7] The Interim Agreement did include a phrase on "the non-use of force" and pledged continued efforts to reach a peace agreement, but as such it was limited in both time and scope.[8] If the same channel had been continued, these talks would be worth examining as the prelude to the diplomatic success at Camp David. But, in fact, it took an entirely new factor, albeit within the circumstances created by the 1973 war, to move matters in that direction.

Leadership Change in the United States and Israel

The election of Jimmy Carter and the appointment of Zbigniew Brzezinski as his national security adviser ushered in a change in the U.S. approach, from step-to-step diplomacy to comprehensive negotiations through a resumed Geneva Conference of all the parties to the Arab-Israeli conflict. For the Israeli government, this was anathema, not only because it meant facing all the Arab states together, thereby virtually linking success with one to success with all, but, under the Carter administration, this would now mean dealing with the Palestinians as well, possibly even in the form of the PLO.[9] President Carter told the Israelis this in so many words,[10] and on March 16, 1977, President Carter said publicly at a Clinton, Massachusetts, town hall meeting that "an ultimate requirement for peace is to deal with the Palestinian problem. . . . There has to be a homeland provided for the Palestinian refugees who have suffered for many, many years."[11] The introduction into American diplomatic parlance of a "homeland" for the Palestinians had not been discussed with Carter's aides, including Brzezinski, nor coordinated with the State Department; it did reflect Carter's direct manner and disdain for diplomatic nuances or taboo buzzwords (as William Quandt has described him), along with the idealism so characteristic of his presidency. To Israel's dismay, however, Carter's positions on the conflict appeared to coincide with a Brookings Institution paper ("Towards Peace in the Middle East") that had been published earlier outlining a settlement that involved both resolution of the Palestinian issue and Israeli withdrawal to the June 4, 1967 lines (with minor adjustments). Combined

with the intensive preparations undertaken by the new administration for convening Geneva, Carter's public statements, particularly on the Palestinian
issue, were of grave concern to the Israeli leadership.

Within Israel, however, another more startling drama was soon to take
place. The elections of May 1977 brought about what Israelis call a "maapach,"
roughly translated as "upset"—in which the right wing came to power for the
first time in Israel's brief history (dating back even to prestate times). The oust-
ing of the Labor Alignment was in fact the unexpected but belated reaction to
the Yom Kippur War and to the disillusionment of the public with the country's leadership at that time. In fact, Labor's votes went not to the right-wing
Likud Party but to a new Center Party, which then joined the Likud to form a
coalition government under the leadership of Menachem Begin. It may seem
strange to credit (at least in part) a diplomatic breakthrough with the election
of a government led by opponents to UNSC resolution 242 and to the "land for
peace" policy of its predecessors. Indeed, it is conceivable that if not for the
leadership change in the United States and the emergence of Carter's worrisome (for Israel) policy, the government change in Israel might not have led to
a breakthrough. But Prime Minister Begin entered office in what he perceived
as a hostile international climate: the UNGA resolution in 1975 labeling Zion-
ism as racism; the growing strength of the PLO (Arafat had been invited to
address the United Nations);, an unsympathetic American president; and advanced preparations for an international conference in which Israel would be
heavily pressed to make unacceptable territorial concessions. "Unacceptable
territorial concessions" for Begin meant any compromise of the "Land of
Israel" (Eretz Israel) of biblical times, which in the post-1967 context meant
the West Bank, including East Jerusalem. As he told the Israeli Knesset upon
presenting his government in June 1977: "The Jewish people has an eternal
historic right to the Land of Israel. The inalienable legacy of our forefathers...,"
and in his party's platform: "Any plan that involves surrendering parts of Western *Eretz Israel* militates against our right to the Land."[12]

Primarily to avoid pressure regarding a comprehensive agreement, or, more
specifically, concessions on the West Bank, Begin was interested in an agreement with Egypt. For Begin, Sinai was not an integral part of Eretz Israel; as a
member of the government following the 1967 war, he had supported the decision to return the Sinai (without Gaza), to the Egyptians.[13] Now in power, he
returned to this idea, believing that peace with Egypt (or Syria) would weaken
the challengers to Israeli control over the West Bank, be they Jordan or the
Palestinians.[14] Furthermore, an agreement with Egypt could be presented
(and eventually was) as Israeli fulfillment of the withdrawal demand in UNSC
resolution 242 (because the resolution did not explicitly state either "all" or
even "the" territories occupied in 1967). Additionally, Begin believed that

Egypt constituted an existential threat to Israel, but without Egypt any Arab assault would be seriously weakened or even prevented.

Two parallel diplomatic paths were initiated. One path consisted of official talks conducted by the United States with the Egyptians and with the Israelis, which included visits to the region by Secretary of State Cyrus Vance (in February and August 1977). These talks were part of the preparations for a resumed Geneva, and they were most contentious with regard to procedures and especially what form, if any, Palestinian participation would take. However, these preparatory efforts also focused numerous times on the nature of an Egyptian-Israeli peace agreement. Sadat told the Americans that the agreement should be reached before convening in Geneva, where it was to be signed, and he further asserted that if Egypt were to reach such an agreement, Syria would quickly follow. He actually presented the Americans with a draft treaty during Vance's visit in August 1977.[15] Quandt has reported that the two foreign ministers, Ismail Fahmy of Egypt and Moshe Dayan of Israel, were a bit more forthcoming in these meetings than their respective leaders.[16] Yet there are reports that a certain degree of warmth developed between Carter and Begin, as well as Carter and Sadat, in the course of the 1977 meetings.

The second path was Begin's preferred way. Presenting his government to the Knesset in June 1977, he called upon Sadat, King Hussein, and Hafiz al Asad to meet with him, "in our capitals or on neutral soil, in public or away from the spotlights of publicity,"[17] And he indeed followed this by seeking a personal meeting with Sadat. He used a back channel as well as third-party intermediaries to determine if, and under what conditions, the two leaders might reach an agreement. Begin informed the Americans that he was seeking direct talks with Egypt (and Syria), though he apparently did not keep them informed of the meetings as they took place. In July, Begin dispatched the head of the Mossad to meet with an emissary of Sadat's in Morocco, and he himself raised the matter in talks with Romanian President Ceaucescu during his August 25–30 visit to Romania.[18] Other intermediaries, especially King Hassan of Morocco and Austrian prime minister Kreisky, played a role as well. For his part, Sadat apparently used these channels to determine Begin's intentions. Sadat demurred regarding a summit, suggesting instead that Deputy Prime Minister Hassan Tuhami meet with Moshe Dayan (who had left the Labor Party to join Begin's government as foreign minister). This meeting took place September 16, 1977, in Morocco, with the direct involvement of King Hassan, and apparently established to Sadat's satisfaction that a deal would be possible. Dayan insists that he did not promise an Israeli withdrawal from all of Sinai,[19] but Tuhami believed, and conveyed to Sadat, that this is what he understood to be the case. A second meeting was scheduled for the end of the month and reportedly went less smoothly, but there is no protocol nor mention of it in Israeli archives.[20]

For Sadat, these meetings were in fact a continuation of his prewar policy of linking peace with the rebuilding of Egypt. The war had indeed served the purpose of breaking the stalemate, but the progress exemplified by the limited disengagement and the Interim Agreement still left most of Sinai in Israeli hands, and the old "no war, no peace" stalemate threatened to return. Food riots in Egypt in January 1977 drove home the continued need for the economic and morale boost that peace might bring, and criticism was heard over what was seen by some as Sadat's squandering of the gains achieved by the war.[21] Yet, what stands out in this period prior to Sadat's historic visit is a general atmosphere of mistrust—with Begin and Sadat seeking assurances of the other's "seriousness," while keeping both the Americans (and also many of their own advisers) in the dark about the talks or at least the content of the talks. Their mutual distrust is not surprising given the history of wars between the two countries, and, from Sadat's point of view, Begin's decidedly hard-line public position and party platform. Neither side kept the fact of their bilateral talks entirely secret from the United States, but apparently neither provided Washington with any detail (in the Rabat meeting it had been agreed not to inform the United States). The reason most likely was that Begin and Sadat, each for his own reasons, preferred the conduct of secret bilateral negotiations to the comprehensive forum planned by Washington, and therefore both were wary of a clash with Washington over priorities. Thus, Israel and Egypt continued to work with the United States on the various difficult procedural issues for getting all the parties, including the Palestinians,[22] to open negotiations at the Geneva conference, while they secretly worked to eliminate the need for anything but a final signature on a bilateral peace agreement at the conference.

However, still a third diplomatic process was going on at the same time, and one which would justify whatever mistrust Israel and Egypt might have been nurturing regarding the Americans. Unbeknown to the parties in the Middle East, Washington and Moscow, as cochairs of the Geneva Conference, had been quietly working on a joint statement that would form the basis for the reconvening of the conference. The Americans did actually show the finished joint statement to the Israelis three days before publication, but no consultation was apparently offered or sought. When the American-Soviet statement was published on October 1, 1977, Israel responded as if surprised, but mainly it was angry both because of the content and because it gave the impression that the United States had worked out a deal with the Soviets that might be imposed on Israel. The latter was a long-time concern of the Israelis, expressed explicitly by both Golda Meir and Itzhak Rabin during the negotiations conducted before the 1973 war and repeated by both Rabin and Dayan in immediate response to the joint statement. Begin was no less suspicious, although he had once conveyed to Meir that he believed Israel could have its way with Washington because, as he told the Israeli Knesset upon his election, the United States needed Israel more than Israel needed the United States.[23] Having to accommodate the Soviets as well as the Arab states was of great concern to the Israelis, but Begin also saw the statement as a step that ruled out (or at best ignored) the bilateral talks undertaken between Israel and Egypt. And of no less concern was the Americans' agreement to what Israel perceived as a new position on the Palestinians by omitting any direct reference to resolution 242. Usually, Begin opposed references to resolution 242 because of the possible interpretation that Israeli withdrawal was meant to be from all the territories occupied in 1967.[24] The omission from the statement, however, was viewed as a way of allowing for PLO participation in Geneva, as Dayan explained in an interview: "We are going to Geneva on the basis of 242 and in 242 there is no PLO."[25] Moreover, going beyond resolution 242's reference to the Palestinians only as refugees, the American-Soviet statement introduced a new formulation calling for "insuring the legitimate rights of the Palestinian people." Thus, the United States was acknowledging that the Palestinians were not only a nation (people) but also a people with "legitimate rights." This still fell short of the formula of "national rights" espoused by Moscow, but it went further than any previous American position.

Sadat, too, was unhappy with the introduction of the Soviet Union in this major way. He had by this time disengaged almost entirely from the Soviets, having dealt exclusively with the Americans for the 1975 Interim Agreement and in the current round of Middle East talks; he was also wary of the backing Moscow could give the Syrians against Egyptian bilateral moves with Israel. Yet, Sadat had known all along that the Soviets would be cochairs of the conference. Perhaps, therefore, what was of greater concern was this clear sign that Washington was determined to have the Geneva conference—a forum in which Egypt's hands would be tied in deference to its Arab coparticipants, leading to endless debates and procedural hassles.[26] At stake as well, Begin believed, was the potential for success in the bilateral track already under way. In a message Sadat sent the United States on October 4, he urged the Americans not to do anything that might impede direct Egyptian-Israeli negotiations, with the United States acting as the intermediary before or after Geneva.[27] Sadat's concerns, however, might have turned to alarm following still another surprise from Washington.

Israel had responded publicly and angrily to the Soviet-American statement, at least indirectly employing a traditional arm of Israeli diplomacy, the American Jewish diaspora and the official Israeli lobby in Washington, AIPAC. The leaders of Amercian Jewish groups, organized under the umbrella of the

Conference of Presidents of Major Jewish Organizations, along with AIPAC, were engaged to sponsor a national speaking tour for Dayan denouncing the administration's policy; similarly, they issued public statements, including comments by Israeli supporters in the Senate such as Henry Jackson, and conveyed them directly to the White House. Presumably in response to this, Carter decided to meet with Dayan in New York in what became a decidedly acrimonious meeting, described later by Dayan as having been "brutal."[28] After some five hours of discussion, a U.S.-Israel "working paper" was drawn up, effectively burying the Soviet-American statement inasmuch as it briefly outlined almost entirely different parameters for the Geneva conference. For all intents and purposes, the United States conceded to the Israeli demands concerning content as well as procedural measures for the conference. If Sadat had thought that the United States would be an unbiased intermediary or even a supporter at a conference, he was sadly disillusioned now.

The Sadat Visit to Israel

In the weeks that followed, Sadat made his decision to meet Begin in Jerusalem.[29] He had already considered the meeting, as clearly indicated by the bilateral talks meant to prepare such a summit, and he had apparently considered various venues inside and beyond the region. He also considered and even publicly proposed an international conference—broader than the planned Geneva Conference—to take place in East Jerusalem, but he finally settled on the idea of the solo visit.[30] There was and remains much speculation as to why Sadat chose this path. Although he had preferred the bilateral track all along, he had also pursued the path of Geneva, presumably not only to please the Americans but also because that platform could be used, ultimately, to endorse a bilateral agreement as if it were a step toward other agreements rather than a separate peace. The interminable preparations for the conference, which itself promised only further delays and complications that would tie Egypt to the broader comprehensive Arab demands, plus the realization (after the U.S.-Israeli working paper) that the United States could not be counted on to provide added weight for Egypt vis-à-vis Israel, apparently persuaded Sadat that the time had come to take the bilateral track to its conclusion.

There were those, most notably his foreign minister, Ismail Fahmy—who claims to have been the first to know of Sadat's decision—for whom the idea of going to Jerusalem was due to Sadat's penchant for drama.[31] Indeed, drama would be part of Sadat's effort to deal with the psychological aspect of the conflict, which he saw as a critical factor. Announcing the decision in a public speech, to the Egyptian National Assembly, was less of a surprise than it appeared, for Sadat had apparently informed not only his entourage, but also King Hussein.[32] Having made his speech, Sadat sought formal communication with the Israelis through the American ambassador to Cairo, Hermann Eilts. Sadat employed this conventional diplomatic channel, receiving and accepting Begin's formal invitation via Eilts and the U.S. ambassador Samuel Lewis in Tel Aviv, but an unconventional channel was also used and is often cited as the new role of the media in conflict diplomacy.[33] In what was still an atmosphere of skepticism—at least among the general public—regarding Sadat's surprising declaration, Sadat gave an interview to Walter Cronkite for CBS television via satellite, repeating his offer to go to Jerusalem, saying, "I am just waiting for the proper invitation." In answer to Cronkite's question "You must get something direct from Mr. Begin, not through the press?" Sadat answered that it could be transmitted through the Americans. Cronkite pressed: "If you get that formal invitation, how soon are you prepared to go?" Sadat answered that he would go "in the earliest time possible," and when Cronkite pressed further, ". . . within a week?" Sadat replied, "You can say that, yes." Although this was aired on CBS, Cronkite also conveyed the content to Begin in an interview the same day. In response, Begin told Cronkite that "I will not hesitate to send such a letter [of invitation]." Thus, the media were added to the backchannel contacts and third-party intermediaries in addition to the official exchanges conducted by the Carter administration. All of these played a role, along with the indirect roles played by the Soviet-American statement and the American-Israeli working paper and possibly even that of the American Jewish diaspora, in making possible the direct high-level talks that both Begin and Sadat, each for his own reasons, had decided to pursue.

Although the preliminary talks had revealed Sadat's demands as no less than a full Israeli withdrawal and agreements with all the countries involved—conditions that Begin was not willing to accept—the Israeli prime minister responded immediately to Sadat's speech. Yet there were many doubters in Jerusalem, not least of which was Chief of Staff Mota Gur, who feared a trick, possibly a prelude to an Egyptian military attack. Even as late as the day before Sadat was to arrive, Defense Minister Ezer Weizman had to intervene by phone from his hospital bed (following a serious traffic accident) to prevent an Israeli mobilization of two armored divisions requested by Deputy Prime Minister Yigael Yadin (himself a former general) at a meeting of Begin with security chiefs.[34] Somewhat less critical but no less important on the eve of this extraordinary diplomatic event was that Israel occupied itself with the arrangements and procedures for the visit, without addressing the potential substance. At least two attempts, one by the chief of military intelligence and the second by members of the Knesset Committee for Foreign and Security Affairs, were rebuffed when the officials sought a discussion of just what Israel might or might not provide by way of concessions or at least responses to the substantive questions Sadat was likely to raise. Some members, in addition to the head of the Mossad (who had been privy to the content of the earlier encounters) and the head of military intelligence, argued that Sadat could not leave Jerusalem without some achievement—which should be discussed.[35] Shlomo Gazit, then head of military intelligence, wrote that he later understood Begin's refusal to conduct a substantive discussion: "Begin did not want to tie his own hands before the talks began. He realized that it would have been impossible to convene the government without its making such decisions."[36]

Skepticism notwithstanding, the Israeli government understood the magnitude of the approaching visit, and, indeed, Sadat's visit constituted the single most important element in the diplomacy that led to the Egyptian-Israeli Peace Treaty. It was the fact of the visit itself, the dramatic personal step by Sadat, that addressed the most basic and important obstacle to peace for Israelis: the psychological barriers, the deep-seated mistrust and fears, generated and reinforced by the years of war, hostility, propaganda, and incitement. Indeed, tackling the psychological barriers had been Sadat's intention in the symbolic act of coming to the controversial city of Jerusalem and speaking at the Knesset, seat of the unrecognized capital of Israel.[37] There could be no more genuine signal of peaceful intent than the willingness of an Egyptian leader to take the risk (political as well as physical) of such a trip. Indeed, this is exactly what the chief of Israeli military intelligence told his staff the day before the visit.[38] As Sadat explained it, "If indeed we wanted to get to grips with the substance of the dispute—with the basis of the problem—in order to establish a durable peace, I reasoned, we ought to find a completely new approach that would by-pass all formalities and procedural technicalities by pulling down the barriers of mutual mistrust."[39]

This approach was evidenced by the visit, but one other element was perhaps critical, contained in the speech Sadat made to the Knesset.[40] In the speech, Sadat repeated the usual demands for Israeli withdrawal from all the territories occupied in 1967, including "Arab Jerusalem," and the need to create a Palestinian state. He also said that he did not intend to make a separate peace, demanding a comprehensive agreement and resolution of all the issues. Nothing new or all that promising here. However, interspersed in this, Sadat addressed Israel's most visceral need for Arab recognition of the country's legitimacy as part of the region. Although Begin himself had maintained that he was in no need of anyone to recognize what was Israel's right to exist,[41] the idea that the Arab world would never accept the state of Israel was basic to the mistrust and insecurity that had characterized Israeli policies and beliefs since 1948. Golda Meir had said in 1973, "The Arab leaders pretend that their real objective is limited to reaching the lines of 4 June 1967, but we know their true

objective: the total subjugation of the State of Israel." And in her 1975 autobi-
ography she wrote, "I have never doubted for an instant that the true aim of the
Arab states has always been, and still is, the total destruction of the State of
Israel [or that] . . . even if we had gone back far beyond the 1967 lines to some
miniature enclave, they would still have tried to eradicate it and us."[42] Even
Itzhak Rabin had declared to President Ford during the talks for the Interim
Agreement that "no Arab ruler is prepared to make true peace and normalization of relations with Israel,"[43] although he had allowed that the situation could
change. And opinion polls tended to indicate the same pessimistic view of the
Arabs' intentions. In the decade before the visit, only a minority of Jewish Israelis, some 20 to 40 percent, believed that the Arab countries as a whole were
interested in peace.[44]

Sadat's speech to the Knesset, therefore, was designed also to deal with this
aspect of the psychological barrier. He did this when he advocated several
times "an Israel that lives in the region with her Arab neighbors in security and
safety," adding, "In all sincerity I tell you we welcome you among us with full
security and safety. . . . Yes, today I tell you, and I declare it to the whole world,
that we accept to live with you in permanent peace based on justice." And "as
we really and truly seek peace we really and truly welcome you to live among
us in peace and security."[45] Following the speech, in televised appearances
over the next few days, Sadat's repeated declarations of "no more war" re-
sounded for all. The clearest evidence of the effects of the visit was the stark
change in opinion polls; public attitudes on the issue of returning all of the
Egyptian territories occupied in 1967 were melted. According to opinion
polls, opposition to returning the Sinai plummeted from 39 percent in 1976 to
just 16 percent from November to December 1977.[46] And gone was the pessi-
mism regarding the Arab countries as a whole. Surveys showed that the belief
that the Arabs were willing to make peace jumped to 64 percent just before the
actual visit, and to 80 percent following the visit.[47] Sadat, too, felt the success,
commenting on the warm reception he had received driving through Jerusalem streets lined with cheering Israelis, including women carrying babies—
one may assume he knew that governments can organize schoolchildren and
party loyalists waving flags, but mothers with babies were almost certainly a
sign of genuine support.

On the substantive side of the visit, there was no real negotiation attempted,
though Begin asserted that he believed Sadat to be sincerely interested in
peace with Israel.[48] In his private conversation with Begin, Sadat demanded
Israel withdraw from Sinai and promised a UN force for Sharm el-Sheikh and
a declaration that the Straits of Tiran were international waters. According to
Begin's account to Dayan, Sadat also promised there would be no Egyptian
troops east of the passes.[49] Begin reported to the American ambassador,

Samuel Lewis, that it had not been clear from the talks if Sadat was willing to make a separate peace with Israel; in fact, Israel did not believe that would be the case until some months later. According to Begin's report to the Israeli government (cabinet), there was no discussion of the Palestinian issue;[50] in fact, Sadat respected Begin's request not to mention the PLO in his speech to the Knesset so as not to necessitate a negative Israeli response, though he did speak of a Palestinian state in the speech as well as in the talks.[51] Warning that Sadat would demand Israeli concessions, Begin told the government that Israel was much stronger and had nothing to fear from Egypt, but he quoted a saying that one should respect people but not trust them too much. He concluded, nonetheless, that he did not believe Sadat to be deceiving him.[52]

Once the heady atmosphere of the visit subsided, diplomacy shifted to the more usual pattern of meetings between state officials and direct communications between the leaders, although for these two adversaries such communication was by no means "usual."[53] The purely bilateral aspect was not entirely maintained, however. Although American plans for a resumption of the Geneva talks were shelved by December, Washington—and Sadat—still sought a comprehensive agreement, and Israel, for its part, tried to engage the Americans on its behalf. Begin traveled to Washington in mid-December, where he presented a plan for a self-rule arrangement in the West Bank and Gaza, announcing somewhat inaccurately that Carter supported his proposals. At the same time, Sadat organized what was called a preliminary meeting in Cairo (the Mena House Conference) that was to deal with the broader issues and invited the PLO, Jordan, Syria, and Lebanon, but only representatives of the United States, Israel, and Egypt attended given the strong negative reaction to the Sadat visit by almost all the Arab states. In fact, Arab states created a "Steadfastness Front" led in large part by Syria.

As early as Begin's postvisit meeting with Sadat on December 25 in Ismailia, site of a battle in the last stages of the 1973 war, the virtual abyss between the positions of the two leaders was fully apparent.[54] The issues revolved not only around broader concerns such as the Palestinians, Jerusalem, the West Bank, and so on, which Sadat was not willing to abandon, but also, more specifically, the question of just how much of Egypt's territory Israel was willing to return. Retention of airfields, settlements, Sharm el-Sheikh, and land access to Sharm were all part of Begin's "plan." Dividing into a military committee, meeting in Cairo, and a political committee, meeting in Jerusalem, the ensuing talks were far from easy, with each side publicly claiming progress while complaining, separately, to the Americans. The problems were not only issue related but also involved matters of style and protocol. Sadat felt insulted by Begin, whom he likened to a "shop-keeper" offering "nickel and dime" little proposals.[55] And Sadat's new foreign minister, Mohammed Ibrahim Kamel, actually left his first set of meetings in Jerusalem after Begin, in a toast at dinner, referred to him as a "young man" who did not understand history, implying that he was a poor diplomat. Israelis, too, had their sensitivities, with the delegation to the Mena House meeting threatening to leave unless the flags (of the other Arab states and the PLO) were removed from the meeting room and hotel entrance.

Sadat suspended the meetings of both committees after their initial failures, not, apparently, because of the Kamel incident but because he despaired of getting what he needed from Begin. On January 12, 1978, he told an Israeli paper that "Begin gave me nothing.... I gave him security and legitimacy, and I got nothing in return."[56] In the following months, each leader traveled to Washington seeking U.S. backing for his position, and Carter sought nobly to keep negotiations going by proposing formulations and also by trying to engage King Hussein and the Saudis. Nonetheless, little progress was made, and both Israel and Egypt publicly expressed mutual recriminations, and the American Jewish diaspora contributed its share as well. By the summer, following meetings in the United States with Dayan and Kamel and a trip to the region by Secretary of State Vance, the Americans came to the conclusion that presidential intervention was needed to try to bring the two leaders together. The decision was taken to hold a three-way meeting at Camp David.

The Camp David Accord

The Camp David talks have been amply documented, most notably Carter's own daily diary of the talks and William Quandt's authoritative accounts of the substantive issues.[57] The meeting was an interesting process itself, demonstrating many aspects of diplomacy as well as its versatility. Having discussed the matter with his wife (perhaps not the most customary approach to diplomacy), Carter envisaged the undertaking as "perhaps unprecedented in history."[58] Rejecting any press coverage (so as to minimizing posturing), the meeting would be what Carter termed an "all or nothing gamble" in which "three leaders of nations would be isolated from the outside world. An intensely personal effort would be required."[59] And in preparation for this personal effort, Carter assiduously studied psychological profiles of Begin and Sadat. In keeping with this approach, he brought his wife and young daughter to Camp David; Rosalynn Carter opened the first meal there with a prayer—vetted beforehand by Begin.[60] In addition, the atmosphere was the opposite of formal diplomatic meetings; the rustic surroundings and cottages, the informal attire, and the absence of virtually any formalities were unusual—even disconcerting, particularly for the Egyptians.[61]

The objective of Camp David was to draw up a framework agreement that would serve as a basis for the final peace accord. In essence it was to resolve the many issues already hotly contested between the two countries. At Camp David, disagreements revolved primarily around Israel's earlier demands to retain two military airfields and the settlements in Sinai, but also the sensitive issue of Begin's autonomy plan for the Palestinians—both its parameters and, mainly, its relationship to the peace agreement with Egypt. It was left to Carter and the Americans to initiate virtually everything because relations between Begin and Sadat were so poor that they rarely met face to face after the first two days. Virtually everything had to go through the Americans, including phone calls between the cabins, and the Egyptian and Israeli delegations ate at separate tables with only rare social contact.[62] The Americans drew up over twenty drafts, dealing simultaneously not only with the Sinai-connected issues of the settlements and security measures but also with the content of the plan for the West Bank and the even more difficult issue of linkage between the two, as demanded by Sadat.[63] A significant, indeed critical, factor in the negotiations was the personal role of Carter as mediator, moving skillfully between each of the leaders separately, sometimes angrily—with Sadat as well as Begin. Quandt has described the moment on the eleventh day of the talks when Sadat, apparently upset particularly by Dayan in connection with the issue of the settlements, threatened to leave. Carter, who was usually more annoyed with Begin's hardline positions, nonetheless responded less than diplomatically to Sadat's threat, persuading him to remain. One participant, Boutros-Ghali, described Carter's tactics as threatening U.S.-Israeli relations when confronted with obstinacy on the part of Begin but using the danger to his, Carter's, political future and power when persuading Sadat to comply with this or that position.[64]

Boutros-Ghali and others on the Egyptian team were in fact very dissatisfied with Sadat's leadership—indeed exclusive leadership—of the negotiations, as they were often surprised by decisions. Sadat was said to be too flexible whereas his delegation was rigid, in contrast to Begin's rigidity despite the Israeli delegations' flexibility.[65] Yet, there were positive personal interactions between members of the Egyptian and Israeli teams, particularly between Aharon Barak, Begin's legal adviser, and Osama el Baz, Sadat's political adviser, contributing significantly to the ultimate success. They resolved the sensitive issue of just how the agreement should refer to resolution 242 (discussed later), and the Israeli defense minister, Ezer Weizman, and the U.S. secretary of defense, Harold Brown, resolved the issue of the airfields demanded by Israel (Brown offered to provide Israel with substitutes).[66] One personal intervention might actually have been critical: on the same day as Sadat's threatened departure, Begin received a phone call from Israel from his minister of

agriculture, Ariel Sharon, with the message that there was "no military objection" to the evacuation of the settlements.[67] Albeit a famous general, Sharon
was also known as the father of the settlement enterprise; for that reason he
had been given the agriculture ministry. Therefore, his call could and did make
the difference for Begin on the issue that seemed to be the last major obstacle
in the talks.[68]

Sadat was not particularly interested in detail, whereas Begin was literal to
the extreme. As a result of Begin's approach, another element of diplomacy
that played a crucial role was that of complicated, sometimes ambiguous formulations, "understandings," and side letters to accommodate the needs or
objections of each side. Some of these "solutions" later proved problematic, for
example, the case of sharp disagreement between Carter and Begin over the
period of a freeze of settlement building in the West Bank.[69] One compromise
even produced contradictory statements in the form of letters from Begin and
Sadat to Carter on the status of Jerusalem. Recalling an Israeli decree of 1967,
Begin asserted that "Jerusalem is one city, indivisible, the Capital of the State
of Israel," and Sadat wrote, "Arab Jerusalem is an integral part of the West
Bank." Additionally, in all of his accompanying letters, Begin used the name
"Judaea and Samaria" rather than "West Bank," and the term "Arabs of *Eretz
Israel*" instead of "Palestinians."

These were not the only ideologically motivated semantics. Begin was most
cautious with regard to any mention of resolution 242. According to Quandt,
"First, the text said that 'the results of the negotiations' should be based on all
the principles of UN Resolution 242, and the principles, including withdrawal,
were then enumerated. Begin argued that the wording should be changed to
read 'the negotiations' should be based on 242, not 'the results of the negotiations.' By this he meant that any party could raise the points mentioned in 242
during the negotiations, but that the final agreement need not reflect these
principles."[70] Nor, Begin insisted, should the principles be listed, including
"withdrawal." Although the Americans understood this as a "watering down"
to merely a vague reference to resolution 242, for Begin it was a reflection of
his sensitivity (actually opposition) to resolution 242 and his suspicions regarding the real intentions of Carter and Sadat (namely, to obtain Israeli withdrawal on all fronts).[71] On a formulation regarding Egypt, Begin's concern was
that, Sadat's Knesset speech notwithstanding, Egypt's loyalty to its Arab
brothers would take precedence over the agreement with Israel.[72] Therefore,
Begin insisted upon the inclusion in article VI of the final peace agreement the
phrase ". . . in the event of a conflict between the obligations of the Parties
under the present Treaty and any of the other obligations, the obligations
under this Treaty will be binding and implemented."[73] Throughout the Camp
David talks Begin also resisted mention of resolution 242's reference to "the

inadmissibility of the acquisition of territory by war." Aharon Barak and Osama el Baz managed to forge agreement to drop this in exchange for Begin's acceptance of "the legitimate rights of the Palestinians" in the autonomy plan.[74] To satisfy Sadat, an annex to the final Camp David agreement contained the entire text of resolution 242.

Of particular significance was the ambiguity regarding the linkage demanded by Sadat between the Israeli-Egyptian peace accord and the autonomy plan for the Palestinians in the West Bank and Gaza. Originally Begin's own idea, the autonomy plan adopted at Camp David left the final status of the area (after a five-year period of autonomy) open-ended, without any prior claim to Israeli sovereignty (although the Likud Party platform of 1977 said clearly "between the sea and the Jordan, there will be Jewish sovereignty alone. Any plan that involves surrendering parts of Western *Eretz Israel* militates against our right to the Land.")[75] This also meant, however, that there was no commitment to an Israeli withdrawal. Nor was there clear or direct linkage, in the form of conditionality or otherwise, between the autonomy plan and the peace agreement with Egypt. Instead of actual linkage, both "agreements" were simply presented in parallel. The Egyptians struggled repeatedly over this issue, but it is more than conceivable that the absence of linkage was entirely intentional on the part of Begin; he might have had no intention of implementing the autonomy plan. Indeed, when Dayan and Weizman later understood this, they actually resigned from the autonomy talks team and later from the government.[76] For Begin, the final version of the autonomy plan, ultimately forced upon him by the Americans (due to Egyptian insistence), was no more than a face-saving device to enable Sadat to make a separate peace with Israel. Having reportedly told Secretary of State Cyrus Vance that he would "never preside over the transfer of one inch of the Land of Israel to anyone else's sovereignty," he is said to have replied, when asked by Vance what would be the fate of the West Bank once the allotted five-year autonomy period ended, "By the end of the five-year period I may not be around."[77] Presumably with the same vague future in mind, this was the reason he was willing to include the phrase about "the legitimate rights of the Palestinians," stating later, according to one account, that it had "little meaning in reality."[78]

Yet, much of Begin's insistence upon side letters, ambiguous formulations, and niceties of language derived from a basic mistrust that the Arabs, including Sadat, would be willing to make peace with Israel. Even after Sadat's visit and his Knesset speech, with its unprecedented acceptance of Israel in the region, Begin was not fully confident Egypt could be trusted. As already noted, he told the government immediately after the visit, quoting a traditional saying, "one should respect people but not trust them too much."

This was just one more example of the basic mistrust and suspicions underlying Begin's approach. Weizman, who did trust Sadat's intentions, nonetheless told an interviewer later that he had told Sadat, "Do you really imagine that
because of [your visit] we can place all our trust in your hands? Today you are
president, tomorrow not. Israel's existence cannot be dependent on you."[79]
And, referring later to these talks, Elyakim Rubinstein, also a member of the
delegation, referred to Israeli mistrust, attributing it to "an inherited suspicion
. . . derived from Jewish history and psychology" that plays a major role in Israeli decision-making.[80]

The diplomatic compromises and "solutions" were not motivated only by
mistrust and matters of principle for the two leaders; they were also connected
to the fact that both leaders also had to deal with their own political interests
and domestic situations. Thus, Sadat's insistence upon the nature of the references to resolution 242, the autonomy plan, and the Palestinians' legitimate
rights as well as his view of Jerusalem were motivated by his claim to the Arab
world that Egypt was not making a separate peace with Israel. He had been
accused by the Syrians of planning to do just that even before his visit to Jerusalem; there was little chance that the Camp David formulations and compromises could change Arab opinion.

Yet, even members of Sadat's team at Camp David, notably Foreign Minister Kamel, believed that Sadat had "surrendered" to American pressure at the
meeting.[81] Kamel in fact resigned after Camp David, publicly expressing his
objections. This resembled the resignation in November 1977 of his predecessor, Ismail Fahmy, who had opposed the idea of going to Jerusalem on the
grounds that this would constitute de facto recognition of Israel. Fahmy
claimed later that Minister of War Mohammed Abdel Gamasy also opposed
the trip when Sadat had initially mentioned it to the Egyptian National Security Council on November 5, 1977.[82] Yet, immediately after the visit, according
to Weizman, Gamasy had publicly declared the event "a courageous step
toward a just peace."[83] In his report on the visit to the U.S. ambassador to
Israel, Samuel Lewis, Begin had conveyed his understanding (presumably
from Sadat) that the Egyptian army supported Sadat's move, and during subsequent negotiations, Weizman had surmised that the Egyptian military was
far more "open to Israel's proposals" than were personnel in the Egyptian Ministry of Foreign Affairs.[84] Indeed, Boutros-Ghali later wrote at length of his
and other Foreign Ministry personnel's dissatisfaction during and after Camp
David, believing that Sadat was interested only in the peace agreement with
Israel—regardless of the broader Arab world and the Palestinian issue.[85] According to Boutros-Ghali, "Sadat's one goal, it was clear to me, was to regain
Egyptian land—the return of Sinai to the motherland. All other issues were
secondary and could wait until the first priority was achieved."[86] When the

talks broke down prior to Camp David, there had been reports that even the Egyptian army was losing patience; Gamasy reportedly told Weizman, "You ought to know that certain officers are demanding that we harden our positions. And those demands are on the rise."[87] It later became apparent—though it was probably known to Sadat and his colleagues at Camp David—that both left-wing intellectuals and the Muslim Brotherhood in Egypt opposed any agreement with Israel, the former primarily because Israel continued to occupy Arab territory, the latter for reasons of ideology.

Begin, too, had to deal with domestic opinion. Public opinion was strongly in favor of making peace with Egypt, with some 75 percent of Israelis supporting the Framework Agreement achieved at Camp David, and even 70 percent supporting removal of the Sinai settlements.[88] In fact, when the process had appeared on the verge of collapse in the spring of 1978, Israel's first and only mass peace movement emerged to urge the government not to let the opportunity for peace fall through its fingers. This was expressed first in an open letter signed by 348 reserve officers and soldiers from combat units and then, on the eve of Begin's trip to Camp David, in a massive demonstration in Tel Aviv. Begin later wrote Israeli writer Amos Oz that he was not able to shake off the impression of the "100,000 rally," and, according to one account, Begin told Weizman that he could not return empty-handed in view of this public outpouring.[89] Yet, Weizman himself has written that although he was "charmed" by the movement, no cabinet decision was influenced by its protests.[90] Nonetheless, there was also pressure from within the government coalition, for the center party Dash (Democratic Movement for Change) threatened to bolt if peace with Sadat was not achieved.[91]

The major domestic problem for Begin, however, lay in his own camp, primarily the settler community and its main representative in the coalition, the National Religious Party (NRP). He also had to face strong opposition from leading figures of his own party, for example, Itzhak Shamir and Shmuel Katz (who resigned his position as information minister in protest). Opposition was expressed by some on the basis of security considerations; Moshe Arens—at the time Israeli ambassador to Washington—reportedly believed that Begin's concessions regarding security demands had been due in part to the pressure of the peace demonstration.[92] Others, such as Itzhak Shamir, opposed relinquishing any territory, viewing Sinai as part of the biblical Land of Israel. Indeed, for the most part, objections were based on ideological and, for the NRP, religious considerations, regardless of how they were framed.

One participant in Camp David, legal adviser Elyakim Rubinstein, later asserted that these potential spoilers were ineffectual in part because the press was not allowed to cover the Camp David talks, so pressure from these circles could not find its way into the talks. He went so far as to say that "the peace would not have been obtained if the media had been allowed to cover the [meeting]."[93] Begin did in fact respond directly by conditioning the Framework Agreement upon a Knesset vote regarding the evacuation of the Sinai settlements. Yet, he managed to undermine these same opponents by ultimately demanding a vote on the agreement as a whole, rather than the specific clauses.[94] Another way in which he sought to deal with potential spoilers was to explain, repeatedly, that he had made no commitment to withdraw from the West Bank nor had even used that term (rather than Judaea and Samaria) or the word "Palestinians."[95] On the whole, however, even his stature among right-wing members of the Knesset (MKs), based primarily on his role in the prestate underground struggle for independence, was insufficient to gain the support of his whole party or the whole coalition. In the Knesset vote on the Camp David agreement, only nine MKs from Begin's twenty-one member Herut faction of the Likud voted in favor (seven voted against, and five abstained), and only five of the NRP's twelve MKs voted in favor (three voted against, and four abstained). Even four prosettlement Labor MKs voted against the Camp David agreement, and three abstained. Although Shimon Peres, head of the opposition in the Knesset, voted in favor, he frequently expressed his belief that Labor could have made a better agreement, saving the settlements.[96]

Potential spoilers notwithstanding, the Camp David agreement was accepted by the Israeli Knesset, albeit only thanks to the votes of the parliamentary opposition, Labor, the Arab parties, and the parties on the left. Another two hundred days were needed to pound out the actual peace accord between Egypt and Israel. Some of the old issues resurfaced, mainly the matter of linkage with the autonomy plan for the Palestinians, and some new ones came into play, such as the Israeli resumption of settlement building in the West Bank and Gaza, despite what the Americans had understood to have been an Israeli promise for a freeze. The same pattern of American mediation and suggested compromises, particularly on the part of Carter, along with person-to-person contacts at the lower level (now mainly between the Egyptian prime minister Khalil and Dayan) were once again critical. These took place in an atmosphere of increasingly vociferous opposition from the Arab states and demonstrations from the Israeli right wing. Although the final vote in the Israeli Knesset was overwhelmingly in favor of the Peace Accord, ninety-five to eighteen, two ministers in Begin's government (one of whom was the "savior" of Camp David, Ariel Sharon) actually voted against the accord.

Sadat, too, had his problems among his own supporters, but his major opposition was that of his colleagues in the Arab world. With the signing of the Peace Accord, the Arab League removed its headquarters from Egypt, and Cairo found itself almost totally isolated. Sadat's failure to condition the Peace Accord upon a genuine link to the autonomy plan for the West Bank and Gaza—which resulted in the failure to even begin implementation of autonomy—simply confirmed the accusations from Syria and others that Sadat had planned all along to make a separate peace with Israel. Sadat had confidentially told Carter as early as April 1977, and often repeated it subsequently, that if it proved impossible to reach a comprehensive agreement, Egypt would have to go it alone.[97] As hard as he did, in fact, strive for at least some progress on the Palestinian issue in the form of the autonomy plan, it is difficult to believe that Sadat had not understood from the outset that Begin would not budge on this issue. The best Sadat could achieve was two parallel agreements, which, with regard to autonomy, Israel never implemented. For Begin, a certain risk was involved in giving up military airports and other security demands, such as a position in Sharm el-Sheikh or early warning stations in Sinai, as well as an ideological concession in evacuating the settlements. But for Begin, the risk and even the ideological issue—as well as the potential political cost—were worth it in exchange for the matter that was of ultimate interest to him, namely, avoiding pressures to relinquish any part of what he considered Eretz Israel. For Sadat, too, there was a risk involved, some might say far greater than for Begin. This risk was primarily of a political nature, within Egypt but mainly within the Arab world. In this calculation, Sadat put what he saw as Egypt's interests before those of his Arab allies.[98] And Egypt in fact suffered a degree of isolation and intensive recrimination among the Arab states for a number of years. Sadat was assassinated in 1981 by Muslim Brotherhood elements, although not entirely because of the agreement with Israel. Yet, inasmuch as it served Egypt's national interests, the peace agreement with Israel held.

Conclusions

One might call Camp David the Sadat-Begin-Carter gamble that became an example of successful diplomacy. Many factors set the stage for this success, including, in fact, unsuccessful diplomacy that ultimately resulted in the outbreak of war in 1973. The war itself became a contributing factor to the subsequent success—for Egypt it restored the country's honor, providing it with greater confidence in entering talks with Israel; for Israel it shattered some of the public's confidence both in the country's leaders and in its military might, spurring an interest in achieving an agreement; for the United States the breakthrough appeared to even the playing field for the pursuit of step-by-step movement between Egypt and Israel. Yet, it is most unlikely that any of these would have been sufficient had it not been for the leadership changes that occurred in all three countries before or after the 1973 war. These leadership changes carried with them a shift in the views of each regarding the

Arab-Israeli conflict. Sadat's leadership—his vision and policies since taking office in late 1970—constituted the first elements in the ultimate diplomatic success. Shifting from the pan-Arab aspirations of Nasser to a more Egypt-centered policy, geared especially to economic recovery and movement away from Soviet support to improved relations (and aid) with the United States, Sadat sought a diplomatic breakthrough as a way to regain Egypt's lost territory and place Egypt domestically as well as internationally on a sorely needed new path. Peace with Israel, with U.S. assistance, was key to this. The ascent of an ideologically motivated right-wing government to power in Israel (itself a reaction to the 1973 war) brought a leader, Begin, who sought first and foremost to protect Israel's hold on the West Bank. Begin saw agreement with Egypt as a measure that would weaken both regional and international pressure to relinquish this territory, as well as eliminate a major existential threat to Israel. The more acute sense of pressure was due to the leadership change in Washington: Carter's shift to (1) a more balanced attitude (regarding Palestinian rights, for example) and (2) a comprehensive approach—namely, a re-convening of the Geneva conference to resolve the conflict. In both cases, Begin responded by seeking a bilateral agreement with Egypt to reduce or avoid the pressures for movement vis-à-vis the Palestinians and the West Bank, which would be the major pitfall for Israel in a comprehensive peace conference. Sadat joined him in opposing the comprehensive approach of a conference—as a starting point—for fear of having his hands tied, perhaps indefinitely, by the demands of the other Arab states.

If it was the advent of these leaders, and their approaches to the conflict, that opened the diplomatic path, it was the diplomacy actually conducted by these three—the process and procedures as well as the individual roles (and those of their coparticipants), bolstered by sufficient domestic support to overcome potential spoilers, that led to the ultimate success. Various channels were used to prepare the ground as well as to move negotiations forward prior to, during, and even after Camp David.[99] These included third-country leaders as well as intelligence and military figures in secret meetings, along with open direct talks and, of course, Sadat's dramatic gesture in his historic visit to Jerusalem. American mediation was critical, particularly at Camp David, due to the very different personalities and negotiating styles of Begin and Sadat, but also due to the large degree of mistrust between them. Carter's personal involvement, along with innumerable proposals from the U.S. team, sustained the talks and provided solutions. These solutions were also part of the diplomatic success: the use of side letters, alternative and sometimes ambiguous formulations, and quiet commitments all designed to accommodate both sides were essential parts of the diplomatic arsenal. These were provided mainly by the Americans, but also in informal contacts between the Egyptian and Israeli negotiators and, in the case of Israel, with the political echelon in Jerusalem. On the whole, negotiations were facilitated by domestic support at home, including, generally, that of the military, in dealing with potential spoilers, though there were important "doubters" on both sides.

No one quality or step may be credited with the success of the Camp David talks, but some stand out. Carter prepared thoroughly and engaged personally, even emotionally. Sadat grasped the importance of the psychological aspects of the conflict for Israelis, and Begin ultimately listened to his advisers. The key was political will—a determination to succeed and therefore a willingness to find solutions such as diplomatic "devices," that is, terminology that could be interpreted as each saw fit, and, most important, a form of linkage that was at best implied. Some said, and still say, that Sadat gave in too much, primarily in connection with the absence of conditional linkage of the peace agreement to the autonomy plan. This was indeed Begin's "victory," for Israel received a separate peace with Egypt. Yet, many Israelis would argue that Begin gave up all of Sinai, military bases, settlements, Sharm el-Sheikh—down to the last grain of sand captured in 1967—and in so doing set a precedent for future agreements as well. Indeed, there have been subsequent attempts to emulate the Camp David model of diplomacy: direct negotiations with the assistance of the United States. Most notable of these were the 2000 Camp David talks between Israel and the Palestinians with the help of President Clinton, but all such attempts have failed. The failures suggest that the crucial factor for successful diplomacy was indeed the "political will" of the leaders involved, combined with the approach of the third party, yet many other factors of both structure and agency played a role, most notably the creative use of diplomatic skills and tools of the trade.

Notes

1. Anwar el-Sadat, *In Search of Identity* (New York: Harper and Row, 1978), 304, and in his speech at the Knesset ("Documents Related to the Peace Process Between Israel and Her Neighbors," www.knesset.gov.il).
2. *Foreign Relations of the United States (FRUS)*, vol. 25, 1969–1976, Arab-Israeli Crisis 1973, Doc. 28, Memorandum from the President's Assistant for National Security (Kissinger) to President Nixon, Washington, February 25–26, 1973.
3. "All this system [of Egyptian war threats] is the outcome of the fact that we are not ready to return to the former [1967] line. Apparently, if you take what Hafiz [Ismail] had said . . . the starting point is that they are ready for peace and a system of agreements and international guarantees etc. — all these on condition that we fully return to the former border." Galili, according to stenographic record of the meeting, cited in Uri Bar-Josef, "Last Chance to Avoid War: Sadat's Peace Initiative of 1973 and Its Failure, *Journal of Contemporary History* 41 (no. 3): 545–556.
4. This is discussed in greater detail in my forthcoming book, *Israeli Peacemaking Since 1967—Factors Behind the Breakthroughs and Failures* (Routledge, 2014).

5. Similarly, settlers on the Golan had to be evacuated when the Syrians attacked, putting to rest the idea that settlements provided security.

6. Asher Arian, *Security Threatened* (Cambridge: Cambridge University Press, 1995), 102. On Sinai, percentages fell from 69 percent to 36 percent just one month after the war and continued to decline steadily. The drop was somewhat less dramatic regarding return of Sharm el-Sheikh (from 94 percent to 86 percent).

7. The reassessment also included the suspension of certain military contracts and other steps. Once Israel agreed to the requested withdrawal (to a line east of the passes in the desert), the United States made certain commitments to Israel regarding U.S. positions (on the Golan, the PLO, and others) along with promises regarding weapons acquisitions, oil, and aid. ("Agreements Published by the Foreign Affairs Committee of the U.S. Senate Regarding the Interim Agreement of 1975," in *Foreign Policy of Israel—Documents* I [in Hebrew], Tel Aviv, Open University, 2004, pp. 336–340). Certain promises of a more general nature were also made to Egypt, among them a commitment to seek a second disengagement on the Golan and an agreement regarding the Palestinians.

8. Rabin did continue to explore the possibility of new talks with Sadat, and Sadat also told a visiting U.S. Senate delegation that he was interested in making a peace deal, but between the U.S. elections due in 1976, Israeli elections due in May 1977, and the outbreak of civil war in Lebanon, nothing of significance was undertaken on the Israel-Egyptian path.

9. One of the commitments made by Kissinger to Israel in securing the Interim Agreement was that the United States would not talk with the PLO until and unless the organization recognized Israel's right to exist and accepted resolution 242. ("Agreements Published by the Foreign Affairs Committee of the U.S. Senate Regarding the Interim Agreement of 1975," in *Foreign Policy of Israel—Documents* I [in Hebrew], Tel Aviv, Open University, 2004, p. 341).

10. To Rabin, during a meeting in Washington, March 7, 1977 (see William Quandt, *Camp David*, Washington, DC: Brookings Institution Press, 1986), 46.

11. Ibid. This quote from the Clinton, Massachusetts, meeting.

12. Colin Shindler, *Israel, Likud and the Zionist Dream* (New York: I.B. Tauris, 1995), 85; Likud Platform for the Ninth Knesset (1977), Likud Archives, Tel Aviv.

13. Israeli cabinet decision of June 19, 1967, to return Sinai (but not Gaza) and also the Golan Heights. There is conflicting evidence as to whether these decisions were conveyed to the respective countries although Abba Eban told the Americans in September 1967 that Israel had passed a message to Egypt, but Egypt apparently was not willing to give up Gaza. Egyptian foreign minister Fawzi met with U.S. Secretary of State Dean Rusk on June 21, 1967, but there is no mention of the Israeli offer in the record of the conversation. (*FRUS* 19, 1964–1968 Arab-Israeli Crisis and War, 1967, Doc. 327, July 27, 1969). A Jordanian source—Samir Mutawi, *Jordan in the 1967 War* (Cambridge: Cambridge University Press, 2002), 180—claims the offer was conveyed to the Arab states, but they did not respond because Jordan was not included. Abba Eban, September 25, 1967, in *FRUS* 19, Doc. 449, "Telegram of the Mission of the United States to the Department of State," September 26, 1967.

14. Aryeh Naor, *Begin in Power* [in Hebrew] (Tel Aviv: Yediot Aharonot, 1993), 99, 106.

15. According to Ismail Fahmy, this was in response to an American suggestion that a draft be proposed. Israel Fahmy, *Negotiating for Peace in the Middle East* (London: Croom-Helm, 1983), 217–219. It was agreed during Vance's visit that a foreign ministers' working committee would meet prior to Geneva, but the idea was dropped when Syria rejected it.

16. Quandt, *Camp David*, 92–93. This perception of Dayan was not to last.

17. Speech to Knesset, July 20, 1977.

18. Fahmy, *Peace in the Middle East*, 252–253, claimed that Sadat had rejected requests by various diaspora "world Zionist leaders" presumably to suggest a meeting with Begin.

19. The Moroccan channel had been established earlier under Golda Meir. The protocol of the meeting composed by the Mossad supports Dayan's claim that he told Tuhami that he, Dayan, could make no commitment without reporting back to Begin, which he did September 17 (Israel State Archives [ISA], [in Hebrew], 4313/4-a, "Report of the Mossad

of the Meeting of Foreign Minister Dayan with Deputy Prime Minister of the Egyptian Government Hassan Tuhami 18 September 1977." Yet, two reliable Israeli sources, former senior Mossad official David Kimche and then General Avraham Tamir, both claimed later that Dayan had in fact assured Tuhami of Israel's willingness to return all of Sinai. Avraham Tamir, *A Soldier in Search of Peace* (London: Weidenfeld and Nicholson, 1988), 17; David Kimche (*The Last Option* [London: Weidenfeld and Nicholson, 1991], 78) actually said this was put in writing.

20. Kenneth Stein, *Heroic Diplomacy* (New York: Routledge, 1999), 208.

21. For example, Mohammed Riad, *The Struggle for Peace in the Middle East* (New York: Quartet Books, 1981), 256, and Arabic sources cited in Yoram Meital, *Egypt's Struggle for Peace* (Gainesville: University Press of Florida, 1997), 139.

22. The role of the Palestinians the major issue, but there were also other procedural questions due not only to Israel's wish to avoid dealing with all their Arab opponents collectively but also because of Syria's strong suspicions that Egypt would try to use Geneva as a cover for making a separate deal with Israel.

23. Golda Meir, *My Life* (New York: Putnam and Sons, 1975), 322–333, according to the account of a foreign correspondent present at the session (Eric Silver, *Begin—A Biography* [London: Weidenfeld and Nicholson, 1984], 67), though in the official record of the speech Begin merely implied this.

24. He actually resigned from the national unity government in 1970 because of Israeli agreement to a reference to 242 in the government's acceptance of the Rogers's initiative for a cease-fire in the war of attrition.

25. Interview to Israel radio, October 15, 1977 (Ministry of Foreign Affairs, Historic Documents, 1977–1979)

26. See Meital, *Egypt's Struggle*, 163–167, regarding Sadat and Geneva.

27. Jimmy Carter, *Keeping Faith: Memoirs of a President* (New York: Bantam, 1982), 294.

28. Interview to Israel radio, October 15, 1977.

29. He took the final decision during his visit to Romania, at which time Ceauşescu assured him that Begin was "serious."

30. Sadat, *In Search of Identity*, 307–308; Fahmy, *Peace in the Middle East*, 255, 259–264 (Fahmy claimed the idea of a broader conference actually was his); Moshe Dayan, *Breakthrough* (London: Weidenfeld and Nicholson, 1981), 87.

31. Fahmy, *Peace in the Middle East*, 224; see also Adel Safty, "Sadat's Negotiations with the United States and Israel: From Sinai to Camp David," *American Journal of Economics and Sociology* 50, no. 3 (July 1991): 199, 285–299; Ibrahim Karawan, "Sadat and the Egyptian-Israeli Peace Revisited," *Middle East Studies* 26 (1994): 249–266. Fahmy claims Sadat told him on October 28 of the idea but that Sadat actually added the announcement unexpectedly during his speech to the National Assembly and even asked him to delete it from the official version (Fahmy, 266).

32. Sadat had Arafat flown to Cairo to hear the speech, but Fahmy says that this was connected with the preparations for Geneva, not the announcement of the visit. Sadat had, however, informed a meeting of his National Security Council on November 5 (Fahmy, *Peace in the Middle East*, 266). Sadat traveled to Damascus the day after the speech, but he neither expected nor received Asad's approval for the move.

33. For example, Eytan Gilboa, "Diplomacy in the Media Age: Three Models of Uses and Effects," *Diplomacy and Statecraft* 12, no. 2 (2001): 1–28.

34. Shlomo Gazit [at the time head of Military Intelligence and present at the meeting Begin called to discuss this proposal with the chief of staff and the head of the Mossad], "Israel-Egypt: What Went Wrong? Nothing," in Edwin Corr, Joseph Ginat, and Shaul Gabbay (eds.), *The Search for Israeli-Arab Peace* (Brighton: Sussex Academic Press, 2007), 105–106.

35. ISA, a-240/1, "Meeting of the Foreign and Security Affairs Committee," November 18, 1977; Gazit, "Israel-Egypt," 95–107.

36. Gazit, "Israel-Egypt," 106.

37. In his memoirs, Sadat discusses this, likening Israeli's psychological barrier to the "Australian Great Barrier Reef" (Sadat, *In Search of Identity*, 302–303).

38. Gazit, "Israel-Egypt," 98.

39. Sadat, *In Search of Identity*, 303–304.

40. Demonstrative of their skepticism, Chief of Staff Motta Gur and Acting Defense Minister Yigal Yadin viewed Sadat's offer to visit as a cover for war preparations (*Yedioth Aharonot*, November 14, 1977, interview of Gur); both actually urged Begin to mobilize two armored divisions. Begin's response was rather to call Sadat's bluff. (Naor, *Begin in Power*, 145; Gazit, "Israel-Egypt" 105–106.

41. Begin said this in a conversation with Carter, over the Kissinger promise to Rabin that the United States would not negotiate with the PLO unless the organization recognized Israel's right to exist (and accepted resolution 242). (Yehuda Avner, *The Prime Ministers* (London: The Toby Press, 2010), 426, and a second time, 440.) Silver, *Begin*, 167, has the full quote, in which Begin added, "God gave us that right 4,000 years ago." Begin also said this in presenting his government to the Knesset on June 20, 1977, but he clarified that he did want mutual recognition of "sovereignty."

42. Both citations, Meir, *My Life*, 365, 364.

43. Yitzhak Rabin, *Service File* [in Hebrew] (Tel Aviv: Maariv, 1979), 263.

44. Louis Guttman, *The Israeli Public, Peace and Territory: The Impact of the Sadat Initiative*, (Jerusalem: Israel Institute of Applied Social Research, 1978), 2.

45. Knesset, Israel Ministry of Foreign Affairs, "Statement to the Knesset by President Sadat, 2 November 1977." Available from http://knesset.com.

46. Arian, *Security Threatened*, 102.

47. Ibid.

48. ISA, a-4270/1, "Meeting of the Government; 24 November 1977."

49. ISA, het-tzdi 6911/2, "Stenographic report to Foreign Minister Moshe Dayan on Conversation with Prime Minister Menachem Begin; 21 November 1977." Later, Begin was to accuse Sadat of having gone back on this promise.

50. Sadat told Begin it was a matter for the Arab states.

51. Begin made the request on the drive from the airport to Jerusalem, according to his report to Ambassador Lewis (ISA, a-4350/3, "Meeting of the Prime Minister and the Minister of Foreign Affairs with Ambassador Lewis at the Prime Minister's Residence, Jerusalem, November 23, 1977, at 6 p.m."). In his private talk, Sadat asked Begin why he was afraid of a Palestinian state, commenting, according to Begin, that "the PLO will eat each other." ISA het-tzdi 6911/2.

52. ISA, a-4270/1.

53. This was the first topic discussed in the private Begin-Sadat meeting; Sadat agreed to the subsequent meetings and a telephone link (ISA het-tzdi 6911/200).

54. Actually already apparent in the first postvisit talks, between Dayan and Tuhami, again in Morocco (4082/3a, "Report of the Mossad ... on the Meeting of Foreign Minister Dayan with Egyptian deputy Prime Minister Hassan Tuhami in Morocco, 2–3 December," December 6, 1977).

55. Stein, *Heroic Diplomacy*, 242, citing remarks made by Quandt at a Washington meeting.

56. *Jerusalem Post*, January 12, 1978.

57. Carter, *Memoirs*, 326–412, and William Quandt; also Ezer Weizman, *The Battle for Peace* (New York: Bantam, 1981), 340–377.

58. Carter, *Memoirs*, 326–327.

59. Carter, *Memoirs*, 325, 327.

60. Weizman, *Battle for Peace*, 345.

61. Boutros Boutros-Ghali, *Egypt's Road to Jerusalem* (New York: Random House, 1997), 136.

62. Weizman, *Battle for Peace*, 343.

63. Howard Raiffa, *The Art and Science of Negotiation* (Cambridge, MA: Harvard University Press, 2003) has an analysis of the method of negotiation at Camp David.

64. Boutros-Ghali, *Egypt's Road to Jerusalem*, 150.

65. Ibid.

66. Weizman, *Battle for Peace*, 371. Brown put this in a letter to Weizman, September 28, 1978 (Quandt, *Camp David*, Appendix G, 387–388).

67. Weizman, *Battle for Peace*, 370.

68. The call was the idea of Weizman and Chief of Planning Gen. Avraham Tamir.

69. There was subsequent serious disagreement between Begin and the Americans, with Begin insisting he had meant it to be only three months and the United States claiming Begin had agreed to a freeze for the entire period of negotiations during the autonomy period. (Quandt, *Camp David*, 248; 263–264; for further details, see Carter, *Memoirs*, 397, and Benny Morris, *Righteous Victims* (New York: Alfred Knopf, 1999), 479.

70. Quandt, *Camp David*, 246.

71. Silver, *Begin*, 197.

72. Naor, *Begin in Power*, 186–187; Quandt, *Camp David*, 304–311 regarding this and Begin's suspicions over Sadat's addition of the words "comprehensive peace."

73. Foreign Ministry of Israel, *Israel-Egypt Peace Treaty*, March 26, 1979, http://www.mfa.gov.il/mfa/foreignpolicy/peace/guide/pages/israel-egypt%20peace%20treaty.aspx.

74. Silver, *Begin*, 197.

75. Shindler, *Zionist Dream*, 85; Likud Platform for the Ninth Knesset (1977), Likud Archives, Tel Aviv.

76. Dayan, *Breakthrough*, 303–305; Weizman, *Battle for Peace*, 384. For the demise of the post-1979 autonomy talks, see Yaacov Bar-Siman-Tov, *Israel and the Peace Process: In Search of Legitimacy* (New York: SUNY Press, 1994), 195–202.

77. Quoted by Silver, *Begin*, 203, based on his interview with Vance; also cited by Begin's aide Yehuda Avner, *The Prime Ministers*, 496, based on interviews and his own notes.

78. Weizman, *Battle for Peace*, 373. Begin accepted this previously rejected phrase (known as Carter's Aswan formula) so as to avoid any mention of eventual statehood as demanded by Sadat. (Dayan, *Breakthrough*, 110, 174)

79. *Maariv*, March 24, 1978.

80. Elyakim Rubinstein, *Paths of Peace* [in Hebrew] (Tel Aviv: Ministry of Defense Press, 1992), 93.

81. Mohammed Ibrahim Kamel, "The Lost Peace in the Camp David Accords," cited by Quandt, *Camp David*, 238–239. See also Safty, "Sadat's Negotiations," 472–484.

82. Fahmy, *Peace in the Middle East*, 266.

83. Weizman, *Battle for Peace*, 73.

84. ISA, a-4350/3; Weizman, *Battle for Peace*, 328.

85. Boutros-Ghali, *Egypt's Road to Jerusalem*, 133–240

86. Boutros-Ghali, *Egypt's Road to Jerusalem*, 46; also 133.

87. Weizman, *Battle for Peace*, 328.

88. Bar-Siman-Tov, *Israel and the Peace Process*, 150–152.

89. Mordecai Bar, *Peace Now: A Portrait of a Movement* [in Hebrew] (Tel Aviv: Kibbutz Meuchad Press, 1985), 31–32.

90. Weizman, *Battle for Peace*, 306.

91. Bar-Siman-Tov, *Israel and the Peace Process*, 150–152.

92. Morris, *Righteous Victims* 463.

93. Rubinstein, *Paths of Peace*, 99–100.

94. Morris and Shindler discuss the differences within the Likud.

95. Shindler, *Zionist Dream*, 96–97. See also Morris, *Righteous Victims*, 474.

96. Comments to the Labor Party and the author.

97. Carter, *Memoirs*, 310.

98. Until the 1993 Oslo agreement, which was in fact the same as the autonomy plan except for the elimination of the role of Jordan.

99. Particularly after Camp David, a back channel was used to overcome last-minute difficulties: this was done by telephone when Weizman used his friend Leon Cherney to convey messages to Carter through White House adviser Robert Lifschitz.

7

American Diplomacy and the End of the Cold War in Europe

ROBERT HUTCHINGS

Even after a quarter century, the events of 1989–1991 continue to astonish. At the beginning of 1989 and as late as midsummer, Communist regimes were in power across Eastern Europe, most of them seemingly well entrenched. By the end of the year, all were gone, swept away by a revolutionary tide that few had imagined possible. Several months later, Germany was reunified, ending the long division of the country and the continent. A year after that, the Soviet Union collapsed.

American diplomacy during this period has been widely credited with skillfully navigating the peaceful end of the Cold War in Europe, throwing U.S. support behind democratic change in Eastern Europe while managing relations with Moscow in a way that facilitated Soviet acceptance of the precipitous loss of empire. Even scholars who dissented from what they considered a triumphalist interpretation of the U.S. role during the period nonetheless credited American policy for its skill in averting a hard-line Soviet backlash that might have set the clock back a decade or more.[1]

The purpose of this chapter is not to review this well-told story but rather to extract from it the key lessons for diplomacy.[2] Its premise is that we should learn from our failures but also acknowledge our successes and learn from those as well.

Interpreting the Cold War's Ending

In the recent literature on the end of the Cold War in Europe, many writers credit Mikhail Gorbachev for purposefully or inadvertently creating the opening that made the Cold War's end possible. Gorbachev surely deserves great credit, but more for what he *refrained from* doing than what he actually did. Although he was clearly prepared to tolerate and encourage change, even radical change, in the Soviet empire, it is equally clear that he was swept along by events that he never imagined. The diary of Gorbachev's senior adviser, Anatoly Chernyaev, is instructive in this regard. Here is a particularly telling entry from May 2, 1989:

> Inside me, depression and alarm are growing, the sense of crisis of the Gorbachevian idea. He is prepared to go far. But what does it mean? . . . He feels that he is losing the levers of power irreversibly, and this realization prevents him from "going far." For this reason he holds to conventional methods but acts with "velvet gloves." He has no concept of where we are going.[3]

Others give credit to Ronald Reagan, conveniently overlooking the fact that most of the decisive events occurred after Reagan's term of office.[4] In January 1989, when Reagan's term ended, the Soviet one-party state was still intact, some half a million Soviet forces remained in Eastern Europe, and genuinely free elections had yet to be held anywhere in the region. What we were dealing with in early 1989 was the potential and the hope but not yet the reality of fundamental change.

Still other observers downplay human agency altogether, citing the growing sclerosis of the Soviet system, the acute crises developing in Poland and Hungary, and the magnetic attraction of a prosperous and more united Western Europe, among other factors and forces.[5] Clearly, these forces were the necessary preconditions for revolutionary change, but were they *sufficient?* Did the momentous events of 1989 and 1990 just "happen," or did diplomacy play a critical role?

Those building a simple narrative structure for understanding such historic turning points tend to omit, or dismiss as mere bureaucratic detail work, the role of diplomacy. Such approaches offer an incomplete and misleading understanding of how history actually happens. By succumbing to what the French philosopher Henri Bergson has called "illusions of retrospective determinism," and what a contemporary writer calls the "narrative fallacy"[6] that ignores the contingencies that might have turned events in a different direction, they are ahistorical.

The tension between structure and agency is a theme running through the cases in this book. Was it the essential structure of the situation in 1989–1990, or was it the behavior of political leaders and their diplomats that made the difference? The contention here is not that diplomacy was *more* important than the deeper structural forces at work, but that structure and agency were *both* important. Structure surely should be accorded primacy, because the relaxation of control from the imperial center in Moscow, coupled with the economic and political crises that had been building up in Eastern Europe and in Poland especially, created the preconditions that made revolutionary breakthrough conceivable. Without those essential preconditions, none of the momentous events of 1989–1991 would have occurred. Yet, as anyone following those events at close range during this period understood very well, the outcome was by no means foreordained. At several critical junctures, the transformations in Poland and Hungary, and later in Germany and the USSR itself, could have been derailed or suppressed.

The history of Communist Eastern Europe is replete with instances of failed revolutionary attempts: East Germany in 1953; Hungary and Poland, 1956; Czechoslovakia, 1968; and recurrent challenges in Poland, 1968, 1970, and 1980–1981. Those following the rise of the Polish trade union Solidarity in 1980 and 1981 remember how firmly many observers believed that the Solidarity movement had so thoroughly taken over the social and political life of the country that it had become irreversible—right up to the moment in December 1981 that martial law was declared, Solidarity leaders imprisoned, and the union "delegalized."[7] In the period under investigation in this chapter, but half a world away in China, many also held great hopes for the swelling democracy movement in Beijing's Tiananmen Square in the spring of 1989—only to see that movement brutally suppressed in the June 4 massacre. Neither the successful revolutions in Eastern Europe nor the ultimate suppression of China's democracy movement were inevitable. They were, rather, among a number of possible outcomes to the revolutionary upheavals of 1989.

The prevalent concern in Eastern Europe in the summer and fall of 1989 was that these hardened and brutal Communist regimes would opt for a "Chinese solution," as indeed some were actively considering. In East Germany, a regime-directed bloodbath was narrowly averted by a last-minute agreement among local authorities and demonstration leaders in Leipzig on October 9,[8] and in late November, just hours before the party leadership resigned en masse, the Czechoslovak defense minister's proposal for a massive military crackdown was narrowly defeated by the Communist party's central committee.[9] At year's end, the Ceauşescu regime in Romania did launch a massacre of demonstrators in Timişoara, only to see protests spread to other cities, leading to the swift collapse of the Ceauşescu dictatorship.

In short, this complex and consequential period cannot be reduced to a single cause, nor can it be understood as the inevitable denouement of broad and impersonal historical forces. The Berlin Wall did not "fall"; it was made of steel and concrete and could have stood for many decades more. The Iron Curtain did not "part"; it was cut by human hands, beginning with those belonging to Hungarian Foreign Minister Gyula Horn and his Austrian counterpart, Alois Mock, on June 27, 1989.

Preparation and Patience

Revolutionary change was in the air in early 1989. Mikhail Gorbachev had been in power for four years, ushering in a new and hopeful climate in East-West relations, signaled most dramatically in his December 1988 speech to the United Nations General Assembly announcing the unilateral reduction of five hundred thousand Soviet forces. Domestically within the Soviet Union, Gorbachev's early policies of glasnost (openness) and perestroika (economic restructuring) were cautious and incremental, exciting hopes and expectations of more sweeping change without ameliorating the deepening economic crisis.

Nowhere were Gorbachev's reforms more keenly felt than in Eastern Europe, where the winds of change blowing from Moscow emboldened opposition forces in Poland and Hungary particularly. In Poland, negotiations in February and March between Solidarity and the Communist regime led to the early April 1989 Polish Round Table Agreement, which promised openly contested elections that summer. This agreement, whose negotiation was being closely followed back in Washington, was seen as the most important harbinger so far of fundamental change in the region. Our judgment then—the product of considerable strategic analysis in the spring of 1989—was that if the Polish elections were held as scheduled, this was the beginning of the end of Communist rule in Poland, and if Communist rule was coming to an end in Poland, it was finished everywhere in Eastern Europe—including East Germany, which meant that "the German Question" had just leapt onto the international agenda.[10] Already in March, more than six months before the breach of the Berlin Wall, a National Security Council staff memorandum to the president made the case: "Today the top priority for American foreign policy in Europe should be the fate of the Federal Republic of Germany. . . . Here we cannot promise immediate reunification, but we should offer some promise of change."[11]

It was on the basis of this assessment that the administration concluded that Central and Eastern Europe, where the Cold War began, was also where it had to end. It was not just about the fate of these countries, important as that was, but also about the forward deployment of half a million Soviet troops in the heart of Europe, the forcible division of Germany and of Berlin, and a Soviet worldview that demanded a ring of "satellite" states on key borders. Thus, the objectives of American policy were to address and ameliorate these conditions, which went to the heart of the Cold War division of Europe. It was an ambitious agenda that aimed at overcoming the sources and not just the manifestations of East-West conflict.

The approach of the George H. W. Bush administration stood in marked contrast to that of the outgoing Reagan administration, which focused on U.S.-Soviet relations and strategic arms negotiations as the central foci of U.S. foreign policy. Indeed, the differences in world-views between the two presidents were substantial. Reagan believed deeply in American exceptionalism and in the unilateral exercise of American power in a world characterized by a Manichaean struggle between the forces of good and the forces of evil, with the dominant feature the U.S.-Soviet relationship. Eastern Europe as well as divided Germany figured in this world-view as objects and victims of Soviet malfeasance but not as international subjects in their own rights. Indeed, in light of all that transpired in Eastern Europe in 1989, it is noteworthy that President Reagan hardly mentioned this region—or indeed Europe at all—in any of his four summit meetings with Gorbachev from 1985 to late 1988.[12]

Bush, by contrast, was far less ideological and unilateralist in orientation. He saw the East-West struggle more in political than in ideological terms, and he was less fixated on arms control as the essential metric of international security. "Arms are a symptom, not a source of tension," Bush said in his first foreign policy address as president, echoing the words of then-political prisoner and future Czechoslovak president Václav Havel.[13] Bush also had a long-standing interest in Eastern Europe, reflected in a blunt 1983 speech delivered in Vienna as vice president, in which he challenged Soviet domination of Eastern Europe, and a dramatic 1987 trip to Poland, where he met with Lech Wałesa and other Solidarity leaders and pressed the Polish authorities to restore the union to legal status. In his first televised debate in 1988 with his Democratic challenger for the presidency, Governor Michael Dukakis, Bush observed that "one of the things that fascinates me about this *perestroika* and *glasnost* is what's going to happen in Eastern Europe."[14]

In seizing what he knew could be a fleeting opportunity, President Bush showed himself to be a bold leader—not in the sense of being a great strategic thinker, which he surely was not, but rather as a president who understood his moment in history and the role he and his office needed to play. His diagnosis was far clearer and more accurate than that of his predecessor, and he knew how to align his administration and deploy his diplomats accordingly.

Just as the administration inherited a European dynamic ripe for major change, it also inherited a hostile Congress deeply divided by the fallout from the Iran-contra scandal, an arms-for-hostages scheme in which members of the Reagan administration engaged in weapons sales to Iran to fund the anti-Communist Nicaraguan contra rebels in contravention of the congressional prohibition, via the Boland Amendment, against funding the contras. Left unresolved, this partisan divide might have complicated and impeded an ambitious European policy. Thus, the road to central Europe started in Central America, with Secretary of State James Baker's successful brokering of a bipartisan accord with congressional Democrats, removing an irritant in executive-legislative relations.[15]

A second essential preparatory step was to condition and mobilize the foreign policy bureaucracy to a new set of priorities. Large organizations tend to act according to established policies and procedures, from which they can be moved only with great effort. Foreign policy bureaucracies tend to carry over strategic priorities and policy objectives from one administration to another; the "talking points" used by diplomats to convey U.S. positions on key foreign policy issues often live on unchanged through multiple administrations. For the most part, such consistency is a positive attribute of diplomacy and statecraft, but it can also produce ingrained habits that inhibit bringing about major policy change.

This aspect of diplomacy is often ignored by scholars, who tend to consign the management of foreign policy agencies to a separate field of inquiry. The contention here, as previewed in the introduction to this volume, is that the two fields of study should be closely linked. Strategic decision-making by senior leaders operating at the political level, the management and coordination of foreign policy and intelligence agencies, and the work of diplomats are integral and irreducible components of the conduct of foreign policy. Foreign policy is conducted and implemented by hundreds if not thousands of officials, and effective diplomacy calls for coherence among the foreign policy agencies, consistency in diplomatic signaling, and careful consideration of policy options beginning well below the level of senior policymakers.

It was for these reasons that President Bush issued a wave of national security directives for policy reviews spanning every region and every major substantive issue. The actual conduct of these reviews was tedious in the extreme, as can be imagined by anyone who has ever engaged in making policy by committee, but the reviews served to signal a decisive break with the policies of the outgoing Reagan administration and galvanize new and creative thinking down to the lower levels of the foreign policy agencies. They also sought to restore executive branch coherence in the wake of the deeply divided Reagan administration, in which the principal national security agencies were running what amounted to their own independent foreign policies. The Bush administration drew criticism for the delays attending these policy reviews, but critics misunderstood the purposes behind them, which were focused as much on the internal management of foreign policy as they were on the topics under review.

This issue touches on more fundamental ones: the need for patience in the conduct of diplomacy and the importance of making time work for rather than against one's policies. It is a quality that comes hard for "can-do" Americans, but not every critical issue needs to be addressed hurriedly. In this case, with President Bush being pressured to "meet Gorbachev halfway" and seek a "strategic understanding" with the Soviet leader, there was a positive reason to decelerate the U.S.-Soviet dynamic and develop our own strategic approach. The "pause" or *pauza*," as it came to be known, also related to the critical importance of setting the agenda. The terms of U.S.-Soviet, and indeed East-West, interaction were being set by the Soviet side through a steady stream of "peace proposals," most of which were tangential or irrelevant to the principal issues dividing East and West. Instead of succumbing to pressure to respond to Gorbachev's agenda, President Bush and his key advisers determined to set a new, more ambitious agenda of their own.

The essential choices for American diplomacy at this juncture were (1) do nothing, letting the European dynamic unfold on its own, (2) seek a strategic understanding with Gorbachev, or (3) throw U.S. weight behind the processes of democratic change in Eastern Europe. The do-nothing option (1), not a bad one under many circumstances, was really no option in early 1989, because the forces about to be unleashed by the Polish Round Table Agreement were going to transform the European landscape in ways that required American engagement. Option (2) was embodied in the so-called Kissinger Plan for a U.S.-Soviet "understanding" on Eastern Europe.[16] It had a superficial attraction, which is why so many pundits embraced it, but its fundamental flaw was that it would not have worked, even if the United States could have mustered the utter cynicism of presuming to dictate the limits of change for those seeking a peaceful democratic transformation in Poland and Hungary. Eastern Europe was not some sort of shared "problem" for the United States and the Soviet Union to work out; besides, the leaders of the East European revolutions of 1989 were not about to await the convenience of the two superpowers. However obvious the choice of option (3) may seem with the benefit of hindsight, it is worth underscoring that this was not the preferred option being thrust on the administration by most outside critics, whose fixation was on answering Gorbachev's appeals.

Rather than being drawn into a tit-for-tat exchange of "peace proposals" with an increasingly desperate Mikhail Gorbachev, the administration determined to let him wait on us, develop our own set of well-considered initiatives, and challenge the Soviet Union to address the underlying sources of East-West discord. It cost us little to unveil our proposals in April-May of 1989, in a set of five interconnected presidential speeches,[17] rather than in January or February; indeed, we benefited by having the U.S.-Soviet agenda set on our terms rather than Moscow's. Of course, there was some risk associated with this delay—namely, Gorbachev might have been unseated for failure to gain a positive Western response to his initiatives. It was a risk we were willing to take, our reasoning being that if Gorbachev's grip on power were really that tenuous, we were unlikely to advance our goals anyway.

Engagement in Eastern Europe

Meanwhile, we focused not on the U.S.-Soviet relationship but on Eastern Europe. To lend tangible U.S. support to the Polish opposition led by Solidarity in the run-up to the coming elections, President Bush announced that he would visit Poland (as well as Hungary, where democratizing change was also under way) in July to address the first freely elected Polish parliament (Sejm) since the imposition of Communist rule.

In May I went to Warsaw and Gdansk (and then Budapest) to prepare the president's trip and to consult with Solidarity advisers about how best to use this trip, and U.S. influence generally, to advance their tenuous agreement with the Polish authorities. "We do not want you to support *us*," I was told by Solidarity adviser (and later foreign minister) Bronisław Geremek, because this would only mobilize hard-liners in Warsaw and Moscow. "We want you to support a *process*," engaging the regime of Polish president Wojciech Jaruzelski as well as the moderate mainstream of Solidarity. This formed the basis of our approaches to Poland in the late spring and summer of 1989, while we also worked to preempt potential Soviet opposition by effectively holding the U.S.-Soviet relationship hostage to Soviet acceptance of peaceful democratic change in the region. We also deployed a modest financial assistance package, coupled with additional West European, World Bank, and IMF support, so as to provide further incentives for political and economic reform.

One episode in particular warrants explanation. The terms of the Round Table Agreement specified that whatever the results of the elections, General Jaruzelski would remain as Polish president and the Communist Party would retain the key defense, interior, and transportation ministries. Yet, when Solidarity scored an unexpected landslide victory, there were pressures within the movement to claim their electoral mandate and displace Jaruzelski. This struck us—and more to the point, the top leaders of Solidarity—as a very risky idea, given the considerable coercive power still possessed by the regime and by Soviet forces stationed in Poland. We and the Solidarity leadership agreed that it was far preferable to show some patience by observing the terms of the Round Table Agreement, establishing a non-Communist government but with Jaruzelski in the largely ceremonial role of president, and keeping hard-liners at bay as the process unfolded.

It is worth noting here the critical role played by the U.S. Embassy in Warsaw, which maintained the closest of contacts with Solidarity advisers and had done so for many years. The U.S. ambassador's residence was home away from home for Polish dissidents, even during the darkest days of martial law. It was where Vice President Bush met with Solidarity leaders in 1987, and where countless congressional delegations met with opposition figures from Solidarity and other groups.[18] This gave us enormous influence—of the kind that can only be acquired by steadfast support over decades. In 1989, we relied on the embassy's well-informed and wise counsel, including its analysis of "the enigmatic, unpopular, but indispensable General Jaruzelski."[19] As one of the many cables back to Washington observed, "Most of the Solidarity leaders with whom we have spoken in recent days are convinced (in varying degrees) . . . if Jaruzelski is not elected president, there is a genuine danger of civil war ending, in most scenarios, with a reluctant but brutal Soviet intervention."[20]

One can question whether this deference to the terms of the Round Table Agreement was necessary, and of course we will never know how history might have turned out had Jaruzelski been unseated, but the charge made by some writers that the president of the United States actually preferred stability and Jaruzelski over democracy and Solidarity is simply preposterous.[21] Had President Bush wished to discourage democratic change in Poland, he would have visited Moscow instead of Warsaw and Solidarity's birthplace in Gdansk.

Jaruzelski's election, secured by the margin of a single vote, cleared the way for negotiations toward a new Polish government headed by veteran Solidarity adviser Tadeusz Mazowiecki, whose pitch-perfect combination of reassurance and firmness helped steer Poland through a very delicate period. In his first major speech, Mazowiecki declared that "we separate ourselves from the past with a thick line," but he also reassured those listening in Moscow that his government would seek "friendly relations with the Soviet Union" and respect "the obligations resulting from the Warsaw Pact."[22] Had the Polish opposition and the new Polish government—with full U.S. support—not acted as skill-fully as it did, the revolutionary year of 1989 might have ended right there. Scholars looking back at this period may have the luxury of believing that fears of military reprisals, emanating from Moscow or Poland itself, were ground-less; leaders of Solidarity, facing a situation that presented both opportunity and risk, did not.

Poland's breakthrough in the summer of 1989 sent a powerful signal throughout the region: if Poland, with its geostrategic importance in Soviet eyes, could elect a non-Communist government, what was left to prop up dis-credited Communist regimes elsewhere? For most of them, moreover, the option of a modest reform agenda had been overtaken by the dramatic turn of events in Poland. As an East German party official put it—all too presciently—in an August 1989 interview, "What right to exist would a capitalist GDR [German Democratic Republic, or East Germany] have alongside a capitalist Federal Republic [West Germany]?"[23] He might also have questioned what right to exist a Communist East Germany would have, sandwiched between a democratic West Germany and a democratizing Poland.

From this point on, events moved with bewildering speed. Not to be outdone by the Poles, the Hungarian government began dismantling the barbed wire along the border with Austria, opening an escape route whereby East German tourists visiting Hungary could immigrate to West Germany via Austria. This "escape valve" only heightened pressures back in East Germany. In late summer and fall, protests spread and intensified in Dresden, Leipzig, East Berlin, and other East German cities. As I observed in a visit to Berlin in early October, hopes of a popular uprising were matched by fears of a "Chinese solution." In a November 3 memorandum to General Brent Scowcroft, I reported that estimates of the next day's demonstration in East Berlin had risen to nearly a million, and that the U.S. Mission and U.S. Military Command in Berlin had prepared crisis contingency measures.[24]

Less than a week later, in what East German authorities later termed "a slight mistake," a vaguely worded Politburo decision to liberalize emigration procedures was interpreted—understandably, perhaps—by harried border guards to mean free access through the Berlin Wall into West Berlin.[25] Within days, the wall was being physically as well as symbolically demolished, and the revolutionary dynamic spread rapidly throughout the region. In stunning succession in the late fall of 1989, Communist regimes fell in East Germany, Bulgaria, Czechoslovakia, and, at year's end, Romania.

Strategy and Improvisation

Historic breakthroughs rarely follow well-marked paths. To the extent that scholars and policy makers considered the possibility that the Cold War might end someday, the presumed scenarios were either revolutionary upheaval (accompanied by East-West armed conflict) or a negotiated truce and evolutionary convergence in which the two sides remained in two different alliance systems. Neither scenario played out in 1989–1991. There was no blueprint for the self-liberation of Eastern Europe, no road map to German unity, and no file drawer labeled "what to do if the USSR disintegrates." No one imagined that hard-line Communist regimes that had already shown themselves capable of brutal suppression would collapse so quickly—in the Czechoslovak case, in just ten days.

Under such conditions, innovation, improvisation, and experimentation were imperative. We and our European allies created new institutions—some essential, such as the "Two-Plus-Four" forum for negotiating German unification (the two German states plus the U.S., Britain, France, and the Soviet Union), others short-lived and ineffective, such as the North Atlantic Cooperation Council which aimed at creating a forum for East-West security dialogue after the demise of the Warsaw Pact. We created ad hoc mechanisms within government, assembling the European Strategy Steering Group (aka the "Gates group," after its chair, Deputy National Security Adviser Bob Gates) to ensure that we kept our eyes on larger strategic goals even as near-term operational matters inevitably claimed most of our attention. To oversee the U.S. official assistance program for Eastern Europe, we created an entirely new mechanism headed by the deputy secretary of state and including the deputy treasury secretary, chairman of the council of economic advisers, and USAID administrator.[26]

Strategic planning was critical—not strategic plans, which suggest semi-permanence, but strategic planning as an ongoing process, including an ability to shift course abruptly as yesterday's well-conceived plan was rendered useless by today's new reality. Foreign policy strategists should take a lesson from Woodrow Call, the veteran Texas Ranger in Larry McMurtry's *Lonesome Dove:* "Though he had always been a careful planner, life . . . had long ago convinced him of the fragility of plans. The truth was, most plans did fail, to one degree or another, for one reason or another. He had survived . . . because he was quick to respond to what he had actually found, not because his planning was infallible."[27] For policymakers, the crucial test is *how* they react to unexpected events: whether the responses are haphazard and episodic, or take place within a larger strategic framework. Achieving the latter requires planning as a continual, ongoing process, with a disciplined willingness to discard plans in the face of new and unforeseen developments.

For 1989 and the first half of 1990, U.S. strategy toward Europe was immensely aided by the fact that this region was accorded the highest priority by the president, his national security adviser, and the secretaries of state and defense. (Thereafter, as principals became preoccupied with the Iraqi invasion of Kuwait and preparations for the Gulf War of 1991, attention was diverted from Europe, with a concomitant loss of focus.) These senior policymakers were aided by key advisers such as Robert Blackwill, Robert Zoellick, and Dennis Ross, gifted and disciplined strategic thinkers who kept government continually monitoring, reassessing, and updating our strategies as circumstances changed. Successful diplomacy requires the integration and coordination of all these elements: policymaking, strategy, organizational management, negotiation, and diplomacy abroad.

We employed useful devices like scenario analysis, thinking forward (to imagine a desired end state), and reasoning backward to chart a course that might take us to where we wanted to get (or avert an undesirable outcome). The "GDR Crisis Contingencies" paper cited earlier (see note 24) laid out five distinct crisis scenarios, each describing how the scenario might unfold and laying out the recommended diplomatic, public affairs, and (if any) military responses.[28] Earlier, an intelligence community report laid out a possible scenario for a revolutionary upheaval in Romania: a "brushfire of popular unrest" leading to the precipitous collapse of the Ceauşescu regime.[29] Although the actual course of events followed that sequence fairly closely, the scenario was not meant to be a prediction but rather a device to help anticipate a high-impact "wild card" development.

There was exceptionally close intragovernmental coordination, owing to the president's intense engagement, intimate knowledge of the machinery of government, and insistence on an orderly presentation of issues for decision, as well as the collegiality among Bush, Baker, and Scowcroft, which filtered down to the next levels of government. There was a close-knit National Security Council staff, which worked well with Secretary Baker's inner circle, and Deputy Secretary Lawrence Eagleburger effectively managed the larger State Department bureaucracy. Close working relations between the policy and intelligence communities, owing partly to Bush's prior service as director of Central Intelligence and Bob Gates's as deputy director of Central Intelligence, were useful in the diplomacy of German unification, as we on the policy side commissioned a wide range of analysis from the CIA's Office of European Analysis.[30] The intelligence–policy nexus was not perfect, particularly as regards Soviet analysis, but it was a substantial improvement over the highly politicized relationship under Reagan and the benign neglect of intelligence under Clinton.

The breach of the Berlin Wall the night of November 9–10, 1989, changed everything. Up until that point, even the dramatic developments in Poland and Hungary were tentative and reversible. Soviet forces were still stationed in Eastern Europe, and the other countries in the region had not yet experienced a revolutionary breakthrough. But the opening of the Berlin Wall made it clear that the entire structure of the Soviet empire in Eastern Europe was now up for grabs. The stakes could hardly have been higher.

On November 20, just ten days after the fall of the Berlin Wall, I forwarded to Brent Scowcroft a detailed ten-page strategy paper (the product of a restricted interagency group) entitled "Handling the German Question" in preparation for the president's early December meeting with Gorbachev off the coast of Malta. It is a fascinating document, now declassified in full, which laid out a comprehensive strategy for American diplomacy.[31] It began with a careful delineation of Soviet, British, French, and German interests. "Because they are constantly undergoing self-criticism and reexamination, Soviet interests are perhaps hardest to define," the paper argued. "The Soviet Union seems to be endorsing progress toward democracy in the GDR, while continuing to exclude the possibility of reunification . . . [though] one cannot exclude that the force of events might lead [Gorbachev] in this direction." The paper then explored a range of outcomes—a two-state solution, some form of confederation, and a united, federal Germany—along with ways of steering a process toward unification despite the inherent unpredictability of the fast-moving dynamic.

After Chancellor Kohl's November 28 "ten-point" speech outlining a pathway to unification—causing alarm in Moscow, London, Paris, and other capitals—we further developed the strategy, concluding that a "gradual, step-by-step" approach would be the best way of reassuring an increasingly anxious Soviet leadership and securing Soviet acquiescence. (It was also necessary to reassure and also constrain the French and British, who were colluding with each other and with Moscow to impede what they considered a headlong rush to unification.) Accordingly, in a statement the day after the ten-point speech, Secretary Baker underscored that this should be a "peaceful, gradual . . . step-by-step process" within the context of "Germany's continuing alignment with NATO and an increasingly integrated European Community."[32] These same principles, give or take a few words here or there, were endorsed by European Community and NATO leaders in their mid-December summit meetings.

Yet, these carefully developed plans were very promptly overtaken by events, owing to the virtual implosion of the East German state. On January 19, 1990, National Security Council Senior Director Robert Blackwill sent a memo to General Scowcroft that began, "I am worried from where I sit that events in Europe are threatening the policy framework we worked so hard to construct last year." He continued, in vintage Blackwill style, dripping with sarcasm: "Meanwhile, we seem to be proceeding with business as usual— . . . extended interagency disputes on issues too small to be seen without the aid of a magnifying glass, routine and episodic exchanges with our allies, etc."[33] In a January 26 memo to Scowcroft, I also stressed that the plans we had laid out the previous month were "fast being overtaken by events. Reunification is coming rapidly, not gradually and step by step." I offered a new plan that replaced "gradual and step by step" with "the faster the better"—taking stock of the new situation and devising a new strategy to allow time to work for us.[34] Deliberate acceleration like this can sometimes backfire, but in this case the risks were manageable, inasmuch as all we needed from Moscow was passive acquiescence, meaning that there were few opportunities for effective blocking actions.

On January 30, we forwarded to the president an almost identical document entitled "A Strategy for German Unification."[35] It repeated that "unification is coming rapidly, not 'gradually and step by step,' and the process will not await 'an increasingly integrated European Community.'" The memo went on to explain "why we cannot leave it to the Europeans" and outlined three dangers that needed to be offset: a Soviet *Nyet*, preemptive West German actions, and the isolation the Federal Republic of Germany if it were forced by its allies to go it alone (*Alleingang*). The strategy laid out eight principles to guide U.S. policy, beginning with U.S. support for "rapid and orderly unification."

Policymakers are typically reluctant to revisit decisions already taken, especially difficult ones, even as evidence accumulates that the hoped-for results are not materializing.[36] Psychologists call this syndrome "premature cognitive closure," and it can vitiate many a well-laid plan.[37] As the Blackwill memo to Scowcroft cited previously suggests, we at senior staff level encountered such resistance in early 1990 and had to work for the better part of a month to overcome it. The senior levels of government, starting with President Bush, had expended great effort to implement the "gradual, step-by-step" strategy, from our response to Kohl's ten-point plan, Bush's discussions with Gorbachev off the coast of Malta, and his and Baker's strenuous negotiations at the NATO summit in early December. Understandably, they were not easily persuaded that these huge efforts, which their senior staff had so insistently urged on them, were now to be replaced by a very different approach. It took half a dozen memos and an equal number of face-to-face meetings to successfully make the case to Scowcroft and Bush, with Baker's advisers making similar overtures to him. It is not that Bush, Baker, and Scowcroft were closed to new ideas, but that they were always and appropriately hesitant to accept at face value the latest new proposal coming from their senior staffs.

To return to the general point: the best antidote to the danger of premature cognitive closure is to develop a rigorous decision-making process that includes regular and disciplined review to determine whether the stated objectives and strategies are in fact achieving the expected results—and to take appropriate action if they are not.[38] In this case, we made an almost 180-degree turn from the strategy we had put in place just a few months before.

Negotiation: The Diplomacy of German Unification

The 329 days between the fall of the Berlin Wall on November 10, 1989, and the formal achievement of German unity on October 3, 1990, have been described as the most intensive period of bilateral and multilateral negotiation in modern history. The most critical events are shown in Figure 7.1. In the

Nov. 9, 1989: the Berlin Wall comes down

Soviet, British, French try to invoke Four Power authority

Nov. 28: Kohl's "ten-point" speech

Dec. 2 – 3: Bush and Gorbachev meet off Malta

NATO, EU support goal of unification as "step-by-step" process

Dec. '89 – Jan. '90: East German state implodes

Feb. 13: creation of the "Two-Plus-Four"

March 18: East Germans vote for unity

May 30 – June 2: Bush-Gorbachev summit in Washington

July 5 – 6: NATO declares a "transformed North Atlantic alliance"

July 16: Gorbachev and Kohl agree on united Germany (in NATO)

Sep 12: treaty on German unification signed in Moscow

Oct. 3: East and West Germany unite

Figure 7.1 Chronology of German Unification, 1989–90.

summer of 1990, according to Karl Kaiser's count, President Bush and Chancellor Kohl met four times, and Secretary Baker met his West German and Soviet counterparts 11 and 10 times, respectively.[39] There were, as well, countless telephone calls from Bush and Baker to their Soviet and European counterparts.

Alexander Moens, in his analysis of American diplomacy during the period, identified four points at which it was critical: "First, it shielded Chancellor Kohl in early December 1989, when he jumped ahead of other world leaders on the unification issue. Second, it committed France, the UK and the USSR to the Two-Plus-Four negotiating framework in February 1990. Third, it forged a common Western position on German membership in NATO in late February. Fourth, it brokered a package of guarantees in May and June that led the USSR to accept the idea of a united Germany being in NATO."[40] As then German foreign minister Hans-Dietrich Genscher later put it, "If America had so much as hesitated . . . we could have stood on our heads" and gotten nowhere.[41]

These negotiations have been well covered from the U.S., West German, and Soviet perspectives, and to a lesser extent from the French and British, but the existing narratives have not analyzed the negotiations from the perspective of negotiation theory. This section attempts to do so—to extract from this period some general lessons for the conduct of bilateral and multilateral negotiations.

Inasmuch as there had been no peace treaty after World War II, the four wartime allies—Britain, France, the Soviet Union, and the United States—continued to exercise legal rights and responsibilities in divided Berlin and divided Germany that had to be discharged before German unification could be accomplished. This authority also gave the Four Powers numerous opportunities to interfere, which British, French, and, of course, Soviet leaders were actively doing in late 1989 and early 1990. Many other countries, notably Poland, also had a strong stake in the outcome.

In the immediate aftermath of the fall of the Berlin Wall, only the United States among the four wartime allies welcomed and supported unification. British prime minister Margaret Thatcher colluded with French president François Mitterrand in hopes of forging an "Anglo-French axis," and both conspired with Gorbachev.[42] Thatcher, we now know from the Soviet minutes of her meeting with Gorbachev on September 24, told him that "Britain and Western Europe are not interested in the unification of Germany. The words written in the NATO communique may sound different, but disregard them."[43] In telephone calls and a meeting conspicuously held in Kiev, Mitterrand likewise tried to enlist Soviet support to slow down and impede unification in the period immediately after the fall of the Berlin Wall.[44]

To begin breaking down British, French, and Soviet resistance, timing and sequence were critical. First, we needed to forge the closest possible relationship with West Germany—not as easy or automatic as outside observers imagined.[45] Then, we needed to neutralize French and British opposition by negotiating a set of principles endorsed by the whole of NATO. Only at the end of the process, and after securing the support of the East Europeans as well, would we engage Moscow. This strategy, also known as "salami tactics," involved peeling or slicing away opponents one by one, developing cross-cutting coalitions to counter blocking coalitions of the kind that were developing among London, Paris, and Moscow.

One of the fundamentals of negotiating strategy is to negotiate interests rather than positions.[46] This was particularly critical in this case, because as Figure 7.2 illustrates, U.S. and Soviet positions were utterly antithetical. As we probed, however, we discovered that the underlying Soviet interests, while problematic, were neither unreasonable nor irreconcilable. For example, Foreign Minister Eduard Shevardnadze's "seven questions," delivered in a speech

Positions

US	USSR
Germany should be united.	Germany should stay divided.
... should regain sovereignty.	... should be subject to 4 powers.
... should stay in NATO.	... should not remain in NATO.

Interests

US	USSR
Germany in cooperative	Soviet security not compromised
security order	USSR should not be humiliated
US in Europe as stabilizer	Avoid chaos in Eastern Europe
Avert "another Versailles"	Avoid domestic backlash in USSR

Figure 7.2 Analysis of the Negotiations: Positions v. Interests.

in late December, constituted an expression of fundamental Soviet interests, to which Secretary Baker responded with "nine assurances" aimed at addressing those concerns. In short, we worked to solve the other side's problems while advancing our own goals—another principle that is familiar in the popular literature on negotiation.[47]

Negotiating on the basis of interests demands a high level of understanding of the other side's needs, objectives, and likely tactics. Before crucial summit meetings, we would typically include in the president's briefing material a section called "Gorbachev's Talking Points" or "Kohl's Talking Points," anticipating the arguments and even the language the president's counterpart would use. Similarly, the key memorandum cited earlier, "Handling the German Question," began with four single-spaced pages examining the interests of all the key protagonists—including the United States—before outlining the strategy and tactics for pursuing our goals.

A key element of the "getting to yes" negotiating method is the concept of BATNA ("best alternative to a negotiated agreement"), which holds that the negotiating team that has a better alternative outside the negotiating framework has a distinct advantage in the negotiations. Our task during the diplomacy of German unification was to improve our BATNA while diminishing

Moscow's, to make it harder for Soviet leaders to say *"Nyet"* while making it easier for them to say *"Da"*—by foreclosing their options to cut separate deals or simply to stall and stonewall. This is where we tried to make time work in our favor, believing that "the faster the better" approach would present Gorbachev with a series of faits accomplis that would make resistance increasingly difficult.

In the prenegotiation phase—from November 1989 to early February 1990, it was essential to control the number of participants and the scope of the negotiating process. We resisted invoking the Four Powers, not only for reasons of principle but also as a matter of political arithmetic, because we could see ourselves outnumbered three to one. At the other end of the spectrum, we also resisted Soviet (and other) calls for a pan-European peace conference to ratify or approve German unification, fearing that such a forum would be open season for any country with a grievance. The Two-Plus-Four process was right on principled grounds—ensuring that the two German states had pride of place in determining their own national future—and was also one that both diluted the prerogatives of the four powers and excluded other countries from matters that were not really theirs to decide. Our position, presented by Secretary Baker at the first Two-Plus-Four meeting on May 18 and repeated many times thereafter, was that the purpose of the Two-Plus-Four talks was to "facilitate the unity of the two Germanys as the German people decide their future." "The timing and form of unification are internal issues to be decided by the Germans themselves," we insisted. "Once a unified and democratic Germany exists . . ., there will be no basis for any remaining [Four Power] rights."[48]

By "framing" the key issues in this way, we aimed at altering the perceptions of Soviet (and other) leaders and steering them toward the outcomes we hoped to achieve. As negotiations proceeded, the role of information—providing, withholding, "spinning"—was likewise essential to maintaining a pro-unification coalition and helping Gorbachev manage hardline critics at home. After every important development, we communicated intensely with the Germans, our other allies, the East European governments, and others, tailoring each message to address the recipient's specific issues and concerns. After the critical NATO Summit in July 1990, President Bush and Secretary Baker both sent immediate messages to their Soviet counterparts, aimed at helping them preempt hardline critics at the Communist Party Congress with news that NATO was in fact transforming in ways consistent with Soviet security interests. (Whether this was an accurate characterization is another, more complicated matter. It is not true that the United States pledged not to expand NATO eastward into Eastern Europe,[49] but it is fair to say that we did not transform the institution into one that offered Moscow a real seat at the table.)

Two-level games, a concept developed some years ago by Robert Putnam, also came into play.[50] This tactic, familiar in trade negotiations, applies to other forms of negotiation as well. One of the elements of the concept is that the latitude a negotiator has is circumscribed by domestic constraints. Negotiators on one side can work to broaden the other side's scope of domestic support—increasing the domestic "win-set," in Putnam's language—and so improve the chances of gaining important concessions. On the question of united Germany's remaining in NATO, we needed to provide Gorbachev with a foreign policy "win" so as to counter growing hard-line opposition back in the Soviet Union. The stronger Gorbachev's position at home, we reasoned, the more likely it was that he could deliver on his commitments regarding German unification. Thus, at the Washington summit in early June 1990, President Bush made the decision to buck congressional opposition and move forward on a U.S.-Soviet trade deal, precisely in order to give Gorbachev a "win" that he could take back with him to his Party Congress, held shortly thereafter.

We used normative leverage as well, invoking the UN Charter and the Helsinki Final Act, which affirm the right of countries to join and leave international alliances. When President Bush, at the Washington summit, asked Gorbachev whether he supported this principle, the Soviet leader agreed and then allowed the official communiqué to reflect that the two sides agreed that NATO membership would be "a matter for the Germans to decide."[51]

Negotiating virtuosity also played a role, and Baker was a master of the art. An example was the resolution of the final sticking point on the treaty on German unification—the insertion, late in the negotiations, of a clause that read, "Foreign armed forces and nuclear weapons or their carriers will not be stationed in [the territory of the former East Germany] or deployed there." We had long since agreed that allied forces would not be stationed in that part of Germany, but the word "deployed" gave us pause. Did this mean that NATO forces could not even enter that part of Germany in the event of some future contingency, or that Allied servicemen could not take their families there for a holiday? Would united Germany be half in, half out of NATO? At the final Two-Plus-Four meeting, on September 12, 1990, in Moscow, the solution was brokered by Baker on the spot,[52] via the device of an "Agreed Minute" to the treaty: "Any questions with respect to the application of the word 'deployed' . . . will be decided by the Government of the united Germany in a reasonable and responsible way. . . ." It was a clever formulation and indeed might have been a unique case in international law, whereby the interpretation of a key provision of a multilateral treaty was left to the sole discretion of only one signatory. Figure 7.3 summarizes the key negotiating principles that came into play in the negotiations leading to German unification.

Control participants, agenda
- ➤ German case: Two-Plus-Four negotiating framework, limited in number and scope

Information: providing, withholding, "spinning"
- ➤ US-German coordination; messages to stakeholders; countless bilateral meetings and phone calls
- ➤ Close coordination of signaling between White House and State Department

Solve the other party's problems while advancing your own goals
- ➤ Shevardnadze's "7 questions"; Baker's "9 assurances"

Cross-cutting coalitions to counteract blocking coalitions
- ➤ Use of NATO, EU to counter "Anglo-French axis"

Use of "salami tactics" to slice away opponents
- ➤ Sequence: first West Germany, then NATO and EU (to isolate the French and British), other parties (East Europeans, especially), only then the USSR

Making time work for you
- ➤ from "step by step" to "the faster, the better"

Division of labor
- ➤ West Germany (internal aspects) and U.S. (external)

Engage in logrolling (two-level gaming)
- ➤ Targeted key constituencies in USSR: June 1990 ("Gorbachev needed a successful summit, and we meant to give him one.")

Using normative leverage
- ➤ Germany in NATO? "President Gorbachev and I... are in full agreement that the matter of alliance membership is, in accordance with the Helsinki Final Act, a matter for the Germans to decide."

Figure 7.3 Analysis of the Negotiations: Applying Negotiating Principles.

Conclusion

It is a mistake to conceive of diplomacy as being defined by diplomatic virtuosity alone. Successful diplomacy, as this case study has tried to show, is the result of a large number of factors, including strategic design, decision-making, interagency coherence, alliance management, negotiating skills, and many others. At the end of the Cold War, Lady Luck played a role as well: we were dealing with a Soviet leadership strong enough to deliver, but too weak to offer effective resistance. American diplomacy in the period immediately after the Cold War was less successful, for we were dealing with a much more fluid and uncertain set of challenges for which the administration was not well prepared. But in the period 1989–1990, all our main objectives were achieved and far exceeded. The Cold War had ended peacefully—not with a bang but a whimper—with the states of Eastern Europe on their way toward democratic change and with Germany united in peace and freedom.

American policymakers are used to hearing that when something bad happens in the world, it is their fault, but when something good happens, they are not a factor. My contention in this case study is not that the United States caused the revolutions of 1989 or the unification of Germany; those developments grew out of deep historical roots. Rather, my argument is that the United States played an important facilitative role by throwing its weight fully behind the processes of peaceful democratic change in Eastern Europe, and that the U.S. role in German unification was decisive in ensuring that it came out right, with Germany united and its sovereignty fully restored.

Political leadership was critical in this case, but effective political leadership is not the same as personal charisma. American presidents in particular wield enormous political power by virtue of their office; personal charisma is an asset for certain aspects of presidential leadership, but many other attributes are more important. In this case, President Bush's leadership skill issued from his masterful command of his own government, his knowledge of and sense of efficacy on foreign policy issues, his understanding of effective alliance management, and, on a personal level, his enormous stamina, emotional intelligence, and disciplined process for reaching decisions. Scowcroft's style fit Bush's perfectly: he served both as key adviser and as manager/honest broker of a national security system that is widely considered the standard by which others are measured. Secretary Baker's exceptionally close relationship with the president allowed him to serve as virtual alter ego in his interaction with foreign leaders, and his steel-trap lawyer's mind and mastery of detail gave him the upper hand in every negotiating setting. In short, leadership matters, but the attributes of leadership that count most are not the ones most readily visible to outside observers.

Some of the elements of successful diplomacy at the end of the Cold War were perhaps unique to this particular setting, but many of those regarding strategic decision-making, policy implementation, crisis management, multilateral negotiation, and others are more durable and transferable. The elements of diplomacy covered in this case are particularly relevant in that they were tested during one of the most fast-moving and high-stakes periods in diplomatic history.

Notes

1. See, for example, Mary Elise Sarotte, *1989: The Struggle to Create Post-Cold War Europe* (Princeton, NJ: Princeton University Press, 2009); Frédéric Bozo, *Mitterrand, the End of the Cold War, and German Unification* (New York: Berghahn Books, 2009); Gregory F. Domber, "Skepticism and Stability: Reevaluating U.S. Policy during Poland's Democratic Transformation in 1989," *Journal of Cold War Studies* 13, no. 3 (Summer 2011): 52–82.

2. Robert L. Hutchings, *American Diplomacy and the End of the Cold War: An Insider's Account of U.S. Policy in Europe, 1989–1992* (Baltimore: Johns Hopkins University Press, 1997). The study here tracks with that larger work and adds to it some of the newer scholarship on this period as well as newly declassified archival material from the United States, Germany, Russia, Great Britain, France, and other countries. For other authoritative accounts on the American side, see George Bush and Brent Scowcroft, *A World Transformed* (New York: Alfred A. Knopf, 1998); James A. Baker III with Thomas M. DeFrank, *The Politics of Diplomacy: Revolution, War & Peace, 1989–1992* (New York: G.P. Putnam's Sons, 1995); and Philip Zelikow and Condoleezza Rice, *Germany United and Europe Transformed: A Study in Statecraft* (Cambridge, MA: Harvard University Press, 1995).

3. Anatoly Chernyaev, *1991: The Diary of an Assistant to the President of the USSR* (Moscow: TERRA, 1997). Translated by Vladislav Zubok ("Making the History of 1989," #362, The National Security Archive). See The Diary of Anatoly Chernyaev, maintained by The National Security Archive, George Washington University, http://www.gwu.edu/~nsarchiv/NSAEBB/NSAEBB192/.

4. John Lewis Gaddis, *The Cold War: A New History* (New York: Penguin, 2005); Melvyn P. Leffler, *For the Soul of Mankind: The United States, The Soviet Union and the Cold War* (New York: Hill and Wang, 2007); Vladimir M. Zubok, *A Failed Empire: The Soviet Union in the Cold War from Stalin to Gorbachev* (Chapel Hill: University of North Carolina Press, 2007); Don Oberdorfer, *From the Cold War a New Era: The United States and the Soviet Union, 1983–1991* (Baltimore: Johns Hopkins University Press, 1998); Jack F. Matlock, Jr., *Reagan and Gorbachev: How the Cold War Ended* (New York: Random House, 2005); Tony Judt, *Postwar: A History of Europe Since 1945* (New York: Penguin, 2006).

5. See, for example, Stephen Kotkin, *Armageddon Averted: The Soviet Collapse, 1970–2000* (New York: Oxford University Press, 2008) and Charles S. Meier, *Among Empires: American Ascendancy and Its Predecessors* (Cambridge, MA: Harvard University Press, 2007). I myself made a similar point in a preface entitled "Gorbachev and Eastern Europe" to the paperback edition of my *Soviet-East European Relations: Consolidation and Conflict* (Madison: University of Wisconsin Press, 1987), as well as in my chapter "Europe Between the Superpowers," in *Turning Points in Ending the Cold War*, ed. Kiron Skinner (Stanford, CA: Hoover Institution Press, 2008), 191–217.

6. Nassim Nicholas Taleb, *The Black Swan: The Impact of the Highly Improbable* (New York: Random House, 2010), especially chap. 6. The narrative fallacy, he argues, "causes us to see past events as more predictable, more expected, and less random than they actually were" (p. 73). "So we pull memories along narrative lines, revising them involuntarily and unconsciously. We continuously re-narrate past events in the light of what appears to make what we think of as logical sense after these events occur" (p. 71).

7. I was deputy director of Radio Free Europe during this period and confess to being one of those who felt the movement could no longer be reversed—which perhaps made me more attuned than others to the tenuousness of Solidarity's renewed challenge to Communist rule in 1989.

8. Elizabeth Pond, *Beyond the Wall: Germany's Road to Unification* (Washington, DC: Brookings Institution Press, 1993), 112–120.

9. "Report of the Commission of Enquiry on the Events Surrounding November 17," published October 1990, as cited in Bernard Wheaton and Zdeněk Kavan, *The Velvet Revolution: Czechoslovakia, 1988–91* (Boulder, CO: Westview Press, 1992), 72. Czechoslovak premier Adamec's call for a "political solution" at that Central Committee meeting has now been declassified in full: "Speech by Premier Ladislav Adamec at the Extraordinary Session of the Czechoslovak Communist Party Central Committee," November 24, 1989, History and Public Policy Program Digital Archive, State Central Archive, Prague, CC CPCz record group, W-0154/89. Published in National Security Archive Electronic Briefing Book No. 22. Translated from the Czech by Todd Hammond.

10. Outside government, in an interview with Don Oberdorfer in early May, William Hyland made essentially the same point: "If there is some kind of new order in Hungary, Poland

and perhaps Czechoslovakia, with less of a Soviet presence . . . and liberalization inside the countries . . ., then the question is whether that can be applied to East Germany. And if it is, aren't you just a step away from the unification of Germany?" (Don Oberdorfer, *The Turn: From the Cold War to a New Era* [New York: Simon & Schuster, 1991], 346.)

11. "The NATO Summit," March 20, 1989, as cited in Zelikow and Rice, *Germany Unified and Europe Transformed*, 28.

12. The full transcripts of these summit meetings—Geneva (1985), Reykjavik (1986), Washington (1987), and New York (1988)—are available at the National Security Archive (http://www.gwu.edu/~nsarchiv/) as well as on "The Reagan Files" website (http://www.thereaganfiles.com/).

13. Hutchings, *American Diplomacy*, 28.

14. Cited in Oberdorfer, *The Turn*, 330.

15. Baker, *Politics of Diplomacy*, 47–60.

16. The plan and Secretary Baker's rejection of any "understanding" on Eastern Europe are described in Thomas L. Friedman, "Baker, Outlining World View, Assesses Plan for Soviet Bloc," *New York Times*, March 27, 1989.

17. Hutchings, *American Diplomacy*, chap. 1, pp. 6–47.

18. In spring 1988, I accompanied a prominent congressional delegation led by Senator John Glenn for meetings in the ambassador's residence with Geremek and others, who were then negotiating with the Communist authorities the so-called anti-crisis pact—a precursor to the Round Table Agreement.

19. American Embassy Warsaw to SecState, "Poland Looks to President Bush," June 27, 1989 (Case ID 199,702,122, 1 April 1999, Doc. No. 89Warsaw08512).

20. American Embassy Warsaw to SecState, "How to Elect Jaruzelski without Voting for Him," June 23, 1989 (Case ID 199,702,122, 1 April 1999, Doc. No. 89Warsaw08679).

21. See, for example, Domber, "Skepticism and Stability," 71–74.

22. Hutchings, *American Diplomacy*, 74.

23. Radio GDR II interview with Otto Reinhold, rector of the party's Academy of Social Sciences, August 19, 1989, as cited by J.F. Brown, *Surge to Freedom: The End of Communist Rule in Eastern Europe* (Durham, NC: Duke University Press, 1991), 125.

24. Hutchings to Scowcroft, "Berlin," declassified per Executive Order 12,958, 2008-0664-MR, 3/30/09. See also the detailed contingency paper prepared by a restricted interagency group: "GDR Crisis Contingencies," November 6, 1989, declassified by Executive Order 12,958, 2008-0655-MR.

25. Michael J. Sodaro, *Moscow, Germany, and the West from Khrushchev to Gorbachev* (Ithaca, NY: Cornell University Press, 1990), 379.

26. Day-to-day operations were coordinated by a special assistant to the deputy secretary, a position I held in 1992 and 1993.

27. Larry McMurtry, *Lonesome Dove: A Novel* (New York: Simon & Schuster, 1985), 125–126.

28. The scenarios included nonviolent political crisis, widespread and severe violence, refugee crisis, martial law, and, at the extreme end, Soviet military intervention.

29. I have no citation for this document, but I remember it well, because I wrote it when I was serving as deputy national intelligence officer for Europe up until March 1989.

30. This period is captured in Jack Davis's interview with Robert Blackwill: "A Policymaker's Perspective on Intelligence Analysis," in Loch K. Johnson and James J. Wirtz, eds. *Strategic Intelligence: Windows into a Secret World* (Los Angeles: Roxbury Publishing Company, 2004), 120–126.

31. Hutchings to Scowcroft, "Handling the German Question," declassified per Executive Order 13,526, 2008-0710-MR, 9/13/10.

32. "Statement by Secretary Baker, November 29, 1989," in *American Foreign Policy: Current Documents, 1989*, ed. Nancy L. Golden and Sherrill Brown Wells (Washington: DC: U.S. Department of State, 1990), 346–347.

33. Blackwill to Scowcroft, "1990," Declassified per Executive Order 12,958, 2008-0655-MR, 4/14/2010.

34. Hutchings to Scowcroft, "Your Breakfast with Kissinger: Managing the German Question," declassified per Executive Order 12,958, 2008-0655-MR, 4/14/2010.

35. Scowcroft to the President, "A Strategy for German Unification," declassified per Executive Order 12,958, 2008-0804-MR, 5/7/10.

36. A more recent case was the refusal of the George W. Bush administration to acknowledge, much less correct, the disastrously flawed U.S. occupation of Iraq after the 2003 invasion. This was also a classic case of "Groupthink," as developed in Irving L. Janis, *Groupthink* (Boston: Houghton Mifflin, 1982).

37. See, for example, the discussion of "premature cognitive closure" in Richard Ned Lebow, *Between Peace and War: The Nature of International Crisis* (Baltimore: Johns Hopkins University Press, 1981), 101–119.

38. For one such process, see Philip Zelikow (one of the key members of the team that negotiated German unification), "Foreign Policy Engineering: From Theory to Practice and Back Again," *International Security* 18, no. 4 (Spring 1994): 143–171.

39. Karl Kaiser, "German Unification," *Foreign Affairs* 70, no. 1 (1991): 179; Horst Teltschik, *329 Tage: Innenansichten der Einigung* (329 Days: Inside Views of Unifications) (Berlin: Siedler Verlag, 1991). See also the chronology at the end of this chapter.

40. Alexander Moens, "American Diplomacy and German Unification," *Survival* 33, no. 6 (November/December 1991): 531.

41. Elizabeth Pond, *Beyond the Wall: Germany's Road to Unification* (Washington, DC: Brookings Institution Press, 1993), 186.

42. Margaret Thatcher, *The Downing Street Years* (New York: HarperCollins, 1993), 796–799. The French scholar Frédéric Bozo has offered an alternative, more generous interpretation of French policy during the period. See especially his *Mitterrand, the End of the Cold War, and German Unification* (New York: Berghahn Books, 2009).

43. "The End of the Cold War in Europe, 1989: 'New Thinking' and New Evidence. Transcript of the Proceedings of the Musgrove Conference on the Openness in Russia and Eastern Europe Project, Musgrove Plantation, St. Simon's Island, Ga., May 1–3, 1998, prepared by Svetlana Savranskaya under the auspices of the National Security Archives, George Washington University. Doc. 53.

44. See R. L. Hutchings, "The US, German Unification and European Integration," in *Europe and the End of the Cold War: A Reappraisal* (London: Routledge, 2008), 119–132, especially 124–125. Nothing much came of these efforts, owing partly to U.S. diplomatic countermeasures but also to the fact that British diplomats failed to turn Thatcher's strictures into British policy. For their part, the French came to realize by early 1990 that such resistance was futile and self-defeating, so French policy shifted toward a more constructive approach, in the end securing French interests rather well.

45. See especially Hutchings, *American Diplomacy*, 109–112. In the period immediately following the fall of the wall, there was intense jockeying for position between the West German and American governments, with the Germans wanting, understandably, the widest possible latitude to achieve their most deeply held national ambition, the unification of their country, and the United States, although strongly supportive, wanting to ensure that this process did not come at the expense of European security and the transatlantic alliance.

46. Roger Fisher and William Ury, *Getting to Yes: Negotiating Agreement without Giving In* (New York: Penguin Books, 1981); G. Richard Shell, *Bargaining for Advantage: Negotiation Strategies for Reasonable People* (New York: Penguin, 1999); P. Terrence Hopmann, "Bargaining and Problem-Solving: Two Perspectives in International Negotiation," in *Turbulent Peace: The Challenges of Managing International Conflict*, ed. Chester A. Crocker, Fen Osler Hampson, and Pamela Aall (Washington, DC: U.S. Institute of Peace Press, 2001), 445–468.

47. See, for example, Roger Fisher, Elizabeth Kopelman, and Andrea Kupfer Schneider, *Beyond Machiavelli: Tools for Coping with Conflict* (New York: Penguin, 1996), "See Changing Their Choice as Our Problem," p. 56–66.

48. State Department cable State 159968, 18.5.1990, declassified on 29.5.1997 (FOIA #9504381).

49. For an authoritative rebuttal, see Mark Kramer, "The Myth of a No-NATO-Enlargement Pledge to Russia, *Washington Quarterly* 32, no. 2 (April 2009): 39–61.

50. Robert Putnam, "Diplomacy and Domestic Politics: The Logic of Two-Level Games," *International Organization* 42, no. 3 (Summer 1988): 427–460.

51. Record of Conversation, M.S. Gorbachev and G. Bush, Washington D.C., The White House, 31 May 1990, National Security Archive Electronic Briefing Book No. 320, http://www.gwu.edu/~nsarchiv/NSAEBB/NSAEBB320/.

52. Zelikow and Rice, *Germany Unified and Europe Transformed*, 359–362.

8

The European Union as a Community of Law

Achieving Diplomatic Goals through Legal Means?

MARK DAWSON

Introduction

Understanding European integration through the lens of diplomacy is a diffi-cult task.[1] The very emergence of the EU as a transnational polity that has dis-placed its member states in a number of key fields of policymaking seems to contradict a traditional understanding of diplomacy as the interaction of actors representing distinct sovereign states.[2] The EU's development seems to add a new layer of actors—transnational officials and institutions—into the conventional landscape of diplomacy.[3]

In spite of this, however, the establishment and functioning of European in-tegration is also a diplomatic achievement. The structure that is the present-day EU did not—contra one popular theory of EU integration[4]—develop through a magical inherent dynamic of its own; rather, it was built by individuals both defending national interests and aiming toward a long-term project of Euro-pean unity. In October 2012, this project was famously recognized when the EU—in the midst of one of its worst ever crises—was awarded the Nobel Peace Prize. The basis for its award was the EU's "successful struggle for peace and reconciliation and for democracy and human rights" over the half century since its creation.[5] The award of the Peace Prize encourages reflection on the factors and conditions which forged the path of European integration from the rubble of the late 1940s to the present-day Euro crisis. If we accept the Nobel Commit-tee's conclusion that the EU is a successful example of postnational cooperation and reconciliation, what were some of the ingredients of this success?

The answer to this question is of course complex: it takes up a litany of aca-demic books and articles.[6] The purpose of this study, however, will be to highlight one particular key element of the EU's success: its ability to legally institutionalize diplomatic conflicts, that is, to act as a "community of law." The concept of a legal community in this work refers not only to formal legal institutions (such as courts) but also to broader processes of institutionalized and rule-based governance, from the "soft" rules of the European Monetary Union to the "conditionality criteria" applied to states seeking to join the EU.

Although the notion that political leaders may be significantly constrained by their legal or political bureaucracies is by no means a new insight,[7] the EU represents a significant deepening of legal institutionalization at a transnational level. By anchoring political cooperation not only in political bargaining between governments but also in general rules overseen by strong countermajoritarian institutions, the EU was able to bind its different national constituents into a common normative framework. This framework helped to both stabilize the integration project at moments of crisis and "deepen" that project into new fields of cooperation.

To develop this argument, this chapter investigates two policy fields in greater depth. The first is economic integration. In anchoring the early European communities in a common European market, early European leaders were aiming primarily toward a diplomatic goal—the achievement of Franco-German reconciliation. Their innovation was to achieve this not only by encouraging closer cooperation between governments but also by establishing a legal and institutional structure whereby individual market citizens could advance and reinforce processes of economic liberalization. This process of institutionalization was advanced through an alliance of political leaders on the one hand and legal and bureaucratic entrepreneurs on the other seeking to expand the influence of transnational institutions.

The second field is human rights and democratization. The successful integration of ten new member states into the EU in 2004 (a process of enlargement that is still ongoing) depended in large part on establishing a regime of institutional monitoring and reform designed to embed the rule of law and the EU's *acquis communautaire* (the acquired body of EU law) in aspiring member states. Again in this case, transnational institutions played a crucial role in defusing diplomatic conflicts, reframing enlargement as a question not just of national self-interest but also of particular overarching norms. These transnational actors succeeded in "domesticizing" many of the traditional concerns of international diplomacy within the confines of established and widely respected institutions.

As discussed later, the model of "the European Community of law" faces key challenges in the twenty-first century. Its design was based on a limited model of integration whereby responsibility for key social and political questions remained a national matter. The Euro crisis and challenges to the rule of law in several "new" EU member states, particularly Hungary and Romania, have stretched that model, requiring greater political intervention at the European level. Achieving diplomatic goals through legal means—an at least partially successful formula for the first half century of EU integration—might appear in a very different form during the next half century of the EU's existence.

The Foundations of the European Union

To put it in simple terms, the immediate postwar years created a daunting diplomatic task for Europe's postwar leadership, a task that would eventually lead to the founding of the EU:[8] How could European leaders limit German power without producing a spiral of resentment and economic instability that might revive tensions between Germany and its neighbors?[9] The French government in particular was mindful of the experience of the previous war, in which a punitive economic settlement was perceived as both promoting German exclusion from international institutions and thwarting long-term German economic recovery, precipitating the destabilizing inflationary crises of the 1920s. These crises had been exploited by extremist parties of both right and left as a club with which to beat Weimar democracy.

This memory did not, however, stop France from repeating some of its early mistakes in the immediate postwar years. Ironically, it was Jean Monnet, that later zealous pioneer of European integration, whose 1946 Monnet Plan turned German coal and steel production areas into French hands in the immediate postwar era.[10] His plan even turned one coal-rich region, the Saarland, into an independent French protectorate from 1947 until its return to German administration in 1957.

Gradually, however, the 1950s saw the development of a new approach. Germany's economic development was to be promoted, particularly through the famous Marshall Plan, formally known as the European Recovery Program.[11] That development, however, should be tied to the equal prosperity and development of its neighbors. Rather than repeat the first postwar strategy of excluding Germany from international organizations, Germany would be hugged ever tighter into international frameworks, with *Völkerrechts Freundlichkeit*—openness to international law—embedded as a foundational principle of the German constitution itself.[12]

The move from promoting German integration into the international order to the creation of European institutions was aided by two important factors. The first was renewed interest in Federalist ideas during the war and the immediate postwar period.[13] By 1941, Altiero Spinelli and other detained democratic socialists had smuggled out the *Manifesto for a Free and United Europe.* Drawing on a tradition of Italian federalism dating from the nineteenth century, the manifesto called for a postwar federation, including Germany, to ensure peace in Europe. The second factor was policy entrepreneurs who were willing to advance national interests through long-term projects that might limit national sovereignty in the short term.[14] It was one such entrepreneur in particular, the French foreign minister Robert Schuman, who leveraged federalist ideas into a concrete vision for achieving Franco-German reconciliation.

The centerpiece of Schuman's vision was his famous declaration issued on May 9, 1950, which envisaged the pooling of Franco-German coal and steel production.[15] The plan would lead to the signing of the Treaty of Paris, creating the European Coal and Steel Community, by France, Germany, Italy, Belgium, Luxembourg, and the Netherlands in April 1951. As the declaration proclaimed,

> Europe will not be made all at once, or according to a single plan. It will be built through concrete achievements which first create a de facto solidarity. The coming together of the nations of Europe requires the elimination of the age-old opposition of France and Germany. Any action taken must in the first place concern these two countries. With this aim in view, the French Government proposes that action be taken immediately on one limited but decisive point: It proposes that Franco-German production of coal and steel as a whole be placed under a common High Authority. . . . The pooling of coal and steel production should immediately provide for the setting up of common foundations for economic development as a first step in the federation of Europe, and will change the destinies of those regions which have long been devoted to the manufacture of munitions of war, of which they have been the most constant victims. The solidarity in production thus established will make it plain that any war between France and Germany becomes not merely unthinkable, but materially impossible.

The plan was thus focused on two central ideas. The first idea—a key insight of "neofunctionalist" accounts of EU integration to this day—was that gradualism would be a cornerstone of European integration.[16] The idea of first pooling coal and steel was based on the assumption that concrete achievements in particular domains would lay the foundations for broader integration in the future. Ironically, as others have noted, even the failure of the European Coal and Steel Community to achieve its early objectives did not prevent it from being used as an inspiration for further integration in other domains.[17]

The second crucial idea was that economic interdependence was the cornerstone of peace. By pooling the means of war production, and creating economic links that would make conflict economically disastrous, Schuman hoped to render "economic nationalism" obsolete as a trigger for future warfare.[18] Institutions, and even a depoliticization of core decisions, were central to this vision.[19] Decision-making in the European Coal and Steel Community was handed over to the High Authority (the executive branch of the community), made up of representatives of the member states who were to operate independently of their national governments. The idea here was that credible distributive decisions that would otherwise trigger conflict between participating states (for example, over aid to particular industrialized regions or how and when to remove barriers to free movement) would be made by an independent authority, one seen as a neutral arbiter of the common interest.

As Schuman predicted (and himself did much to bring about), the Coal and Steel Community paved the way for the more ambitious economic union that would follow. In 1956, a committee designed to explore economic integration, chaired by the Belgian prime minister, Paul-Henri Spaak, published its findings, laying out the economic case for a single European market.[20] The report articulated the foundation for a treaty providing for free trade between European states in four main areas—goods, workers, services, and capital. The Treaty of Rome, formally known as the Treaty establishing the European Economic Community (TEEC), was eventually signed in Rome in March 1957, both economically committing its member states to removing trade barriers and politically aiming toward the famous "ever closer Union between the peoples of Europe" promised in the treaty's preamble.

The institutional design of the European Economic Community was in fact more reminiscent of a classical international organization than its forebear, the European Coal and Steel Community. Whereas the European Economic Community also carried its own independent and politically insulated initiator of legislative proposals—the European Commission—those proposals were to be subject to the agreement of an intergovernmental council designed, as the first president of the commission put it, "to reconcile the interests of the Member States with those of the Community."[21] As the early European Economic Community would observe in the decade to follow, the difficulties in achieving agreement even in a relatively small community of six—on issues ranging from sex discrimination to the level of support member governments could give farmers without distorting the single market—had the capacity to provoke significant conflict among the member states.

How could one prevent such "diplomatic" conflicts from either blocking progress on the completion of the common market or eroding trust in the early European Communities as a project of political, as well as economic, union? The tentative answer may be that many of the broad goals that the Treaty establishing the European Economic Community attempted to pursue were in fact developed through nonmajoritarian institutions capable of both driving integration forward and fleshing out treaty provisions in the face of intergovernmental disagreement. Development of a robust legal system in this sense served as a device to insulate European integration from the diplomatic disagreements and political tensions that drove European policymaking in the founding decades of the European Economic Community.

Europe as a Community of Law

When the treaty establishing the European Coal and Steel Community was first negotiated, there was in fact disagreement between the member states as to whether their new organization required a central court at all.[22] The French government, steeped in a suspicion of a nonaccountable *gouvernement des juges* (government of the judges), rejected the idea of a "Supreme Court for Europe" as unnecessary. The German delegation, headed by Walter Hallstein and his legal adviser Carl Ophüls, were in favor of a permanent court of justice. As a compromise solution, the European Court of Justice was created in 1952, but it was modeled on the more modest French Conseil d'État (Council of State). Its primary function would be to police the European institutions themselves: the court carried a capacity to annul European Coal and Steel Community, and later European Economic Community, measures whenever the EU institutions acted beyond their powers. The application of European measures at the national level, however, would remain a matter for the national authorities.

This seemingly innocuous first step in the direction of a European legal order was of course only the beginning. As observed in Joseph Weiler's often-cited article from 1991, Europe's early jurists used law to transform the European Union—and European societies—from a bundle of competing states, fighting for supremacy within a classical international organization, into a constitutionalized entity that bears closer analogy to a federal state.[23] The "constitutional" quality of the EU legal order was recognized very early on and explicitly promoted by key actors in the integration process.[24] Foremost among them was the first president of the European Commission, and the man who secured the Court of Justice's institutional position in the early negotiations of the European Steel and Coal Community, Walter Hallstein. This speech, from 1965, demonstrates his vision quite clearly:

> The main novelty of the Rome Treaty is not, however, that it is an "outline-treaty." What commands even more attention in our Treaty is the procedures by which it can be amplified, adapted or elaborated. The Treaty does not assign these duties to the Member States, acting alone or meeting in inter-governmental councils, but to Community bodies having their own freedom of action. These Community bodies—we call them "Institutions"—are empowered to take decisions. And these decisions are as fully binding on the Member States as the Treaty itself, without any further action, such as approval by the national Parliaments, being required of the States. Far more important, certain of the decisions which the Community Institutions have the power to take are embodied in "regulations," which are "directly enforceable in all the Member States" and which therefore directly create rights and obligations for every citizen. Thus the Treaty controls not only the relationships of the Member States with each other or with the Community, or again with the Community Institutions, it also controls, of itself or by legal acts stemming from it, the legal position of private individuals. What should we conclude from these facts? ... More than a traditional convention in international law, this "outline-treaty," embodying active policies, forming the basis of institutions with wide powers, creating rights and obligations for each citizen as much as for the highest authorities of the State, does it not remind us of the constitution of a modern State?[25]

The development of a "constitutionalized" European Community legal order was a decisive lever for diffusing conflict. It protected against a major danger: that structures of transnational cooperation would fail as a result of selective noncompliance. One does not have to look far into other historical examples—from early examples of transnational economic cooperation (such as the Latin Monetary Union established by four European states in the 1860s) to security cooperation (and the failed League of Nations)—to find organizations in which "free riding" and weak levels of compliance broke bonds of trust between national participants. Once states see that a cooperation mechanism can be easily flouted, the incentives to breach the rules oneself, and thus to precipitate complete collapse, heighten.[26] The development of the early European Community's legal order was both precipitated and accepted by reluctant member states, on the basis of its ability to tackle this structural weakness.[27]

The key element in doing so was the development by the Court of Justice of the supremacy principle. Under classical public international law, the legal effects of international treaties in the domestic legal order were largely a matter for domestic constitutional law. States assumed obligations through treaties in the international sphere, and there was no prima facie assumption either that international treaties could be applied in domestic courts or that those treaties "trumped" domestic law.[28] In two seminal judgments of the 1960s, however, the Court of Justice gave EU law precisely this quality.

This move began via a Dutch reference to the Court of Justice in 1962. In *Van Gend & Loos*, the court argued that—contrary to the ordinary rules of international law—EU law created rights for individuals "which become part of their legal heritage." As such, rights granted under EU law, so the Court argued, were directly enforceable in front of domestic courts.[29] The radical effect of *Van Gend* was accentuated even further two years later, in *Costa v ENEL*.[30] Facing a question from an Italian court over how a domestic court should act where norms of EU and domestic law collide, the court argued that EU law carried presumed supremacy over conflicting national law. Through these judgments, the EU courts created the building blocks for a European legal order that was quite different from ordinary international law. This was not just a law of states that political actors could apply or ignore according to the ordinary diktats of power politics, but a legal order that could operate independently of changing national preferences.

In effect, the supremacy principle prohibited member states from "picking and choosing" between which aspects of EU policies to apply and which to ignore. As Hallstein recognized, the key to doctrines like supremacy and direct effect was not just their ability to build trust at the supranational level but also lay in their recasting of the relationship between the state and the individual. Insofar as EU law's "direct effect" allowed individuals to challenge national law—in national courts—on the grounds that it violated EU rules, EU law created both a novel channel by which individuals could "discipline the state" and a new army of private persons, nongovernmental organizations, and companies able to hold states to common EU rules. Flouting supranational provisions was much more difficult if compliance was secured not just by a limited pool of Brussels administrators but also by an army of individual litigators, incentivized to "make EU law stick" as a matter of self-interest.[31] The decentralization of enforcement through direct effect was thus crucial in maintaining an embedded system of transnational cooperation—and a robust market—over time.

Law's centrality was highlighted during moments of crisis or impasse. A key turning point was 1965. The 1958 election of Charles de Gaulle as president of France was a vital event.[32] Distrusting American influence over the early integration project, as well as the supranational nature of existing institutions established by the Rome Treaty, de Gaulle agitated for a more intergovernmentalist Europe, proposing in 1960 a new political union (the Fouchet Plan) that would operate alongside the then European Economic Community.[33] In contrast to the European Economic Community, however, this organization would be governed by an intergovernmental council and checked by a parliament made up of national representatives.[34]

Although this plan failed, de Gaulle would prove a thorn in the side of the European Economic Community throughout the 1960s. In 1965, he rejected a proposal from the European Commission to establish for the Community its own direct sources of revenue for the purposes of funding the Common Agricultural Policy (CAP), as well as proposals to strengthen the European Assembly (now the European Parliament). Unable to negotiate a solution favorable to both France and smaller member states, de Gaulle instructed his ministers to boycott meetings of the Council of the European Union (hereafter, the EU Council) for over six months, making agreement on new legislation impossible. This "empty chair" crisis was only resolved in January 1966 through the Luxembourg Compromise—an agreement that future legislation could only be passed by the unanimous agreement of all member states.[35]

The impact on the Community of the compromise was dire. The unanimity rule made the agreement on legislation increasingly difficult, requiring elaborate negotiations between the European Commission and the COREPER (the body of permanent representatives of the member states) prior to adoption. The effective veto established via the "compromise" was exercised not just by France but by a number of other states, including vetoes over initiatives seemingly unrelated to core national interests.[36] In essence, the late 1960s and 1970s have often been described as "a lost decade," with multiple initiatives launched by the Community (e.g., the ambitious 1970 Werner Plan for an economic and monetary union and the 1974 Social Action Programme, designed to develop a more robust "social dimension" to the EU's activities) failing as a consequence of the inability of member states with divergent political preferences and historical traditions to agree on a common program for reform.[37]

Even though *political* integration had stalled, however, *legal* integration continued. The core thesis in this regard is that legal integration played an important role both in stabilizing the Community in times of political disagreement and in expanding the reach of central areas of policy integration, such as the single market, in periods when political paralysis was the norm. As noted earlier, processes of litigation could resolve certain interstate conflicts and further develop integration, even in the absence of explicit agreement between political leaders. The key element here was an interaction between a policy entrepreneur and a key doctrine to emerge from the Court of Justice in the 1970s.

The entrepreneur was Jacques Delors; the doctrine he espoused was the mechanism of "mutual recognition."

Let us start with the doctrine first. From the beginning of the Communities, it was relatively clear that although all member states were committed to the goal of a single European market, their interpretation of what was required to fulfill this market varied significantly. The main challenge to the market's "completion" by the late 1970s was no longer customs or other economic tariffs, but nontariff barriers to trade such as the numerous regulations existing on the national level that could make cross-border trade cumbersome.[38] Disentangling these barriers was no easy task. Unlike barriers to tariffs, many nontariff barriers reflected important political and cultural choices that were deeply embedded in national legal systems and cultures. To give just one often-cited example, Germany's famous *Reinheitsgebot*, its beer purity law, had for centuries restricted the ability of beer manufacturers to use additives in beer. This law was no mere public health measure but reflected centuries-old tradition. It also, of course, clearly restricted the ability of beer manufacturers outside of Germany to export their beers freely across the continent.[39] How could the member states—faced with a deadlocked EU Council—agree on a system for determining which nontariff barriers were justifiable and which had to be eliminated on the grounds of ensuring a free and undistorted single market? A deadlocked political decision-making system was completely unable to advance the single market beyond its initial stages.

This was precisely the gap that the European courts began to fill. In an important decision from 1974—*Dassonville*—the Court of Justice established that nontariff barriers to trade that restricted the market access of foreign providers were contrary to the Treaty of Rome.[40] At the same time, national governments could still justify these measures by demonstrating that they fell within an open list of public policy justifications, from public health and safety to consumer protection. In effect, *Dassonville* again allowed private litigation to do what political integration could not: break down trade barriers to the completion of the internal market while simultaneously providing member states with an outlet to defend national laws that safeguarded important policy objectives. As Fritz Scharpf famously observed, for the decades that followed, the primary instrument of European integration became not "positive integration" (i.e., the creation of common European rules through transnational regulation), but "negative integration" (i.e., the use of EU rules to remove and strike down national barriers to trade).[41]

The Court of Justice reinforced this tendency through a second important decision. In 1979, its decision in *Cassis de Dijon* established an equally important building block for the single market—the doctrine of mutual recognition.[42] The case concerned a classical interstate trade conflict: a dispute between France and Germany over the marketing and sale of alcohol. Cassis is a French liqueur that had been successfully produced in France in keeping with national regulations. Its import into Germany was restricted, however, on the grounds that fruit liqueur sold in Germany was required to have a minimum alcohol content of 25 percent. Germany alleged that this was necessary to protect German consumers. The Court of Justice held that the same objective could also have been achieved by a less restrictive means: labeling the bottles and thereby allowing consumers to make an informed choice. It concluded,

> There is therefore no valid reason why, provided that they have been lawfully produced and marketed in one of the Member States, alcoholic beverages should not be introduced into any other Member State.[43]

Cassis de Dijon produced an assumption of "mutual recognition" between national regulatory regimes. If a particular product was produced in keeping with the rules of any one European state, other states should recognize the product *as if it had been produced according to national standards*. The same principle today allows professionals to use national qualifications (e.g., as a lawyer in Belgium or a plumber in Greece) to carry out equivalent services in other member states. Once again, *Cassis* opened up channels of free movement that had previously been restricted, producing an operating presumption that states should trust and accept the regulatory regimes of their neighbors.

Even though legal entrepreneurship was vital in effecting European integration, so were political entrepreneurs. The EU's political leaders quickly realized the implications and potential of these rulings. This was particularly so for the European Commission. During the 1970s, much of its work was spent in exhaustive negotiations on legislation designed to liberalize various elements of the European economy. An ambitious new commission president, Jacques Delors, the policy entrepreneur who espoused the doctrine of mutual recognition, used widespread frustration with the economic torpor of the early 1980s to argue for a renewed commitment to "completing the single market." The central thrust of the new policy was laid out in an ambitious white paper published in June 1985 that latched on to mutual recognition as the cornerstone of removing remaining barriers to trade:

> While the elimination of physical barriers provides benefits for traders, . . . [it] is through the elimination of technical barriers that the Community will give the large market its economic and industrial

dimension by enabling industries to make economies of scale and therefore to become more competitive. . . . The general thrust of the Commission's approach in this area will be to move away from the concept of harmonization towards that of mutual recognition and equivalence.[44]

This was a full-throated embrace of the judicial route to a free market. It also, however, entailed a different approach to legislating. The white paper suggested a "new approach" whereby future legislation agreed to by political leaders in the internal market would not elaborate technical detail but "in future be restricted to laying down essential health and safety requirements which will be obligatory in all Member States."[45] The remainder—technical details—would be left to the member states with a presumption of "mutual recognition" of national rules and standards. In essence, in the face of a high unanimity rule in the EU Council, mutual recognition was used by Delors to change the dynamics of political bargaining. Legislation would focus only on essential and generalized health and safety standards, and the rest left to national administrations (policed of course by the courts). In one fell swoop, much of the source of disagreement between the member states—an inability to agree on comprehensive harmonizing measures—was removed. Through mutual recognition, a source of conflict—how to agree on the harmonization of sensitive national standards—was delegated from the legislative to the judicial level.

The larger question may be over why national governments agreed to such a move. The acceleration of the single market could easily have been seen as limiting national sovereignty, handing control over sensitive areas of policy to actors—courts—not subject to political censure. Many explanations have been given for national acquiescence to these changes. One important factor was the surrounding political context, such as the rise of the "new right" of monetarist and/or Christian Democratic governments in the early 1980s, backed by corporate interests and far more amenable to a liberalization agenda.[46] Another might have been interstate bargaining.[47] One should not, however, underestimate the influence of key individuals in the process of national acceptance. Take, for example, the principles of supremacy and direct effect, which were such essential features of the nascent EU order. It was not simply a matter of "announcing" these principles and assuming obedience from national administrations and judiciaries. Instead, they were explicitly promoted by key actors at the European level in concert with national judges and politicians sympathetic to the cause of further transnational integration.

As Antonin Cohen has pointed out, the ability of the early Court of Justice to embed its doctrines has to be understood in light of the heterogeneous nature of the legal profession in the 1950s and 1960s.[48] Many of the judges who made up the early court enjoyed political careers prior to taking office. The first Belgian judge, for example, had been an MP and minister for agriculture before entering the court; the Dutch judge had been secretary general of the International Confederation of Trade Unions, as well as an MP. Others had been chief judges of their national constitutional courts, such as Otto Riese, who was president of the Federal Constitutional Court of Germany and who served as a judge on the Court of Justice from 1952 to 1963. These judges were thus in a particularly powerful position to disseminate their "constitutional" reading of EU law into national legal and political orders.

They did so with gusto. As Antoine Vauchez has demonstrated, within days of the rendering of the *Van Gend* decision, members of the court conducted numerous speeches to influential audiences highlighting the significance of the judgment as well as their own new reading of the direct effect of EU law.[49] Among many examples, the French justice, Robert Lecourt, writing in *Le Monde* just a few weeks after the decision, explained that "in the core of the Brussels crisis, the judicial world has just brought an important stone to the building of the European entity."[50] *Van Gend* was held up as heralding a turning point in the European legal order. In this sense, the acceptance of doctrines like direct effect and supremacy at the national level can be seen not just as a legal enterprise but also as a personal one, in which Europeanized elites forwarded and argued for a particular "constitutional" reading of EU law.[51]

This "personal" dimension should be seen not as antithetical but as complementary to the broader idea of a European community of law. European law created a common frame of reference through which transnational integration could occur beyond the bargaining and subjective conflicts of states. At the same time, as much as EU lawyers have often portrayed the EU treaties and their interpretation as a "given" legal order from which principles like supremacy could be objectively "deduced," the EU legal order was anything but a matter of logical deduction.[52] Rather than a matter of deduction, the normative frame of European law was molded and shaped both by jurists, who used it to assert the development of a new legal order, and by policymakers, such as Schuman and Delors, who saw it as a way out of decision-making inertia. Although later EU policies—for example, enlargement of the union—had unique characteristics, they would also adopt elements of this model, providing lessons for diplomats and policymakers to this day. Nonmajoritarian institutions would prove useful allies in forwarding the supranational political agenda.

Enlarging European Integration

In their pursuit of a united European order, Jean Monnet (whose post–World War II Monnet Plan had turned German coal and steel production areas into French hands) and Robert Schuman (who in the early 1950s had leveraged federalist ideas into a concrete vision for achieving Franco-German reconciliation), were of course constrained by a natural geopolitical limit: the Iron Curtain, which had descended across Europe in the late 1940s.[53] By the time the Berlin wall fell in late 1989, the EU had gone through several enlargements from the entry of the United Kingdom, Denmark, and Ireland in 1973 to Spain and Portugal's accession, after peaceful democratic revolutions, in 1986. The fall of the wall, however, precipitated a much more significant move: toward a European Union that could meaningfully claim to incorporate (or at least aspire to incorporate) the entire European continent.

Enlargement policy always carried both a political and a legal dimension. Legally speaking, the original Treaty of Rome was designed as an "open treaty" under international law. According to article 237 of the EEC treaty, "any European state may apply to become a member of the European Community" provided this membership is approved by all of the member states in the European Council under a unanimous vote and through national ratification. The treaty gave scant detail on the kinds of criteria aspiring member states would have to meet, or even whether they would have to bring their legal and political orders in line with EU law prior to accession.

In effect, this meant that the procedure for entry was highly politicized. Individual member states could (and did) hold the process up indefinitely on the basis of threats to specific national interests. The foremost example of this was the first enlargement attempt, which arose from the application of the UK Macmillan government to join the Communities in the early 1960s. Twice—in 1963 and again (under Harold Wilson) in 1967—Charles de Gaulle vetoed British entry, accusing Britain of a "deep-seated hostility" to the European construct and arguing that the UK economy was unfit to be integrated within the common European market.[54] Early enlargement procedures were also highly noninterventionist.[55] It was largely left to the candidates themselves to prepare for the obligations arising from accession to the Communities, with little financial or technical assistance coming from the EU institutions.

The system of enlargement faced by the new member states seeking to join three decades later was significantly different. Responding to the democratic revolutions breaking out across Europe in 1989–1990, EU leaders developed much more detailed enlargement criteria at the Copenhagen European Council in June 1993. This led to a far more *institutionalized* form of interaction between future members and the existing EU member states.

The first step in the Copenhagen system was the elaboration of certain over-arching normative benchmarks for future enlargement. The Copenhagen Council listed three requirements in particular:

> Membership requires that the candidate country has achieved sta-bility of institutions guaranteeing democracy, the rule of law, human rights and respect for and protection of minorities, the existence of a functioning market economy as well as the capacity to cope with competitive pressure and market forces within the Union. Member-ship presupposes the candidate's ability to take on the obligations of membership including adherence to the aims of political, economic and monetary union.[56]

Reflecting the "transitional" nature of democratic rule in the new states of Eastern and Central Europe, accession was conditional not just upon market reforms and the adoption of the EU *acquis* (existing laws) but also upon em-bedding core constitutional values such as democracy, human rights, and the rule of law within the national legal order.[57] These normative benchmarks were applied and elaborated not just by the EU but also by other interna-tional organizations (the Council of Europe, the Organization for Security and Co-operation in Europe [OSCE], NATO, and others) using a cumulative approach. Understandably, these bodies were most able to exercise norma-tive pressure when they acted together. To take one example, Latvia's reluc-tance to alter its stance toward its Russian-speaking minority was gradually overturned in the late 1990s through the European Commission's strict ad-herence to the guidelines of the OSCE's high commissioner on national minorities.[58]

Copenhagen's second novelty was in moving away from the noninterven-tionist approach of prior enlargements. The post–Copenhagen EU demanded that aspiring member states engage in extensive partnership and dialogue with the EU institutions prior to accession.[59] As with the economic integration ex-ample, the key actor in the enlargement story quickly became a nonmajoritar-ian institution, the European Commission, which established a separate unit (the Directorate General, "DG") for enlargement in 1999.

At the core of the DG's activities were detailed "accession agreements" with aspiring entrants, which established more concrete indicators by which the Copenhagen criteria could be measured and laid out steps for accession states to meet in the short to medium term.[60] These agreements demanded periodi-cal reporting and were subject to annual review by the European Commis-sion.[61] From 1998 on, the agreements were replaced by more robust "accession partnerships," which also allowed for sanctions ("negative conditionality") in the case of serious noncompliance with democratic principles, human rights, the rule of law or essential principles of the market economy.[62] The commission's annual reports on national compliance with the partnership agreements were the key barometer measuring a country's readiness for accession. The commission also drafted the common position presented by the presidency of the European Council in accession negotiations. In effect, a depoliticized actor—with no official role in enlargement under the EU treaties—quickly became the principal policeman of the enlargement process.

A final element of the Copenhagen system was its attempts to intervene in accession states not only procedurally but also in terms of funding and capacity building.[63] The PHARE (Poland and Hungary: Assistance for Reconstructing their Economies) program was quickly extended to other transition countries preparing for EU membership. At its peak, it provided €1.5 billion per year of financial assistance to prepare candidates for accession via institution building and technical assistance. This was designed to aid accession states in adopting the EU *acquis* (i.e., its existing laws), and to distribute and audit structural and other EU funds. Its main instruments, TAIEX (the Technical Assistance Information Exchange Office) and Twinning (the matching of civil servants of candidate countries and existing member states) were also designed to facilitate the transfer of knowledge from existing EU states to accession countries.[64]

In combination, these three elements—fixed normative criteria, institutional monitoring, and financial and technical assistance—amounted to an EU enlargement policy in the late 1990s that was quite different from the hands-off approach of the earlier Communities. As discussed next, the institutionalization of enlargement policy played an important role in insulating and dampening diplomatic conflicts.

Institutionalizing Enlargement

What was the practical effect of the accession partnerships? The advantage of institutionalization could be seen from both sides. From the perspective of aspiring member states, a clear road map to accession was intended not only to prepare new members for the obligations of EU membership but also to embed democratic and free-market reforms in the Central and Eastern European Countries (CEECs).[65] The partnerships carried both a carrot and a stick. The carrot was the promise of access to new European markets and goods, and the stick was "negative conditionality" and the possible revocation of EU financial assistance were specific aspects of the accession partnerships breached.

In practice, there was much more carrot than stick (negative conditionality was rarely applied in practice).[66] Nonetheless, the possibility of EU membership and the obligations which this entailed were frequently cited by national politicians in the CEECs throughout the late 1990s as important reasons to complete the transition to more liberal and democratic forms of rule.[67] For liberal elements in the political system, accession partnerships could be a useful political tool: opponents of, for example, strong constitutional courts, high human rights standards, or market liberalization, could more easily be characterized not just as making bad political choices but as imperiling a core national interest: the achievement of EU membership.

An example in this regard is Slovakia. Slovakia's perceived authoritarian backsliding in the mid-1990s under Vladimír Mečiar's government led in 1997 to a negative assessment by the European Commission, which reprimanded "the instability of Slovakia's institutions, their lack of rootedness in political life and the shortcoming in the functioning of its democracy."[68] In the face of increasing isolation from the West, the Mečiar government gradually lost electoral support.[69] The new and more liberally minded prime minister, Mikuláš Dzurinda (1998–2006), was able to win EU agreement on reopening accession negotiations at the Helsinki European summit in December 1999. This was not a uniform picture—other authors have stressed key failings of conditionality in Eastern and Central Europe, from an inability to properly embed rule of law and democratic norms beyond formalities to a too interventionist approach (whereby EU sympathetic governments were too easily tarred as "agents of the West").[70] Nevertheless, the ability of the accession process to frame and influence national discourses can be observed to this day.[71]

An even more important effect of institutionalization might have been its impact on existing members of the EU. Institutionalization also carried the advantage of making unilateral objections to further expansion, which had been characteristic of earlier enlargement attempts, more difficult. As it would prove, the creation of a well-defined path to accession, with objective criteria, would make it harder for reluctant member states to refuse to endorse specific enlargement rounds. Even national resistance to enlargement now had to have a different character. After Copenhagen, unilateral objections based on naked national self-interests had to be framed in a more universal language, to wit, had the accession state in question fulfilled objective criteria (criteria that the member states had already agreed to, and which created legitimate expectations for future members of the club)?

To understand this point requires engaging with the political conflicts that EU enlargement precipitated. Certainly, one should not understand the politics of enlargement as an easy, overlapping consensus. As Frank Schimmelfennig has argued in an influential essay from 2001, EU enlargement saw frequent divides between "driver" states that powerfully forwarded the enlargement agenda and "brakemen" who perceived greater risks and financial costs from the EU's eastern expansion.[72] The positions of these states in either camp are closely correlated with their capacity to win or lose from enlargement. Among the most enthusiastic were border states, such as Austria and Finland, which had significant existing trade with the CEECs and stood to benefit even further in the future.[73] Among the most reluctant states were France, Spain, and Italy, which either received significant subsidies from the EU budget that were likely to be reduced upon enlargement (e.g., because of competition from poorer Eastern European competitors) or faced an influx of cheap labor and goods that could place a downward pressure on living and working standards. States thus disagreed significantly on the pace of enlargement and on the states that should be given priority in the enlargement process.

In these circumstances the dominant features of the Copenhagen system— the normative criteria for enlargement and the presence of a "neutral" coordinating actor (the European Commission)—played an important role in binding the EU as a whole to a proenlargement agenda. In the first place, the overarching normative commitment to enlargement made it difficult for member states to oppose specific enlargement rounds. It was common, for example, for the French and Spanish governments to insist upon specific reforms either at the European level, or in the CEECs, as a precondition for further enlargement.[74] It was difficult, however, for these governments to move beyond specific reform demands toward a larger *political* objection to further enlargement without contradicting earlier rhetorical statements.

Other, more supportive member states, and overarching EU institutions, were quick to remind the reluctant of their historical commitments.[75] The European Parliament, for example, intervened to end blockage in the European Council over agreement on early preaccession negotiations with Bulgaria in 1993, arguing that the impasse was "undermining the European Community's credibility in Eastern Europe."[76] Similar appeals to the credibility of the EU on the European and global stage were made by the European Commission.[77] One can see the Bulgarian case as an example of using rhetorical "shaming" and the framing effect of commonly accepted norms, such as the Copenhagen criteria, to bring reluctant member states in line with overarching European Community values. As these EU-level actors were quick to point out, once negotiations have reached a certain level of institutionalization—with firm promises to meet an objective road map to EU accession—breaking negotiations carries a broader political cost: that the wider foundations of the community will be brought into disrepute. By the late 1990s, the political weight of "brakemen" states seemed to be in full retreat. When France demanded in a declaration to be attached to the Amsterdam Treaty that further institutional

reform was an "indispensable condition of enlargement," it found little support among other member states.[78]

A second important factor in binding the EU to an enlargement agenda was
the role of the European Commission.[79] As earlier indicated, the commission
was the principal investigator of the reform process in accession states and able
to control the supply of information upon which decisions in other EU institutions on enlargement were based. The general political direction of the commission vis-à-vis enlargement was set early on. When preparing its submission
on enlargement to the Lisbon European Council in 1992, the commission was
quick to remind the member states of its historic responsibilities:

> The Community has never been a closed club and cannot now refuse
> the historic challenge to assume its continental responsibilities and
> contribute to the development of a political and economic order for
> the whole of Europe.[80]

Subsequent assessments of national progress, therefore, often assumed that
accession was an agreed-upon political objective, with the main "sticking
point" being various technical and economic criteria that had been only "partially fulfilled." The most common opening line of such reports was, "The
Commission must report regularly to the European Council on progress
made by each of the candidate countries of Central and Eastern Europe in
preparations for membership."[81] Membership is cast as an inevitable destination, with the European Commission as a "neutral" actor able to determine
the rate of gradual progress toward that objective. This can be seen as an important lesson for diplomacy in a broader sense. Rather than negotiate immediately on a far-reaching goal (in this case, EU accession), the commission
adopted a gradualist approach. Agreement on smaller and "technical" details,
as part of an institutionalized process, was crucial in building up bonds of
trust between existing and aspiring states, as well as in creating momentum
toward the end goal.

This gradualism can be observed at several points in the accession process.
One element concerned preaccession negotiations. Prior to official negotiations for entry, the European Commission adopted a staggered approach, recognizing that certain elements of the EU *acquis* might be more difficult to
implement than others. Costly social and environmental regulation could
therefore wait for later stages in the accession process, but the commission insisted that measures necessary for the single market should be applied immediately. This had the added benefit of illustrating, at a crucial moment, some of
the tangible benefits of enlargement for existing members: trade between the
ten main CEECs and the EU doubled in the period from 1995 to 2000.[82]

The gradualist approach can also be seen in the four main phases of official negotiations. In the first stage—the prescreening process—the European Commission scrutinized the existing implementation of the *acquis* with two groups of applicants, supplemented by bilateral meetings. In the second stage, reporting on the screening process led to the opening of "chapters" of the *acquis* with the six most advanced candidate countries in late 1998. (Chapters of the *acqui* are particular issue areas to be negotiated between the commission and states aspiring to EU membership). Position papers were passed back and forth between national governments and Brussels. The easiest and least controversial chapters were tackled first, and the more contentious issues (e.g. agricultural policy, where the need for transitional periods was likely) left to the end.

In a third stage, beginning in the second half of 1999, six more countries were brought into negotiations after the European Council reluctantly agreed to a European Commission recommendation that accession negotiations be extended. The main opponents, ironically, were not existing members but the advanced group of applicants who feared delay. In the fourth and final phase, in November 2000, the commission published a much more detailed "road map," providing for the first time a concrete timetable for completion of the chapters. The timetable was designed to pressure both sides: accession countries to speed up implementation, and the rotating presidencies of the council (composed of heads of government) to complete negotiations on chapters within a designated time frame. In each of these stages, the commission used its power over the pace of accession to nudge both of the main parties to negotiations: the accession states who had to adopt the *acquis*, and the member states who finally agreed to the entry of ten new states at the Copenhagen European Council in December 2002.

The importance of institutionalization can be seen by contrasting the countries that entered the EU in 2004 with the more recent rounds of enlargement. Many have pointed to an increasing "renationalization" of the enlargement process after 2006.[83] In part, this can be attributed to increasing popular hostility (particularly in Western Europe) toward further expansion. Some features are of particular import here, such as an increase in the use of conditionality during the discussions prior to the opening of enlargement negotiations and the introduction of greater national "firewalls" against expansion.[84] Increasingly, member states have sought to multiply the procedural hurdles and criteria prior to even referring an application for membership to the European Commission for consideration. The agreement of the European Council to open accession negotiations with Serbia was made conditional upon its reaching an agreement with Kosovo over its international recognition.[85] Equally, Slovenia blocked the opening of negotiations with neighboring Croatia for almost a year, from December 2008 to October 2009, over a border dispute concerning Slovenia's access to the Adriatic Sea.[86]

These cases signal growing recognition from some "reluctant" member states of the dynamics of enlargement. Institutionalizing enlargement through overarching and independently monitored rules makes both national contestation of enlargement and *national control* more precarious (even in circumstances where "ultimate" decision-making power remains with the member states). To return to the idea of a community of law, whereas Copenhagen's rule-bound process was successful in integrating ten new states into the EU, its mitigation of interstate conflict was to an extent a *deferral* of conflict, with an increasing number of both member states and national populations voicing a political backlash against further enlargement.[87] The European Union as a community of law thus faces serious challenges in the coming decades.

Conclusion: The Community of Law in Peril?

When leaders such as Jean Monnet and Robert Schuman advanced the early blueprints for EU integration, they did so in uncertain times, and without obvious models for imitation. Europe had of course been riven by interstate conflict, creating both a challenge and opportunity. The opportunity was the will to move beyond the harrowing cycle of violence that had characterized the preceding eighty years. The challenge was how to make that political will survive the winds of political change and evolving divergences in national interest. The argument set forth here is that this diplomatic challenge was met, at least in part, through the legal institutionalization of conflict. Through both the design of economic integration and the criteria for the EU's enlargement, EU leaders have sought to embed core political projects in abstract rules and procedures, overseen by nonmajoritarian institutions. These institutions have played a crucial role in moving processes of transnational integration forward in circumstances wherein political leadership has failed or political dialogue would likely increase rather than diffuse interstate conflict. As Monnet observed, "Rien n'est possible sans les hommes, rien n'est durable sans les institutions."[88]

In so doing, early EU leaders, and the political and bureaucratic entrepreneurs that followed them, significantly expanded the landscape of conventional diplomacy. In many regards, they succeeded in "domesticizing" international diplomacy, making actors—such as transnational courts and administrations—not merely the *objects* of national diplomacy but also its *subjects*. To take the enlargement example, expanding the EU became not only a battle of competing national positions, but also a value-based process in which a "European" interest in having a more democratic and peaceful continent also had to be accommodated. This new "domestic" international diplomacy has added new players to the diplomatic game, even if, as the example of contemporary enlargement negotiations has shown, it has not rendered more "traditional" forms of diplomacy obsolete. Diplomacy, in Europe at least, may now be carried out not just through traditional diplomatic actors working at an international level, but by domestic institutions such as courts acting in concert with their transnational counterparts.

Although the community of law was a useful model for transnational cooperation in the twentieth century, what are its prospects today? And what lessons does it offer for diplomats? In effect, the EU's receiving a Nobel Prize in 2012 is a reflection of its weakness as much as its strength. The EU faces significant challenges in economic integration as well as the spread of democracy and the rule of law. These challenges have led EU leaders to disregard many of the elements of the community of law forged in the European Communities' founding decades.

In regard to economic integration, the trigger for this change has been the crisis in the eurozone. Attributing the collapse in market confidence in the euro to the weak instruments by which the EU can control national fiscal policies, the EU has introduced a number of measures designed to strengthen economic policy coordination.[89] Although these measures have "supranationalized" economic governance, they have often done so through very different methods. The dominant actor in steering the reforms has been an intergovernmental body, the European Council (made up of heads of government), rather than the supranational European Commission. Similarly, two of the centerpieces of the reform package—the European Stability Mechanism (a European-style International Monetary Fund) and the Fiscal Compact (designed to encourage budgetary discipline)—have been adopted as intergovernmental treaties lacking the doctrines of direct effect and supremacy enjoyed by the regular EU treaties. Desperate to increase market confidence in the euro, yet unwilling to cede control over vast tracts of government money to supranational institutions, EU member states have turned away from the community of law ideal in their pursuit of economic integration.[90]

Similar problems have also emerged in the enlargement process. A key problem here is not only the stalling of enlargement per se but also the transition to democratic and law-based rule in those countries that are already part of the EU.[91] International institutions—such as the Venice Commission of the Council of Europe—have questioned whether recent reforms to the Hungarian Constitution are throwing into doubt the commitment of Hungary to rule of law values. Of particular concern to the EU was action by the prime minister, Viktor Orban, in 2011, to lower the mandatory retirement age of judges to sixty-two, removing at a stroke a number of critical justices of the Constitutional Court.[92] The EU has also voiced concerns over other constitutional reforms.[93] Ironically, the enlargement process allows significant EU monitoring of democracy and the rule of law in the accession process, but most of these review powers vanish upon official accession. These developments throw into doubt the long-term success of the EU in embedding rule of law and democratic values in its member states.

Although these developments question the long-term durability of an EU community of Law, the lessons of the first half century of the EU's existence should not be forgotten, even when constructing responses to quite different challenges today. One important lesson concerns individual agency and leadership. As both the economic integration and enlargement examples show, "strong" diplomatic leadership does not always equate with the accumulation of knowledge and power by a diplomat. In the case of the early European Community leaders, the value of their vision was in creating an institutional framework that was independent of their short-term preferences yet which embodied a long-term vision of transnational cooperation. Independent and nonmajoritarian institutions may offer credibility in delivering long-term diplomatic goals that direct negotiations cannot provide, provided that leaders have the vision to commit to common institutions (and respect their rules). "Successful diplomacy" can be found even in examples in which diplomats displace themselves as the central actors.

A second lesson concerns the relationship between diplomatic "vision" and the technical negotiations necessary to secure diplomatic agreement. The EU case illustrates the need for attention to both. To take the enlargement process as a foremost example, EU leaders and administrators succeeded in projecting an overall endpoint: the unification of Europe. At the same time, the most difficult question—who should enter the union and when—was consistently deferred or subordinated to the more technical and managerial issue of whether aspiring states carried the administrative and legal capacity to become EU members. Once these technical steps had been achieved, it became increasingly difficult for reluctant member states to bring the enlargement process to a halt. In sum, "small victories" over technical detail may be just as important as a common "big vision" in building the necessary trust and confidence to make diplomacy work in the long term.

The capacity of institutions—both "legal" and "administrative"—to foster diplomatic goals has been bruised in the last decade but ought not to be forgotten in the race to build an EU fit for the demands of supranational governance in the twenty-first century. As Monnet argued, both individual will and institutional support will remain crucial ingredients for the next generation of successful diplomats.

Notes

1. See, for example, the special issue "Diplomacy and the European Union," *Hague Journal of Diplomacy* 4 (2009).
2. Michael Smith, "The EU as an International Actor," in *European Union: Power and Policy-Making*, ed. J. Richardson (London: Routledge, 1996), 290–309
3. See also Christopher J. Lee, *The Rise of Third World Diplomacy: Success and Its Meanings at the 1955 Asian-African Conference in Bandung, Indonesia*, in this volume.
4. See, for example, Ernst B. Haas, *The Uniting of Europe: Political, Social and Economic Forces 1950–1957* (Stanford, CA: Stanford University Press, 1958)
5. See "The Nobel Peace Prize for 2012" (press release), http://www.nobelprize.org/nobel_prizes/peace/laureates/2012/press.html).
6. See for an overview, Ben Rosamond, *Theories of European Integration* (Basingstoke, UK: Palgrave Macmillan, 2000).
7. See, for example, the "models" of Graham Allison in *Essence of Decision: Explaining the Cuban Missile Crisis* (London: Longman, 1999).
8. To clarify terminology, the European Union per se was formed in 1993 through the adoption of the Maastricht Treaty, the early EU was commonly understood as the "European Community," made up of three original organizations: the 1952 European Steel and Coal Community (1951 Treaty of Paris), plus the 1958 European Economic Community and Euratom (1957 Rome Treaties)
9. See Tony Judt, *Postwar* (London: Pimlico Random House, 2007), 63–99
10. See Philippe Mioche, *Le Plan Monnet: Genèse et élaboration, 1941–1947* (Paris: Publications de la Sorbonne, 1987).
11. One should note, of course, that the plan included many European states—France and the UK benefited as much as, or arguably more than, Germany from its provisions.
12. See, for example, the "integral" nature of general principles of international law according to Article 25 BVerfG.
13. See Antonin Cohen, "Constitutionalism without Constitution: Trans-national Elites between Political Mobilization and Legal Expertise in the Making of a Constitution for Europe" *Law and Social Inquiry* 32 (2007): 109–135. Even prominent Nazis were influenced by this wave. Referring to a meeting with the French minister of production in September 1943, Albert Speer told an interviewer, "We agreed that in the future we would avoid the mistakes of the First World War generation, who were now at the helm. Irrespective of national frontiers, Europe had to be economically integrated." Desmond Dinan, *Europe Recast: A History of European Union* (Boulder, CO: Lynne Rienner, 2005), 4–5.
14. On policy entrepreneurs, see Andrew Moravcsik, "A New Statecraft? Supranational Entrepreneurs and International Cooperation," *International Organization* 53, no. 2 (1999): 267–306.
15. Fontaine, Pascal, *Europe, a Fresh Start: The Schuman Declaration* (Luxembourg: Office for Official Publications of the European Communities, 1990).
16. Haas, *The Uniting of Europe*, 4; Gráinne de Burca, "Re-thinking Law in Neo-functionalist Theory," *Journal of European Public Policy* 12, no. 2 (2005): 310–326
17. John Gillingham, *Coal, Steel, and the Rebirth of Europe, 1945–1955: The Germans and French from Ruhr Conflict to Economic Community* (Cambridge: Cambridge University Press, 1991).
18. This idea was not, of course, peculiar to Europe but can be traced also within the context of other international institutions such as the Bretton Woods system. See, for example, John Gerard Ruggie, "Embedded Liberalism and the Postwar Economic Regimes," in Ruggie, *Constructing the World Polity: Essays in International Institutionalization* (London: Routledge, 1998).
19. On the legacy of depoliticization in the present-day EU, see Jan-Werner Müller, "Beyond Militant Democracy?" *New Left Review* 73 (2012): 39.

20. *Rapport des Chefs de Délégations aux Ministres des Affaires Etrangères*, (Brussels: Secretariat April 21, 1956).

21. Walter Hallstein, *The Role of the Community Institutions in European Unification* (statement by Walter Hallstein, president of the European Commission), Strasbourg, October 12, 1960.

22. See Ditlev Tamm, "The History of the Court of Justice and the European Union Since its Origin," in *The Court of Justice and the Construction of Europe: Analysis and Perspectives on Sixty Years of Case-law*, ed. Court of Justice of the European Union (Heidelberg: Springer, 2012)

23. See Joseph H. H. Weiler, "The Transformation of Europe," *Yale Law Journal* 100 (1991): 8.

24. Interestingly, the one institution rather slow to adopt this language of constitutionalism was the European Court itself. By the 1980s, however, this had changed. See, for example, its description of the treaty in the 1983 case of *Les Verts* as the European Community's "basic constitutional charter." Case 294/83, *Parti Écologiste "Les Verts" v. European Parliament* [1986] E.C.R. 1339 at [23].

25. Walter Hallstein, *The Commission, a new factor in international life*, Address by Professor Dr. Walter Hallstein, President by of the European Commission, given at the British Institute of International and Comparative Law, London, 25 March 1965, http://aei.pitt.edu/13638/.

26. See Weiler, "The Transformation of Europe," 22, 31–38.

27. This is a common explanation offered by, for example, intergovernmental theories of EU integration (i.e., that a strong court is accepted in order to circumvent national free-riding and moral hazard. See Andrew Moravscik, "Preferences and Power in the European Community: A Liberal Inter-governmentalist Approach," *Journal of Common Market Studies* 31 no. 4 (1993): 473–524.

28. See Bruno de Witte, "Direct Effect, Primacy and the Nature of the Legal Order," in *The Evolution of EU Law*, ed. Paul Craig and Gráinne de Burca (Oxford: Oxford University Press, 2011), 324–326.

29. Case C-26/62, *Van Gend & Loos.*

30. Case C-6/64, *Costa v ENEL.*

31. See R. Daniel Kelemen, *Eurolegalism: The Transformation of Law and Regulation in the European Union* (Cambridge, MA: Harvard University Press, 2011), 22–28.

32. See Andrew Moravcsik, "De Gaulle Between Grain and Grandeur: The Political Economy of French EC Policy, 1958–1970," *Journal of Cold War Studies* 2, no. 3 (2000): 4–68.

33. "The Fouchet Plan" (first draft, November 2, 1961), http://www.cvce.eu/viewer/-/content/485fa02e-f21e-4e4d-9665-92f0820a0c22/en.

34. On (reasons for) this proposal's failure, see Jeffrey W. Vanke, "An Impossible Union: Dutch Objections to the Fouchet Plan, 1959–1962," *Cold War History* 2, no. 1 (2001): 95–112.

35. On the impact of the compromise, see Jean-Marie Palayret, Helen Wallace, and Pascaline Winand, *Visions, Votes, and Vetoes: The Empty Chair Crisis and the Luxembourg Compromise Forty Years On* (Brussels: Peter Lang, 2006).

36. See, as one example, the use of the compromise by Germany to veto in 1985 a decrease in the price of cooking oil grain. Damian Chalmers, Gareth Davies, and Giorgio Monti, *European Union Law* (Cambridge: Cambridge University Press, 2014), 16; M. Vasey, "The 1985 Farm Price Negotiations and the Reform of the Common Agricultural Policy," *Common Market Law Review* 22 (1985): 664–666.

37. See, for example, Gerda Falkner, *EU Social Policy in the 1990s: Towards a Corporatist Policy Community* (London: Routledge, 1998), 55–77; Joseph H. H. Weiler, "The Genscher-Colombo Draft European Act: The Politics of Indecision," *Journal of European Integration* 6 (1983): 129.

38. See Neil Fligstein and Iona Mara-Drita, "How to Make a Market: Reflections on the Attempt to Create a Single Market in the European Union," *American Journal of Sociology* 102, no. 1 (1996): 11–13.

39. See Case 178/84, *Commission v Germany (German Beer)* [1987] ECR 1227.

40. Case 8/74, *Procureur du Roi v Benoit & Gustav Dassonville* [1974] ECR 837.

41. Fritz Scharpf, "Negative and Positive Integration in the Political Economy of European Welfare States," in *Governance in the European Union*, ed. Gary Marks et al. (London: SAGE, 1996).
42. Case 120/78, *Rewe-Zentral AG v Bundesmonopolverwaltung fur Branntwein (Cassis de Dijon)* [1979] ECR 649.
43. Case 120/78 [14], 40.
44. European Commission, *Completing the Internal Market* (white paper), COM(85)310 final at para. 13.
45. Ibid., 65.
46. See, for example, Keith Middlemas and Virginia Crowe, *Orchestrating Europe: The Informal Politics of European Union 1973–1995* (Waukegan, IL: Fontana Press, 1995), 115–135.
47. Andrew Moravcsik, *The Choice for Europe: Social Purpose and State Power from Messina to Maastricht* (Ithaca, NY: Cornell University Press, 1998), chap. 5.
48. Cohen, "Constitutionalism," 128.
49. Antoine Vauchez, "The Trans-national Politics of Judicialization: Van Gend en Loos and the Making of the EU Polity," *European Law Journal* 16, no. 1 (2010): 1–28.
50. Robert Lecourt, "L'Europe dans le prétoire," *Le Monde*, February 23, 1963.
51. On this broader topic, see Antoine Vauchez and Bruno de Witte, *Lawyering Europe: European Law as a Trans-national Social Field* (Oxford: Hart, 2013).
52. As well as Vauchez and de Witte above, see Mark Dawson, Elise Muir, and Bruno de Witte, *Judicial Activism at the European Court of Justice* (Cheltenham: Edward Elgar, 2013), 1–10.
53. Nonetheless, the idea of enlargement was hinted to in the Treaty of Rome itself. See, for example, the preamble, which called "upon the other peoples of Europe who share their ideal to join in their efforts."
54. Press conference given by General de Gaulle at the Elysée (November 27, 1967), http://www.cvce.eu/content/publication/1999/1/1/fe79955c-ef62-4b76-9677-dce44151be53/publishable_en.pdf.
55. See Christophe Hillion, "EU Enlargement," in *The Evolution of EU Law*, ed. Paul Craig and Gráinne de Burca (Oxford: Oxford University Press, 2011), 193.
56. Presidency Conclusions, Copenhagen European Council, June 21–22, 1993.
57. The success of conditionality in this field is certainly contested. See, for example, Anneli Albi, "Ironies in Human Rights Protection in the EU: Pre-Accession Conditionality and Post-Accession Conundrums," *European Law Journal* 15, no. 1 (2009): 46; Dimitry Kochenov, *EU Enlargement and the Failure of Conditionality* (Alphen aan den Rijn: Kluwer Law International, 2008).
58. Wojciech Sadurski, "Accession's Democracy Dividend: The Impact of the EU Enlargement upon Democracy in the New Member States of Central and Eastern Europe," *Yearbook of Polish European Studies* 7(2003): 40–41.
59. See also Presidency Conclusions, Madrid European Council, December 15–16, 1995.
60. Between 1991 and 1996, the EU signed twelve association agreements, with Poland, Hungary, and Czechoslovakia in 1991; Bulgaria, Romania, the Czech Republic, Slovakia, Estonia, Latvia, and Lithuania in 1995; and Slovenia in 1996.
61. See Marc Maresceau, "Pre-Accession," in *The Enlargement of the European Union*, ed. Marise Cremona (Oxford: Oxford University Press, 2003).
62. Tanja Börzel and Thomas Risse, "Venus Approaching Mars? The European Union's Approaches to Democracy Promotion in Comparative Perspective," in *Promoting Democracy and the Rule of Law: America and European Strategies*, ed. Amichai Magen, Thomas Risse, and Michael A. McFaul (Basingstoke, UK: Palgrave Macmillan, 2009), 40.
63. One should also note the important contribution of non-European programmes to post-Communist development in CEE states. See, for example, the U.S. "Support for Eastern Democracy" (or SEED) program.
64. On these (and further related) programs, see Tanja Börzel and Thomas Risse, "One Size Fits All! EU Policies for the Promotion of Human Rights, Democracy and the Rule of

Law" (paper presented at the Conference on Democracy Promotion, Stanford University, October 4–5, 2004, p. 11).

65. Sadurski, "Accession's Democracy Dividend," 33.

66. Börzel and Risse, "One Size Fits All," 41.

67. ilada Anna Vachudova, *Europe Undivided: Democracy, Leverage, and Integration after Communism* (Oxford: Oxford University Press, 2005).

68. Conclusion, "Commission Opinion on Slovakia's Application for Membership of the European Union," DOC/97/20, July 15, 1997.

69. On the domestic effects of accession negotiations in Slovakia, see Ján Figel and Miroslav Adamiš, "The Accession of the Slovak Republic," in *The Accession Story: The EU from 15 to 25 Countries*, ed.George Vassiliou (Oxford: Oxford University Press, 2007).

70. On the former, see Gwendolyn Sasse, "The Politics of Conditionality: The Norm of Minority Protection before and after EU Accession," *Journal of European Public Policy* 15, no. 6 (2008): 842–860; on the latter, see Grigore Pop-Eleches, "Between Historical Legacies and the Promise of Western Integration: Democratic Conditionality after Communism," *East European Politics and Societies* 21, no. 4 (2007): 153.

71. See, for example, the most recent example of Serbian agreement to normalize relations with Kosovo after an EU-brokered deal allowing the opening of accession negotiations with Serbia. See Vanessa Mock and Gordon Fairclough, "Serbia, Kosovo Advance Toward Bloc," *Wall Street Journal*, April 22, 2013, http://online.wsj.com/article/SB1000 1424127887324874204578438123563817706.html.

72. Frank Schimmelfennig, "The Community Trap: Liberal Norms, Rhetorical Action and Eastern Enlargement of the European Union," *International Organization* 55, no. 1 (2001): 49–56.

73. See, for example, the disproportionately high share of Austria in total EU exports to CEE countries (8.8 percent). Ibid., 51.

74. See, for example, the decisive negotiations in 2001 over levels of access for the 2004 accession states to European labor and goods markets. The French and Spanish governments attempted yet failed in these negotiations to link the access of new members to these markets to special guarantees on the distribution of agricultural and cohesion funding. See "EU Objections to Enlargement Dropped," Radio Free Europe, May 31, 2001, http://www.rferl.org/content/article/1096579.html.

75. As Margaret Thatcher, one of the most prominent proponents, argued in an Aspen speech in August 1990, "We can't say on one breath that they are part of Europe and in the next our European Community club is so exclusive that we won't admit them." *Financial Times* report, August 21, 1991.

76. European Parliament, Press Release No. 5564, October 27, 1993.

77. See, for example, Leon Brittan's statement that blocking association negotiations "could affect the Community's credibility." Quoted in Schimmelfennig, "The Community Trap," 72.

78. Only Belgium, France, and Italy adopted Declaration No. 6, "on the Protocol on the institutions with the prospect of enlargement of the European Union," www.europarl.europa.eu/summits/mad3_en.htm.

79. On the impact of enlargement on the Commission itself, see John Petersen, "Enlargement, Reform and the European Commission: Weathering a Perfect Storm?" *Journal of European Public Policy* 15, no. 5 (2008): 761–780.

80. European Commission, *Europe and the Challenge of Enlargement* (Brussels: Official Publications of the European Communities, 1992), 9–10.

81. This is an opening line from Slovakia's "2001 Regular Report on Progress Towards Accession" http://ec.europa.eu/enlargment/archives/pdf/key-documents/2001/sk-en.pdf.

82. Graham Avery, "The Enlargement Negotiations," in *The Future of Europe: Integration and Enlargement*, ed. Fraser Cameron (London: Routledge, 2004), 37.

83. See Hillion, "EU Enlargement," 200.

84. An example being the amendment to art. 88(5) of the French Constitution in 2008, which demands future accession treaties to be subject to a national referendum.

85. See the conclusions of the General Affairs Council (press release, September 13, 2010, No. 13420/10).

86. This impasse was finally resolved (after a full public referendum in Slovenia) via an agreement to submit the case to a binding international arbitration panel. See "EU Relieved After Slovenian Vote on Border Dispute," *EU Observer*, June 7, 2010, http://euobserver.com/enlargement/30222.

87. See, for example, the blocking of Romania and Bulgaria's participation in the Schengen area by the Council of Ministers in September of 2012 in spite of commission recommendations that the formal criteria for entry had been met. See "Council Conclusions on Cooperation and Verification Mechanism for Bulgaria and Romania," September 24, 2012, http://www.consilium.europa.eu/uedocs/cms_data/docs/pressdata/EN/genaff/132536.pdf.

88. My thanks go to Lorinc Redei for this insightful observation.

89. These measures (the so-called six pack) include five regulations and a directive. See the commission's introduction to the legislative proposals at http://ec.europa.eu/economy_finance/economic_governance/index_en.htm.

90. On the implications of the crisis for the EU's legal structure, see Mark Dawson and Floris de Witte, "Constitutional Balance in the European Union after the Euro Crisis" *Modern Law Review*, 76, 5(2013), 817–844.

91. See Mark Dawson and Elise Muir, "Enforcing Fundamental Values: EU Law and Governance in Hungary and Romania," *Maastricht Journal of European & Comparative Law* 19, no. 4 (2012), 469–476.

92. Venice Commission, "Opinion on three legal questions arising in the process of drafting the New Constitution of Hungary" (CDL-AD(2011)001, 25-26.3.2011), http://www.venice.coe.int/docs/2011/CDL-AD(2011)001-e.pdf.

93. This led to the launch by the EU of infringement actions against Hungary before the Court of Justice. See European Commission, "Hungary: Commission continues accelerated infringement procedure ..." (press release, March 7, 2012), http://europa.eu/rapid/pressReleasesAction.do?reference=IP/12/222&format=HTML&aged=0&language=EN&guiLanguage=en.

9

Economic Statecraft through the Use of Two-Level Games

Mexico's Successful Diplomacy in NAFTA and the Pacific Alliance

RAFAEL FERNÁNDEZ DE CASTRO AND BEATRIZ LEYCEGUI

According to U.S. president Harry S. Truman (1945–1953), "foreign and economic relationships are indivisible."[1] The truth of this statement is evidenced by Mexico's successful use of diplomacy in negotiations leading to signature economic treaties. To achieve this success, Mexico undertook a process of concerted actions with clear goals that encompassed domestic and foreign interests while utilizing presidential leadership, trained negotiators, and professional lobbyists. In this chapter, we examine Mexico's effective use of diplomacy to achieve economic ends through the North American Free Trade Agreement (NAFTA) and the Pacific Alliance—a new free-trade pact comprising Chile, Colombia, Peru, and Mexico. The Pacific Alliance was launched in 2011, and the four countries' negotiators concluded the first stage of liberalization in February 2014 through the signing of the Additional Protocol to the Framework Agreement of the Pacific Alliance. These two negotiation processes represented the intimate intertwining of both foreign and domestic economic policies for Mexico.

It is no exaggeration to say that NAFTA marked a sea change in U.S.-Mexico relations. The agreement, which went into effect in 1994, prompted bilateral cooperation beyond the core issues of trade and economic matters. In a similar fashion, the Pacific Alliance has allowed Mexico to foster cooperation beyond just trade and economic issues in order to consolidate a new subregion in Latin America that will provide for the free mobility of persons as well as a special outlook for economic relations with Asian Pacific countries.

NAFTA and the Pacific Alliance are cases of successful diplomacy because Mexico negotiated each in such a way that permitted it to conclude both agreements. Moreover, the goals of the treaties have been achieved: the deepening of Mexico's trade and economic relations with the world has favorably influenced Mexico's foreign policy and international prestige—both directly and through substantial spillover effects. In regard to direct results, by using economic tools and promoting a free-trade agenda, Mexico has strengthened its diplomacy and presence abroad. Regarding indirect effects, it is thought that a greater Mexican diplomatic and economic presence in the United States and Latin America will strengthen its economic security, and also that there have already been other positive results related to democratic gains.[2]

Why are the negotiations of NAFTA and the Pacific Alliance worthy of being singled out as cases of truly successful diplomacy? It is because both of these cases resulted in permanent changes in foreign and domestic policy that not only fundamentally changed visions of Mexico's place in the world but also resulted in significant alterations to Mexico's economy. Given the asymmetry of power between Mexico and the United States, it is no surprise that the prime objective of Mexico's diplomacy for many years was to protect its sovereignty. As a result, the traditional Mexican diplomatic agenda did not generally embrace the types of negotiations that promote either strong or heterogeneous domestic constituencies. With economic treaties, however, there will always be strong domestic constituencies as well as long-lasting policy consequences. Thus, although the preceding trade negotiations in the early 1980s were deemed to be a diplomatic success (especially vis-à-vis the United States), there were few domestic spillovers and even fewer permanent policy changes.[3]

This chapter relies on Robert Putnam's two-level game concept as an analytical tool to explain the success of both the NAFTA and the Pacific Alliance negotiations.[4] This approach takes into account several factors that are important to understanding the success of the negotiations, including how domestic constituents are handled and engaged, and what the expected spillover effects are. First, it sets forth that to be successful, central decision-makers must strive to reconcile domestic and international imperatives simultaneously.[5] Second, it recognizes that negotiations lead to adoption of policies different from those that would have been pursued in the absence of international negotiations, and that agreement is often possible only because a powerful minority within each government favors the internationally demanded policy due to domestic realities.[6] Furthermore, it is often the case that in the absence of international pressure, policy changes would likely not have been pursued, and that even if they were pursued, they would certainly not be implemented on the same scale or even within the same time frame.[7] This seems to be particularly true of economic negotiations.[8]

Mexico's negotiations of NAFTA and the Pacific Alliance offer parallels to the two-level game concept. Presidential involvement was strongly present in the negotiations of each treaty, as the agreements were at the top of the respective agendas. During the NAFTA negotiations, President Carlos Salinas (1988–1994) exercised important leadership by building a strong negotiating team. Regarding the Pacific Alliance, President Felipe Calderón (2006–2012) personally attended six meetings and promoted effective coordination between the foreign and economic ministries dealing with the negotiations. Subsequently, President Enrique Peña Nieto (2012–2018) followed up with a series of five summits with the leaders of the other Pacific Alliance countries. It is important to note that in both cases, Presidents Salinas (with NAFTA) and Calderón and Peña Nieto (with the Pacific Alliance) played Level II (domestic-focused) games by placing special attention on two constituencies: the Mexican Senate and the private sector. Even though there are clear differences in the scope and details of both cases, there are also numerous similarities, including the existence of prior agreements that paved the way for a later deepening of the economic relationship, the involvement of the private sector, and the coincidence of both agreements with significant internal economic reforms.

In these two cases, it is also intriguing how Mexico was able to turn what should have theoretically been its primary negotiation weakness into a source of strength. The supposed weakness was due to a paradox inherent in the two-level game concept: that institutional arrangements which strengthen decision-makers at home may weaken their international bargaining positions, and vice versa.[9] That is, a system that should make domestic ratification easy also makes the preceding international negotiation much more difficult. With regard to Mexico, its political arrangement features a heavily centralized system with a strong executive and relatively weak legislative and civil sectors. This system seems to present negotiators with few real limits to their capacity to make promises, and it is within this context that we see the paradox at work.

We can begin to understand the paradox when we observe that government negotiators typically must negotiate simultaneously with government officials from other countries as well as their own domestic agencies or constituencies.[10] The two-level game is therefore usually played with foreign counterparts (Level I, or international negotiation) and with domestic constituencies (Level II, or domestic ratification). As a result, what is agreed to with the foreign counterparts must be perceived as acceptable to domestic constituencies in order for a treaty to be ratified.

The perceived interest of the domestic constituency is routinely used as a powerful bargaining chip. This is what Thomas Schelling referred to when he wrote that "the power of a negotiator often rests on a manifest *inability* to make concessions." That is, the more constrained negotiators are seen to be, the more credible any statements that they *could not possibly* yield to the demands of their counterparts sitting across the table will be. Schelling noted that U.S. negotiators generally make effective use of the constraints imposed upon them by Congress.[11]

How President Salinas and later President Peña Nieto (to a lesser but still significant degree) were able to overcome the constraints placed upon them by domestic forces is an important part of the story of why the NAFTA and Pacific Trade Alliance negotiations can be seen to go beyond mere diplomatic successes to constitute successful diplomacy.

Background: Mexico's Trade Policy

Since 2006, Mexico's international trade policy has focused on (1) deepening and improving its relations with its existing trade partners and creating new agreements with emerging economies and (2) integrating wider free-trade areas through treaties to promote specialization, economies of scale, and the integration of production value chains. In its international trade policy, Mexico has prioritized its relationships with North America and Latin America.

North America

In 2013, North America's gross domestic product (GDP) constituted 26.9 percent of world GDP (the European Union participated with 23.4 percent).[12] The three North American countries composing NAFTA represent a potential market of 473 million consumers with high purchasing power.[13] In the NAFTA area, trilateral commerce reached 1.1 trillion dollars in 2013, a figure accounting for 5.8 percent of world trade.[14] In that year, North America registered 82.6 percent of Mexico's exports and 48 percent of its imports.[15] Since 1999, Mexico has received 191.3 billion dollars in foreign direct investment (FDI) from Canada and the United States, an amount that accounts for 53 percent of the total FDI received during that period.[16]

Latin America

During the last decade, Latin America[17] has become the second most dynamic economic region in the world, with only Asia ahead. Between 2000 and 2012, its gross domestic product (GDP) grew at an annual average rate of 3.21 percent (European Union, 1.25 percent; Japan, 0.71 percent; United States, 1.74 percent).[18] It is a market with over 560 million potential consumers.[19] Latin America also has increasing purchasing power: from 2000 to 2012, its GDP per capita grew 20.3 percent (whereas North America's grew 8.9 percent, the European Union's 10.8 percent, and East and Pacific Asia's 32.2 percent).[20] In 2012, 75 percent of Latin American imports were manufactured goods, an area in which Mexico has a comparative advantage as witnessed by the fact that manufactured goods constituted 74.3 percent of its global exports that year.[21] Latin America is a natural market for Mexican companies, particularly for small and medium enterprises (SMEs). In 2011, almost 60 percent of the Mexican companies that exported to this region were SMEs.[22]

The North American Free Trade Agreement
Economic Background

Mexican foreign trade has historically been and continues to be concentrated in the United States, which is the main destination for Mexican exports and the main source of its imports. Table 9.1 shows three major trends in this regard. First, the U.S. share of Mexico's total trade remains at approximately 70 percent from the 1970s to the present. Second, Mexican international trade shows an impressive increase during the 1970s and 1980s. This can be explained by the transition of the Mexican economy from an import substitution industrialization model to one based on exports, with important participation of the oil sector. Finally, both Mexican exports to the United States and imports from the United States showed a sharp increase from 1993 to 2000. This can be explained by the significant effect of NAFTA as a facilitator of trade.

Table 9.2 shows a comparison of total trade for North America, the European Union, and East Asia from 1990 to 2012. Of the three economic regions, North America has the largest asymmetry between the markets. In 1990, when NAFTA was launched, the United States accounted for 74 percent of total trade in the three North American countries, and Mexico had only 7 percent. This asymmetry represented both a challenge and an opportunity for Mexico. The challenge was the heavy dependence of Mexican trade on the U.S. market. The opportunity was for Mexico to negotiate a free trade agreement that would enhance its economic standing in North America.

Tables 9.2 and 9.3 show some of the trade dynamics caused by NAFTA. Mexico's participation in North American total trade increased from 7 percent in 1990 to 13.5 percent in 2012 (see Table 9.2). Table 9.3 shows the impact that NAFTA had in increasing Canadian and Mexican trade with the United States. Total U.S. trade with Canada and Mexico increased from US$ 340.5 billion in

Table 9.1 **Mexican Merchandise Trade, 1990–2013**

Year	Exports to U.S. (US$ billion)	Imports from U.S. (US$ billion)	Trade with U.S. as % of global	Trade with Canada as % of global
1970	0.90	1.6	66	N/A
1980	9.90	12.60	64	N/A
1993	37.89	43.46	75.79	2.41
1995	59.75	51.68	79.20	2.33
2000	135.22	121.02	80.96	2.20
2005	158.32	106.12	68.19	2.46
2009	159.10	97.28	62.10	3.58
2013	263.46	154.08	62.24	2.84

Source: 1970 and 1980 data - Revista Mexicana de Comercio Exterior, 1994; and 1993 to 2013 data - estimates using data from Banco de México available at: <www.banxico.org.mx/estadisticas/index.html>.

1993 to 729.3 billion in 2000. In contrast, during this same time period, Japanese and Chinese trade with the United States grew less dynamically, as did German and British trade (see Table 9.3). It is also noteworthy that Canadian and Mexican trade with the United States reduced its rate of growth in the first decade of the twenty-first century. Moreover, due to the U.S. economic crisis in 2008 and 2009, North American trade showed a decline.

The NAFTA Negotiations

NAFTA marked a watershed in the U.S.-Mexico relationship. By embracing NAFTA, the Salinas administration put an end to the traditional resistance to further economic integration with its neighbor to the north. For the Mexican government, the essential goal of the agreement was to take advantage of being next door to the largest world market.

NAFTA had an enormous scope, encompassing almost all economic sectors. However, Mexico excluded the energy sector from the negotiations on political grounds, and the United States set aside immigration. Although the primary impact of NAFTA was economic, there were important spillovers into other areas of the bilateral relationship. For example, the three signatory countries agreed to an unprecedented level of cooperation and to monitor one another's compliance with national regulations concerning environmental and labor issues. Moreover, Mexico and the United States engaged together in the peace process in El Salvador. It is for these reasons that Mexican historian

Table 9.2 **Total Trade for North America, the European Union, and East Asia: 1990–2012**

Group or Country	Total trade (US$ billion) and % of total trade for each country (in parentheses)	
	1990	2012
North America	1,539,655	5,563,789
U.S.	1,141,609	3,882,657
	(74)	(69.8)
Canada	296,702	929,740
	(19)	(16.7)
Mexico	101,544	751,391
	(7)	(13.5)
European Union	3,066,830	11,646,951
Germany	776,786	2,574,521
	(25)	(22.1)
U.K.	408,149	1,148,778
	(13)	(9.8)
East Asia	720,566	6,618,749
China	57,645	3,866,883
	(8)	(58.4)
Japan	533,218	1,684,412
	(74)	(25.4)
South Korea	129,701	1,067,454
	(18)	(16.1)

Source: 1990 data - Robert A. Pastor, *The North American Idea: A Vision of a Continental Future*, 2011; 2012 data - estimates using data of the World Bank, available at: <databank. worldbank.org>.

Lorenzo Meyer wrote, "The year 1990 (when NAFTA negotiations were launched) shall be considered an historic date in the evolution of U.S.-Mexican relations," because Mexican elites brought about "an historic shift in the definition of the national interest facing its powerful northern neighbor."[23]

NAFTA inaugurated a new period in Mexican foreign policy in which one of its long-standing end goals—autonomy from Washington—came to an end. During the Cold War, Mexico's most internally celebrated diplomatic triumphs were the decisions to oppose the U.S.-backed resolution in

Table 9.3 **Total U.S. Trade of Goods and Services with Partners in North America, Asia, and Europe, 1986–2013 ($US million)**

Countries	1986	1993	2000	2007	2009	2010	2013
Canada and Mexico	179,694	340,535	729,299	1,027,573	918,655	1,038,171	1,296,243
Japan and China	134,172	234,791	387,803	684,046	727,880	746,508	900,597
Germany and the United Kingdom	91,658	152,440	266,138	411,378	518,730	378,915	433,742

Source: 1986 to 2010 data - Robert A. Pastor, *The North American Idea: A Vision of a Continental Future*, 2011; 2013 data - estimates using data of the U.S. Department of Commerce: available at: <www.bea.gov/international/index.htm>.

the Organization of American States (OAS) to oust Cuba from the Inter-American System in 1962 and the creation of the Contadora Group in 1983 (Mexico, Colombia, Panama, and Venezuela), which sought alternatives for peace in Central America that were sometimes in marked opposition to U.S. perspectives. In contrast, starting from the 1990s, there was a greater convergence in U.S. and Mexican foreign policies.[24] This is not to say that the two countries became totally free from differences and frictions. For example, in February of 2003, Mexico opposed the U.S.-backed resolution in the UN Security Council to invade Iraq. However, in this instance the goal of Mexico was not to mark its opposition publicly, but rather to avert the possibility of retaliation from Al Qaeda, which later struck in Spain in March 2004 and the United Kingdom in July 2005. Mexico later supported the United States in the Security Council in 2010 when it backed the U.S. and Germany's efforts to impede Iran from developing nuclear weapons.[25]

Paving the Way to NAFTA

In the aftermath of World War II, the United States became the leading force behind free trade in the Western Hemisphere, and the General Agreement on Tariffs and Trade (GATT) became its favorite international institution to foster global trade. In contrast, Mexico developed a highly protectionist trade regime as part of a strategy of import substitution industrialization, and as a result did not join GATT until 1986—forty years after its creation. These wildly divergent foreign trade strategies caused continual friction between the United States and Mexico. Surprisingly, these tensions did not seem to have a detrimental effect on either of the two economies during the 1960s and 1970s. As Sidney Weintraub noted, trade conflicts between the United States and Mexico were the result of these two worldviews, but as long as both countries prospered, as they did until the 1970s, the conflict was muted.[26]

In the 1980s, Mexico underwent important economic reforms, the most important of which was trade liberalization. This was achieved through a unilateral reduction of both tariff and nontariff trade barriers. The import substitution industrialization model (implemented from the 1950s to the 1970s) was replaced by an economy oriented toward manufacturing and export. As noted earlier, the sharp increase in Mexican exports to the United States during the 1970s and 1980s made the continued openness of the U.S. market very important to Mexico.

Paradoxically, just when Mexico opened up its economy and increased its reliance on exports in the 1980s, trade frictions between Mexico and the United States intensified, with the United States showing incipient signs of protectionism. Mexico's accusations of unfair trade practices on the part of the United States mounted, resulting in substantial uncertainty concerning Mexican exports. Meanwhile, there was a sharp rise in countervailing duty and antidumping suits against Mexican exports, and restrictive quotas were placed on Mexican steel exports. Canadian ambassador Rodney Grey described the antidumping and countervailing duty measures as "contingent protectionism." Imports were limited or supplemental duties were imposed in retaliation for what were considered unfair trade practices.[27] In 1984, Mexico signed the Voluntary Export Restraint (VER) on steel, a new U.S. trade protectionist mechanism. Through this agreement, Mexico "voluntarily" diminished its steel exports to the United States by half. Put another way, Mexico was assigned a quota that compelled a necessary reduction of steel exports.[28] Mexico had neither recourse nor resources to cope with rising U.S. protectionism. Despite the fact that the U.S. market was the main destination of Mexican exports, there was no legal framework with which to adjudicate U.S.-Mexico trade relations. Moreover, Mexico was not yet a member of GATT. In fact, Mexico had not signed a single trade agreement with the United States from 1942 through the 1980s.[29] To deal with its increasingly conflicting trade relations with the United States, Mexico decided to build a legal trade framework through a series of bilateral agreements during the second half of the 1980s, and it finally joined GATT in 1986.

Between 1985 and 1989, Mexico and the United States signed six bilateral agreements. The most relevant ones were the Subsidies and Countervailing Duties Agreement of 1985, the Legal Trade Framework I of 1987, and the

Legal Trade Framework II of 1989. In the Subsidies and Countervailing Duties Agreement, Mexico promised to stop subsidizing exports and in return was granted the "injury test," making the imposition of duties on Mexico more difficult by requiring U.S. industries to demonstrate proof of domestic injury.[30] The Legal Framework I was a mechanism for bilateral consultations preventing trade disputes, furthering trade and investment liberalization.[31] The Legal Trade Framework II went a step further by deepening and actively promoting the liberalization of trade and investment.[32] This emerging legal trade framework between the two countries paved the way to NAFTA, a surprise proposal made by Mexico in 1990.

Presidential Leadership in the NAFTA Negotiations

President Salinas had an ambitious agenda to foster foreign investment in Mexico and to promote exports. He believed Mexico's economic reforms in the late 1980s had made it an attractive market for foreign investors. The reforms consisted of four main elements: trade liberalization, deregulation, the privatization of state enterprises, and the setting in order of public finances.[33] Despite these improvements, Salinas and his trade minister, Jaime Serra, realized while at the 1989 World Economic Forum in Davos that the European Community and Japan were not ready to invest in Mexico. Europe was too busy managing the collapse of the Soviet Union—the wealthy Western European countries were entirely occupied with the reconstruction of Eastern Europe, and Germany's priority was reunification. Europe's goal seemed to be to build democratic, market-oriented regimes that would eventually become part of the European Union. Meanwhile, Japan had domestic deflationary pressures to contend with.

While at Davos, Salinas recalled that President George H. W. Bush (1989–1993) had proposed the possibility of a free trade agreement during a meeting in 1988 in Houston, Texas:

> I realized the advancement of globalization made urgent the negotiation of a Free Trade Agreement. . . . Once we decided to negotiate a Free Trade Agreement it was necessary to find out where the U.S. interest stood since I had rejected the offer (of soon-to-be President Bush) in 1988.[34]

The meeting had taken place before either man had been sworn into office. At that time, Salinas thought it was too early to negotiate an agreement of such great magnitude, but after realizing that neither the European Union nor Japan (the second- and third-largest world economies) were ready to invest in

Mexico, he decided to open the Mexican economy to the possibility of free trade with the United States.

Soon after returning from Davos in April 1990, Salinas dispatched some of his most trusted economic officials to Washington, D.C., to explore the possibility of initiating free trade negotiations with Bush's economic and trade teams. The Mexican contingent encountered initial resistance from the U.S. trade representative, Ambassador Carla Hills, who was devoted to the Uruguay Round of GATT. But President Salinas and his economic team had decided that the best way to foster the growth of the recently reformed Mexican economy was to initiate free trade negotiations with its neighbor to the north.

On June 10, 1990, Salinas traveled to Washington, D.C., with the sole purpose of convincing President Bush to launch free trade negotiations.[35] The two presidents met at Camp David, where President Bush hosted a dinner for his Mexican counterpart. The reception preceding the dinner was attended only by Bush's closest economic and trade advisers.[36] According to Bush's press secretary, Marlin Fitzwater, "Both leaders believe[d] that the United States and Mexico would each derive substantial and long-term benefits from a comprehensive bilateral trade agreement. They agreed that bilateral efforts to maximize trade and investment opportunities [could] and should complement the trade liberalization achieved in the Uruguay round of the GATT."[37] In the end, Salinas and his team's perseverance paid off. President Bush acquiesced to bilateral meetings in preparation for the negotiations. Even though American trade negotiators were busy with the Uruguay Round of GATT, it was difficult for President Bush to deny Salinas a negotiation that he had first suggested.

To prepare for the negotiations, the Mexican government established a new office in Washington, D.C., dedicated solely to the negotiating effort. President Salinas and Trade Minister Serra also put together an impressive team of technocrats located in both Mexico City and Washington. The team included dozens of highly trained professionals with prestigious graduate degrees.[38] For example the top negotiator, Trade Minister Serra, had a Ph.D. in economics from Yale University.

Although Mexico was well prepared to enter negotiations, it is not clear whether these preparations in and of themselves would have been sufficient to guarantee success. At the time of the NAFTA negotiation's launching, Mexico and the United States revealed important contrasts in their decision-making processes. Formally, both governments were presidential regimes with separation of powers; but in practice, there were deep differences, the most emblematic was that in Mexico, the same party (the Institutional Revolutionary Party, or PRI, using its Spanish acronym) had been in power for sixty-five years.[39] Another key difference was that in Mexico in the early 1990s, power was highly centralized in the Mexican presidency, with neither Congress nor the courts, to say nothing of civil society, providing a sufficient balancing force. As noted earlier, the paradox noted in Robert Putnam's two-level game concept signifies that international negotiation is much more difficult when domestic ratification is seen to be easy, meaning that the differences in the Mexican and U.S. policymaking processes should have had a significant impact on Mexico's negotiating capacities vis-à-vis the United States.

Thus, during the NAFTA negotiations, it was expected that American negotiators were to keep in mind both their Mexican counterparts and their domestic constituencies, but there was no equivalent expectation out of Mexico.[40] As described by Jorge Dominguez, "Mexican President Salinas would have been literally 'incredible' if he had attempted to argue, in negotiation with the United States, that he was constrained by Congress or the courts in making or unmaking commitments."[41] In that case, how were the negotiations necessary to create successful diplomacy accomplished?

President Salinas's skill in playing Level II (domestic) games was an important factor in the success of Mexico's negotiations. Salinas unexpectedly placed special attention on two domestic constituencies: the Mexican Senate and the private sector. In addition, he was also able to successfully capture much of the U.S. domestic constituency.

Once President Bush acquiesced to launching negotiations leading to NAFTA, President Salinas formally asked the upper chamber of the Mexican Congress to establish a consultative process on whether it would be in the national interest to negotiate a free trade agreement with the United States. The Senate proceeded with the consultation and soon thereafter announced that such an agreement would result in great benefit to the Mexican economy.[42]

To secure the backing of the private sector, the administration facilitated the creation of the Business Coordination of Foreign Trade (Coordinadora de Organizaciones Empresariales de Comercio Exterior, or COECE in its Spanish acronym). COECE integrated each economic sector: steel, cement, textiles, construction, toys, agribusiness, and many others.[43] COECE business leaders became the inseparable companions of Mexican NAFTA negotiators, or in negotiation jargon, the "next-door chamber." Always present and ready with assessments on how NAFTA was going to affect their own economic sectors, COECE became an effective negotiation tool. Moreover, COECE leadership was asked by President Salinas to engage in a lobbying campaign in the United States in order to secure the successful negotiation of NAFTA and its eventual approval by the U.S. Congress. COECE hired lobbyists in Washington, D.C., who shepherded top Mexican businesspeople within the corridors of the Capitol. At the same time, Minister Serra and Chief Negotiator Blanco hired over a dozen lobbying firms in Washington as well as in key states such as California and Texas. The lobbying firms centered their efforts on key members of Congress and crucial constituencies such as Latinos, states bordering Mexico, and business organizations.

In this way, President Salinas transformed his negotiating weakness—that is, not having domestic constituencies that would limit his negotiation capacities—into a strength for his negotiators. Instead of ignoring the Mexican Congress and the private sector due to their relative lack of strength, President Salinas recruited them, especially the business sector, as an integral part of the negotiating team.

NAFTA became President Salinas's single most important foreign policy initiative. He and his entire economic team became very engaged in securing the approval of NAFTA. One can argue that Salinas became Mexico's number one self-taught lobbyist. He traveled extensively to the United States to popularize the idea of the agreement. To counter the accusations of U.S. environmental groups that Mexico did not properly implement its own environmental laws, President Salinas took bold steps such as closing the largest oil refinery in Mexico City and implementing dolphin-safe fishing practices. When problems arose in other areas of the bilateral relationship, President Salinas rushed his cabinet ministers to resolve them. For example, as a result of the 1985 murder of U.S. Drug Enforcement Administration agent Enrique "Kiki" Camarena, the agency kidnapped a Mexican doctor, Humberto Álvarez Machain, in 1992. Mexico used all of its diplomatic leverage to make sure that this bilateral friction did not negatively affect the NAFTA negotiations.

For the first time in Mexican diplomatic history, the Mexican government made full use of every resource available in the U.S. policymaking processes in order to pass NAFTA. In addition to hiring lobbying firms, the Mexican negotiating team encouraged the United States' most prominent business organizations and think tanks to come out with favorable reports on the projected impact of NAFTA. The Washington-based think tanks, the Center for Strategic and International Studies and the Overseas Development Council, created programs almost entirely dedicated to fostering the passage of the agreement. In addition, Mexico created a national program to nurture Mexican-American organizations. These organizations were very helpful in places like California and Texas in ensuring that their congressional delegations were favorable to NAFTA.

In sum, Mexico's successful negotiation of NAFTA and the eventual passage of the agreement by the U.S. Congress were the product of effective diplomacy. President Salinas's success was the result of a three-pronged game. First, Mexico's negotiating team played a Level I game with the U.S. and Canadian negotiators. At the same time, Salinas played two Level II games, the first with Mexican domestic economic and political constituencies, and the second—through his lobbying efforts—with U.S. economic constituencies and Congress.

The Pacific Alliance

Economic Background

The Pacific Alliance has become one of the most dynamic economic integration processes in Latin America and has caught the attention of the international community. The Pacific Alliance represents a potential market of 216 million consumers with rising purchasing power. Although intrabloc exports are low (less than 5 percent) and the added value of Pacific Alliance inputs in each country's exports is small (12 percent in Peru, 10 percent in Colombia and Chile, and close to 2.5 percent in Mexico), there is great potential for further integration of each member's value chains in sectors such as mining, chemicals, textiles and apparel, and the agroindustry.[44] See Table 9.4 for a comparison of its economic weight with other regional initiatives.

Table 9.4 **Economic Weight of Various Regional Initiatives, 2012**

	Pacific Alliance	*Mercosur*	*ASEAN*	*TPP*
GDP (US$ million)	2,015,684	3,307,835	2,281,023	28,117,758
% Latin America	35	58	N/A	N/A
GDP per capita (US$ million)	9,331	11,822	3,749	35,351
Total trade (US$ million)	1,116,965	822,021	2,474,969	7,860,831
Exports (US$ million)	556,033	437,139	1,253,513	3,555,479
% Latin America	51	40	N/A	N/A
Imports (US$ million)	560,932	384,882	1,221,456	4,305,352
% Latin America	52	36	N/A	N/A
Population (millions)	216	279	608	795
% Latin America	38	49	N/A	N/A

Notes: Latin America includes Argentina, Belize, Bolivia, Brazil, Chile, Colombia, Costa Rica, Ecuador, El Salvador, Guatemala, Honduras, Mexico, Nicaragua, Panama, Paraguay, Peru, Uruguay, and Venezuela. The Pacific Alliance comprises Chile, Colombia, Mexico, and Peru.

Mercosur includes Argentina, Brazil, Paraguay, Uruguay, and Venezuela. The

ASEAN countries are Brunei, Cambodia, Indonesia, Laos, Malaysia, Myanmar, Philippines, Singapore, Thailand, and Vietnam (GDP estimates do not include data from Myanmar).

TPP includes Australia, Brunei, Canada, Chile, Japan, Malaysia, Mexico, New Zealand, Peru, Singapore, the United States, and Vietnam.

Source: estimates using data of the World Bank, available at: <databank.worldbank.org>.

The Pacific Alliance is not only a trade agreement designed for ongoing economic and commercial integration. It has also created mobility for citizens of the four member nations. For instance, Mexico eliminated visitor visas for Colombian and Peruvian nationals, an important change in its immigration practices. Mexico had previously applied very strict security measures regarding Colombians traveling to Mexico due the strength of Colombia's drug cartels. As a result, Colombian nationals often had to wait months to get visas, and many were denied entry to Mexico altogether.

The Pacific Alliance also serves as a foreign policy pact. It is a club for like-minded countries that share the ideas of trade liberalization, economic development based on market-oriented economic policies, and a foreign policy that is not antagonistic toward the United States. Moreover, this subregional integration model can be seen as a subtle liberal response to the Bolivarian Alliance of the Americas (Alianza Bolivariana para las Américas, or ALBA in its Spanish acronym). The Pacific Alliance directly contradicts ALBA's protectionist trade policies and statist and populist economic development policies.

Previous Economic Integration Efforts in Latin America

Efforts at economic integration in Latin America date back to 1960, the signing of the Treaty of Montevideo, and the creation of the Latin American Free Trade Association, which in 1980 was reorganized to become the Latin American Integration Association (ALADI in its Spanish acronym). Although the member countries have signed various commitments through ALADI, the agreement has not been able to achieve its desired integration of the region.

Another regional trade agreement was attempted in 1994. Under the leadership of the United States, thirty-four American countries started negotiations to create the Free Trade Area of the Americas. Despite the complex negotiation process, which lasted nearly a decade, the initiative did not succeed.

In 2007, eleven Latin American countries—Chile, Colombia, Costa Rica, Ecuador, El Salvador, Guatemala, Honduras, Mexico, Nicaragua, Panama, and Peru—created the Latin American Pacific Arc Forum. The member countries intended to form a space for dialogue, cooperation, and convergence on economic and trade issues, as well as to commit themselves to developing a strategy to project themselves in a more coordinated and competitive manner toward the Asia Pacific region.[45] The Pacific Arc did not ultimately produce specific results, due to various factors, among them the number of countries involved, conflicting priorities, the existence of other ongoing negotiations, and the fact that not all the countries had preferential agreements with each other.

Negotiations

In October of 2010, due to the impossibility of building consensus under the Pacific Arc, the former president of Peru, Alan García (1985–1990 and 2006–2011), proposed a new negotiation with fewer participating countries. At first, García only sent the proposal to Chile, Colombia, Ecuador, and Panama. Mexico was excluded because of the perceived difficulties of its being able to conclude a bilateral free trade agreement with Peru.

However, owing to Mexico's standing in the region and the restart of bilateral negotiations with Peru after a long period of stalemate, in December 2010 the president of Mexico joined the presidents of Chile, Colombia, and Peru in laying out a road map for a deep integration initiative, establishing specific commitments for its advancement. The presidents agreed that there was no time to lose, and they instructed their trade and foreign ministers to commence work on the agreement in the first days of January 2011. By June 2012, they had completed and signed the Pacific Alliance Framework Agreement, which established an integration area in which to seek progressive advancement concerning the liberalization of goods, services, capital, and the movement of people. The agreement also serves as a platform for foreign policy coordination, economic and trade integration, and the projection of the member countries as a bloc to the world, with emphasis on the Asia-Pacific region.

The network of preexisting trade agreements between members was key to the successful creation of the Pacific Alliance. During the negotiations, Peru's lack of a trade agreement with Mexico and other Latin American countries placed it in a disadvantageous position relative to the other parties that had agreements between themselves. This hindered the possibility of advancing in the negotiations. Mexico and Peru's conclusion of a bilateral agreement became Mexico's ticket to the Pacific Alliance and the Trans-Pacific Partnership negotiations. President Calderón had to surmount significant opposition from the Mexican private sector, particularly agricultural interests, to conclude the Free Trade Area of the Americas agreement with Peru. If this negotiation had not succeeded, that is, if it had failed at Level II (domestic affairs) and caused defection, Mexico would not have had the credibility to participate in more ambitious negotiations in the future.

All countries participating in the Pacific Alliance have free trade agreements (FTAs) with each other. Mexico has an FTA with Chile, and in recent years has adjusted and deepened its FTA with Colombia. The signing of the Mexico-Peru Trade Integration Agreement in 2011 was fundamental to further progress, as it was the only major trade relationship that remained undeveloped. Having a network of preexisting trade agreements among the countries negotiating the Pacific Alliance established a level playing field that allowed negotiators to seek more ambitious commitments.

The countries that negotiated the Pacific Alliance share values and principles that were essential to achieving a successful result. The four countries' governments share the idea of trade liberalization and the promotion of foreign investment as engines to drive their economic development. The continuity of the respective countries' international trade policies by their new administrations has also been fundamental to the integration process.

Former presidents Calderón of Mexico and García of Peru were important promoters of their countries' trade liberalization, and they played a vital role in creating the initiative. Despite the occurrence of presidential elections and a resulting change in governing political parties in these countries while the negotiations were taking place, there has been continuity in their trade policies. Since taking office, Mexico's current president, Peña Nieto, has decisively promoted economic liberalization, and even Peru's new president, Ollanta Humala (2012–2016), who is characterized as "left wing," has favored and driven the negotiations. Likewise, the president of Chile, Michelle Bachelet (2006–2010 and 2014–2018), also supported the integration process.

In the last two decades, the four countries that are members to the alliance have established ambitious trade agendas, continuously negotiating FTAs with the world. The members' shared ideals were a determinant in driving the negotiations to a successful result. As Mexico's minister of economy, Ildefonso Guajardo, has noted: "the countries involved in the Pacific Alliance are those that reflect the greatest dynamism in Latin America."[46]

Presidential Leadership

Chile, Colombia, Mexico, and Peru have shown genuine interest in the Pacific Alliance, which has clearly become a high priority in their trade and economic agendas. This interest has been led by the highest levels of each country. From the initiative's launching in December 2010 to the signing of the first liberalization agreement in February 2014, the member country presidents held eight summits and then met again four months later (in contrast, the Pacific Arc gathered the presidents only once during the span of five years). In some cases, the presidents have even connected through sophisticated video conference systems. In addition to engaging the presidents, the Pacific Alliance has secured active participation and leadership from high-level officials, particularly deputy ministers.

The Pacific Alliance has prioritized the following areas, for which technical groups have been established:

- the movement of businessmen and the facilitation of transit migration, including police cooperation;
- trade and integration, including trade facilitation and customs cooperation;
- services and capital, including the integration of stock exchanges; and
- cooperation and dispute settlement mechanisms.

The Pacific Alliance concluded a first stage of the integration process on February 10, 2014, with the signing of the Additional Protocol to the Framework Agreement of the Pacific Alliance. The members agreed to a complete trade liberalization of goods (92 percent immediately and the remaining 8 percent to be reached by 2030). The liberalization of services is also covered, although less forcefully.

The countries also agreed to a practically complete harmonization of rules of origin; regulatory cooperation through the promotion of mutual recognition agreements on technical standards; elimination of visa requirements; establishment of mechanisms for trade facilitation and customs cooperation (through, for example, the connection of each country's single window for trade operations and electronic certificates of origin); cooperation on many fronts (the opening of common embassies and trade and investment promotion agencies, environment and climate change, science and technology, tourism, and scholarship programs for academic exchanges); and introduction of agreements in the financial, transportation, and telecommunications sectors.

In addition, the members sought to advance their negotiations on the free mobility of investments. The Mexican Stock Exchange was integrated into the Latin America Integrated Market, which already comprises the stock exchanges of Santiago, Bogotá, and Lima. There is also an agreement to regulate government procurement within the four countries. Good regulatory practices and e-commerce are part of the agreement as well. The countries have also signed the Agreement for the Establishment of the Pacific Alliance Cooperation Fund, which through equal contributions will finance cooperation projects as well as a scholarship system to facilitate the exchange of students between the countries.

The level of ambition of the Pacific Alliance has caught the attention of the international community, resulting in a growing number of country observers. These now include Australia, Belgium, Canada, China, Costa Rica, the Dominican Republic, Ecuador, El Salvador, Finland, France, Germany, Guatemala, Honduras, India, Israel, Italy, Japan, Morocco, the Netherlands, New Zealand,

Panama, Paraguay, Portugal, Singapore, South Korea, Spain, Switzerland, Trinidad and Tobago, Turkey, the United Kingdom, the United States, and Uruguay.

Costa Rica and Panama are candidates to become members of the Alliance. The Pacific Alliance could also grow to include not only more Latin American countries but also other countries that have expressed interest in participating as observers. The integration of Latin America will give the region greater bargaining power vis-à-vis other regions; successfully integrate it into global and regional value chains; and resolve many common economic, social, and political challenges.

Two-Level Games in the Pacific Alliance Negotiations

The paradoxical nature of two-level games—players that have a high degree of power in Level II negotiations also have decreased power in Level I negotiations—was important during the NAFTA negotiations due to the significant structural differences between the Mexican and U.S. political systems. In the case of the Pacific Alliance negotiations, the issue was less pronounced because the countries involved shared more similar power structures. Also, Mexico was perceived to have changed structurally in the previous twenty years. In contrast with NAFTA, for which President Salinas strategically empowered domestic constituencies (the private sector and Congress) to increase his negotiating power in Level I, under the Pacific Alliance, Mexico's domestic stakeholders arguably had a real possibility of blocking the agreement. In particular, President Calderón faced greater adversity because of the opposition of certain producers within the agricultural sector, and because his political party did not have a majority in Congress.

But as the saying goes, what's past is prologue, and it could be argued that perhaps Mexico has not changed that much. The return in 2012 of the PRI as the ruling party after twelve years out of power meant that President Peña Nieto had practically all the votes needed to pass trade agreements, even though he did not have the comfortable majority in Congress enjoyed by President Salinas. Mexican international trade agreements require approval by a simple majority of the Senate, which is composed of 128 senators. The ruling PRI and its ally, the Partido Verde Ecologista de México (PVEM), together hold 61 seats out of the total of 128. Thus, the current administration needs only a couple of votes from the opposition to obtain the majority needed to pass international treaties.

Despite this increased room to maneuver provided by the current makeup of the Senate, the Peña administration's negotiators could still reasonably allege in

Level I negotiations that they needed to address internal demands, particularly from the agricultural sector. Moreover, they were further constrained because the administration was in negotiations with opposition parties regarding structural reforms and so could not risk compromising the internal consensus President Peña Nieto had begun to construct even before coming into office.

Aside from the effects caused by the paradoxical nature of the two-level games, Putnam's theory also describes many of the directions taken in the negotiations that helped to create successful diplomacy.

As in NAFTA, the scope of the agenda of the Pacific Alliance went beyond trade issues. Thus, there was both political and economic content that had to be addressed by the countries' policymakers. In Mexico's case, presidential leadership under Calderón and Peña Nieto translated into a fine-tuned coordination among the governmental agencies involved, especially the foreign affairs and the economy ministries. In an analogous fashion to NAFTA, the teams negotiating the Pacific Alliance were highly experienced, technically trained officials. Many were career public servants, involved in previous negotiations, who knew each other well.

Also recalling the NAFTA process, the Peña Nieto administration had undertaken reforms in various key sectors of the economy, including telecommunications, economic competition, labor, and fiscal and energy policy, as well as in education.[47] As a consequence, Mexico once again liberalized major sectors of the economy that had been historically closed to private investment.

The crucial domestic constituencies of the Senate and the private sector were again mobilized to achieve the necessary consensus to pass the agreement. While Mexico's private sector evinced a favorable opinion of the Pacific Alliance,[48] the trade pact—and its associated economic reforms—still faced opposition from a significant part of civil society. In contrast, Chile, Colombia, and Peru all had high levels of trade negotiation activity with scarce public opposition to liberalization policies.

By linking the ongoing trade and investment negotiations to the momentum to drive structural reforms in the country, Mexico essentially sought to obtain concessions from its most important trading partners in exchange for domestic liberalization. In other words, for Mexico's counterparts, binding market access through a trade or investment agreement created value by constraining the ability of future Mexican administrations to impose new restrictions.

Finally, similar to the process during the NAFTA negotiations, the parties to the Pacific Alliance committed to comply with specific deadlines. This was a clear sign of the countries' intention to achieve an ambitious integration of their economies.

Conclusion

NAFTA and the Pacific Alliance are two prime examples of Mexico's successful diplomacy through economic statecraft. Although the agreements are more than two decades apart and involve different geographical regions, both negotiations shared a similar strategy and a series of actions that allowed for the successful conclusion of the agreements.

Among the most important shared elements were: recognition from the outset that the pacts represented more than mere trade issues and were pivotal to Mexico's foreign and domestic interests; strong presidential leadership and a prioritization that limited opportunities for bureaucratic battles; establishment of specific goals, tied to a series of economic liberalization reforms that preceded them; and use of well-trained negotiators. Finally, success in these negotiations was also dependent upon the skillful employment of presidential outreach to domestic constituencies—particularly to the Senate and the private sector—which strengthened Mexico's Level I game by turning its primary negotiation weakness into a source of strength.

Both trade agreements also had important implications not only for other aspects of Mexican diplomacy but also for the social and political development of the country. Trade agreements institutionalize ties—they establish rules, working groups, follow-up mechanisms, and even institutions that bring high-level policymakers and officials in contact on a regular basis, thus creating better coordination and understanding among nations. Trade agreements can also establish dispute settlement provisions outside the political arena to address issues that cannot be solved solely with technical means. As Robert Keohane argued, negotiated international orders help reduce transaction costs and increase confidence among policymakers, which allows for better coordination among nations.[49] We thus conclude that NAFTA helped to accomplish more optimal economic results, benefiting the consumers of the United States, Mexico, and Canada. We expect that the Pacific Alliance will produce similar benefits for Mexico, Chile, Colombia, and Peru.

NAFTA was implemented in January 1994. It dramatically changed the manner in which Mexico interacted with its North American neighbors, Canada and the United States. NAFTA also helped to institutionalize other areas of the bilateral relationship. The U.S.-Mexico Binational Commission, created in 1991 to coordinate three areas of the relationship, expanded to include sixteen working groups, including education, cultural affairs, immigration, consular affairs, and border issues. NAFTA also stimulated a series of spillover effects in U.S.-Mexican relations. For example, just a year after NAFTA went into effect in January 1995, the renewed U.S.-Mexico partnership was put to a test. In what became known as the "tequila effect," Mexico's difficulties in servicing its foreign debt shattered global confidence in emerging markets. To help Mexico confront its international debt payments, President Bill Clinton used executive action to issue a multibillion dollar loan to Mexico (US$50 billion).[50] The U.S. loan had a crucial effect in raising global confidence concerning Mexico's capacity to face its financial problems.

By joining NAFTA, Mexico's diplomacy moved closer to Washington's. This perception opened some doors for Mexico and closed others. For example, Mexico intensified its relations with Japan, a close U.S. ally in Asia. Not only did Mexico negotiate an FTA with Japan, which went into effect in 2004, it also expanded its bilateral cooperation with what was then the world's second-largest economy. However, in some Latin American countries, such as Brazil, Mexico was precluded from participating in new regional groups such as UNASUR on the grounds that it was already part of NAFTA.

Similarly, the Pacific Alliance is already having an important effect not only on bilateral relationships, but also on Latin American regional integration, as well as its relations with other regional blocs. The alliance is as much a foreign policy pact as a trade agreement and has caused Mexican diplomacy to be perceived as moving closer to that of Latin America. For example, within the Pacific Alliance, Mexican-Colombian cooperation has been expanding not only in the area of the economy, but also concerning citizen security, as evidenced by the new bilateral initiative to train Mexican police in the Andean country. In the same vein, Mexico's decision to eliminate visitor visas for Colombian and Peruvian citizens is creating closer ties. In addition to relationships with members of the alliance, the agreement has served to strengthen Mexico's presence across Latin America.

In addition, there are various similarities between NAFTA and the Pacific Alliance negotiation processes that explain why the first succeeded and the latter continues on a path toward successful integration. From the Mexican perspective, there are important elements that are worth underscoring. First, there were preexisting networks of agreements that served as ready-made building blocks for creating the structures necessary for further liberalization and integration. In the case of NAFTA, this included Mexico's entrance into GATT and the Legal Trade Framework agreements of the 1980s. In the case of the Pacific Alliance, Mexico's existing bilateral FTAs with the group's members provided a critical foundation.

During both the NAFTA and Pacific Alliance negotiations, all parties involved had a common mindset regarding the desirability of expanding trade. In the case of the Pacific Alliance, Chile, Colombia, Mexico, and Peru all had signed bilateral FTAs. As a result of these shared goals, the leaders (and by extension their administrations) of the countries involved were able to give the negotiations a high level of priority. In the case of Mexico, the presence of strong presidential leadership ensured lack of bureaucratic infighting. The combination of these shared priorities and the attention of leaders encouraged effective coordination between government agencies.

For Mexico, the high priority given to these negotiations by the respective presidents led directly to the creation and then to the active participation of heterogeneous Level II constituencies, which included the Senate and the private sector. Furthermore, once constituted and active, these constituencies had effects that went well beyond the scope of the original aims. It is striking how important the inclusion of the Senate was in these negotiations for the active instrumentation of heterogeneous Level II constituencies in both cases.

Finally, the two international negotiations coincided with a previous determination of the urgent need for extensive domestic structural reforms. In the case of NAFTA, these were centered on the need to end the era of import substitution industrialization and to open Mexico to the world economy. In the case of the Pacific Alliance, Mexico had ambitious plans to reform the telecommunications and energy sectors and to address the pending competitiveness agenda.

Taken together, these two cases make it quite clear that Mexico's economic statecraft has provided a solid basis for successful diplomacy. That is, in intertwining both foreign and domestic economic imperatives, Mexico created the conditions necessary to play a series of Level I and II games successfully in the negotiations of NAFTA and the Pacific Alliance. It did so by undertaking a process of concerted actions to achieve clear goals, and by leveraging presidential leadership to harness the political and bureaucratic apparatus in order to capture domestic and foreign interests for the benefit of Mexico.

Notes

1. Quoted in Hillary Clinton, "Delivering on the Promise of Economic Statecraft" (November 17, 2012), http://m.state.gov/md200664.htm.
2. Although these democratic gains are beyond the scope of this chapter, it is worth mentioning a few examples. For one, it can be argued that NAFTA was a necessary precondition to the alternation of power in 2000 and that the insertion of the "Democratic Clause" in the negotiations for a free trade agreement between Mexico and the European Union in the late 1990s was fundamental to changes in how Mexico conceived of human rights. See Marcela Szymanski's discussion of the acceptance by Mexico of "the Democratic Clause" during negotiations with the European Union: "El nuevo acuerdo entre México y la Unión Europea: El primer vínculo de libre comercio entre Europa y el TLC," in *México-Unión Europea: El acuerdo de asociación económica, concentración política y cooperación*, ed. Alicia Lebrija and Stephan Sberro (Mexico City: Miguel Ángel Porrúa, 2002), 30–32.
3. The Contadora Group was created in 1983 and comprised Colombia, Mexico, Panama, and Venezuela. The goal was to pacify Central American countries independently from U.S. involvement in the region. Marisol de Gonzalo, "La significación del Grupo Contadora

como actor internacional y hemisférico y sus implicaciones diplomáticas en el ámbito latinoamericano," *Política Internacional*, 3 (July–September 1986): 16–32.

4. Robert D. Putnam, "Diplomacy and Domestic Politics: The Logic of Two-Level Games," *International Organization* 42, no. 3 (Summer 1988): 427–460.
5. Putnam, "The Logic of Two-Level Games," 460.
6. Putnam, "The Logic of Two-Level Games," 428.
7. Putnam, "The Logic of Two-Level Games," 429.
8. Putnam, "The Logic of Two-Level Games," 455.
9. Putnam, "The Logic of Two-Level Games," 460.
10. Putnam, "The Logic of Two-Level Games," 427–460.
11. Thomas C. Schelling, *The Strategy of Conflict* (Cambridge, MA: Harvard University Press, 1960), 19 (emphasis ours).
12. Measured in nominal terms. The European Union includes the twenty-seven countries that currently constitute it. Estimates using data from the International Monetary Fund.
13. Estimates using data from the World Bank (2012), databank.worldbank.org.
14. Trilateral commerce is estimated with data of the importing country (Banco de México, Statistics Canada, U.S. Department of Commerce). World trade is estimated with data of the World Bank, databank.worldbank.org.
15. Estimates using data of Banco de México, www.banxico.org.mx/estadisticas/index.html.
16. Estimates using data of the Mexican Ministry of the Economy, www.economia.gob.mx/comunidad-negocios/competitividad-normatividad/inversion-extranjera-directa/estadistica-oficial-de-ied-en-mexico. FDI received to March 31, 2014.
17. Includes Argentina, Belize, Bolivia, Brazil, Chile, Colombia, Costa Rica, Ecuador, El Salvador, Guatemala, Honduras, Mexico, Nicaragua, Panama, Paraguay, Peru, Uruguay, and Venezuela.
18. Estimates using data from the World Bank, databank.worldbank.org.
19. Estimates using data from the World Bank (2012) databank.worldbank.org.
20. Estimates using data from the World Bank, databank.worldbank.org. The definition of East Asia is according to the World Bank.
21. Estimates using data from the World Bank, databank.worldbank.org.
22. Estimates using data from the Mexican Ministry of the Economy. In this case, SMEs are defined as companies with exports valued from five thousand to two and one-half million dollars during 2011.
23. Lorenzo Meyer, "La crisis de la élite mexicana y su relación con Estados Unidos: Raíces históricas del Tratado de Libre Comercio," in *México-Estados Unidos*, 1990, ed. Gustavo Vega (Mexico: El Colegio de México, 1992), 73.
24. René Herrera and Manuel Chavarría, "México en Contadora: Una búsqueda de límites a su compromiso con Centroamérica," in *Foro Internacional 96* (Mexico: El Colegio de México, 1984), 458–483.
25. Roberto Dondisch, *México en el Consejo de Seguridad de la ONU, La historia tras bambalinas* (Mexico: Debate, 2012).
26. Sydney Weintraub, *A Marriage of Convenience* (New York: Oxford University Press, 1990), 72.
27. See Gary C. Hufbauer, *The Free Trade Debate* (New York: Twentieth Century Fund, 1989), 146.
28. See Rafael Fernández de Castro and Judith Mariscal, "La industria siderúrgica mexicana ante el TLC," in *México y el acuerdo trilateral de comercio*, ed. Eduardo Andere and Georgina Kessel (Mexico: ITAM-McGraw-Hill, 1992).
29. Gustavo Vega, *El Tratado de Libre Comercio en América del Norte: Visión retrospectiva y retos a futuro* (Mexico: El Colegio de México, 2010), 67.
30. Vega, *El Tratado de Libre Comercio en América del Norte*, 79.
31. Vega, *El Tratado de Libre Comercio en América del Norte*, 87.
32. Vega, *El Tratado de Libre Comercio en América del Norte*, 89.
33. See Nora Lustig, *Mexico: The Remaking of an Economy* (Washington, DC: Brookings Institution Press, 1998).

34. Carlos Salinas, *México: Un paso difícil a la modernidad* (Mexico: Plaza & Janés Editores, 2000), 50.

35. Maxwell A. Cameron and Brian W. Tomlin, *The Making of NAFTA: How the Deal was Done* (Ithaca, NY: Cornell University Press, 2000), 68.

36. These included Vice President Quayle, Secretary of the Treasury Brady, Secretary of Commerce Mosbacher, U.S. Trade Representative Hills, National Security Adviser Scowcroft; U.S. Ambassador to Mexico Negroponte, and William Pryce, of the National Security Council.

37. Statement by Press Secretary Fitzwater on President Bush's dinner with President Carlos Salinas of Mexico, June 10, 1990.

38. Hermann Von Bertrab, *Negotiating NAFTA: A Mexican Envoy's Account* (Westport, CT: Praeger and CSIS, 1997), 6–7, 44.

39. In the end, the PRI governed Mexico for 71 years, from 1929 to 2000, and won the presidency again in 2012.

40. Putnam, "The Logic of Two-Level Games," 427–460.

41. Jorge I. Dominguez, "Widening Scholarly Horizons: Theoretical Approaches for the Study of U.S.-Mexican Relations, " The David Rockefeller Center for Latin American Studies: Working Paper Series, no. 96-91, Cambridge, MA, 1996, p. 2.

42. Cameron and Tomlin, *The Making of NAFTA*, 62–63.

43. Cameron and Tomlin, *The Making of NAFTA*, 63, and Von Bertrab, *Negotiating NAFTA*, 6.

44. Perspectives of Production Integration among Pacific Alliance Countries (preliminary version), Inter-American Development Bank, April 2013, pp. 4, 10, 22–32.

45. Declaración de Urubamba, 2010, VI Reunión Ministerial del Foro del Arco del Pacífico Latinoamericano, Urubamba, Cusco, Peru, October 15, http://www.economia.gob.mx/files/comunidad_negocios/tlcs/tlcs_americalatina/06DeclaracionMinisterialUrubamba2010.pdf.

46. Ildefonso Guajardo (remarks third meeting of Ministers of the Pacific Alliance (March 14, 2013).

47. President Peña Nieto created the Pacto (Pact), a gentleman's agreement among the three major political parties—PAN, PRD, and PRI—to secure the passage of structural refoms. See Shannon O'Neil, "Viva las Reformas," *Foreign Affairs*, vol. 93, pp. 11–16 (January–February 2014).

48. "Business sectors want more countries in the Pacific Alliance," *El Economista*, http://eleconomista.com.mx/internacional/2013/08/04/sectores-empresariales-quieren-mas-paises-alianza-pacifico

49. Robert Keohane, *International Institutions and State Power* (Boulder, CO: Westview Press, 1989), 9.

50. William Glasgall, "Welcome to the New World Order of Finance," *Business Week*, February 13, 1995.

10

Displaced Diplomacies

Reframing Development and Humanitarianism in Taliban-Era Afghanistan

PAULA R. NEWBERG

The period that began on February 15, 1989 (when the last Soviet troops departed Afghanistan after a ten-year war against Western-backed Afghan *mujahideen*) and ended on October 7, 2001 (when U.S.-led coalition forces arrived in Afghanistan to retaliate for al-Qaeda's September 11 terrorist attacks in New York and Washington, D.C.) bracketed the near-end of the Soviet Union and the beginning of an era in which armed nonstate actors and new global ideological movements took center stage. The Taliban movement, which began its active quest to redirect Afghan politics in 1994, exercised power in ways both centralized and piecemeal. It mired the failed Afghan state in repression and poverty as it pursued conquest through war, a process that led ultimately— by hosting al-Qaeda—to its diplomatic exclusion.

This was Afghanistan's lost diplomatic decade. The marginalized Afghan state, with neither traditional government nor traditional engagement with the international community, became the place where foreign assistance providers experimented with different ways of undertaking the business of humanitarianism. Confronting new power holders in Afghanistan who were often spurned by foreign capitals, aid providers were often the only interlocutors with Afghan communities and the Taliban. In this sense, the assistance community— donors, nongovernmental organizations (NGOs), and UN bodies—took on roles that would otherwise be the province of formal diplomacy. Without clear policies regarding engagements, however, the community was left to devise its own. The result was a process of community consultation—coined a "strategic framework" by the United Nations—that tried to reconcile aid principles and practices with a quickly evolving environment that was continually buffeted by the changing winds of war and diplomacy by omission.

By the time the Taliban seized Kabul in September 1996 (after more than two years of intermittent fighting), the international community was sharply divided about its own role in, and toward, a barely governed country torn apart by war since the 1970s. There was little agreement about whether, how, and with whom diplomacy might be pursued, what the appropriate agendas should be, and how to handle cascading humanitarian, developmental, and political crises within Afghanistan. The Taliban's relationships across southern and western Asia made every problem regional, if not global, but divergent opinions among foreign governments about the Taliban's role in Afghanistan occasionally turned potential diplomatic interlocutors into protagonists, defenders, or victims of events within the country. The Taliban's social practices (as well as its ideology, allies, and fighting) easily conflated problems of diplomacy with problems of principle, and the cumulative effects of decades-long war made humanitarian assistance a front-line issue for Afghanistan and its neighbors. Interested governments, near and far, had already watched as the Afghan state faltered and then failed in the years following the Soviet withdrawal in 1989; the Geneva Accords of 1988 orchestrated the withdrawal of Soviet troops, but did not include peace negotiations or create a basis for a future stable peace in the country. Except for occasional UN-initiated discussions about the country's political future, Afghanistan remained almost a place apart—literally and diplomatically—until the Taliban's gathering momentum in the mid-1990s returned the country to international headlines.

Even then—and while many of the same humanitarian actors were working among brutal conflicts in Africa and Europe—Afghanistan languished relatively far from diplomatic front lines. During this period, Afghanistan's primary relationship to outsiders was through a patchwork of humanitarian assistance providers: the ravages of war were corrosive and devastating to the state and its people, and aid organizations had maintained a consistent presence there for more than fifteen years. When the Taliban arrived in Kandahar in 1994, Herat in 1995, and Kabul in September of 1996, its impact on Afghanistan was inevitably felt in the social, economic, and humanitarian spheres, as much as—if not more than—in politics.

Practical problems of engagement—who should talk with whom, about what, and why, and how the provision of aid would or would not help to mitigate violence—were complicated by two critical problems. First, the early Taliban movement was, to outsiders, a remarkably diffused and disorganized group. Its spiritual home was Kandahar, where Mullah Mohammed Omar was based; its military members included the members of former mujahideen groups who had signed on with the Taliban propitiously or after being defeated; and after 1996, its leaders included individuals who held government titles (such as governor or minister) but did not appear consistently to hold portfolios that outsiders would recognize. Second, the absence of foreign diplomats in the capital made intelligence gathering and institutional authority distant and often disorganized. Most embassies had closed shortly after the Soviet intervention in late 1979, and the Taliban's human rights practices deterred their return.

Assistance providers became a community of serendipity, and the community's agenda of emergency response, recovery, and planning—all of which required working relationships with the Taliban and its opponents to secure humanitarian access—became a form of quasi-diplomatic engagement created by sheer necessity. As in other conflict zones and countries, this community included the agencies, funds, and programs of intergovernmental organizations, including the United Nations (whose political mission—the UN's interlocutor with armed groups and quasi-political organizations—worked alongside the economic and social sector agencies) and the European Union, with many organizations working in response to missions and mandates established by their own boards of directors; an array of foreign nongovernmental organizations, each with its own mission and financial resources (both private and public); and donor governments that funded many of these activities. And as in most emergency situations, the interests of these organizations and their patrons alternately converged and diverged as operating policies—such as they were—encountered the conditions of Afghanistan's ground wars and ideological fights. The interests of neighboring governments—themselves refugee-receiving states with complex foreign policies and economic interests in everything from food exports to natural gas pipelines—formed a diplomatic backdrop that influenced the daily work of relief, rehabilitation, and prospective reconstruction in Afghanistan and was closely entwined with the ambitions of southern, western, and central Asia.

From 1996 onward, this evolving community pursued its work in an increasingly troubled and changeable environment. Joining political, development, humanitarian, and rights issues on their collective agendas, these actors invested more than three years seeking ways to respond to a gathering complex emergency. At the same time, they responded to the growing imperatives of a broader international community that, under the leadership of Secretary-General Kofi Annan of the United Nations, was already rethinking the ways that assistance and political negotiations could be conducted in conflict and postconflict environments. Afghanistan—a failing state without a formal government—was among the most difficult of these crises for international actors to navigate. To accomplish its daily tasks, the assistance community found it necessary to reexamine its habits and principles, experiment with guidelines around which assistance providers could appropriately organize their work, consult as broadly as possible across Afghan society, and test standards for appropriate action at the intersections of humanitarian, development, and diplomatic engagement. In this way, and sometimes unintentionally, it organized its interactions with the Taliban to try to fulfill the humanitarian imperatives that initially brought assistance to the country.

Afghanistan's story in this period is therefore as much a tale of displaced diplomacies as it is about responding to the Taliban and Afghanistan's deep humanitarian crisis. The narrative of an emergency in a failed state, when negotiations about rights, relief, and development temporarily substituted for traditional diplomacy, offered lessons to be learned (but certainly not explicit instruction) for crisis negotiations in other conflict regions later, and indirectly set the stage for Afghanistan's external engagements after 2001. Perhaps most important, they provided a venue—physical, political, economic, and, in a sense, ethical—to continue discussions about diplomacy and aid during combat and principled engagement with nonstate actors that began long before the drafting of the Geneva Conventions and continues today.

Context

In the early 1990s, central Asia's newly independent states were seeking their individual and collective diplomatic moorings, with keen interest in reshaping their attitudes toward Afghanistan's continuing conflicts (while seeking to quell their own). This was also the first time that most south Asian states were democratically elected—with all the benefits and tensions that electoral politics brought to diplomacy. Pipeline politics joined east to west, creating a common agenda for western, central, and southern Asia (with Iran as an outlier for western Asia, but a significant actor in central and southern Asia). At the same time, the microeconomies that narcotics trade created across Afghanistan's borders created new financial and political incentives within these border states and beyond; patronage from Gulf states and Saudi Arabia (toward Afghanistan and Pakistan in particular) underscored a diplomatic dynamic that would persistently influence the region's sectarian and economic policies. These diplomatic shifts were both global in orientation and locally critical with regard to Afghanistan.

While regional power alignments were shifting, traditional diplomatic efforts toward Afghanistan were devoted primarily to confronting—or optimistically, staving off—the regional effects of the failing Afghan state. The newly independent states of central Asia had inherited their interests in Afghanistan from the Soviet Union; their close borders to Afghanistan turned their occasional meddling and cross-border patronage of warlords, as well as

narcotics trafficking, into concern for their own domestic stability and regional influence. For the larger economies of Turkey and Iran, Afghanistan's
changing conflict environment offered seeming opportunities for recasting
their regional commercial and ideological ambitions. Turmoil in Afghanistan
was both a cause and a consequence of Pakistan's civil-military uncertainties
and expansive foreign policies. Competition between India and Pakistan for
central Asian trade, continuing tensions between Pakistan and India about Afghanistan's governance, and the volatile Afghanistan-Pakistan border, as well
as the presence of millions of Afghan refugees in Iran and Pakistan heightened
regional involvement in Afghanistan's war and peace (and Pakistan in particular had played an active role in Afghan politics for decades). Russia and China
hovered nearby, as participants in UN discussions and benefactors to Afghanistan's neighbors, if not to Kabul itself. A long list of issues—narcotics and
arms trafficking, nuclear proliferation, emerging markets for oil and natural
gas—at once brought these states together and also underscored profound differences in their interests and behavior. Given the breadth of these agendas,
and the difficulties of working in Afghanistan, regional powers, small and
large, often treated the country as a project—to be manipulated—rather than
a diplomatic actor in its own right.

In the two years before the Taliban seized Kabul (in September 1996), the
question of how to deal with this new political movement was a serious but
secondary challenge for most concerned diplomatic actors. Aid organizations
sought ways to respond to the imposition of Islamic punishments and edicts
that barred girls from schools and women from jobs—sometimes through discussion, sometimes by closing operations, and regardless of their mode of engagement, usually unsuccessfully. But when the Taliban began to assert
something that resembled national authority, albeit in piecemeal and sometimes erratic ways, its role became a diplomatic problem of a different sort. The
same issue that had languished on diplomatic back burners for years—how to
handle armed nonstate actors that initially eschewed power and then began to
exercise control while continuing to fight for more territory—was now a
global, regional, and local problem. Sorting it out was to take a very long time.
In the interim, difficult questions of authority, power, influence and intention
were left to an assistance community that dealt directly with the Taliban and
was most affected by its actions.

Afghanistan's grave problems were shadowed by events elsewhere, earlier
in the decade: wars in the former Yugoslavia, genocide in Rwanda, and the
continuing travails of Somalia. An undercurrent of dissatisfaction, dismay,
and occasional desperation about missing or misled interventions, and the
weaknesses of bilateral and multilateral responses to each of these tragedies,
weighed heavily on the United Nations and its member states. When U.S.

embassies in eastern Africa were attacked (assumedly by al-Qaeda) in the summer of 1998—with retributive bombings in Sudan and then Afghanistan (as presumed hosts for al-Qaeda) and the temporary withdrawal of aid workers from Afghanistan—the political context for assistance began to limit opportunities for assistance negotiations, which nevertheless continued until late 2001.

Twenty-first-century war in Afghanistan—following civil strife in the 1970s, the decade of the anti-Soviet war, factional fighting through the post–Geneva Accord years, and arriving in 1994 at what became known as the Taliban period—has often been viewed as a problem apart, a piece of the post–Cold War puzzle gone terribly awry. The 1988 Geneva Accords had brought no peace, and UN-sponsored negotiations continually—and weakly and misleadingly—hailed the need for all parties to conflict to come together.[1] But post-1988 Afghanistan had been loosely joined to its neighbors by arms bazaars and heroin refineries; training for young fighters; patronage relationships among intelligence, military, and political actors; and the corrosive effects of permeable borders: millions of refugees, cross-border labor markets, and irrepressible irredentism pursued under the cover of ethnic and tribal affinities. These habits, which continued long after 2001, were nonetheless colored by the way the international community responded to them.

Political disarray, state incapacity, and resource shortages have long defined the scope and duration of Afghanistan's humanitarian disasters, which—particularly for outsiders—in turn defined Afghanistan. With great-power interests focused on the architecture of the post–Cold War world after 1989, the United Nations and its closest partners improvised in Afghanistan by concentrating on the diplomacy surrounding humanitarian relief. The 1990s encounter with Afghanistan—during a relatively cheap and contained war, pervasive human rights abuses, the absence of a credible state, and relative disinterest from great powers—provided an unplanned space for assistance providers to experiment once the Taliban seized power. The results were incomplete and frequently unworkable, unintentionally fragmented and always underfinanced—characteristics of what might be assumed to be short-sighted, inevitable diplomatic failure. But institutional incremental policy reform in a situation of profound instability and state failure can also be optimistic, and in some instances, even visionary. In Afghanistan, it was a bit of everything.

Perhaps most important, the actors, issues, and policies concerned with Afghanistan helped to crystallize an opportunity in the international response to complex emergencies. The conflicts of the late 1980s and early 1990s represented the first adjustments of a post–Cold War world; those after 2001 reflected an increasingly different environment, to which multilateral diplomacy is still accommodating itself. Taliban-era Afghanistan encompassed a transition in the ways that local politics intersected with evolving global political movements across Asia and the Middle East.[2] Institutionally and diplomatically, the ways that outside actors responded to a world they did not, and perhaps could not, understand combined tactical response and wishful thinking.[3] The relief and development community in Afghanistan, along with colleagues working under somewhat similar conditions in Africa, learned to identify and confront complex emergencies and test their capacities to heal the wounds of war when fighting would not stop. The process of analyzing, learning, testing, and applying new ideas about institutional collaboration became a different kind of diplomacy toward failed and failing states divided by insurgency, ideology, and persistent crisis.

Setting the Stage: Afghanistan in the 1990s

The last Soviet troops left Afghanistan in February 1989, leaving Najibullah Ahmadzai in place as head of government in a minimally functional state. In 1992, a Western-backed plan facilitated his removal from office and replaced him with mujahideen parties whose internecine warfare led to the further breakdown of the state. The rule of those commanders inaugurated a period of pillage across the country, antigovernance that fed on itself and victimized Afghan citizens. Refugees and internally displaced persons, ethnic parties based on fighting factions, increasing localism and traditionalism in the absence of national government, and massive corruption in all sectors of public life created conditions that were impossible to sustain. Afghans were beholden to two vastly different groups, warlord-led criminal parties and international assistance organizations that dealt with each other in local, ad hoc, sometimes backhanded, and often inconsistent ways. Afghans often viewed both as interlopers.

The slow erosion of security accompanied a military stalemate that blurred the distinction between war and peace. UN statements, exhortations, and resolutions urging everyone to get along failed as profoundly as had the Afghan state itself.[4] Some diplomatic observers therefore hoped the Taliban would repair the effects of chaos and corruption and help restore equilibrium to the country. Others thought it was a solution waiting to happen: an organized group sorting out grass-roots problems, taking on warlord mafias, instituting a blunt justice that was, possibly, more justice than had been previously available. This was temporizing, in a way: the Taliban movement did not suddenly appear but had been slowly nurtured;[5] it did not respond to a call from within Afghanistan for ideological purity but took advantage of war weariness to quash dissent before it might arise, and never sought agreement with its ideas or actions. Its seeming good works—dismantling roadblocks, ending targeted killings, robberies, and allegedly rapes, and quashing anarchic conditions throughout the country—contrasted sharply with its violent punishments and personal sanctions against allegedly non-Islamic practices. Afghans seemed to be at the mercy of those who claimed to rescue them from the predation and anarchy.

The Taliban's arrival in Kabul did not translate into new diplomatic efforts by Kabul, or toward it. Most embassies to Afghanistan had been closed for years, and diplomatic and World Bank watching briefs were undertaken from afar—literally watching as the Taliban first insisted that it was a placeholder for a future government and then gradually assumed control of the territory it had won. Some governments thought that after years without a single governmental interlocutor, the Taliban would simplify the process of dealing with humanitarian access, shorten the war, and relieve a growing development emergency, but repressive Taliban edicts quickly belied this impression. (Connecting the dots among the Taliban, the "Afghan Arabs" who dotted the pre-Taliban landscape, and the global al-Qaeda movement took longer and changed diplomatic calculations far more, and far beyond, the more parochial concerns of the first years.) Even after the 1998 U.S. bombings in Sudan and Afghanistan, foreign governments continued to seek ways to include the Taliban as a form of governing body—if not a government per se—that could speak for itself and on behalf of a country that it did not govern, even though it was neither recognized formally by the United Nations nor formally legitimized within Afghanistan.

The costs of the failure of the Afghan state remained high. Diplomats and aid workers found themselves dealing with complex issues that thwarted their initial efforts to work with the Taliban. (No doubt the complex and decentralized aid community puzzled the Taliban as well.) The devastating humanitarian and development consequences of the war were exacerbated by the absence of government and the limited presence of foreign aid providers in Kabul. The lion's share of work was done by Afghans, under the banners of UN agencies and foreign-based aid organizations,[6] who labored under increasingly dangerous Taliban strictures. Foreign-funded relief organizations—many of which had survived more than two decades of war—were now viewed with suspicion, and all sides found fault with others for failures that were everyone's responsibility.

These challenges highlighted the sharp differences between and among belligerent nonstate actors (now sitting in government offices), nongovernmental humanitarian organizations, and worried and distracted governments. Each actor was an agent for a different kind of interest, and the diversity of these communities became the collective reason that decision-making within the international community turned into a policy issue all its own. Negotiating a process that could accommodate a common principled denominator became the international community's critical diplomatic decision for the early Taliban period.

Rights and Politics

Human rights abuses, particularly those targeting women and religious and ethnic minorities, colored the Taliban's reputation from the moment it first occupied Kandahar and Herat in 1994 and 1995 and fundamentally changed the way that outside powers were willing to interact with Afghanistan by late 1996. A few NGOs and UN agencies protested Taliban practices early: UNICEF suspended some education programs in 1995, and Save the Children did the same.[7] Taliban representatives initially compared themselves favorably to previous regimes, whose records of imprisonment and torture were legendary. The Taliban's explicitly Islamist program, which replaced the principles on which humanitarianism is usually grounded with its own notions of propriety, shifted international rights discourse from politics (where, it can be argued, it belonged) to culture and religion, a nod to practices that the international community did not fully comprehend and had little experience confronting, positively or negatively. Diplomacy about rights—usually voiced through conditions and sanctions—could not succeed when confronting a movement that was not a government. To many women in Afghanistan and assistance providers elsewhere, mere lament without action seemed close to excusing Taliban actions.[8] Rights and assistance were therefore drawn quite close, in discomfiting ways, setting a tone that was curious, unforgiving, and unremittingly frustrating on all sides.

The Taliban's list of edicts, published soon after its arrival in Kabul, constituted rights abuse in the minds of many Afghans and foreigners alike. Although some edicts might have seemed trivial—women were prohibited from wearing white socks, men forced to grow beards—almost all were profoundly repressive: thwarting free expression and political activity, reviving conscription, ending most education, closing women's hospitals, and discriminating against religious and ethnic minorities. "All of these changed and limited society." Most edicts initially seemed to focus on preventing women from leaving their homes, and in urban Afghanistan, with untold numbers of female-headed households, this prohibition was stunningly punitive. The World Food Programme, for example, supported Kabul's families through its female-staffed bakeries; without them, the bakeries would cease to function; without bread, families would starve. From 1996 to 2001, the food program struggled to feed Afghan families while maintaining the safety of its Afghan workers. It was still fighting this battle in June 2001, when news headlines broadcast the imminent closure of the bakeries program because the Taliban still could not agree on conditions for female employment.[9]

The Taliban might not have meant the issue of women's rights to become the lightning rod for its first dealings with the international community; it is possible that the ideological tail wagged the diplomatic dog far too soon, before the Taliban consolidated its rule in Kabul, realized just how complicated its position would be internationally, and then did not know how to move away from early positions taken by its most conservative leaders.[10] But the issue hardened the views of the international community about Taliban means and objectives, affected the ways assistance and diplomatic communities were willing or able to work with Taliban counterparts, and created an increasingly brittle response from the Taliban itself.

It also exposed differences within and among the diplomatic, rights, and assistance communities: the place of rights in discussions with the Taliban—and whether rights were understood and recognized as such by the Taliban—depended on the developmental, humanitarian, and political contexts for tactical discussions. (It was too early for strategy, except in the most general sense of the word, and divisions within the assistance community and among UN member states changed rapidly.) Questions about whether to engage with the Taliban, and how to engage with the Taliban, seemed to merge into one normative vacuum.[11] The differences between and among aid providers, donors, and UN member states resembled a sine curve: high in response to specific abuses, lower when long-range policy was needed.

Principled Humanitarianism and Rights

Gaining agreement about how to establish a normative basis for international engagement with the Taliban became a problem that NGOs and the UN were forced to confront together: rights became the sharp edge of the wedge of international engagement, with humanitarian assistance as its first arena. In the name of Afghanistan's sovereignty, the Taliban restricted access to poverty-stricken communities, violated Afghanistan's obligations to respect the rights and privileges of the United Nations, and threatened aid providers—if not to restrict women, then in similar spirit. In response, some aid donors withdrew assistance, or threatened to do so, and assistance organizations limited their work. Occasionally in their own eyes, and often in the view of the Taliban, these policies undercut the universality, impartiality, and neutrality that theoretically informed the provision of assistance. This was a classic example of incommensurability: each set of actors understood its own reasons, but not those of others; each answered to different parties in rigid ways that occasionally came close to ending any discussion at all.

Taliban practices highlighted the deep, if quiet, relationship between humanitarian action and respect for human rights—one that rights and assistance organizations had difficulty heeding, particularly given the fundamental absence of free choice that such abuses represented.[12] From 1994 until 2001, the Taliban was the de facto ruling body of Afghanistan, and for some aid providers, a necessary, if unfortunate link between them and the communities they served. For others, the simple fact of working with this de facto authority— never acknowledged de jure—invited further rights abuse. For them, respect for rights set the terms for the provision of aid. But the Taliban answered only to itself. Its regime of edicts seemed to focus exclusively on "no" when aid workers were looking for "yes."

These large-bore issues invited small-bore, circumstantial responses. If the Taliban refused to admit women from international organizations to meetings, should the meetings be canceled, should women be excluded, or, more abrasively, required to attend—and if so, how should they be attired? Would marginal attendance (behind a curtain, simulating purdah) suit anyone, or everyone? In some ways, even if not intended, the Taliban exposed to the international community incremental prejudices and fault lines that the community did not want to recognize in itself, and the picture it drew was disturbing. The mirror image was no clearer: when the issue was political influence—for example, when meeting a senior female diplomat, Taliban leaders would carefully set aside their own restrictions, presumably in the hope of gaining recognition or resources. This was not a new game, certainly, but one that created maximum discomfort among external interlocutors who had worked alongside affected communities for years.

Relief and Development

The uneasy relationship between Taliban rules and international practices exposed an old divide between development and relief, an artifact of the post–World War II architecture of international assistance that was strained in Taliban-controlled Afghanistan. By 1994, Afghanistan had lived with war and its effects for almost twenty years. Every humanitarian emergency was a development emergency: the distinction meant little to affected populations. But in assistance terms, relief is often viewed as a short-term, mitigating measure (even when precipitating conditions continue for decades), and development is assumed to be long-term, demanding a planning process, government oversight, and accountability provisions. Relief is quick and humanitarian, easy to offer and justify; development requires longer commitment and, by habit, a state to organize it. This is a problem based in capitals rather than among assistance providers, most of which recognize that an intellectual commitment to the indivisibility of relief and development runs counter to political prerogatives among those who control the assistance purse.

This issue was raised among donors to Afghanistan almost every time they met.[13] Most government representatives noted that their own legislatures controlled their budgets and were quicker to provide emergency aid than negotiate long-term programs—and in Afghanistan, of course, there was no government as such. Efforts to make aid more effective in the almost twenty years since this period have had some limited success, in part due to the response to protracted conflicts in Afghanistan, Somalia, and Sierra Leone. But twenty years later, this problem is still pervasive: not only is short-term response easier to sell—for budgetary and policy reasons—but it can quickly become the lens through which conflict is seen, to the exclusion of long-term analysis and planning.[14]

This distinction raised uncomfortable questions for donors and aid providers. For example: The Taliban was fighting a territorial as well as an ideological war, and therefore restricted relief in areas not under its control. For aid providers, this raised immediate questions about the intersections of moral choice and political expediency. When international agencies pushed for refugee repatriation from Pakistan after the Taliban took power (continuing a pattern that had been established in the early 1990s, when each political change sparked an immediate effort to return refugees to their homes), decisions about development bordered on the politically efficacious: would refugees be afforded the development assistance needed to resettle—and was this a move to help Pakistan, or Afghans? When the Taliban negotiated with the government of Japan for funds to restore a power plant, was this relief (there was no power), or development (it would aid rebuilding), or a form of diplomatic bargaining? If the former, could the donor-Taliban relationship be "excused"? If not, were donors and aid agencies succumbing to wishful thinking that Taliban behavior would change by a substantial development embrace—or was Taliban agreement simply a tactical decision to sow dissent among donors?

Every decision—where to de-mine, whom to feed, how and where to plant crops, when and where tribal migrants could graze, whom to bribe and how to negotiate, how to protect workers from imprisonment and villages from ransack—raised difficult questions that typified the intersections of relief and development, humanitarianism and human rights, and political convenience and political intractability. Among aid providers—the front-line actors in negotiations with the Taliban—it was clear that more specific and agreed guidance was needed.

Aid, Politics, and Political Aid

The Taliban's unclear political and diplomatic status complicated the diplomacy of assistance. The Taliban movement was viewed as a presumptive authority—neither a government, nor exclusively a fighting force, nor a member of the international community (although explaining to early Taliban leaders the difference between a state and a government raised interesting issues of language and culture). The Taliban presumed to rule, and others responded, inconsistently and often unhappily.

However carefully foreign governments and international agencies tried to traverse this terrain, the Taliban, by sheer stubbornness, nonetheless demanded attention. It had fighters, sought territory, and controlled personal and political behavior. Little serious contest was offered to the few governments that formally recognized the Taliban.[15] The complex military environment, along a north/south-tribal/ethnic divide, was the major preoccupation of the UN political mission in its efforts to prevent fighting from spreading beyond the country's borders. This, of course, was a bit like locking the barn door after everyone escaped: from 1973 onward, Afghanistan's fights had been regional, its wars fought across its borders as much as within them. Nonetheless, the continued availability of support for fighting, the enticement of gaining territory, the prospect of governing according to its own precepts and gaining recognition internationally—all led to vigorous battles through the 1990s and concomitant concern across Asia that the virus of conflict (and failure) would spread. Occasional regional diplomatic parleys would raise the elusive idea of peace, reflecting the concerns of neighboring states. Until September 2001, the Taliban continued to seek to consolidate its territory as others worried about a raft of regional interlocking security concerns.

Taliban actions begged two much larger questions: How does a failed state formulate a foreign policy? And how do other states respond to behavior that resembles policy but doesn't emanate from a recognized form of governance, domestically or internationally?

At one level, these questions underscored a governance issue: a foreign policy based on the will of very few without any formal domestic backing is a hard nut to crack. The Taliban's quest for formal recognition, and the refusal of most UN member states to grant it, underscored their vastly different ambitions from the Taliban's. Their reasons for refusing recognition ranged from the Taliban's incomplete control of Afghan territory to the brutality of its ascent to power, to the backing of Pakistan, to the Taliban's hosting Osama bin Laden, to the Taliban's treatment of women. The distance between these sides was not bridged by deft diplomacy on anyone's part, because there was little mandate for policy anywhere. The UN political mission would talk with

Taliban leaders, but had no mandate for taking decisions, and members of foreign missions (usually based outside the country) would do the same. Although the Taliban wanted to be recognized, much of the world wanted the Taliban to change its behavior and thinking. At the same time, private companies and foreign governments, often represented by a rotating cast of the same individuals, cheerfully wooed Taliban leaders in aid of building a gas pipeline through Afghanistan. In these dealings—never fully realized, always incompletely conceived—the Taliban was at once a private actor and a public one, led less by policy as commonly understood than by positioning, widely understood and rarely applauded. This gap left space, however, for the assistance community to begin to bridge its own divides, and in so doing, attempt to do its business in more self-directed ways.

The special diplomatic circumstances of Afghanistan's failed state and—to most outsiders—faux governance were the underlying causes of many contentious policy issues. Were the country really governed rather than informally ruled, then debates about relief and development would have taken place formally and reciprocally, the political dimensions of these discussions would have been more clearly articulated, and the parameters of war more precisely defined. For the assistance community—charged, in this sense, with doing by chance what diplomats might otherwise do by direction—such conditions differed from its accustomed norms and practices. Without a state, and without government (at any level), aid providers interacted directly with civil society as a political and development actor in its own right. This had potential concrete benefits—community-led development has been widely hailed as an effective assistance tool[16]—but two clear disadvantages: first, decisions might be taken too locally and too specifically, without consistent guidance on either side, and without knowing whether a single decision would be undercut, punished, or used as a precedent; and second, practical decisions—for example, working with individual Taliban leaders in a locality—would be construed as informal recognition and lead to further misapprehension about what was and was not acceptable in relief, development, rights, or political terms.

After decades of war and migration and poverty, Afghanistan was complicated, tired and weak. Substituting civil society engagement for both state direction and diplomatic interlocution was not ideal, but it was the only thing available. Although aid providers often dealt directly with aid recipients (not necessarily a bad thing), they lived with Taliban control in the near background. Afghans who worked directly with aid providers were often at risk, even though aid itself helped a population that the Taliban ignored, or, in some instances, victimized. Most of the usual requirements for aid, including sustainability and accountability, were modified or ignored. The most important characteristic of a failed state—that nothing works—overshadowed transactional details.

The brute fact of the intersections between war and humanitarian crisis are often well known, even if the outcomes are confused; in this instance, however, the necessary links between governance and development were absent.[17] The consequences of Taliban rule could be observed, but few individuals or groups were privy to the intentions behind Taliban behavior. Each negotiation was undertaken relatively informally, often sui generis, and without agreement among all interested parties.

(Re)-Framing a Debate: Diplomacy and Aid

Coordination among donors and aid providers is often a substitute for policy agreement.[18] In the late twentieth century, the absence of day-to-day coordination and policy coherence proved costly in every way in a range of conflicts across the globe: Cambodia, Rwanda, Somalia, Bosnia, and Haiti all challenged diplomats, politicians, and aid providers to deal more effectively with the combined effects of political fragmentation, politicized refugee populations, cross-border military engagement, environmental degradation, profound poverty, and improvised assistance practices.

The role of political missions—tireless negotiators on behalf of elusive peace among fighters who were often loath to talk with one another or with anyone else—was often assumed to be at odds with aid providers, in Afghanistan and elsewhere. But cooperation among the political and assistance branches of the UN and embassies sometimes left the field open to misinterpretation: that outside actors could be spoilers or bargaining agents whose portfolio had hidden objectives, including the indirect recognition of malign actors; and that cooperation among humanitarian and diplomatic actors could, in the eyes of Afghans, taint both diplomacy and assistance. The role of foreign assistance in building peace was challenged all the more in these situations by aid practices unintentionally at once duplicative, unclear, or contradictory. By the mid-1990s, having struggled to provide assistance to states scarred by too many wars and far too many deaths, the United Nations began to rethink the way it was doing business. Its first test—no doubt among the most complicated of choices—was Afghanistan.

The effect of rights abuse on the provision of humanitarian assistance had already forced serious discussions about principles and coherence in Afghanistan. It led to uncomfortable discussions, desperately needed and almost inevitable, among NGOs, UN agencies, diplomats charged with bilateral and multilateral relationships, and, when possible, Afghan citizens. When the Taliban reached Kabul, however, conversations about theory were rapidly replaced by discussions about practice and principle in several dimensions.

When aid providers discuss the ownership of assistance, they generally mean that the "beneficiaries" of aid should "own" that aid by participating in decisions about providing, monitoring, and accounting for aid. In Afghanistan, however, the aid community owned assistance because no one else really could. Restrictions on its operations, on the one hand, and respect for rights on the other, highlighted the security, validity, effectiveness, and inclusion dimensions of assistance that so easily eroded the role of aid in improving Afghanistan—and was a counterpoint to the Taliban's arguments for recognition. At the same time, conflicting institutional demands within the international community—particularly concerning the independence of donors and the mandates of organizations—were preexisting obstacles to cooperation.

Assistance is both a diplomatic carrot and a diplomatic stick, and the Taliban, like its foreign interlocutors, quickly learned to conflate humanitarianism and political advantage. With assistance conditionality came the promise of future arguments: women today, demobilization tomorrow, recognition the day after that. Every policy actor in Afghanistan in the mid-1990s knew three things: (1) the 1988 Geneva Accords had created as many problems as they had solved by postponing hard questions about Afghanistan's future; (2) the failure of ceasefire negotiations (and therefore, any hope of a peace shepherded by external actors) exposed deep divisions between the Taliban and its opponents on the one hand (and it appeared, divisions of opinion within the Taliban itself) and the UN peace efforts on the other; and (3) time would not solve these or future conflicts without clear decisions about political responsibility, and the real meaning of sovereignty.

As a first effort to counter Taliban restrictions on women and girls, the UN's Emergency Commission on Humanitarian Affairs developed a "principle-centered approach" to gender and capacity building, in contrast to an assistance-based approach that set human rights principles to the side in order to maximize the amount of assistance provided to Afghanistan. The former view assumed a counterproductively rigid divide between aid and rights and acknowledged another divide—not always rigid, but present in early 1990s Afghanistan—between political negotiations and assistance negotiations. Taliban-controlled Afghanistan joined every rights issue to every other issue: the violations of rights of personal integrity, free expression, and freedom from torture affected the same communities whose women and girls were confined to their homes, and this limited the scope of community involvement in social and economic decisions.

But each aid provider also followed its own practices and preferences: some, like the World Health Organization (and usually the UN Development Programme and its affiliated funds), required direct relationships with government and saw their roles as building the state, and others, like UNICEF, were willing to work with an array of partners and did not always require "government" sanction. The World Food Programme, at the front lines of food delivery, found itself in the crosshairs of the Taliban leadership rather than in its accustomed role as a partner with government. NGOs were more flexible than intergovernmental agencies and could sometimes ignore the state, but they were subject to the same pressures of insecurity and conflicts with Taliban leaders; some donor governments required government-to-government agreements, but others could experiment at the community level. In all instances, prevailing rights abuses were a problem across the board. Every donor government, after all, was a UN member state, with responsibilities that ranged beyond the provision of assistance, including responsibilities for the political (and rights) consequences of aid. The stakes for Afghans were high: no one wanted the provision of aid to lead to further repression; no one wanted bad blood between the Taliban and outsiders to harm the population; and no one wanted to give up on the idea of peace or, for that matter, a future functioning Afghan state—even the Taliban, whose initial understanding of UN membership might have been hazy, but in matters relating to diplomatic recognition was unyielding.

Strategic Framing

The Strategic Framework for Afghanistan,[19] a UN idea that began in New York and Geneva and was expanded and carried out by organizations in Afghanistan, offered an opportunity to tackle these problems—and particularly the question of policy and organizational coherence—all at once. The focus on Afghanistan moved the goalposts from the level of global policy—creating a way for the UN Department of Political Affairs to work more easily with UN development and relief organizations—to the most vexing problems of working in Afghanistan, and for a much broader community. A seemingly straightforward, UN headquarters-based bureaucratic exercise turned into a referendum of sorts on humanitarianism, development, and rights in Afghanistan, undertaken by almost all assistance actors working there.[20] The consultative process, rather than single victories, became its signal, and hard-won, accomplishment.

Afghanistan was among the hardest cases the United Nations could have chosen for experimenting, but the rigors of the case placed problems of complex emergencies into sharp relief. Following a New York-led mission comprised of senior bureaucrats and representatives of the UN coordinator for Afghanistan as well as NGO leaders, a Kabul-based initiative took up the immediate challenges of working in Afghanistan, and equally important, the enormous difficulties that Afghans faced as the Taliban continued to fight for territory and political victory. High-level visits to Afghanistan—relationship building combined with firefighting—confirmed the difficulties of the environment: the executive director of UNICEF, Carol Bellamy, visited Kabul, as did the European Union's Emma Bonino (who chose to violate Taliban rules and found herself and her entourage on the verge of being jailed during a one-day excursion to Kabul). The UN secretary-general sent his gender adviser, Angela King;[21] the U.S. president sent cabinet member Bill Richardson to discuss security. Separately, but with increasing coordination and consultation across the humanitarian community, the UN secretary-general's special representative for Afghanistan and head of the UN Assistance Mission for Afghanistan, former Algerian foreign minister Lakhdar Brahimi, began an intensive campaign to gather local knowledge, convene a consultative group of Afghanistan's neighbors (the 6 + 2 group), confer with the full range of Afghan leaders and foreign offices (including the Islamic Conference), and pave the way for cooperation with the UN assistance leadership for Afghanistan—a marked change from earlier efforts to draft tenuous agreements among warring factions.

These efforts signaled the importance of diplomatic issues that ranged beyond international assistance: narcotics and arms trades, insecure borders, and the patronage of neighboring governments for fighting factions in Afghanistan.[22] They also provided support for the heads of UN agencies based in and around Afghanistan, and for the UN's first combined humanitarian and development coordinator, Alfredo Witschi-Cestari, whose background working with the principle-driven International Committee of the Red Cross (ICRC) and with the United Nations High Commissioner for Refugees (UNHCR) in Afghanistan years earlier influenced the Strategic Framework's governance and normative approach.[23]

The Strategic Framework would have been radically incomplete without the participation of the NGOs that had provided a backbone of assistance for decades. Their inclusion in what might otherwise have been a UN-centric process underscored the essential difficulties of crafting principles to suit all people and purposes. The Peshawar-based NGO coordinating committee for Afghanistan, ACBAR (the Agency Coordinating Body for Afghan Relief), represented hundreds of local and cross-border assistance groups in addition to international organizations like Save the Children and the Swedish Committee for Afghanistan. Coming to agreement about the parameters of engagement with local Taliban authorities was particularly challenging for its membership.

For these reasons, the noun became a verb: the framing *process* was a different way of doing business, rather than a way to do a different kind of business.

UN protocol and habit might have established a process that concentrated almost solely on member states and UN agencies. The Afghanistan method was fundamentally and broadly consultative and included donor governments (with particular assistance from governments in Scandinavia and from the United Kingdom's Department for International Development) as well as small community organizations. Its work was, by necessity, of a piece with the daily work of aid: this was a time of war and massacres, natural disasters, desperate food shortages, health crises, and rising insecurity—all problems exacerbated by the diplomatic impasses created by Taliban rights violations.

Framing was meant in part to rebalance the humanitarian, rights, and political elements of foreign aid through long examinations of current practice and common principles and programming. Over time, it created a consensual form of meeting and decision-making at the field level (in Afghanistan, or wherever Afghanistan-related assistance actors were able to operate); concentrated on long-term planning based on impact rather than intention (a challenge in Afghanistan, where predicting outcomes would seem almost impossible); and established—again, consensually—self-governing, although largely unenforceable, principles to guide everyday work. Bringing in the Taliban was unlikely—although conversations with individual members continued throughout—and with the exception of interactions associated with operational requirements, rarely occurred as part of this process. The UN political mission was able to maintain communications with the Taliban leadership as part of its own mission, and for the rest of the UN family. As Taliban positions hardened (as did the policies of major UN actors), the Strategic Framework became a careful, if time-consuming, instrument for considering common responses to obstacles and restrictions—the assistance community's equivalent of negotiated diplomatic policies.[24]

The process was improvisational by necessity: the same people responsible for crafting guidance for the future were, day to day, coping with earthquakes, famines, disease, rights abuses, retributive Taliban actions toward the assistance community itself, and the effects of repression in Afghanistan. Timing, if not everything, was certainly something. It can be argued that decisions taken during emergencies are inevitably incomplete. In this three-year-long instance, the urgency of daily tasks lent realism to talk of concepts and principles, but also tagged every generality with a task, every small problem with the weight of future precedent.

Recognizing that Afghanistan's emergency was deteriorating markedly under Taliban rule (even more when donor states began to limit or withdraw funds), the primacy of the humanitarian over other goals—saving lives, even if only in the short term—became a driving element of this process. Under other circumstances, this might not have been the correct decision; but in this instance, a moral imperative for some became practical need for others. The framework process negotiated a settlement about the facts and principles of engagement, as well as the substance of respect for rights over the formalities of rights vested in international treaties—highly contentious issues, brought to local and immediate concerns. It was also the only explicit statement of purpose, from the international and domestic Afghan communities alike, that articulated a rationale (peace building) and a basis (principled respect for communities, rights, and relief) for engagement with those who would lead Afghanistan.

The framework reflected these immediate concerns. It had two premises: (1) underlining the need for agreement about priorities among all assistance actors[25] and (2) reinforcing inclusiveness—inside and outside Afghanistan and among all external assistance actors for Afghanistan—in an otherwise highly fractured environment. It was a UN-directed framework, without a doubt, but enfranchised non-UN actors as (almost) equals in developing consensus about policies and actions.[26] These two premises were matched by simple principles—guidance for working in Afghanistan, which was also to be guidance for judging success concerning rights, humanitarianism, aid as an element of peace building, neutrality with regard to warring parties, local participation, and accountability.[27] In all, this was an effort to bring together actors from the development, rights, political, and humanitarian communities (each of which included diversity of opinion as well). The final framework created programming and monitoring bodies that included the assistance and political wings of the United Nations, as well as nongovernmental bodies, the ICRC, and multilateral development banks.

The initial imperative was to find ways for assistance groups to act with a shared analysis of the political and assistance environment, with common purpose (and perhaps shared programs) and in ways that would not contradict others with regard to rights. The two most important results of the Strategic Framework were nonetheless process based, in two ways that were important for the actions of the assistance community. First, consultation as a means for identifying issues and, later, for vetting text, was broad and not limited to the international community. Draft documents were carried around Afghanistan for community meetings and NGO consultations—not quite a substitute for elections in a functioning state, but a significant effort to ensure that Afghans were participants in discussions about issues that defined their lives and livelihoods. This became an indirect way for Afghan communities to respond to the rights environment in which they were living, to clarify the rights consequences of relief and development decisions (whether about favoring one group over another, or one issue over another), and to emphasize the local consequences of decisions that might otherwise seem to be taken with international or foreign interests at the forefront.

Second, the process of articulating principles for future assistance became more important than the text/agreement itself.[28] When the process began, the international community had been talking about principled assistance for years, provoked by circumstance, interest, humanitarianism and an instinct for survival. The Strategic Framework's principles emphasized humanitarianism, universality, impartiality, and neutrality—the bedrocks of international assistance—but also emphasized the close relationship between politics, rights, development, and relief. It took years to gain agreement on these points, and when it was finally reached in 1999, it was due in some measure to the way that Afghanistan's difficult circumstances affected everyone living and working there.

At the same time, a major focus of the Strategic Framework document itself—to encourage and assist programs that were shared across the assistance community—became almost impossible to implement. Agreeing on principles was easier than providing the same assistance through common programs. It quickly became clear that its programming guidelines were difficult to implement—given the same problems of dispersed authority that continued (and continue) to plague humanitarian and development aid. In Afghanistan, this problem was exacerbated by unfortunate timing: just as the assistance community agreed to its principles, resources for aid were decreasing markedly, and with the absence of funding came a lack of global attention to Afghanistan itself.

Silk Purses, Sows' Ears: The Primacy of Process

Did the Strategic Framework fix Afghanistan? Of course not, and it was not meant to do so. Preliminary conversations about coherence and principles began in 1996; discussions about a framework process began in 1997, and the final version was agreed to in 1999. For a UN-led process, this was relatively short, but for Afghanistan, it was very long indeed. By the end of 1998, however, foreign donors—responding to the deep despair of Afghanistan and the impasses of formal diplomacy—had whittled their contributions to almost nothing: at one point, there was just enough funding to operate the basic radio communications system and run relief planes a few times a week. If the principles of humanitarianism could not demonstrate that they could trump other interests, it was in part because there was less about which to argue. The agenda of the political mission's 6 + 2 regional contact group had shrunk by 2000. The Taliban continued its territorial fighting and engaged in brutal violations of human rights, further marginalizing Afghanistan and its people—but still sought formal recognition and Afghanistan's UN seat. Without funds to spend, however, the aid community's principles were rendered quiet, if not silent, limiting the effect of devolved, assistance-oriented diplomacy.

Did the Strategic Framework change the Taliban? No, and again, it was not meant to do so. It did, however, try to stake out conceptual and practical grounds of agreement for dealing with the Taliban—not to resolve the basic territorial and ideological conflicts of Afghanistan, but to make it possible for needed business to be done transparently and with some dignity.

Did this essentially diplomatic effort fix assistance, or the relationship between formal diplomacy and the diplomacy of assistance?[29] The Strategic Framework itself downplayed politics and governance—issues that were fundamental to the task but inaccessible in this context; ignored difficult issues that typified Taliban rule; and wrapped the UN political mission into an assistance framework without thorough analysis of the strengths and weaknesses of all parties. Moreover, it left out any serious discussion of the roles of neighboring states—all weak in their own ways, but important in either perpetuating Taliban rule or seeking to dislodge it. Critical stones were left unturned: al-Qaeda was never mentioned and rarely discussed in these pre-2001 conversations, and the effects of an evolving pattern of terrorism was an issue left to corridor discussions in the UN Security Council. The assistance community's mandated practice of working within borders rather than across them—with UNHCR as the historical exception to the rule—shortened the view from Afghanistan itself, for which neighboring states and global activities were viewed (as they often are elsewhere) only through the lens of immediate, local concerns. The immediate focus on dealing with the Taliban ignored the enormous economic, military, security, and political roles of neighboring states and the repercussions of global terror emanating from Afghanistan on its neighbors. That this choice was to the advantage of some—Taliban supporters, or their opponents in the wider neighborhood, or actors seeking a foothold in the unsettled diplomatic decade of the 1990s—was often left unspoken.

More than anything else, the process pushed the diplomatic envelope at a long moment of despair: it pushed those working in Afghanistan to agree that their efforts required cooperation and transparency, and to acknowledge that their previous work, under conditions of profound uncertainty, included (and might have fostered) failure as much as incremental success.

Time takes its toll, and it can change behavior. The Strategic Framework consultative processes could not have worked without four essential components: (1) the support of UN headquarters and the overall program of Secretary-General Kofi Annan, whose appointment of the individuals tasked with rethinking Afghanistan's problem distinguished the framework period from those that preceded it and empowered the relief and development sectors at this difficult time; (2) stubbornly cooperative leaders at the field level who became persuaded that relief, development, and respect for rights were integral parts of both development and diplomacy at all phases of war and negotiation; (3) evolving good will among highly experienced assistance actors and diplomats who had labored for years in an increasingly inhospitable environment; and (4) in the language of the framework, the careful development of "a culture that places a premium on cooperation and coordination for effective action," which arose in these special circumstances in part because the primary actors—including donor governments that later led the Strategic Framework's Afghanistan Support Group—were relatively independent by virtue of working in an outlier country.

These last two points became meaningful far beyond Afghanistan. First, the fact of state failure was assumed, but neither the United Nations, nor the nongovernmental sector, nor bilateral diplomatic actors formulated or employed a sophisticated theory of the state to accompany their more polished theories of humanitarianism. For this extended moment, failure simply meant that nothing worked, no one was really in charge, and there was no state apparatus capable of redressing the grievances of its citizens—all correct observations, but not an adequately informed basis for future planning. Assistance actors had become accustomed to filling in when government did not work. Indeed, some aid actors found the absence of government confounding, but others found it easier to work without the burdens of host-government attention.

When the international community installed a new government in Afghanistan in 2002 after consultations in Bonn, its first instincts were to see state institutions as something separate from—even competing with—the NGOs that had worked, independently of a state, during the 1990s. Politically, international habit in places like Taliban-controlled Afghanistan was to reward and punish—a practice that has continued since 2001 as the international community wavers between engagement and sanction, recognition and toleration, and intermittent reconciliation among many of the same actors who set Afghanistan's direction in the 1980s and 1990s. The Strategic Framework did not, and could not, take on such issues: it dealt with the question of aid conditionality obliquely, since its role was to facilitate the kind of engagement that could sustain relationships until policy could be crafted coherently. (In this sense, both the Taliban and the assistance community were in self-imposed holding patterns.) Sustaining relationships meant raising humanitarianism to a primary role, over and above developing a foundation for future governance in Afghanistan. In a sense, the community took over the job of speaking for disenfranchised Afghans who had few ways to speak for themselves. Who speaks for whom, however, is a highly politicized decision with profound effects on diplomacy: raising humanitarian imperatives over politics (and diplomacy)—or at least separating it from its political environment—reflected an acknowledgment of state failure and the international community's inability to fix it.

Organizational change does not substitute for policy, and diplomacy about assistance, while critical in crisis regions, does not replace state-to-state diplomacy. The experience of trying to craft appropriate responses in Afghanistan in the middle to late 1990s—for the active assistance community and diplomats in more distant capitals—contributed to a continuing multilateral conversation about three particularly important questions: how to establish a common assessment of problematic places under conditions of complex humanitarian, development, political, and foreign policy threats; how to craft missions and mandates that can address those analyses; and how to analyze human rights in ways that could protect society and contribute to overall analysis. In the first instance, the Afghanistan assistance community, with UN leadership, established its own analysis wing in the late 1990s, and that organization continued to work and grow (independently) in the years following 2001. More broadly, the issue of systemwide analytical agreement and goals—an issue underscored repeatedly by the UN secretary-general's special representative to Afghanistan, Lakhdar Brahimi—figured in the *Report of the Panel on United Nations Peace Operations* (2000), which Brahimi later chaired.[30]

At the same time, the broad scope of human rights abuses that Afghans encountered under the Taliban—and the assistance community's neither fully absorbing nor fully responding to those conditions, and foreign diplomats attending to them only lightly, along with the varied views held of the importance of this problem in political and humanitarian terms—ultimately contributed to growing international understanding of the need for rights protections in weak, failing, and beleaguered states. The UN high commissioner for human rights began to assign rights monitors to crisis zones ranging from Rwanda to Nepal (followed inevitably by nongovernmental monitors) who could contribute to policy while formulating ways to protect civilians.

The special case of 1990s Afghanistan also highlights issues that could not be confronted directly and that remain immensely challenging. First, strategy is not policy—it is a way to organize participation to craft and execute policy, and in complex emergencies it is meant to help simplify the understanding of complexity and the range of actions that can respond to it. A strategic framework can justify or substitute temporarily for an action framework, but in challenging conditions—and with an unknown timeline—it is also a piece of that complexity and therefore only minimally strategic.

Second, and equally important, strategy cannot help but reflect the actors who design and implement it. Afghanistan's Strategic Framework was largely created by humanitarian actors who focused on questions of direct concern to humanitarian access and effectiveness. This group knew well that broader diplomatic issues colored its opportunities and obstacles, but were beyond its control. Even states that donated aid had many more interests than the framework reflected. An assistance community's interests are more limited and differ markedly from the nonhumanitarian—and more singularly diplomatic— interests of states. With time, and new crises, Afghanistan would become a paramount *diplomatic* issue; assistance strategy filled the space until that happened.

Global conversations about ending war, building peace, and assisting afflicted populations have come far in the years since Afghanistan's humanitarian actors tried to formulate a way to handle problems that much of the world ignored.[31] For a short time, those working in Afghanistan tried to rescue the basic idea of engagement for an international community so taxed by conflicts that it had lost its principled bearings in Afghanistan. Historians are likely to see Afghanistan's Taliban period as a case study in failed states, and even more, as the beginning of a new period of violence. The case of Taliban-era Afghanistan nonetheless helped the international community to begin to clarify the intersections of policy and process, and the close relationships between rights, aid, and, ultimately, diplomacy.

Notes

1. See Bruce Riedel, *What We Won: America's Secret War in Afghanistan, 1979–1989* (Washington DC: Brookings Institution Press, 2014), chap. 8; Riaz M. Khan, *Untying the Afghan Knot: Negotiating Soviet Withdrawal* (Durham, NC: Duke University Press, 1991); Diego Cordovez and Selig Harrison, *Out of Afghanistan: The Inside Story of the Soviet Withdrawal* (New York: Oxford University Press, 1995); Rosanne Klass, "Afghanistan: The Accords," *Foreign Affairs* 66, no. 5 (Summer 1988): 922–945; Dipali Mukohopadhyay, "The Slide from Withdrawal to War: The UN Secretary General's Failed Effort in Afghanistan, 1992," *International Negotiation* 17, no. 3 (2012): 485–517; and Riaz M. Khan, *Afghanistan and Pakistan: Conflict, Extremism and Resistance to Modernity* (Washington, DC: Woodrow Wilson Center Press, 2011), chaps. 1 and 2.
2. See, for example, Khaled Ahmed, *Sectarian War: Pakistan's Sunni-Shia Violence and Its Links to the Middle East* (Karachi: Oxford University Press, 2012).
3. For a nuanced discussion, see Faisal Devji, *Landscapes of Jihad* (Ithaca, NY: Cornell University Press, 2005).
4. A partial list of UN General Assembly resolutions on Afghanistan includes: A/RES/51/195 (December 1996), A/RES/52/211 (February 1998), A/RES/55/243; and UN Security Council Resolutions includeS/RES/1076 (October 22, 1996), S/RES/1193 (August 28, 1998), S/RES/1214 (December 8, 1998), S/RES/1333 (December 19, 2000), A/55/305-S/2000/809 (August 2000) (Brahimi Report), and A/55/305-S/2000/809.
5. See Abdul Salam Zaeef, *My Life with the Taliban* (New York: Columbia University Press, 2010).
6. The number and range of organizations was surprisingly broad, given the limitations of the working environment, and included UNHCR (working across all of Afghanistan's borders), UNICEF, the UN Development Programme and its affiliated organizations, the Food and Agriculture Organization and the World Food Programme, the World

Health Organization, and, critically, a coalition of demining organizations. The European Union as well as the governments of Sweden, Norway, the Netherlands, Japan, and the United Kingdom (among many others) provided critical funding to their own and to UN bodies; and NGOs from across the globe—including the ICRC, Save the Children, the Swedish Committee for Afghanistan, the Norwegian Refugee Council, Doctors Without Borders, some smaller religiously oriented groups, and small local organizations that managed to persist through decades of conflict.

7. On Save the Children, see Angela Kearney, "Why We Closed in Herat," *Aina* 2 (September 1996).
8. Paula Newberg, *Principles, Capacity Building and Gender in Afghanistan: Report to the Afghanistan Support Group* (Kabul, May 1, 1998) "In author's possession."
9. Afghanistan: *AFP Emergency Report* No. 41 of 1996. Reliefweb, October 17, 1996. Taliban seek more talks to keep U.N. bread aid. June 15, 2001: www.Islamweb.net.
10. William Maley, *The Foreign Policy of the Taliban* (New York: Council on Foreign Relations, 2002), http://www.cfr.org/afghanistan/foreign-policy-taliban/p8609.
11. See Antonio Donini, Eric Dudley, and Ron Ockwell, *Afghanistan: Coordination in a Fragmented State* (New York: United Nations Department of Humanitarian Affairs, 1996); Claude Bruderlein and Adeel Ahmed, *Report of the DHA Mission to Afghanistan* (New York: UN Department of Humanitarian Affairs, Policy Analysis Division, 1997); Paula Newberg, *Principles, Capacity Building and Gender: Report to the Afghanistan Support Group* (Kabul, May 1, 1998); Claude Bruderlein, *The Role of Non-state Actors in Building Human Security: The Case of Armed Groups in Intra-state Wars* (Geneva: Centre for Humanitarian Dialogue, 2000); and International Council on Human Rights, *Ends and Means: Human Rights Approaches to Armed Groups* (Versoix, Switzerland: ICHR, 2000), http://www.ichrp.org/files/reports/6/105_report_en.pdf
12. Paula Newberg and Michael Dalton, *Governance in Afghanistan: Report of the UNDP Mission* (Kabul: UNDP, 1997); see also Chris Johnson and Jolyon Leslie, *Afghanistan: The Mirage of Peace* (London: Zed Books, 2004).
13. The assistance community for Afghanistan (based in Islamabad) proposed and accepted a common donor position on aid to Afghanistan within ten days of the Taliban's entry into Kabul, but this agreement quickly frayed. For a discussion of this issue, see Paula R. Newberg, *Politics at the Heart: The Architecture of Humanitarian Assistance to Afghanistan*, Washington, D.C., Carnegie Endowment for International Peace, July 2, 1999, http://carnegieendowment.org/1999/07/02/politics-at-the-heart-architecture-of-humanitarian-assistance-to-afghanistan/3yi.
14. Witness the provision of assistance to the victims of war in Syria in 2013 and 2014. One effort intended to reverse this trend in southern Asia was the United States Senate Enhanced Partnership with Pakistan Act of 2009, W.1707 (known informally as the Kerry-Lugar-Berman bill), an effort to provide long-term development-oriented assistance to Pakistan, which nonetheless had difficulty achieving its spending targets in successive years due to strict, legislatively mandated accountability and burden-sharing requirements. See Nancy Birdsall, Molly Kinder, and Wren Elhai, *Beyond Bullets and Bombs: Fixing the U.S. Approach to Development in Pakistan: Report of the Study Group on a US Development Strategy in Pakistan*, Washington, DC, Center for Global Development, June 1, 2011.
15. The United States and other states argued with Pakistan about its recognition of the Taliban in 1997. Pakistan's weak government was unable to retract its hasty decision, and given the intricacy of overall relationships in the region, including Pakistan's far stronger relationships with Saudi Arabia (which also recognized the Taliban), did not suffer unduly for its decision. Pakistan would later argue privately that its formal recognition of the Taliban gave the United Nations, the United States, and others a conduit for dealing with the Taliban. Not long thereafter, in 1998, Pakistan tested a nuclear weapon (following an Indian test weeks earlier), a move that strained Pakistan's relations with Western capitals even more, including Afghanistan.
16. On community-based relief and development in Afghanistan, see Newberg, *Principles, Capacity Buiding and Gender* and Peter Coleridge, "Community Based Rehabilitation in

a Complex Emergency: Study of Afghanistan," *Asia Pacific Disability Rehabilitation Journal*, January 2002, http://english.aifo.it/disability/apdrj/selread102/contents.htm.

17. See Newberg and Dalton, *Governance*.

18. The problem of "policy coherence" predated the Taliban period in Afghanistan and was, in fact, the initial reason for experimenting with new forms of collaboration in the development community. Most of these efforts had not moved very far before 1996–1997; the experience with Afghanistan provided both an assistance and a diplomatic rationale for raising the importance of the idea—if, in the end, not the practice—of coherence. See Larry Minear, "The InterAgency Strategic Framework Mission to Afghanistan," Humanitarian Exchange Magazine, no. 11 (May 1998), http://www.odihpn.org/humanitarian-exchange-magazine/issue-11/the-interagency-strategic-framework-mission-to-afghanistan; Joanna Macrae and Nicholas Leader, *Shifting Sands: The Search for 'Coherence' between Political and Humanitarian Responses to Complex Emergencies* (London: Overseas Development Institute, 2000); Nicola Reindorp and Peter Wiles, *Humanitarian Coordination: Lessons from Recent Field Experience* (London: Overseas Development Institute, 2001); and Cedric De Coning, *Coherence Dilemma in Peacebuilding and Post-Conflict Reconstruction Systems. African Journal on Conflict Resolution* 8, no. 3 (2008): 85–110.

19. United Nations, *Strategic Framework for Afghanistan: Towards a Principled Approach to Peace and Reconstruction*, 1998. Reprinted January 4, 1999, as *Strategic Framework for Afghanistan Endorsed by UN Agencies*, Reliefweb.int/report/Afghanistan/strategic-framework-afghanistan-endorsed-un-agencies.

20. On trade-offs between humanitarianism and other priorities, see Nicholas Stockton, *Strategic Coordination in Afghanistan* (Kabul: Afghanistan Research and Evaluation Unit, 2002).

21. King's report was far blunter than some others in recommending conditioning relations with the Taliban on respect for women's rights and treated the Taliban as a de facto government. See *Report of the United Nations Interagency Gender Mission to Afghanistan* (New York: United Nations Office of the Special Adviser on Gender Issues and the Advancement of Women, 1997). On the effects of this, see Johnson and Leslie, *Afghanistan* and Newberg, *Principles, Capacity Building and Gender.*

22. The Pakistani government and military were assumed to be supporting the Taliban; Uzbekistan and Tajikistan were assumed to support the Northern Alliance (which contested the Taliban, and whose leader was assassinated just before September 11, 2001); Iran supported the minority Shia community, which found itself under increasing stress.

23. Prior experience with Afghanistan and the region became important in different ways: the UN Political Mission was staffed with old Afghan hands seconded from participating foreign offices; many NGO and UN staff had worked in Afghanistan during the post–Geneva Accord period, with UNHCR or the cross-border assistance program, or with NGOs. Their knowledge and sympathy for an otherwise ignored population and country helped to solidify the interests of otherwise divergent organizations in the 1990s and to cement relationships with some Afghan communities.

24. Antonio Donini, "The Elusive Quest: Integration in the Response to the Afghan Crisis," *Ethics and International Affairs* 18, no. 2 (2004): 21–27; and Mark Duffield, Patricia Gossman, and Nicholas Leader, *Review of the Strategic Framework for Afghanistan* (Kabul: Afghanistan Research and Evaluation Unit, 2001).

25. These principles were (a) life-sustaining humanitarian assistance shall be provided in accordance with the principles of humanity, universality, impartiality, and neutrality; (b) assistance shall be provided as part of an overall effort to achieve peace; (c) international assistance will be provided on the basis of need; it cannot be subjected to any form of discrimination, including of gender; (d) rehabilitation and development assistance shall be provided only where it can be reasonably determined that no direct political or military advantage will accrue to the warring parties in Afghanistan; (e) institution and capacity-building activities must advance human rights and will not seek to provide support to any presumptive state authority which does not fully subscribe to the principles

contained in the founding instruments of the United Nations, the Universal Declaration of Human Rights, the Convention on the Rights of the Child, the Convention on the Elimination of Discrimination against Women and International Humanitarian Law; (f) assistance activities must be designed to ensure increasing indigenous ownership at the village, community, and national levels and to build the country as a whole; (g) assistance activities must attain high standards of transparency and accountability and must be appraised, monitored, measured, and evaluated against clear policy and programmatic objectives.

26. Each participating organization had to answer to its own leadership, locally and at headquarters, including each UN agency, fund, and program separately; UN coordinating and policy bodies in New York and Geneva; all major policy bodies of the European Union, and in some instances, the relief, development, and diplomatic bureaucracies of participating UN donor/member states.

27. Duffield et al. suggested that rights problems were intentionally underplayed, an opinion belied by the conditions that compelled the Strategic Framework itself. See Donini, *The Elusive Quest*, for a response to this assessment.

28. The text reads: "Political, operational and other conditionalities must be subordinated to the humanitarian imperative of saving lives and to the right to receive humanitarian assistance. The day-to-day application of these principles should be informed by the following operational modalities. International assistance partners working in Afghanistan must ensure that assistance works towards the eradication of structural discriminations, by gender, tribe, ethnicity, language, religion or political affiliation; agree to speak with one voice on all issues of principle; agree on the collective conditions for engagement and disengagement when human rights are violated and human distress is increased; consider and reach consensus on the range of non life-threatening activities to which conditionalities may be imposed."

29. See Chris Johnson, "The Strategic Framework Review: Lessons for Post-Taliban Afghanistan," *Humanitarian Exchange Magazine*, no. 20 (2002), http://www.odihpn.org/humanitarian-exchange-magazine/issue-20/the-strategic-framework-review-lessons-for-post-taliban-afghanistan.

30. Known as the Brahimi Report, sections II (F) and II (G) emphasized strategic planning: UN General Assembly/Security Council A/55/305-S/2000.809 (August 21, 2000).

31. See, for example, *Lessons Learned from Peacebuilding Strategic Frameworks since the Late 1990s*. PBSO Briefing Paper, Working Group Lessons Learned. (New York: United Nations Peace Building Support Office, 2007); World Food Programme, *Humanitarian Assistance in Conflict and Complex Emergencies*, June 2009 conference report and background papers; International Crisis Group, 2011; Department for International Development, Government of the United Kingdom, *Understanding Afghanistan: Strategic Conflict Assessment*, 2.4 *Final Report*. (York: The Recovery and Development Consortium, 2008.

11

Conclusion

ROBERT HUTCHINGS AND JEREMI SURI

Diplomacy comes in many shapes and sizes. The chapters in this book track the experience of diplomacy in numerous parts of the world, under the guidance of presidents and prime ministers as well as lawyers, scientists, economists, aid workers, and, of course, ambassadors. As shown, these diverse diplomatic actors pursued their aims through discussions, negotiations, compromises, and various forms of manipulation. They struggled continuously to understand their adversaries, to persuade their publics, and to promote the interests of their government or organization. They exemplified the diversity of potential diplomatic actors, but also the coherence of what we might call the "diplomatic style"—the effort to increase power and influence through innovative partnerships and strategies, rather than unilateral acts of force. As stated in the introduction and as shown throughout the chapters, diplomacy is not an alternative to war; it is a process for broadening the range of policy options beyond the clash of arms alone.

In international relations theory, diplomacy is realistic about material conditions, but it also constructs new arrangements of power based on political, economic, legal, and cultural activities that modify the material order. Each case in this book shows both the realist and constructivist parts of the story. That is why diplomacy is central to all major events and actions in the international system. It helps determine the scale of collaborations and the scope of conflicts. Diplomacy is not just "soft power." The chapters show that it is central to *all* forms of power.

We live in what scholar Hedley Bull has called an "international society" of peoples, states, and organizations. Diplomacy is the oxygen for interactions and associations. Diplomacy connects states and groups seeking to maximize their self-interest, while still maintaining a livable environment beyond their borders. That is the crucial "society" part of the phrase "international society"; it is the most enduring rationale for devoting study and support to the practice of diplomacy.[1]

Diplomacy is about action, not just abstract thought. Policymakers rely on a large number of officials not only to generate the best policy options but also to translate goals into results. Diplomacy is a translational enterprise, turning thought into reality, as it also brings different cultures, traditions, and ambitions together.

Henry Kissinger's key insight as a diplomat was that policymakers need more options to address the difficult problems that they confront. For President Richard Nixon, Cold War rivalry, military quagmire in Vietnam, and rising unrest within the United States were nearly debilitating challenges to effective policy leadership. Nixon's talented but overwhelmed predecessor, President Lyndon Johnson, spent his last years in office on the defensive, reacting to a continuing proliferation of crises, unable to pursue new initiatives. Kissinger's great service for Nixon was in helping the president to formulate and pursue new openings for influence through improved relations with the People's Republic of China, as well as the Soviet Union and numerous countries in the Middle East. Kissinger brilliantly used diplomatic overtures— many of them unilateral and risky—to create new partners, procure assistance with common challenges, redefine inherited problems, and, perhaps most important, mobilize further support. Kissinger's diplomacy multiplied Nixon's options, and it allowed the president to turn the tide of international conflict toward American interests. The United States seemed less under siege because Kissinger and Nixon found major new partners abroad.

Many scholars question the consequences of Kissinger's diplomacy. Did the Nixon administration's policies in China, the Soviet Union, Vietnam, and the Middle East really help American interests? Did these policies improve global conditions? The point of this book is not to judge policy outcomes, although that is certainly a worthwhile historical task. The purpose of our case studies, as stated in the introduction, is to focus on the creation of options and opportunities through skilled diplomacy. How did figures like Kissinger increase the options for policymakers? How did they create opportunities for significant change in the routines of international behavior? The preferences of presidents and other national leaders, as well as the contingencies of interactions between actors (what Clausewitz famously called the "fog" of war and politics), are not controlled by diplomats.[2] The point of diplomacy is to create new options, "to rescue an element of choice from the pressure of circumstance," in Kissinger's words.[3] The value content of the choices made by political leaders is not in the hands of the diplomats, nor should it be.

Each of the chapters in this book analyzes a case in which diplomats, similar to and different from Kissinger, expanded the options and opportunities for political leaders. These are cases of successful diplomacy—in which diplomacy did its job of expanding the policy possibilities. Some cases, including the Nuclear Non-Proliferation Treaty, the evolution of the European Union, and the conclusion of the North America Free Trade Agreement (NAFTA), also had successful policy outcomes, according to many observers. Other cases, especially the Bandung Conference and United Nations aid to Afghanistan, did not result in obvious policy successes. Another set of cases, including the United Nations Relief and Rehabilitation Administration (UNRRA) and Camp David, were decidedly mixed in their results.

Successful diplomacy clearly catalyzes diverse outcomes. It is a necessary, but not a sufficient source of effective policymaking. Ignoring diplomacy will undermine policy, but emphasizing diplomacy alone is not enough. It is one crucial step in giving policymakers a pathway for improving the conditions of their country and their wider environment. The decision-makers at the center of each chapter in this volume used diplomacy to increase their options and give their programs for change a chance. To be strategic, one must also be diplomatic.

There is obviously no formula for successful diplomacy. Historical study does not provide universal guidelines, because each case is unique in its time and its context. Above all, diplomats must be attentive to the particularities of their era, their counterparts, and their geography. Diplomats fundamentally avoid broad generalizations so they can respond to the specific needs of the issue at hand. Diplomats think big, but they master the key details. Each chapter in this volume shows that.

With this caveat about the uniqueness of each case in mind, there are some common themes that are worth articulating as scholars and practitioners think more systematically about diplomacy. These are common experiences that future diplomats should consider. These are also dynamics that practitioners should prepare for and scholars should study in more depth.

Diplomacy Begins with Failure and It Requires Patience

Each chapter in this volume opens with an unsettled strategic issue or an ongoing crisis. Leaders and diplomats had attempted to address these issues and crises in the past, but they had not succeeded. The diplomats who sought to open new options had to begin by understanding past failures. From the founding of UNRRA to the United Nations efforts at aid in Afghanistan, diplomats drew on a long record that identified the sources of suffering on the ground. High-level diplomats, including Henry Kissinger, James Baker, and all the major participants at Camp David, formulated their negotiating positions with knowledge of how and why their predecessors had failed to achieve their goals.

Kissinger, Baker, and other diplomats also encountered many of their own failures before moments of achievement. Kissinger's plans for a negotiated settlement to the Vietnam War in 1969 did not reach fruition, and his early overtures to China elicited no direct reaction from Beijing. Baker and the entire administration of President George H. W. Bush faced intensive criticism for months of indecision about future steps with Soviet leader Mikhail Gorbachev.

Kissinger, Baker, and other diplomats began their tenures with uncertainty about some of their tactics. They also had many reasons for doubt about their goals—doubts often articulated by their internal and external critics. The ability to turn doubt into success required a high tolerance of risk and a patient approach to change. Kissinger and Baker did not seek immediate results, and they did not abandon their goals in the face of initial difficulties. Skilled diplomats turn early troubles into justifications for additional creativity. They convince those around them to redouble their efforts and maintain confidence in diplomatic goals.

Of course, patience requires political bosses willing to invest in long-term goals, despite short-term setbacks. Patience also requires an ability to convey confidence despite apparent odds—not the hubris of believing goals will be achieved, but confidence that the articulated goals are the right ones, even in the face of long odds. If a diplomat can work effectively against contrary short-term pressures, then the diplomat generally adds to his or her credibility with potential foreign partners. The perseverance and commitment shown by Kissinger surely helped to convince his counterparts in Beijing that he could deliver on a mutually beneficial agreement. The intensity and duration of the Camp David talks had a similar effect on all participants: Israeli, Egyptian, and American. Patience and perseverance are difficult to maintain, but they are necessary to turn past failures into current opportunities.

Procrastination Can Pay Off

Driven in part by a twenty-four-hour news cycle, modern politics create pressures for frenetic activity and rapid responses to emerging crises. This is particularly true for the leaders of large states who face daily questions about what they are going to do about a foreign terrorist threat, a distant conflict, or an urgent international economic difficulty. Presidents and prime ministers are often figures who have risen to the top of their society by responding quickly and effectively to diverse challenges throughout their careers. Their urge is to act decisively, covering up any hesitation or indecision with an image of strength and resolve.

Successful diplomacy recognizes that speed is frequently important, but it can also close options too rapidly. It can allow adversaries to set one's priorities, rather than encouraging a careful exploration of interests, goals, and alternatives. Reactivity and crisis management give the appearance that leaders are in command, but they mask the reality of panic and shortsighted policy development.

Diplomacy can help because it can slow down the policy process for reflection and an exploration of options. It often gives adversaries and allies the space to reconsider their goals, as well as their assessments of one another. The great sixteenth-century diplomat Francesco Guicciardini made this point very well: "When you are in difficult straits or involved in troublesome affairs, procrastinate, and wait as long as you can. For often time will enlighten or free you."

Timing matters enormously in politics and foreign policy. There are imperative moments to seize a possibility for agreement. President George H. W. Bush and his policy team did this through their efforts to negotiate a peaceful reunification of Germany. There are also moments when agreement is not possible, and stalling might in fact put off an impending conflict. As Guicciardini explained, the passage of time sometimes softens conflicts and makes agreement possible again. "If you attempt certain things at the right time," he wrote, "they are easy to accomplish—in fact, they almost get done by themselves. If you undertake them before the time is right, not only will they fail, but they will often become impossible to accomplish when the time is right."[4]

In creating UNRRA after the Second World War, Undersecretary of State Dean Acheson effectively stalled for a year on a Soviet proposal. He used this time effectively, according to chapter author Stephen Porter, organizing Anglo-American agreement on postwar relief. Echoing Guicciardini, Porter labels Acheson's actions as "benign delay." Similar words could be used to describe the many diplomatic delays in negotiating the Nuclear Non-Proliferation Treaty and various European integration agreements. As the chapters on these topics show, although the slowness of diplomacy frustrated many policymakers, it ultimately allowed diverse and antagonistic actors to navigate the trade-offs that were necessary to bring agreements to fruition. Faster is not always better; successful diplomacy is often slow and deliberate.

Diplomacy Requires Strategic Planning and Preparation

None of the foreign policy breakthroughs covered in this volume occurred without significant prior planning, embedded in an overarching strategy that integrated the relevant elements of national power and influence. None would have succeeded had key agencies of government been allowed to pursue their own separate courses, as happens more often than not in policymaking. The seemingly obvious judgment that foreign policy should proceed from rigorous strategic planning is made more interesting by the fact that it so rarely does.

Due to the outsized influence of the military in the United States and many other countries, there is a strong imperative to integrate military and diplomatic strategy. In the case of the Nuclear Non-Proliferation Treaty, the creation of the Arms Control and Disarmament Agency (ACDA) helped to overcome resistance from military and other figures in the United States and abroad. In the diplomacy leading to the end of the Cold War, the Bush administration successfully brought both the military and civilian sides of the Pentagon into a strategic decision-making process led by the National Security Council. In China, where the military establishment wields great power, it is instructive to see how Mao Zedong and Zhou Enlai used the report of the four marshals to coopt the senior leaders of the People's Liberation Army.

In the U.S. government, rivalry between senior figures—especially the national security adviser, the secretary of state, and the secretary of defense—is a recurrent theme. Personal and institutional tensions are exacerbated by the fact that strategic planning is normally the province of individual departments, rather than a government-wide, coordinated activity. In coalition governments (which the Federal Republic of Germany has had for most of the last half century) or in constitutional systems that place national security decision-making firmly in the office of a president who shares overall governing power with a prime minister (as in the French Fifth Republic), strategic incoherence is built in.

Despite these challenges, the cases in this volume show that coordinated strategic planning can be achieved, and that it is essential for successful diplomacy. There were extensive multinational and multiagency planning processes leading up to the creation of the UNRRA, the development of an EU enlargement strategy, and the negotiations of the Treaty on the Non-Proliferation of Nuclear Weapons (NPT) and NAFTA. Even in the case of American diplomacy at the end of the Cold War, when a strategic opportunity opened quickly and without the kind of prior preparation that might ideally have occurred, the Bush administration organized the whole of government around a focused and coherent strategy. Policy coherence came at some political cost, and it required the direct role of the president. Top-level leadership is especially crucial in forging overall government strategy.

None of these cases proceeded according to the calculations that guided policy planning at the outset; all of the plans were revised, often radically, in the face of new and unexpected realities. Planning is essential, but plans—meaning fixed statements of purpose and action—are transitory. Wise statesmen know that foreign policy initiatives seldom if ever go according to plan—such is the fog of war and of diplomacy. Effective policymakers build reconsideration and reevaluation into their planning process. They know that no matter how disciplined their thinking, their ability to predict a future course of events is very limited. They must be prepared to respond rapidly to unforeseen developments while also ensuring that those responses fit within a larger and flexible strategic framework.

Strategic planning and preparation allow for calculated opportunism. The opening to China and the reunification of Germany at the end of the Cold War are two examples of what this looks like. Successful diplomacy is flexible and opportunistic because it plans and prepares, always recognizing that it cannot predict the future.

Political Leadership Plays a Crucial Role, But Not Only for the Reasons One Might Think

Leadership at the highest level was central to many of the cases in this book. Richard Nixon's visit to China, Anwar Sadat's visit to Israel, Jimmy Carter's mediation at Camp David, and George H. W. Bush's personal management of a strategy for ending the Cold War were the most dramatic instances—each demonstrating the ability of a political leader to look beyond an existing situation and envision a different future. Each case also entailed a high degree of personal diplomacy and considerable political risk, and each required a disciplined and effective foreign policy team to translate an abstract vision into diplomatic reality. The vision and determination of leaders like Sukarno and Gamal Abdel Nasser were critical to the convening of the Bandung Conference, and presidential leadership in both Mexico and the United States was indispensable for launching the NAFTA negotiations.

Yet, few of the leaders studied here resemble Hegel's "world-historical" figure, Nietzsche's "Great Man," or Weber's charismatic personality. Mao and Sadat embodied some of these heroic attributes, but Nixon, Bush, Zhou Enlai, Carlos Salinas, Menachem Begin, and the others whose statesmanship is examined in this book were not charismatic personalities, masterful strategists, gifted orators, or commanding authority figures. They still exhibited political leadership of a high order.

Which qualities of political leadership did they demonstrate? As Robert Hutchings observes in his discussion of President George H. W. Bush, the key leadership qualities included emotional intelligence, careful judgment, stamina, patience, calm under pressure, task competence (born of easy familiarity with foreign policy issues), deep knowledge of the machinery of government, wisdom in selecting key officials at the cabinet and subcabinet level, skill in dealing with allies, and, not least, empathy. This last quality was revealed in Bush's sensitivity to the needs and motivations of his Soviet counterpart, Mikhail Gorbachev. The same was true for Carter's attention to the personalities of Sadat and Begin, and Nixon's remarkable appreciation for the need to show deference to Chairman Mao. Empathy is an irreducible quality of successful diplomacy, and it is particularly difficult to encourage in a competitive culture that emphasizes victory over adversaries. Great leaders show empathy toward allies and adversaries.

Political Leadership Requires Selective Delegation and Restraint

Since political leadership at the highest level was crucial in some cases, it might be tempting to conclude that it should be deployed for every diplomatic challenge. Yet, some of the cases covered in this book—the creation of UNRRA, the evolution of the European Union as a "community of law" and, by default, the provision of aid to Taliban-era Afghanistan—are cases where decisive leadership came from lower-level and sometimes anonymous officials. Presidents and prime ministers are always pressured to take bold action—by their staffs, the media, and their allies—but they must choose their battles carefully. Effective leaders recognize not only that they must guard their time and energy, but also that engagement at their level carries risks as well as opportunities. In particular, agreements and disagreements between leaders have a finality that does not obtain with their agents.[5] The position of an ambassador or even a foreign minister can be repudiated or "clarified"; it is not so easy to walk back from a position taken by a president or a prime minister. Think of the risks taken by Carter (an "all or nothing gamble") and even more so by Sadat and Begin, or of Nixon in venturing to Beijing without having so much as a scheduled meeting with Mao. We also have the example, not covered in this book, of Ronald Reagan and Mikhail Gorbachev at their 1986 summit meeting in Reykjavik, venturing well off script and far beyond the bounds of policy or prudence.[6]

Harold Nicolson wrote that the worst statesmen are the missionaries and fanatics, and "the best kind are the reasonable and humane skeptics."[7] Leaders on a mission can imbue their task with undue moral certainty, overconfidence in their ability to achieve success, and a reckless tendency to dismiss or ignore countervailing advice. The heedless invasion and occupation of Iraq by the George W. Bush administration after 2003 fits this classic example of "groupthink."[8] Boldness needs to be tempered by "prudence," one of the favorite terms and guiding principles of the first President Bush. Although boldness and prudence must start at the top, they should also echo throughout the lower levels of leadership. Change and reevaluation must flow in two directions, from the top down, and from below to above. Presidents and diplomats must shape one another, based on a continual interplay between a strategic vision and observations from the field.

Diplomacy Demands That Political Leaders and Their Agents Are Aligned

The veteran American diplomat Chas Freeman has offered a revealing statement about diplomatic agency: "To achieve the results sought by his principal, an agent must be intimately familiar with his principal's objectives. He must understand the interests and presuppositions from which these objectives derive. He must possess dispassionate comprehension of the interests, predispositions, and aspirations of those he is seeking to influence."[9] It could hardly be stated better, but stating the case does not make it so. These attributes do not come automatically; they flow out of a decision-making process that engages a wide range of senior officials, so that those officials understand and are vested in the policies they are sent to advance. In addition to communicating goals, leaders must follow a careful process of putting in place senior officials who are skilled, loyal, and prepared. There are no shortcuts to achieving this kind of coordinated and mutually reinforcing relationship between political leaders and their agents. It is, in fact, quite rare.

In the recent history of American diplomacy, the George H. W. Bush administration is widely seen as the "gold standard," for reasons described in the case study on the end of the Cold War in Europe. That chapter describes the long preparation, careful selection of key officials, development of an inclusive decision-making process, coordinated signaling within government as well as toward outsiders, and the careful cultivation of hundreds of officials needed for the effective implementation of policy. Our case study on the opening to China may be a partial counterpoint here, as President Nixon and his national security adviser, Henry Kissinger, kept the Department of State at bay, for reasons of secrecy as well as their antipathy toward their own bureaucracy. That said, within the National Security Council staff, Kissinger created a highly effective and disciplined team, allowing little slippage between principals and agents. The Nixon and Kissinger NSC effectively aligned presidential goals with policy implementation.

Several chapters show the importance of teams of technical experts on humanitarian aid, trade negotiations, arms control, and development assistance—and the development among them of multinational "epistemic communities" of similarly trained and often similarly motivated experts who may advance objectives not shared by their home governments.[10] In the European Union's enlargement process, for example, officials in the European Commission tended to become greater advocates than European political leaders of early admission into the EU for countries that had met the criteria set forth in the *acquis communautaire*. The case of aid to Taliban-era Afghanistan offers an example of an epistemic community achieving coordination without the active participation of governments.

Such communities of experts constitute an increasingly important dimension of contemporary diplomacy. Aligning them to larger foreign policy goals is an increasingly important challenge for national leaders. On the one hand, these epistemic communities may be able to forge international agreement where such consensus would have been impossible to achieve at the political level. As ACDA director William Foster noted with regard to negotiating the nuclear nonproliferation treaty, Geneva was "the *only place* where we have a continuing contact with the Soviet Union outside official channels"; it became a "citadel of learning."

On the other hand, experts can succumb to a kind of diplomatic "Stockholm syndrome," finding common ground among themselves, but taking their governments where those governments may not want to go. For the most part, in the cases covered in this book, the experts and their political leaders were kept closely aligned. Dean Acheson's Special Research Division, for example, prepared for UNRRA three months before the Pearl Harbor attack and remained closely linked to the secretary of state's office. Similarly, President Carlos Salinas and Trade Minister Jaime Serra assembled an impressive team of technocrats and maintained close control over their activities during NAFTA negotiations. When aligned, experts and their political leaders can collaborate through diplomacy to become more than the sum of their parts.

Successful Statesmen Must Learn to Play Two-Level Games

Our NAFTA case is a classic example of a "two-level game," in which governments negotiate simultaneously at the international and domestic levels.[11] The need to satisfy domestic interests limits the ability of a negotiator to strike a deal internationally, and international exigencies may make it impossible to meet the expectations of domestic constituencies. Statesmen obviously must respond to their own domestic constituencies, but they must be attentive to the other side's domestic pressures too. All leaders, even the most repressive dictators, have domestic constraints.

Of course both sides invoke their domestic constraints, real or contrived, to improve their bargaining leverage internationally. This is indeed a complex, multilayered process. President Salinas and Minister Serra created the Business Coordination of Foreign Trade (*Coordinadora de Organizaciones Empresariales de Comercio Exterior*, or COECE in its Spanish acronym), composed of key business leaders, both to secure domestic support and to strengthen their hands in negotiating with the United States. Salinas and Serra also worked hard to understand and influence U.S. domestic interests, employing over a dozen lobbying firms to persuade crucial constituencies in Washington, D.C., California, and Texas.

Two-level games are not confined to trade negotiations. They apply in many other settings as well. They played a key role in the NPT, as U.S. negotiators worked to address the concerns of German domestic constituencies after the cancellation of a cherished weapons program. Similarly, President Bush employed two-level games with Poland to help forge domestic agreement there in the aftermath of the 1989 Polish elections. He did the same a year later with the Soviet Union, to help strengthen Gorbachev's domestic standing so that he could overcome domestic opposition to German unification.

In most of the cases studied here, successful diplomacy was built on strong domestic support for policy initiatives, as well as leaders' respect for the domestic constraints on allies and adversaries. Successful diplomacy offers all participants accomplishments they can advertise to their citizens at home. Successful diplomacy also involves frequent cooperation to keep potentially damaging information secret from domestic critics. In preparing for Camp David, for example, Prime Minister Begin purposely declined to disclose his negotiating objectives lest the military leadership or political rivals in his government tie his hands before the negotiations began. He and Sadat also employed such devices as side letters to allow each side to "spin" the agreement in ways most conducive to winning support back home. On many issues affecting the Middle East peace process, "constructive ambiguity" of this kind was essential for reaching agreement, despite irreconcilable differences on contested issues like the status of Jerusalem or the meaning of "occupied territories." Henry Kissinger also employed constructive ambiguities in his discussions with China about the future of Taiwan. Two-level games make successful diplomacy a delicate and ever-shifting balance between international goals and domestic constraints.

Diplomacy Requires a Careful Mix of Secrecy and Openness

Especially in a democracy, citizens and their elected representatives expect to be informed about key diplomatic overtures. The modern media will demand information for the twenty-four-hour news cycle, and they will exploit government leaks wherever they can. Transparency is indeed imperative for effective policymaking. Its absence will inspire public opposition and jeopardize the long-term viability of diplomatic initiatives.

At the same time, many of the chapters in this volume show how important secrecy remains for signaling potential partners and negotiating new agreements. The broader discussions of nuclear nonproliferation occurred in the United Nations, but the key actors (especially the United States and the Soviet Union) had to work quietly behind the scenes to encourage adherence from their allies, many of whom did not want to foreswear the development of their own nuclear capabilities. Of course, none of these states wanted to reveal the terms of the deals they made with Washington and Moscow. Similarly, Kissinger, Begin, Sadat, Carter, and Baker used secrecy to encourage agreements and minimize public embarrassments. Secrecy increases flexibility and the possibilities for taking risks. It also facilitates difficult trade-offs, especially when the public costs may be high.

The challenge for diplomats is to find the correct balance between openness and secrecy. Public audiences must feel informed, but diplomatic partners must feel protected from public embarrassment. There is no set formula for mixing the two. In each particular moment and context, diplomats must work hard to reach the appropriate balance. They must continually reevaluate and adjust. Secrecy and openness are symbiotic parts of successful diplomacy. Revising President Woodrow Wilson's famous claim in his 1918 speech about democratic war aims: Everyone wants open covenants, but they often must be secretly arrived at.[12]

Statesmen Need to See the Objective of Diplomacy Not as Victory, but as Compromise

Harold Nicolson made the distinction between the "heroic" and the "shopkeeper" models of diplomacy, with the former seeing the aim of negotiation as victory and the latter seeing it as compromise.[13] All of us would rather be heroes than shopkeepers, but the message for diplomats is that negotiations are ultimately successful when they serve the interests of all sides. American diplomats, in particular, are subjected to the public expectation that they should get everything they want, giving up nothing in return. In most cases, this is not only unobtainable; it is unwise. Among the minimum standards for a successful negotiation is sustainability. A negotiator may be able to put one over on the other side, but if the agreement does not hold up over time, it is not much of an achievement.

In several of our cases, statesmen went to great lengths to be attentive to the needs of the other side, even when dealing with adversarial regimes. In forming UNRRA, Secretary of State Cordell Hull and Undersecretary Dean Acheson were acutely aware of the bitter legacy, in Soviet eyes, of the massive humanitarian operation directed by Herbert Hoover during and after the First World War. Hull and Acheson conspicuously included Moscow in the planning for post–World War II relief efforts.

Nixon and Kissinger similarly showed immense sensitivity to Chinese pride, exhibiting deference where less skilled leaders might have been constrained by protocol and presumptions of American superiority. Nixon and Kissinger understood that memories of Western exploitation under the "unequal treaties" were still vivid in China, and they were willing to be seen in China as supplicants.

In our case on the end of the Cold War, Secretary of State James Baker offered "nine assurances" to Soviet foreign minister Eduard Shevardnadze. President Bush knowingly accepted domestic criticism in offering a trade agreement to address Gorbachev's domestic needs. That chapter also questions whether the United States was really as attentive to Soviet concerns as it professed to be—a point that returned to plague U.S.-Russian relations thereafter.

Conceptualizing diplomacy as compromise does not come easily for diplomats and statesmen trained in the Anglo-American tradition. As Raymond Cohen has observed, negotiators from other countries are often surprised by American negotiators' moralistic and legalistic approach, their ignorance of history, their tendency to see issues in black-or-white terms, and their obsession with problem-solving at the expense of the overall relationship. Negotiators from other cultures tend to take "the long view" and value the whole relationship over any specific agreement.[14]

Diplomacy should be seen not as a series of discrete episodes, but as a continuum in which the main objective is in the relationship, rather than the outcome of any particular negotiating event. Successful diplomats do not create winners and losers; they find ways to improve the positions of as many participants as possible. Successful diplomats serve their own nation's interests, but within a broader system of sustainable relations.

When successful, diplomacy does not replace other foreign policy tools; it increases the constructive options for their use. When successful, diplomacy redefines intractable problems as opportunities for negotiation and mutual adjustment. Diplomacy translates intent into action, goals into results. That does not make diplomacy an alternative to war, but instead an *addition* to the resort to arms in times of conflict.

There are no formulas for successful diplomacy, and there is no standard character type for the effective diplomat or statesman. Context and other particularities require continual adjustment. The passage of time means that yesterday's sources of success will not work today or tomorrow. The historical case studies in this book are rich and complex, not reducible to simple "lessons learned" for future diplomats and policymakers. If history offered up clear lessons, we would have learned them long ago. Instead, we need to grapple with historical successes and failures, understanding recurring patterns and dynamics that reappear, but in different forms and at different times. Although the past does not repeat, the future does build on the past.

In this volume we have aimed to show how one can learn from history without succumbing to the false belief that past experience provides a clear guide to future action. We need better diplomacy, and it must begin with deeper understanding of what diplomacy has meant in years past, coupled with the wisdom to apply these insights to the challenges ahead.

Notes

1. Hedley Bull, *The Anarchical Society: A Study of Order in World Politics*, 4th ed. (New York: Columbia University Press, 2012). See also Jeremi Suri, "Non-Governmental Organizations and Non-State Actors," in *Palgrave Advances in International History*, ed. Patrick Finney (London: Palgrave, 2005), 223–245.
2. See Carl von Clausewitz, *On War*, ed. and trans. Michael Howard and Peter Paret (Princeton, NJ: Princeton University Press, 1976), esp. 100–123.
3. Henry Kissinger, *White House Years* (Boston: Little, Brown, 1979), 54.
4. Guicciardini quotations from G. R. Berridge, "Guicciardini," in *Diplomatic Theory from Machiavelli to Kissinger*, ed. G. R. Berridge, Maurice Keens-Soper, and T. G. Otte (London: Palgrave, 2001), 39.
5. Chas. W. Freeman, Jr., *Arts of Power: Statecraft and Diplomacy* (Washington, DC: U.S. Institute of Peace Press, 1997), 113–114.
6. See Ken Adelman, *Reagan at Reykjavik: Forty-Eight Hours That Ended the Cold War* (New York: HarperCollins, 2014); Jack F. Matlock, Jr., *Reagan and Gorbachev: How the Cold War Ended* (New York: Random House, 2004).
7. Harold Nicolson, *Diplomacy*, rev. ed. (1939; repr., Oxford: Oxford University Press, 1977), 24. The actual quote begins, "The worst kind of diplomatists are missionaries, fanatics, and lawyers," but we are not so sure about including lawyers, whose training may encourage an overly legalistic approach to foreign policy problems, but also prepares them for empathy and compromise.
8. Irving L. Janis, *Groupthink: Psychological Studies of Policy Decisions and Fiascoes* (Boston: Houghton Mifflin, 1982).
9. Freeman, *Arts of Power*, 112.
10. See, for example, Anne-Marie Slaughter, *A New World Order* (Princeton, NJ: Princeton University Press, 2004), 36–64.
11. Robert Putnam, "Diplomacy and Domestic Politics: The Logic of Two-Level Games," *International Organization*, 42, no. 3 (Summer 1988): 427–460.
12. Wilson called for "Open covenants of peace, openly arrived at, after which there shall be no private international understandings of any kind but diplomacy shall proceed always frankly and in the public view." See President Woodrow Wilson's Fourteen Points Speech to the U.S. Congress, January 8, 1918, available at http://avalon.law.yale.edu/20th_century/wilson14.asp.
13. See Nicolson, *Diplomacy*.
14. Raymond Cohen, *Negotiating across Cultures: International Communication in an Interdependent World*, rev. ed. (Washington, D.C.: U.S. Institute of Peace Press, 1997), esp. 28–38 and 217.

INDEX